John Chalmers

Ying Yüeh tzu tien

An Englisch and Cantonese Dictionary

John Chalmers

Ying Yüeh tzu tien
An Englisch and Cantonese Dictionary

ISBN/EAN: 9783743394162

Manufactured in Europe, USA, Canada, Australia, Japa

Cover: Foto ©Paul-Georg Meister /pixelio.de

Manufactured and distributed by brebook publishing software (www.brebook.com)

John Chalmers

Ying Yüeh tzu tien

典字粵英

AN

ENGLISH AND CANTONESE

DICTIONARY;

FOR THE

*USE OF THOSE WHO WISH TO LEARN THE SPOKEN
LANGUAGE OF CANTON PROVINCE.*

BY

JOHN CHALMERS, LL.D.

Sixth Edition.

With the Changing Tones marked.

Hongkong:
KELLY & WALSH, LIMITED.
HONGKONG—SHANGHAI—YOKOHAMA—SINGAPORE.

1891.

65365

Registered in accordance with the provisions of Ordinance No. 10 of 1888, at the Office of the Registrar General, Supreme Court House, Hongkong.

DIRECTIONS FOR USING THE ENGLISH AND CANTONESE DICTIONARY.

THE system of spelling here used is adapted from that of Dr. Williams' Tonic Dictionary, only dispensing with his diacritic marks for the sake of convenience in writing and printing, and, it is hoped, also in using the Dictionary. The vowels are to be pronounced as follows:—

aa, and *a* final, as in *father*.
a, not final, as in *company*.
e, as in *they*.
i, as in *machine*, but before *ng* and *k* as in *king*.
o, final as in *no*, and not final, as in *hop*.
oh, as in *horn*.
ŏ, as in *Göthe*.
oo, as in *school*.
u, as in *fun*, (interchanged with short *a*.)
uu, nearly as in *bull*.
ue, as *ü* in *Trübner*.
ai, as *y* in *fly*.
aai, as *a* with *ea* in *far-reaching*.
au, as *ow* in *now*.
aau, as *a* with *u* in *far ruling*.
eu, as *eyo* in *beyond*, or *ayo* in *crayon*.
iu, as *ee* with *ou* in *see you*.
oi, as *oy* in *boy*.
ui, nearly as in *Louis*.
ooi, as in *cooing*.
sze or *sz'* is a mere buzz, with scarcely any vowel sound.

The use of short *u* in many cases where the other Dictionaries have short *a* is to prevent a habit which English learners are very liable to get into of pronouncing, for example, 民 'mun,' people, exactly the same as the English word 'man'; 佛 'Fut,' Buddha, the same as the English word 'fat,' &c. The broader Scotch *a* is a little nearer the Cantonese, but 分 is in any case not 'fan' but 'fun.'

The double *u* is a little different from double *o*. 'Kau-loon' should be written Kau-luung, the second syllable being indeed quite different from the English 'lung,' yet not by any means the same as the Scotch 'loon.'

Words ending in *ue* (*ü*) often vary in Canton so as to be not distinguishable from words ending in *ui;* but it is an exaggeration to make 去 ʽ*hue* rhyme with 水 ʽ*shui*.

The only vowel used with a diacritical mark is *ö;* and it is of rare occurrence. I cannot accept, even on the authority of Mr. Parker, this vowel as a substitute for *eu* in *sheung, sheuk,* &c. There is some truth in the suggestion, but if *sheung* gives too much of a diphthong, *shöng* gives too little. Considering that 郎 *long* and 良 *leung* rhyme with each other in the universal language of China, it would seem almost better to write the Cantonese sounds *long* and *leong*, than to introduce the peculiar *ö*, which, after all, does not represent the Cantonese perfectly. However, students may take Mr. Ball's *shöng, löng*, &c. as a warning not to exaggerate the diphthong.

The 8 Tones.—There are only eight regular tones in the Chinese language, and even these are not all found in many dialects. The upper series of tones is printed in Italics, and the lower series in Roman letters. Syllables printed in Italics must always be pronounced on a higher key than the others. (1) Syllables without any tonal mark are in the 'even' tone.

(2) Those with a tonal mark (‘) on the upper left corner are in the 'rising' tone. (3) Those with a tonal mark (’) on the upper right corner are in the 'going' tone. (4) And words ending in *k*, *p*, or *t* are in the 'abrupt' tone; that is to say, they end in a close consonant which cannot be sung out. It seems to me that the first tone might more properly be called the 'natural' and the third the 'even' tone; for the third or 'going' tone resembles a note of music which continues at the same pitch. It begins rather lower than the first, but does not drop at all.

The following is an example of the eight tones applied to what the Chinese regard as one syllable (*t* being only a modification of *n*) :—

		UPPER SERIES.		LOWER SERIES.	
			Williams.		*Williams.*
平	even	溫 *wun*	₍wan	雲 wun	₍wan
上	rising	穩 ‘*wun*	‘wan	尹 ‘wun	‘wan
去	going	慍 *wun*’	wan’	混 wun’	wan²
入	abrupt	屈 *wut*	wat₃	核 wut	wat₂

Additional Tones:—We are indebted to Mr. E. H. Parker for first calling attention to other tones, besides the above eight, which occur in Canton Colloquial.

First, there are three even tones instead of two, the uppermost one being a sort of cry. A typical case is ₍*maau*, a cat, the name being an imitation of its cry. These *uppermost* even tones are distinguished in this Edition of the Cantonese Dictionary by a tonal mark on the lower left corner of the syllable in addition to its being printed in Italics. I have been guided entirely by a Cantonese Teacher in this and the following distinctions of tones.

Second, there are three abrupt tones instead of two, the middle one being about as much lower than the one above as the upper 'going' tone is lower than the upper 'even.' This lowering of the upper fourth tone takes place almost invariably in connection with long or broad vowels. The first tonal exercise familiar to most beginners affords an example of it—

Sin ʽ*Sin* *Sin*' *Sit*'.

The *i* being long (= *ee*) the fourth tone follows the cadence of the third; so that this middle fourth tone is appropriately marked like the third. What is probably the normal upper fourth tone is heard where the vowel is short, as in—

Sing ʽ*Sing* *Sing*' *Sik*.

Third, all the tones, except perhaps the upper even and the upper abrupt, are liable to be changed into an exaggerated rising tone; <u>the initial letter always following the proper tone of the word, and the raising of the voice commencing from that pitch whatever it may be</u>. This exaggerated rising tone is indicated by an asterisk on the upper left side of the syllable. For example, the character 近 (near) has three pronunciations according to the shades of meaning, kan', ʽk'an, and *kan'. The last is to commence like the first and has no aspirate (ʽ) but it rises even more than the second.

It is well to keep in mind that the lower even and the lower rising tones always take the aspirate after *ch*, *k*, *p*, *t*, and *ts*, while the lower 'going' tone never takes it, and the lower abrupt tone seldom. There is some little help in this to a foreigner in distinguishing so many tones.

More than nine-tenths of the characters given as equivalents of English words in this Dictionary will answer equally well for the general language of China; and I have thought it well with this in view to substitute authorized characters for 唔 ʼm, 嘅 *ke*', 冇 ʽmo, 嚟 lai, &c. in many cases while retaining the colloquial sounds. It seems a little absurd to write 嚟 for 'lai,' to come, when the proper character 來 'loi' is pronounced 'lai' in other dialects. This sort of thing, like the multiplication of 'easy wênli' versions of the Scriptures, will in the end only multiply difficulties.

This Dictionary was from the first intended for English people rather than Chinese, and those who consult it are requested, if they fail to find any particular English word, to look for a synonym or an approximate synonym; and to learn to form parts of speech themselves from the material given, thus:—

Adjectives may be formed at pleasure by adding *ke'* to nouns and verbs.

Verbs may often be formed by placing *'ching* or tso' before adjectives, as *'ching*-paak, to whiten.

Sometimes an alternative pronunciation of a syllable is given in parentheses which will generally be found equally or more colloquial. For example, under 'Adjoin,' foo'-kan' ('k'an), is an abbreviated way of saying, foo'-kan', *or* foo'-'k'an.

J. C.

HONGKONG, 28th March, 1891.

AN
ENGLISH AND CANTONESE
DICTIONARY.

A

A, an, (one) 一 *yat*. [The numerals or classifiers are given after (a) or (an) under different nouns. The most common of all numerals is 個 *koh'*, as 一個人 *yat-koh'-yan*, "one man" or "a man," but where other numerals are given they must be used in connection with the classes of nouns to which they respectively belong, as 一隻獸 *yat-chek'-shau'*, "a beast," 一條魚 *yat-t'iu-*ue*, "a fish."]

Abacus, 筭盤 *suen'-p'oon*, (an), 一個筭盤 *yat ko'-suen'-p'oon*.

Abaft, 向船尾 *heung'-shuen-'mi*.

Abandon, 捨棄 *'she-hi'*.

Abate, 減少 *'kaam-'shiu*.

Abbey, (Bud.) 佛寺 Fut-*tsze', (an) 一間佛寺 *yat-kaan-Fut-*tsze'*, (Tau.) 道觀 To'-koon', (Rom.) 修道院 *sau-to'-*uen'*.

Abbot, (Bud.) 方丈 *fong-cheung'*, (an) 一位方丈 *yat-wai'-fong-cheung'*, (Tau) 道長 To'-'cheung.

Abbreviate, 減短 *'kaam-'tuen*.

Abbreviation, (in writing) 減筆 *'kaam-put*.

Abet, 幫助 *pong-choh'*.

Abhor, 憎嫌 *tsang-im'*.

Abide, 住實 chue⁾-shat, 住吓 chue⁾-ʿha, 耐 noi⁾.
Ability, 才能 tsʿoi-nang, 本領 ʿpoon-ʿling, 能幹 nang-kohn⁾.
Abjure, 誓願絕 *shai⁾-uen⁾-tsuet.
Able, 能 nang, 會 ʿooi.
Aboard, 在船上 tsoi⁾-shuen-sheung⁾, 喺船處 ʿhai-shuen-shue⁾.
Abolish, 廢除 fai⁾-chʿue.
Abominable, 百家憎 paak⁾-ka-tsang.
Abominate, 至憎 chi⁾-tsang.
Aborigines, 土人 ʿtʿo-yan, (of China) 苗子 Miu-ʿtsze.
Abortion, 墮胎 toh⁾-tʿoi 小產 ʿsiu-ʿchʿaan.
Abound, 處處都多 chʿue⁾-chʿue⁾-too-toh, 豐盛 fuung-shing⁾.
About, (round-) 周圍 chau-wai, (more or less) 上下 sheung⁾-*ha⁾, 左右 ʿtsoh-ʿyau, (about to) 將近 tseung-*kan (concerning) 論 luun⁾.

Above, 上 sheung⁾.
Abreast, 並肩 ping⁾-kin, 一拍 yat-pʿaak⁾.
Abridge, 簡畧 ʿkaan-leuk, 整簡畧 ʿching-ʿkaan-leuk.
Abroad, 外 ngoi⁾.
Abrogate, 廢 fai⁾.
Abrupt, 突屹 tat-ngat.
Abruptly, 突然 tat-in.
Abscess, 膿瘡 nuung-ʿchʿong.
Abscond, 躲避 ʿtoh-pi⁾, (with money) 起尾注 ʿhi-ʿmi-chue⁾.
Absent, 不在 ʾm-tsoi⁾.
Absolutely, 必定 pit-ting⁾.
Absolve, 赦 she⁾.
Absorb, 軟去 shok⁾-hue⁾.
Abstain from, 戒 kaai⁾.
Abstracted, 忘形 *mong-ying, 想入神 ʿseung-yup-shan.
Abstruse, 深奧 shum-o⁾.
Absurd, 斷不合理 tuen⁾-ʾm-hop-ʿli, 混賬 wan⁾-cheung⁾.
Abundant, 豐阜 fuung-fau⁾.

Abuse, (things) 亂用 luen'-yuung', (people) 詈罵 li-ma', 殘害 ts'aan-hoi'.
Abyss, 深淵 shum-uen.
Acacia, 金鳳 kum-fuung', 聲息花 shing-sik-fa.
Accept, 收納 shau-naap.
Access, 走近路 ʻtsau-ʻkʻan-lo'.
Accidental, 意外 i'-ngoi', 偶然 ʻngau-in.
Acclamation, 齊聲喝彩 ts'ai-sheng-hoht-ʻts'oi.
Acclimated, 服水土 fuuk-ʻshui-ʻt'o.
Acclivity, 斜坡 ts'e-poh.
Accommodate, 從——便, ts'uung——*pin', 依 i.
Accompany, 同埋 t'uung-maai, 陪 p'ooi.
Accomplice, 從犯 tsuung'-*faan'.
Accomplish, 成 shing.
Accord, 相和 seung-woh.
According to, 照依 chiu'-i.
Accordingly, 噉就 ʻkom-tsau'.

Account, (money) 數目 sho'-muuk, 賬目 cheung'-muuk, 單 taan.
Accountable, 是問 shi'-mun'.
Accountant, 掌匱 ʻcheung-*kwai'.
Accumulate, 集埋 tsaap-maai.
Accumulation, 重重疊疊 ch'uung-ch'uung-tip-tip.
Accurate, 無錯 ʻmo-ts'oh'.
Accusation, 告狀 ko'-*chong'.
Accuse, 告 ko', (a superior) 攻許 kuung-k'it'.
Accustomed, 慣熟 kwaan'-shuuk.
Ache, 痛 t'uung'.
Achieve, 成就 shing-tsau'.
Achievement, 成功 shing-kuung.
Acid, 酸 suen.
Acknowledge, 認 ying'.
Acorn, 石栗 shek-luut.
Acquaintance, 熟識 shuuk-shik, 相識 seung-shik.
Acquire, 得到 tak-ʻto, 獲 wok.

Acquit, 擬無罪 ʻi-ʻmo-tsuiʼ, 審無罪 ʻshum-ʻmo-tsuiʼ.
Acre, (Chinese) 畝 ʻmau (6½ =1 Eng.).
Acrid, 辣 laat.
Across, 橫 waang, 過 kwohʼ.
Act, 做 tsoʼ, 行 hang, 做事幹 tsoʼ-szeʼ-kohnʼ.
Acting officer, 署任 ʻchʻueʼ-yumʼ.
Actions 行爲 hang-wai.
Action-at-law, 訟詞 tsuungʼ-tsʻze.
Actionable, 可告發 ʻhoh-ʻkoʼ-faatʼ.
Active, 手快 ʻshau-faaiʼ, 活動 oot-tuungʼ.
Actor, (play-) 戲子 hiʼ-ʻtsze.
Acute, 尖銳 tsim-yuiʼ, (clever) 伶俐 ling-liʼ.
Adam's apple, 喉欖 hau-ʻlaam.
Adapt, 合 hop.
Add, 加 ka, 添 tʻim.
Addict to, 專務 chuen-moʼ.
Addition (the rule of), 加法 ka-faatʼ.

Addled, 膈 ʻwoh.
Address, (a person) 稱呼 chʻing-foo, (a letter) 寫信皮 ʻse-suunʼ-pʻi, (an) 信皮 suunʼ-pʻi.
Adept, 老手 ʻlo-ʻshau.
Adequate, 够使 kauʼ-ʻshai, 能够 nang-kauʼ.
Adhere, 黏緊 nim-ʻkan, 依實 i-shat.
Adhesive, 翻 chʻi.
Adieu, 好行 ʻho-hang, 望你好咯 mongʼ-ni-ʻho-lok.
Adjoin, 附近 fooʼ-kanʼ (ʻkʻan).
Adjourn, 訂期 tingʼ-kʻi, 訂期再會 tingʼ-kʻi-tsoiʼ-ooiʼ.
Adjust, 整齊 ʻching-tsʻai, 做歸一 tsoʼ-kwai-yat.
Adjutant, 副將 fooʼ-tseungʼ, 協台 hip-tʻoi.
Administer, 總管 ʻtsuung-ʻkoon.
Admiral, 水師提督 ʻshui-sze-tʻai-tuuk.

Admire, 讚羨 tsaan'-sin'.
Admit, 許進 'hue-tsuun', 俾入 'pi-yup, 允准 'wan-'chuun.
Admonish, 勸誡 huen'-kaai'.
Ado, 事做 sze'-tso', 事幹 sze'-kohn'.
Adopt a son, 立義子 laap-i'-'tsze, 立螟蛉 laap-ming-ling.
Adopted, (personally) 契 k'ai', (father, mother) 契爺, 契姆 k'ai'-ye, k'ai'-'na, (by a second marriage) 繼 kai'.
Adore, 崇拜 shuung-paai'.
Adorn, 文飾 mun-shik, 整飾 'ching-shik.
Adrift, 漂流 p'iu-lau.
Adroit, 善精 shin'-tsing.
Adult, 長大成人 'cheung-taai'-shing-yan, 大人 taai'-yan.
Adulterate, 摳雜假貨 k'au-tsaap-'ka-foh'.
Adultery, 姦淫 kaan-yum.

Advance, 進 tsuun', (money) 預先交出 ue'-sin-kaau-ch'uut, 支 chi, (goods on credit) 賒 she.
Advantage, 贏 yeng, 益 yik.
Adventure, 行險 hang-'him.
Adversary, 對頭 tui'-t'au, 對敵 tui'-tik.
Adverse, 凶 huung, 不幸 pat-hang', 逆 yik, ngaak, 滯 chai'.
Advert to, 提起 t'ai-'hi.
Advertise, 通報 t'uung-po', 報告 po'-ko', (by posting bills) 貼街招 tip-'kaai-'chiu.
Advisable, 合勢色 hop-shai'-shik'.
Advise, 勸 huen'.
Advocate, to, 代訴 toi'-so'.
Adze, 鐇 poon.
Aeolian Harp, 响弓 'heung-kuung.
Aeolus, 風神 fuung-shan.
Affable, 好相與 'ho-seung-'ue.
Affair, 事幹 sze'-kohn'.

Affect, 感 ʿkom, (concern) 關 kwaan.
Affectation, 整腥詐靚 ʿching-seng-chaʾ-lengʾ.
Affectionate, 深情 shum-tsʻing.
Affiance, 定親 tingʾ-tsʻan.
Affinity, 姻親 yan-tsʻan.
Affirm, 話係 waʾ-haiʾ.
Afflict, 磨苦 moh-fu.
Afflictions, 痛楚 tʻuungʾ-ʿchʻoh.
Affluent, 豐盛 fuung-shingʾ.
Afford, 供給 kuung-kʻup, (can) 買得起 ʿmaai-tak-ʿhi.
Affront, 相撞 chʻuung-chongʾ, 辱 yuuk.
Afloat, 浮 fau.
Afore-said, 個的前言 kohʾ-tik-tsʻin-in, 上文所講 ʿsheungʾ-mun-ʿshoh-ʿkong.
Afraid, 恐怕 ʿhuung-pʻaʾ.
After, —— 後 —— hauʾ.
After-birth, 後人 hauʾ-*yan, 胎衣 tʻoi-i, 胞衣 paau-i.
Afternoon, 下午 haʾ-ʿng, 晏晝後 aanʾ-chauʾ-hauʾ.

Afterwards, 然後 in-hauʾ, 尾後 ʿmi-hauʾ, 後來 hauʾ-loi.
Again, 再復 tsoiʾ-fuuk, 又試 yauʾ-shi.
Against, 相反 seung-ʿfaan, 逆 yik, ngaak, (over-) 對面 tuiʾ-minʾ, (to rub—) 纜親 kʻwaangʾ-tsʻan.
Agate, 瑪瑙 ʿma-ʿno.
Age, 年紀 nin-ʿki, (what is your?) 你有幾多歲 ʿni-ʿyau-ʿki-tohʾ-sui? (or politely) 貴庚呢 kwaiʾ-kang-ni?; (the) 世 shaiʾ.
Aged, 高壽 ko-shauʾ, 老大 lo-*taaiʾ.
Agent, 代辦人 toiʾ-paanʾ-yan.
Aggravate, 整更關系 ʿching-kangʾ-kwaan-haiʾ, 整重 ʿching-chʻuung.
Aggressor, 先下手 sin-ʿha-ʿshau, 先攻人 sin-kuung-yan.
Agitate, 郁動 yuuk-tuungʾ.
Agitated, 徬徨 pʻong-wong.
Ago, 前 tsʻin.

Agony, 苦極 ʿfoo-kik.
Agree, 和合 woh-hop.
Agreeable, 溫和 wan-woh, (willing) 歡喜 foon-ʿhi, (to one's liking) 合心水 hop-sum-ʿshui.
Agreement, 約 yeukʾ, 合同 hop-tʿuung, 契約 kʿaiʾ-yeukʾ.
Agriculture, 耕種 kang-chuung, 農事 nuung-szeʾ.
Aground, 擱淺 kokʾ-tsʿin, 阬船 hong-shuen.
Ague, 發冷病 faatʾ-ʿlaang-pengʾ.
Ah! 囉 Haai! Ha!
Aha! 嗄嗄 Ha-ha!
Ahead, 在前頭 tsoiʾ-tsʿin-tʿau (to go) 前去 tsʿin-hueʾ.
Ahoy! 喊 Wai!
Aid, 幫助 pong-chohʾ.
Aide-de-camp, 守備 ʿshau-pi².
Aim, 向准 heungʾ-ʿchuun.
Air, 氣 hiʾ.
Air, to, 晾 longʾ, 晾爽 longʾ-ʿshong.

Air-plant, 吊蘭 tiuʾ-laan.
Airy, 涼爽 leung-ʿshong.
Alarm, 震驚 chanʾ-king, (arouse) 儆醒 ʿking-ʿsing.
Alarm-clock, 鬧鐘 naauʾ-chuung.
Alas! 噯呀 Aaiʾ-ya!
Ale-house, 酒店 ʿtsau-timʾ.
Alert, 關心 kwaan-sum.
Aleurites, nuts, 石栗 shek-luut.
Alias, 別名 pit-*meng.
Alien, 外國人 ngoiʾ-kwokʾ-yan, 不相屬 ʾm-seung-shuuk, (他人的) 人哋嘅 yan-ti-ʿkeʾ.
Alight, 落 lok.
Alike, 相似 seung-ʿtsʿze 一樣 yat-*yeungʾ.
Alive, 生活 shaang-oot.
All, 皆 kaai, 攏總 ʿluung-ʿtsuung, 咸崩冷 hamʾ-pangʾ-langʾ, (are) 都係 tooʾ-haiʾ, (before nouns) 衆 chuungʾ, 萬 maanʾ, 百 paakʾ.
All-along, 一路 yat-loʾ.
Allay, 止 ʿchi.
Allegory, 寓言 ueʾ-in.

Alliance, 結親 kit⁾-ts'an, 聯盟 luen-mang.
Alligator, 鱷魚 ngok-ue.
Allot, 照分 chiu⁾-fun, 分派 fun-p'aai⁾.
Allow, 准 ʿchuun.
Alloy, (base metal) 金低 kum-tai, (to), 摳 k'au.
Allure, 引誘 ʿyan-ʿyan.
Allusion, 暗指 om⁾-chi.
Almanac, 通書 t'uung-shue.
Almighty, 無所不能 mo-shoh-pat-nang.
Almond, 杏仁 hang⁾-yan.
Almost, 差不多 ch'a-pat-toh.
Alms, (to give) 施捨 shi-ʿshe.
Aloes, 蘆薈 lo-ooi⁾, 沈香 ch'um-heung.
Alone, 獨一個 tuuk-yat-koh⁾, 孤獨 koo-tuuk.
Along, (lengthwise) 掂 tim⁾, 直 chik, (with) 同埋 t'uung-maai.
Alongside, 在傍 tsoi⁾-p'ong, (to go) 行埋 hang-maai.
Aloud, 大聲 taai⁾-sheng.

Already, 曾經 ts'ang-king, 已經 i-king.
Also, 亦 yik, 都 too, 又 yau⁾.
Altar, 祭壇 tsai⁾-t'aan, 神臺 shan-t'oi.
Alter, 改 ʿkoi.
Alternate, 互相替代 oo⁾-seung-t'ai⁾-toi⁾.
Alternately, (in succession) 輪流 luun-*lau, (every second one) 躝躎 laam⁾-la⁾.
Alternatives, 兩樣任揀 ʿleung-yeung⁾-yum⁾-ʿkaan.
Although, 雖然 sui-in.
Altogether, 總共 ʿtsuung-kuung⁾.
Alum, 白礬 paak-faan.
Always, 時時 shi-shi, 常時 sheung-shi.
Am (I-), 我係 ʿngoh-hai⁾.
Amaze, 驚着 king-cheuk.
Ambassador, 使臣 sze⁾-shan, (an) 一位使臣 yat-wai⁾-sze⁾-shan, (imperial) 欽差 yum-ch'aai.
Amber, 琥珀 foo-paak⁾.
Ambitious, 志氣高 chi⁾-hi⁾-ko.

Ambush, 伏兵 fuuk-ping.
Amend, 改正 ʿkoi-chingʾ.
Amends, (to make) 賠補 pʻooi-ʿpo.
America, 亞美利加 Aʾ-ʿmi-liʾ-ka.
Amiable, 可愛 ʿhoh-oiʾ.
Amiss, 唔着 ʾm-cheuk.
Ammunition, 火藥銃子 ʿfoh-yeuk-chʻuungʾ-tsze.
Among, 在—中 tsoiʾ— chuung.
Amorous, 多情 toh-tsʻing.
Amount, 共計 kuungʾ-kaiʾ.
Amour, 情頭 tsʻing-tʻau.
Amoy, 廈門 Haʾ-moon.
Ample, 廣大 ʿkwong-taaiʾ.
Amputate, 割去 kohtʾ-ʿhue.
Amuse, 開心 hoi-sum, 則劇 tsak-kʻek, (a child) 嗒 tʻumʾ.
Amusement, 頑耍 waan-ʿsha.
Amusing, 趣 tsʻueʾ.
Analyze, 察實 chʻaatʾ-shat, 考究 ʿhaau-kauʾ.
Anarchy, 大亂 taaiʾ-luenʾ.

Ancestor, 祖先 ʿtso-sin, 祖宗 ʿtso-tsuung, 太公 tʻaaiʾ-kuung.
Anchor, 鐵錨 tʻit-naau, 碇 tingʾ, (to) 灣 waan.
Anchovy-sauce, 魚觧 uc-ʿkaai.
Ancient, 古 ʿkoo.
And, 及 kʻaap, 兼 kim, 共 kuungʾ, 又 yau.
Anecdote, (an) 一段故事 yat-tuenʾ-kooʾ-szeʾ.
Angel, 天使 tʻin-szeʾ.
Anger, 嬲 nau, 恨怒 hanʾ-noʾ.
Angle, 角頭 kokʾ-tʻau.
Angle, to 釣魚 tiuʾ-*ue.
Angry, 發怒 faatʾ-noʾ, 嬲怒 nau-noʾ.
Animals, 生靈 shang-ling, 禽獸 kʻum-shauʾ.
Animate, (to) 聳起 ʿsuung-ʿhi.
Animation, 精神 tsing-shan.
Animosity, 恨 hanʾ, 仇 shau.
Aniseed, 茴香 ooi-heung.
Ankle, 脚眼骨 keukʾ-ʿngaan-kwut.

Annex, 接續 tsip-tsuuk, 加 ka.
Annihilation, 歸無 kwai-moo.
Anniversary, 年期日子 nin-kʻi-yat-ʻtze, (first) 對年 tuiʼ-nin.
Annoy, 煩憂 faan-ʻiu.
Annual, 每年 ʻmooi-nin.
Anoint, 搽 chʻa, 搽油 chʻa-yau.
Anonymous placard, 白帖 paak-tʻipʼ.
Another, 別個 pit-kohʼ. 第二 taiʼ-iʼ, 他 tʻa, aanʼ.
Answer, 答應 taap-yingʼ, 回音 ooi-yum, (suit) 着使 cheuk-ʻshai.
Ant, 蟻 ʻngai, (an) 一隻蟻 yat-chekʼ-ʻngai.
Ante-, 先 sin, 一之先 — chi-sin.
Antelope, 羚羊 ling-yeung.
Antennæ, 兩條鬚 ʻleung-tʻiu-so.
Anti-, 逆 yik, 對面 tuiʼ-minʼ.
Anticipate, 預料 ueʼ-liuʼ.

Antidote, 解毒 ʻkaai-tuuk.
Antiquities, 古事 ʻkoo-szeʼ.
Antiquity, 上古 sheungʼ-ʻkoo.
Antler, 丫角 a-kok.
Anus, 肛門 kong-moon, (VULG.) 屎窟 ʻshi-fut.
Anvil, 鐵砧 tʻitʼ-chum.
Anxious, 放心不下 fongʼ-sum-pat-haʼ, 掛心 kwaʼ-sum, (for) 燃 nat.
Any, 無論邊個 mo-luunʼ-ₑpin-kohʼ, 乜野 mat-ʻye, (some) 的 tik.
Anywhere 邊處 ₑpin-chʻueʼ, 邊處都好 ₑpin-chʻueʼ too-ʻho.
Apart, 離開的 li-hoi-tik, 疏 shoh.
Apartment, 房 *fong, (an) 一間房 yat-kaan-*fong.
Apathy, 無感動 ʻmo-ʻkom-tuungʼ.
Ape, 馬騮 ʻma-lau.
Aperient, 輕瀉藥 hing-seʼ-yeuk.
Aperture, 空處 huungʼ-chʻueʼ, 口 ʻhau, 籠 luung.

Apex, 巔頂 tin-ʻting, 尖處 tsim-chʻueʼ.
Apiece, 每一個 ʻmooi-yat-kohʼ.
Apologize, 解說 ʻkaai-shuet, 說開 shuet-hoi, 賠禮 pʻooi-ʻlai.
Apoplexy, 腦血中風 ʻno-huetʼ-chuungʼ-fuung, 腦水中風 ʻno-ʻshui-chuungʼ-fuung.
Apostatize, 背教 pooiʼ-kaauʼ.
Apostle, 使徒 szeʼ-tʻo.
Apparatus, 傢伙 ka-ʻfoh, 器具 hiʼ-kueʼ, (complete set) 一副應當 yat-fooʼ-yingʼ-tongʼ.
Apparel, 衣服 i-fuuk.
Apparition, 顯迹 ʻhin-tsik, 怪物 kwaaiʼ-mat.
Appeal, 控告 huungʼ-koʼ, 上控 sheungʼ-huungʼ.
Appear, 出顯 chʻuut-ʻhin.
Appearance, 貌 maauʼ.
Appease, 息氣 sik-hiʼ.
Appeased, 平息 pʻing-sik.
Appendix, 補遺 ʻpo-wai.
Appetite, 胃口 waiʼ-ʻhau.
Applaud, 喝彩 hoht-ʻtsʻoi.
Apple, 平菓 pʻing-ʻkwoh,
Apply, 着 cheuk, 用 yuungʼ, 哈 up, (ask, &c.) 求 kʻau, 向 heungʼ.
Appoint, 設立 chʻitʼ-laap.
Appraise, 估價 ʻkoo-kaʼ.
Apprehend, (seize) 捉到 chuukʼ-ʻto, (mentally) 曉 ʻhiu, 估 ʻkoo.
Apprentice, 徒弟 tʻo-*taiʼ.
Approach, 就近 tsauʼ-kanʼ, tsauʼ-*kanʼ, 將近 tseung-kanʼ.
Appropriate, (take) 擅取 shinʼ-ʻtsʻue, (fit) 合使 hop-ʻshai.
Approve, 中意 chuung-iʼ.
Apricot, 杏 *hangʼ.
April, 英四月 Ying-szeʼ-uet.
Apron, 圍裙 wai-*kʻwan.
Apt to, 會 ʻooi.
Aquiline nose, 鶯哥鼻 ang-koh-piʼ.
Arbitrate, 公斷 kuung-tuenʼ.
Arbitrator, 和頭 woh-tʻau, 中人 chuung-yan.

Arbute, 楊梅 yeung-mooi.
Arch, 拱 ʽkuung, 彎拱 waan-ʽkuung.
Archer, 箭手 tsinʾ-ʽshau.
Architect, 大匠 taaiʾ-tseungʾ [in Hongkong, waak-chik-keʾ].
Ardent, (hot) 熱 it.
Are, 係 hai, (in) 喺 ʽhai.
Argue, 辯駁 pinʾ-pokʾ.
Arise, 起 ʽhi.
Aristocracy, 世家 shaiʾ-ka.
Arithmetic, 算法 suenʾ-faatʾ.
Arm, (upper-) 手臂 ʽshau-piʾ, (fore-) 手肘 ʽshau-ʽchau, 手瓜 ʽshau-kwa, (the whole) 肩膀 kin-ʽpong.
Arm-chair, 交椅 kaau-ʽi.
Armour, 盔甲 kʽwai-kaapʾ.
Armoury, 軍器局 kwan-hiʾ-*kuuk.
Arm-pits, 胳肋底 kaak-laak-ʽtai.
Arms, 兵器 ping-hiʾ.
Army, 三軍 saam-kwan, 六軍 luuk-kwan.

Aromatic, 香 heung.
Around, 周圍 chau-wai.
Arouse, 醒 ʽseng, 打醒 ʽta-ʽseng.
Arraign, 告 koʾ.
Arrange, 安排 ohn-pʽaai, 整齊 ʽching-tsʽai, 調停 tʽiu-tʽing.
Arrear, 拖欠 tʽoh-himʾ.
Arrest, 捉 chuukʾ.
Arrive, 到 toʾ.
Arrogant, 驕傲 kiu-ngoʾ.
Arrogate, 僭分 tʽsimʾ-funʾ.
Arrow, 箭 tsinʾ.
Arsenal, 軍器局 kwan-hiʾ-*kuuk.
Arsenic, 信石 sunʾ-shek, 人言 yan-in.
Arson, 放火 fongʾ-ʽfoh.
Art, 藝 ngaiʾ, 工藝 kuung-ngaiʾ.
Artemisia, 艾 ngaaiʾ.
Artery, 血脈管 huetʾ-mak-ʽkoon.
Artful, 乖巧 kwaai-ʽhaau.
Article, 件 kinʾ, *kinʾ.
Artifice, 詭計 ʽkwai-kaiʾ.

Artificial, 人手作 yan-ʻshau-tsokʼ.
Artillery, 大炮 taaiʼ-pʻaauʼ, (-men) 砲手 pʻaauʼ-ʻshau.
Artisan, 匠人 tseungʼ-yan, 做工人 tsoʼ-kuung-yan.
Artist, 巧匠 ʻhaau-tseungʼ, 妙手 miuʼ-ʻshau, (painter) 畫師 waʼ-sze.
Artless, 魯鈍 ʻlo-tuunʼ, 純直 shuun-chik.
As, 好似 ʻho-ʻtsʻze, 即如 tsik-ue, 猶之乎 yau-chi-oo.
Asafœtida, 阿魏 oh-ngaiʼ.
Asbestos, 不灰木 pat-fooi-muuk.
Ascend, 上 ʻsheung, 上去 ʻsheung-hueʼ, 升 shing, 登 tang.
Ascent, (way of) 上去之路 ʻsheung-hueʼ-chi-loʼ, 上路 ʻsheung-loʼ.
Ascertain, 查明 chʻa-ming, 查眞 chʻa-chan.
Ascetic, 修鍊 sau-linʼ.
Ascribe to, 歸于 kwai-ue.

Ashamed, 見羞恥 kinʼ-sau-ʻchʻi, 怕醜 pʻaʼ-ʻchʻau.
Ashes, 火灰 foh-fooi.
Ashore, 喺岸上 ʻhai-ngohnʼ-ʻsheungʼ, (to go) 上岸 ʻsheung-ngohnʼ.
Aside, 在傍 tsoiʼ-pʻong, (to put) 收埋 shau-maai.
Ask, 問 munʼ, (invite) 請 ʻtsʻeng, (beg for) 求 kʻau.
Aslant, 斜 tsʻe, tʻse.
Asleep, 睏 ʻfun.
Asparagus, 天門冬 tʻin-moon-tuung, 天冬 tʻin-tuung, 龍鬚菜 luung-so-tsʻoiʼ.
Aspect, 景色 ʻking-shik, 貌 maauʼ, 光景 kwong-ʻking.
Asperse, 講壞 ʻkong-waaiʼ.
Aspirate, 噴氣 pʻunʼ-hiʼ.
Aspire, 想上進 ʻseung-ʻsheungʼ-tsuunʼ, 貪大 tʻaam-taaiʼ.
Ass, 驢 *lue, (an) 隻驢 chekʼ-lue, (a great) 大笨象 taaiʼ-punʼ-tseungʼ.
Assail, 攻 kuung.
Assassin, 刺客 tsʻzeʼ-haakʼ.

Assault, 攻打 kuung-ʻta, (as robbers) 打脚骨 ʻta-keuk'-kwut.
Assay, 考驗 ʻhaau-im', 驗過 im'-kwo'.
Assemble, 聚集 tsue'-tsaap.
Assembly, 會 *ooi'.
Assent, 話肯 wa'-ʻhang, 允 ʻwan.
Assert, 話係 wa'-hai', 力言 lik-in.
Assess, 估稅 ʻkoo-shui'.
Assets, 遺業 wai-ip, 遺產 wai-ʻch'aan.
Assign, 立限 laap-haan', 限定 haan'-ting', (-to) 定歸 ting'-kwai.
Assist, 幫助 pong-choh', 照顧 chiu'-koo'.
Assistant, 二手 i'-ʻshau, (in government) 副 foo'.
Assize, 官擬價 koon-ʻi-ka'.
Associate, to, 相與 seung-ʻue, 往來 ʻwong-loi, (an) 同伴 t'uung-poon'.
Association, 會 *ooi'.
Assort, 排列 p'aai-lit, 安排 ohn-p'aai.

Assuage, 解 ʻkaai.
Assume, 以爲 ʻi-wai, 假借 ʻka-tse', (a name) 冒名 mo'-*meng.
Assuming, 擅自 shin'-tsze'.
Assurance, (faith) 篤信 tuuk-suun', (presumption) 膽 ʻtaam.
Assure, 擔保 taam-ʻpo.
Assuredly, 果然 ʻkwoh-in.
Asthma, 氣喘 hi'-ch'uen.
Astonish, 驚着 king-cheuk.
Astonishing, 出奇 ch'uut-k'i.
Astound, 騾嚇 tsau'-(chaau')-haak.
Astray, 蕩失 tong'-shat.
Astringent, 收濕藥料 shau-shup-yeuk-liu'.
Astrology, 星學 sing-hok.
Astronomy, 天文 t'in-mun.
Asylum, 院 *uen', (for children) 育嬰堂 yuuk-ying-*t'ong.
At, 在 tsoi', 喺 ʻhai, (-last) 卒之 tsuut-chi, 究竟 kau'-ʻking.

Atheist, 話無上帝者 waʼ-ʻmo-sheung ʻtaiʼ-ʻche.
Atlas, 地圖書 tiʼ-tʻo-shue.
Atmosphere, 天氣 tʻin-hiʼ.
Atom, 微末 mi-moot.
At once, 即時 tsik-shi.
Atone, 代贖 toiʼ-shuuk, 使敵和 ʻshai-tik-woh, 做和頭 tsoʼ-woh-tʻau.
Atrocity, 殘認之事 tsʻaan-ʻyan-chi-ʻsze.
Attach, 貼近 tʻipʼ-kanʼ (ʻkʻan) 相連 seung-lin.
Attachment, 貼心 tʻipʼ-sum.
Attack, 攻打 kuung-ʻta, 攻擊 kuung-kik.
Attain, 得到 tak-ʻto, 得至 tak-chiʼ, 及至 kʻaap-chiʼ.
Attempt, 試爲 shiʼ-wai, 試做下 shiʼ-tsoʼ-ha.
Attend to, 留心 lau-sum, (at) 在 tsoiʼ, (upon) 侍奉 shiʼ-fuung, 服事 fuuk-szeʼ, (manage) 打理 ʻta-ʻli.
Attendants, 跟班 kan-paan.
Attentive, 檢點 ʻkim-ʻtim, 細心 saiʼ-sum.

Attest, 作証 tsokʼ-chingʼ.
Attire, 裝扮 chong-paanʼ.
Attitude, 容 yuung, 狀貌 chongʼ-maauʼ.
Attorney, 狀師 chongʼ-sze, 小狀師 ʻsiu-chongʼ-sze, (to act as) 代辦 toiʼ-paanʼ.
Attorney General, 國家律政司 Kwokʼ-ka-luut-ching-sze.
Attract, 招引 chiu-ʻyan.
Auburn, 褐色 hohtʼ-shik.
Auction, (sell by) 投賣 tʻau-maaiʼ, (sale) 喊夜冷 haamʼ-yeʼ-ʻlaang.
Audacious, 果敢 ʻkwoh-ʻkom, 大膽 taaiʼ-ʻtaam.
Auditor General, 考數司 ʻHaau-shoʼ-sze.
Augment, 加增 ka-tsang, 添 tʻim.
August, 英八月 Ying-paatʼ-uet.
Augúst, 皇 wong.
Aunt, (paternal) 姑母 koo-ʻmoo, (maternal) 姨母 i-ʻmoo.

Auspicious, 吉 kat.
Austere, 局肅 kuuk-suuk.
Author, 造主 tso'-ch'ue, 著造之人 chue'-tso'-chi(ke')-yan, 作家 tsok'-ka.
Authority, 權 k'uen, 權勢 k'uen-shai', 權柄 k'uen-ping'.
Autumn, 秋天 ts'au-t'in.
Avail one's self of, 趁 ch'an', 乘 shing, 趁勢 ch'an'-shai', (be of use) 有益 'yau-yik.
Avarice, 貪財 t'aam-ts'oi, 貪婪 t'aam-laam.
Avenge, 報仇 po'-ch'au.
Average, 拉扯筭 laai-'ch'e-suen'.
Averse, 不中意 'm-chuung-i', 不耐煩 'm-noi'-faan.
Avoid, 脫免 t'uet-'min, 避 pi'.
Avouch, 認眞 ying'-chan.
Avow, 直話 chik-wa'.
Await, 等待 'tang-toi'.
Awake, 瞓醒 fun'-'seng, 醒 'seng, (wide-) 醒定 'sing-ting'.

Aware, 知到 chi-to'.
Away, 去 'hue, 離 li.
Awe, 畏懼 wai'-kue'.
Awkward, 粗魯 t'so-'lo, 不(唔)入世 'm-yup-shai'.
Awl, 錐 ch'ui, 'yui.
Awning, 遮帳 che-cheung', 布帳 po'-cheung'.
Awry, 歪 'me.
Axe, 斧頭 'foo-*t'au.
Axle, 轉軸 'chuen-chuuk.
Ay, 係咯 hai'-lok, 係 hai'.
Azalea, 杜鵑花 to'-kuen-fa.
Azure, 蒼色 ts'ong-shik.

B

Babble, 嘹嘈 lo-ts'o, 嘈吵 ts'o-'ch'aau.
Babbler, 嘈吵之人 ts'o-'ch'aau-ke'-yan.
Baby, 亞蘇仔 a'-so-'tsai.
Bachelor 未娶 mi'-*ts'ue'.
Back, (the) 背 pooi', 背脊 pooi'-tsek', (turn-) 返 faan, 回轉 ooi-'chuen, (behind one's) 背後邊 pooi'-hau'-pin.

Back-bite, 背後譭謗 pooi²-hau²-ʻwai-pʻong².
Back-bone, 背脊骨 pooi²-tsek²-kwut.
Back-door, 後門 hau²-*moon.
Backslide, 背道 pooi²-to².
Backstitch, 鈎 kʻau.
Backward, 向後 heung²-hau², 退後 tʻui²-hau², (to walk) 倒行 ʻto-hang.
Bacon, 烟豬肉 in-chue-yuuk.
Bad, 惡 okʼ, 不好 ʼm-ʻho, 醜 ʻchʻau, 滲 sum², 呦 yai.
Badge, 記號 kiʼ-hoʼ.
Badger, 狗貛 ʻkau-foon.
Baffle, 捐阻 kʻangʼ-ʻchoh, 擺佈倒 ʻpaai-poʼ-ʻto, (him) 奈佢何 noiʼ-kʻue-hoh.
Baffled, 無定埋手 ʻmo-tengʼ-maai-ʻshau, 無計 ʻmo-kaiʼ.
Bag, 袋 *toiʼ, 囊 nong.
Baggage, 行李 hang-ʻli.
Bail, 保領 ʻpo-ʻling.
Bait, 餌 niʼ.

Baize, 粗大呢 tsʻo-taaiʼ-ni.
Bake, 炕 hongʼ, 局 kuuk.
Balance, (a) 天平 tʻin-pʻing, (steelyard) 把秤 ʻpa-chʻing², (small do.) 釐戥 li-*tangʼ, (to) 抵 tai, 相抵 seung-ʻtai, 平兌 pʻing-tuiʼ, (the) 剩銀 shing-*ngan.
Bald, 光 kwong, 禿 tʻuuk, (-head) 光頭 kwong-tʻau.
Bale, (a) 包 paau, (to, water) 戽水 fooʼ-ʻshui.
Ball, (a) 毬 kʻau, (cannon) 砲子 pʻaauʼ-tsze, 砲碼 pʻaauʼ-*ma.
Ballad, 曲 kʻuuk, huuk, (a) 一支野 yat-chi-ʻye.
Ballast, 責載 chaak-*tsoiʼ.
Balloon, 輕氣毬 hing-hiʼ-kʻau.
Balsam, (flower) 指甲花 ʻchi-kaapʼ-fa, 鳳仙花 fuungʼ-sin-fa.
Bamboo, 竹 chuuk, (a) 條竹 tʻiu-chuuk.

Bamboo shoots, 竹笋 chuuk-ʿsuun.
Banana, 蕉 ʿtsiu.
Band, (tie) 帶 taaiʾ, (company) 一隊 yat-tuiʾ, 一班 yat-paan.
Bandage, (a) 纏帶 ch'in-taaiʾ (ʿtaai), (to) 纏 chinʾ.
Band-box, 紙盒 ʿchi-*hop.
Banditti, 賊夥 ts'aak-ʿfoh, 匪黨 ʿfi-ʿtong.
Bandy-legged, 曲脛 kuuk-ʿking, 八字脚 paatʾ-tszeʾ-keukʾ, 蜯髀 paangʾ-ʿpi.
Bane, 毒 tuuk.
Bang, 碰 p'uungʾ, 蜯 p'aangʾ, paang.
Bangle, 鈪 aakʾ.
Banian, 榕樹 yuung-shueʾ.
Banish, 充軍 ch'uung-kwun, 問軍 munʾ-kwun.
Bank, (of a river) 河岸 hoh-ngohnʾ, 海邊 ʿhoi-pin, (for money) 銀行 ngan-*hong.
Bankrupt, 倒行 ʿto-*hong, 倒灶 ʿto-tsoʾ.

Banner, 旗 k'i, (large) 大翻 taaiʾ-t'o.
Bannermen, 旗下 k'i-*haʾ.
Banquet, 酒蓆 ʿtsau-tsek.
Banter, 訛諧 fooi-haai, 激笑 kik-siuʿ.
Baptism, 洗禮 ʿsai-ʿlai.
Baptize, 施洗 shi-ʿsai, (to be baptized) 受洗 shauʾ-ʿsai 領洗 ʿling-ʿsai.
Bar, (of a door) 門閂 moon-shaan, 橫遏 waang-aatʾ, (of a cage) 橫櫳 waang-luung, * waang.
Barbarous, 蠻 maan, 蠻夷 maan-i.
Barbel, 嘉魚 ka-ue.
Barber, 剃頭人 t'aiʾ-t'au-yan.
Bare, 裸 ʿloh, 赤 ch'ikʾ, 光 kwong, (to) 剝 mok, 袒 ʿt'aan, 捋 luetʾ, (-faced) 無臉 ʿmo-limʾ.
Bargain, (to) 講價 ʿkong-kaʾ, (settle a) 講定價錢 ʿkong-tingʾ-kaʾ-ts'in.
Bark, (of a tree) 樹皮 shueʾ-p'i.

Bark, (to) 吠 faiʼ.
Barley, 大麥 taaiʼ-maak, (pearl) 苡米 ʻi-mai.
Barn, 田庄 tʻin-ʻchong.
Barometer, 風雨針 fuung-ʻue-chum.
Baron, 男爵 naam-tseukʼ.
Barque, 兩枝半桅船 ʻleung-chi-poonʼ-*wai-shuen.
Barracks, 兵房 ping-fong.
Barrel, 洋酒桶 yeung-ʻtsau-ʻtuung.
Barren, (womb) 石胎 shek-tʻoi (land) 瘠土 tsikʼ-ʻtʻo.
Barricade, 棚欄 chʻaak-laan.
Barrier, 閘 chaap, 保障 ʻpo-cheungʼ, 阻碍 ʻchoh-ngoiʼ.
Barrister, 大狀師 taaiʼ-chongʼ-sze.
Barrow, 手車 ʻshau-chʻe.
Barter, 兌換 tuiʼ-oonʼ.
Base, (bottom) 底 ʻtai, 墩 ʻtun, 基 ki, 脚 keukʼ.
Base, (mean) 鄙陋 ʻpʻi-lauʼ, (bad) 歹 ʻtaai.
Basement, 地牢 tiʼ-loo, 墩 ʻtun.
Bashful, 怕醜 pʻaʼ-ʻchʻau.

Basil, (sweet) 紫蘇 ʻtsze-soo.
Basin, 盆 pʻoon, (small) 碗 ʻoon.
Basket, 籃 *laam, 籮 loh, 筐 hong, kʻwaang, 笠 lap, 篱 li.
Bastard, 野仔 ʻye-ʻtsai, (in abusive language) 龜仔 kwai-ʻtsai.
Baste clothes, 攤衣服 naanʼ-i-fuuk.
Bastinado, 打板子 ʻta-ʻpaan-ʻtsze.
Bat, 飛鼠 fi-ʻshue, (a) 一隻飛鼠 yat-chekʼ-fi-ʻshue.
Bathe, 洗身 ʻsai-shan.
Battery, 炮臺 pʻaauʼ-*tʻoi.
Battle, (a) 打仗一陣 ʻta-cheungʼ-yat-chanʼ.
Bawdy-house, 娼寮 chʻeung-*liu, cheungʼ-*liu.
Bawl, 呼喊 foo-haamʼ.
Bay, (of the sea) 灣 waan, 澳 oʼ.
Bayonet, 鎗頭劍 ʻtsʻeung-tʻau-kimʼ.
Be, 係 haiʼ, (be in) 喺 ʻhai, 在 tsoiʼ.

Beach, 海邊 ʻhoi-pin.
Beacon, 烟墩 in-tuun.
Bead, 珠 chue, (a string of beads) 一串珠 yat-chʻuenʼ-ₑchue, (a bead) 一粒珠 yat-nup-ₑchue.
Beak, 嘴 ʻtsui.
Beam, (a) 梁木 leung-muuk, 條陳 tʻiu-chanʼ.
Beam, (to) 發光 faatʼ-kwong.
Bean, 豆 *tau, (French) 豆角 tauʼ-kokʼ, 邊豆 pin tauʼ, 面豆 minʼ-*tauʼ (sprouts), 芽菜 nga-tsʻoi.
Bean-curd, 豆腐 tauʼ-fooʼ.
Bear, (carry on the shoulder) 擔 taam, (between two) 擡 tʻoi, (on the back) 孭 me, (endure) 抵住 ʻtai-chueʼ, 受 shauʼ, (a child) 生 shang.
Bear, (a) 一隻熊人 yat-chekʼ-huung-*yan.
Beard, 鬚 so, 下爬鬚 haʼ-pʻa-so.
Bearer, (chair-) 擡夫 tʻoi-foo, (letter-) 拈信人 nim-suunʼ-yan.

Beast, 獸 shauʼ, (a) 一隻獸 yat-chekʼ-shauʼ.
Beat, 打 ʻta, (up eggs, &c.) 拂 faakʼ, (defeat) 打敗 ʻta-paaiʼ.
Beau, 大亞官 taaiʼ-aʼ-koon.
Beautiful, 美 ʻmi, 好睇 ʻho-ʻtʻai, 好樣 ʻho-*yeungʼ, 標緻 piu-chiʼ, 威 wai.
Beauty, female, 色 shik.
Beaver, 海騾 ʻhoi-*loh.
Becalmed, 無風駛 ʻmo-fuung-ʻshai, 聽風 tʻingʼ-fuung.
Because, 因爲 yan-wai.
Beche-de-mer, 海參 ʻhoi-shum.
Beckon, 手招 ʻshau-chiu, 噏 ngup.
Become, 成 shing, 爲 wai, 做 tsoʼ, (to grow) 生成 shaang-shing.
Becoming, (fit) 合式 hop-shik.
Bed, 牀 chʻong, (a) 一張牀 yat-cheung-chʻong.

Bed-chamber, 臥房 ngoh`-fong, 瞓房 fun`-fong, *fong.
Bedding, 床鋪 ch'ong-p'oo, 鋪蓋 p'oo-k'oi`, 被 `p'i.
Bee, 蜂 fuung, 蜜蜂 mat-fuung.
Bee-hive, 蜜籠 mat-*luung.
Beef, 牛肉 ngau-yuuk.
Beef-steak, 牛肉耙 ngau-yuuk-*p'a.
Beer, 卑酒 pe-`tsau.
Beet, 莧菜 in`-ts'oi`.
Beet-root, 紅菜頭 huung-ts'oi`-*t'au.
Beetle, 甲蟲 kaap`-ch'uung.
Before, 先 sin, 前 ts'in, (formerly) 從前 ts'uung-ts'in, 先時 sin-shi.
Beforehand, 預先 ue`-sin.
Befriend, 照顧 chiu`-koo`, 體恤 `t'ai-suut.
Beg, 乞 hat, 乞求 hat-k'au.
Beget, 生 shaang.
Beggar, 乞兒 hat-i, 花子 fa-`tsze.

Begin, 初造 ch'oh-tso`, 開手 hoi-`shau, 埋手 maai-`shau, 起首 `hi-`shau, 興工 hing-kuung.
Beginning, 始初 `ch'i-ch'oh, 首 `shau.
Begone, 扯咯 `ch'e-lok`.
Begonia, 春海棠 ch'uun-`hoi-t'ong.
Beguile, 欺 hi, 欺惑 hi-waak.
Behalf, (in) 替代 t'ai`-toi`.
Behave, 行 hang, (towards) 待 toi`.
Behaviour, 品行 `pun-hang`.
Behead, 斬頭 `chaam-\*t'au, 殺頭 shaat`-*t'au.
Behind, 後 hau`, (to be) 喺後頭 `hai-hau`-t'au.
Behold, 顧住 koo`-chue,` 睇 `t'ai, (lo!) 睇嗱 `t'ai-na!
Behoof, 利益 li`-yik.
Behove, 應該 ying-koi.
Being, (existence) 有 `yau, 有者 `yau-`che.
Belch, 打噯氣 `ta-`oi-hi`, (COL.) yeuk-`hi-lai, yeuk.

Believe, 信 suun`.
Bell, 鐘 chuung, 鈴 `ling.
Bell-flower, 吊鐘花 tiu-chuung-fa.
Belladonna, 癲茄 tin-*k`e.
Bellows, 風箱 fuung-seung, 皮排 p`i-p`aai.
Belly, 肚 `t`o, 腹 fuuk.
Belong, 屬 shuuk, 關屬 kwaan-shuuk.
Beloved, 愛 oi`, 所愛 `shoh-oi`.
Below, 下 ha`, 底下 `tai-ha`, 下底 ha`-`tai (tai).
Belt, 腰帶 iu-taai`, 帶圍 taai`-wai.
Bemoan, 悲哀 pi-oi.
Bench, 板凳 `paan-tang`, (magistrate's) 公案 kuung-ohn`.
Bend, (to) 屈曲 wat-huuk (k`uuk), 整曲 `ching-huuk, 曲 `lai, (a) 彎曲 waan-huuk.
Beneath, 在下 tsoi`-ha`, 喺下邊 `hai-ha`-pin (pin).
Benefactor, 恩主 yan-`chue.

Beneficent, 肯賙恤 `hang-chau-suut.
Benefit, 益 yik, (grace) 恩澤 yan-chaak, (to) 滋益 tsze-yik.
Benevolence, 仁愛 yan-oi`, 仁 yan, 仁德 yan-tak.
Benighted, 居黑暗中 kue-hak-om`-chuung.
Bent, 曲 k`uuk, huuk, 拗了 `aau-`liu (hiu).
Bent of mind, 志氣 chi`-hi` 志向 chi`-heung`.
Bequeath, 留落 lau-lok, 遺囑 wai-chuuk.
Bereaved of, 喪失 song` shat.
Berth, 房位 fong-*wai`.
Beseech, 懇求 `han-k`au.
Beset, 圍住 wai-chue`.
Beside, 側邊 chak-pin.
Besides, 另外 ling`-ngoi`.
Besiege, 圍困 wai-k`wun`.
Besotted, 昏迷 fun-mai.
Bespeak, 定 ting`, 講定 `kong-ting`.
Best, 第一好 tai`-yat-`ho, 至好 chi`-`ho, 頂好 `ting-`ho.

Bestow, 施賜 shi-ts'ze', 給 k'up.
Bet, 輸賭 shue-'to.
Betelnut, 檳榔 pun-long.
Betel-pepper-leaf, 荖葉 lau-ip.
Betray, 賣付 maai'-foo', 欺陷 hi-haam'.
Betroth, (of men) 定親 ting'-ts'an, (of women) 許聘 'hue-p'ing'.
Better, 更好 kang'-'ho, (a little) 好的 'ho-tik, (quite) 好嗮 'ho-saai'.
Between, 中間 chuung-,kaan, ——之間 ——chi ,kaan.
Bewail, 哀哭 oi-huuk.
Beware, 提防 t'ai-fong, 關顧 kwaan-koo'.
Bewildered, 心亂 sum-luen', 入迷路 yup-mai-lo', 恍惚 'fong-fut.
Bewitched, 鬼迷 'kwai-mai.
Beyond, ——之外 ——chi-ngoi', ——外 ——ngoi', (to go) 過 kwoh'.
Bezoar, 牛黃 ngau-wong.

Bias, 偏 p'in.
Bib, 口水肩 'hau-'shui-,kin, 'hau-'shui-lau.
Bible, 聖經 shing'-king.
Bid, (order) 囑咐 chuuk-foo, (invite) 請 'ts'ing, (offer) 出 ch'uut.
Bide, 等 'tang, 耐 noi'.
Bier, 運柩架 wun'-kau-ka'.
Big, 大 taai'.
Bignonia, 凌霄花 ling-siu-fa.
Bigoted, 固執 koo'-chup, 泥 ni', 泥住本教 ni'-chue'-'poon-kaau'.
Bile, 膽汁 'taam-chup.
Bill, (beak) 嘴 'tsui, (paper) 張單 cheung-,taan.
Bill of exchange, 匯單 ooi'-,taan.
Bill of lading, 攬載紙 laam'-tsoi'-'chi.
Billiard, 波 poh, (to play) 打波 'ta-poh, (room) 波攊 poh-*lau.
Billows, 波浪 poh-long'.

Bind, 札 chaat', 綁 'pong, 綁住 'pong-chue,' (agree) 約 yeuk' (books) 釘 teng, 釘裝 teng-chong.

Binding, (of clothes) 綑邊 'k'wun-pin, 綑條 'k'wun-*t'iu, 緣 nen'.

Biography, 行狀 hang-chong'.

Birch, 樺木 wa-muuk.

Bird, 鳥 'niu, 雀鳥 tseuk'-'niu, (small) 雀仔 tseuk'-'tsai, (a) 一隻鳥 yat-chek'-'niu, (and beast) 禽獸 k'um-shau'.

Bird-lime, 糍膠 c'hi-kaau.

Bird's-nest, (edible) 燕窩 in'-woh.

Birth, 生 shaang.

Birth-day, 生日 shaang-yat.

Biscuit, 餅乾 'peng-kohn.

Bit, (of a bridle) 馬口鉗 'ma-'hau-k'im, (piece) 塊 faai'.

Bitch, 狗母 'kau-'moo, 狗姆 'kau-'na.

Bite, 咬 'ngaau, (a) 一啖 yat-taam'.

Bitter, 苦 'foo.

Bittern, 朱鷺 chue-lo'.

Bitumen, 瀝青 lik-ts'ing.

Bivalve, 蜆殼 'hin-hok'.

Black, 黑 hak, 黑色 hak-shik.

Blackguard, 光棍 kwong-kwun', 爛仔 laan'-'tsai, 爛口 laan'-'hau.

Blacking, (shoe-) 鞋墨 haai-maak.

Blackleg, 掴家仔 lo-ka-'tsai.

Black-smith, 打鐵匠 'ta-t'it'-*tseung'.

Bladder, 尿胞 niu'-paau, (animal's) 小肚 'siu-'t'o.

Blade, (of grass) 草葉 'ts'u-ip, (of a knife) 刀肉 to-*yuuk, (shoulder-) 飯匙骨 faan'-shi-kwut.

Bladed knife, three, 三開刀 saam-hoi-to.

Blain, 血旺色 huet'-wong'-shik.

Blame, 罪 tsui', (to) 彈 t'aan, 怪 kwaai', 責 chaak'.

Blameless, 無罪 'mo-tsui'.

Blanc-mange, 牛乳凍 ngau-ʻue-*tuung*ʼ.
Blank, 空白 *huung*ʼ-*paak*.
Blanket, 白氈 paak-*chin*.
Blaspheme, 褻瀆 *sit*ʼ-tuuk, 謗讟 *pʻong*ʼ-tuuk.
Blast rocks, 打石炮 ʻ*ta-shek-pʻaau*ʼ.
Blaze, 火熖 ʻ*foh*-*im*ʼ, 火光 ʻ*foh-kwong*, 火氣 ʻ*foh-hi*ʼ, 火猛 ʻ*foh*-maang.
Bleach, 漂白 *pʻiu*ʼ-paak.
Bleat, 咩 *me*, 咩聲 *me-sheng*.
Bleed, 流血 lau-*huet*ʼ.
Blemish, 疙點 *oo*-ʻ*tim*, 病 peng', 毛病 mo-peng', 瑕疵 ha-*tsʻze*.
Blend, 和勻 woh'-wan, 摳勻 *kʻau*-wan.
Bless, 祝 *chuuk*, 祝福 *chuuk-fuuk*.
Blight, 殘 tsʻaan, 弊 paiʼ.
Blind, 盲眼 maang-ʻngaan.
Blind-manʼs-buff, 捉迷蒙 *chuuk*ʼ-*mi*-*muung*, 摸盲 ʻ*moh*-maang.
Blinds, 簾 *lim*, (venetian-) 百葉窻 *paak*ʼ-ip-*chʻeung*.

Blink, 閃 ʻ*shim*, (the eyes) 喎 *ngup*, (elude sight) 閃過眼 ʻ*shim-kwoh*ʼ-ʻngaan.
Bliss, 福 *fuuk*.
Blister, 水泡 ʻ*shui-pʻaau*, (pʻok), (to) 發水泡 *faat*ʼ-ʻ*shui-pʻaau*.
Bloated, 浮腫 fau-ʻ*chuung*.
Block, (of wood, &c.) 頭 tʻau, 俗 kauʼ, (for printing) 板 ʻpaan, (pulley) 律羅 luut-*loh.
Blockade, 阻塞港口 ʻ*choh-sak*-ʻ*kong*-ʻ*hau*, 阻塞津要 ʻ*choh-sak-tsuun-iu*ʼ.
Blockhead, 木偶人 muuk-ʻngau-yan, 吤佬 yai-ʻ*lo*.
Blood, 血 *huet*ʼ.
Bloom, (to) 開花 hoi-*fa*.
Blot, 塗污 tʻo-*oo*, (out) 塗抹 tʻo-*moot*, 搽 chʻa.
Blotch, 酒齇 ʻ*tsau-cha*.
Blow, (strike) 打 ʻ*ta*, (a) 打一下 ʻ*ta-yat*-ʻ*ha*, (as wind) 吹 *chʻui*, (the nose) 擤鼻 sangʼ-piʼ, (out) 吹滅 *chʻui*-mit.
Blue, 藍色 laam-*shik* 靛 tinʼ.

Blunder, 錯誤 ts'oh⁻-'ng⁻.
Blunt, 鈍 tuun⁻, tuen⁻, 痴呆 ch'i-ngoi.
Blur, 矇 muung, 模糊 moo-oo.
Blush, 發紅 面 faat⁻-ʿhuung-ʿnin-min⁻, 含羞 hom-sau.
Bluster, 躁暴 ts'o⁻-po⁻.
Boa-constrictor, 蟒蛇 ʿmong-she.
Boar, 猪郎 chue-long.
Board, (wood) 木板 muuk-ʿpaan, (a) 一塊板 yat-faai⁻-ʿpaan, (department) 部 po⁻.
Board, (to eat with) 同食 t'uung-shik, 搭食 taap⁻-shik, (one's self) 食自已 shik-tsze⁻-ʿki, (ship) 土船 ʿsheung-shuen.
Boast, 矜誇 king-k'wa, 誇 k'wa.
Boat, 艇 ʿt'eng, 三舨 saam-ʿpaan, 船 shuen.
Bob, 夭 ngan⁻.
Bodice, 押胸 moon-huung.

Bodkin, 串帶針 ch'uen⁻-taai⁻-chum.
Body, 身 shan, 身體 shan-ʿt'ai, 體 ʿt'ai.
Bog, 涎池 paan⁻-ch'i.
Bohea-tea, 武彛茶 ʿmoo-i-ch'a.
Boil, (to) 煲 po, 烚 shaap.
Boiled, 熟 shuuk.
Boiling, 滾 ʿkwan, (with rage) 心滾 sum-ʿk'wan.
Boils, 瘡 ch'ong.
Boiler, 鑊 wok, 塔 tap, 煲 po.
Boisterous, 暴 po⁻, 猛 ʿmaang.
Bold, 大膽 taai⁻-ʿtaam, 剛毅 kong-ngai⁻.
Bolster, 大牀枕 taai⁻-ch'ong-ʿchum.
Bolt, 釘 teng, 榫 suut, 鐵貫 t'it⁻-koon⁻, (of a door) 門閂 moon-shaan, (to) 閂 shaan.
Bomb, 開花炮 hoi-fa-p'aau⁻, (COL.) ʿpom-p'aau⁻.
Bombay ducks, 肚魚乾 ʿt'o-*ue-kohn.

Bond, 約單 yeuk²-ₑtaan,
(money-) 借單 tse²-ₑtaan,
(band) 帶 taai².
Bond-servant, 奴僕 no-puuk.
Bone, 骨 kwut.
Bonnet, 女帽 nue-*mo².
Booby, 戇人 ngong²-yan,
大頭蝦 taai²-t'au-ha.
Book, 書 shue, (a) 一部書 yat-po²-shue, 部 *po².
Book case, 書櫃 shue-*kwai².
Bookbinder, 釘書人 teng-shue-yan.
Book-worm, 蠹魚 to²-ue.
Boom, 帆杠 faan-kong².
Boor, 蠻村佬 maan-ts'uen-ᶜlo.
Boot, 靴 hö.
Booth, 茅屋 maau-uuk, 棚 p'aang.
Bo-peep, 覵眼 ₑchong-ᶜnyaan.
Borax, 硼砂 p'ang-sha.
Border, 邊 pin, 界 kaai², 邊境 pin-ᶜking.
Bore, 鑽 tsuen², 穿 ch'uen.
Born, 生 shang, 出世 ch'ut-shai².

Borrow, 借來 tse²-loi, 假借 ᶜka-tse².
Bosom, 胸懷 hung-waai.
Botany, 草木學 ᶜts'o-muuk-hok.
Botch, 弊家伙 pai²-ka-ᶜfoh.
Both, 兩個 ᶜleung-koh².
Bother, 煩擾 faan-ᶜiu, 撈 lo.
Bothered, 厭悶 im-moon².
Bottle, 罇 tsuun.
Bottle-gourd, 葫蘆 oo-*loo.
Bottom, 底 ᶜtai.
Bound, }
Bounce, } 跳 t'iu².
Boundary, 交界 kaau-kaai².
Boundless, 無限 ᶜmo-haan².
Bountiful, 厚重 hau²-chuung².
Bow, (to) 打恭 ᶜta-kuung, 作揖 tsok²-yup.
Bow, (a) 弓 kuung, 一把弓 yat-ᶜpa-kuung.
Bowels, 腸 ch'eung, 肚 ᶜt'o.
Bowl, 碗 ᶜoon.
Bowsprit, 船頭拔 shuen-t'au-pat.

Box, 箱 seung, (to) 舉打 k'uen-ʻta, 打拳頭 ʻta-k'uen-t'au.

Boy, 男仔 naam-ʻtsai, (servant-) 事仔 sze'-ʻtsai, (waiting-) 侍仔 shi'-ʻtsai.

Bracelet, 手鈪 ʻshau-aak'.

Braces, 褲帶 foo'-taai'.

Brag, 誇大 k'wa-taai'.

Braggart, 誇口 k'wa-ʻhau.

Braid, 欄杆 laan-kohn, (to) 編織 pin-chik, 棍 pun'.

Brain, 腦漿 ʻno-tseung.

Bramble, 荊棘 king-kik, 笏 lak.

Bran, 麥糠 mak-hong.

Branch, 枝 chi.

Brand, (a) 火把 ʻfoh-ʻpa, 鐵烙 t'it'-lok', (to) 烙印 lok'-yan'.

Brandish, 舞 ʻmoo, 手舞 ʻshau-ʻmoo.

Brandy, 罷欄地酒 pa'-laan-ti'-ʻtsau.

Brass, 銅 t'uung, 黃銅 wong-t'uung.

Brassica, 白菜 paak-ts'oi'.

Brave, 勇敢 ʻyuung-ʻkom.

Bravo! 好 ʻho!

Brawl, 鬧交 naau'-kaau.

Bray, 驢鳴 lue-ming.

Brazen-faced, 無臉 moo-lim'.

Brazier, 打銅人 ʻta-t'uung-yan, tup-t'uung-yan.

Breach-loader, 後堂（炮）hau'-t'ong (p'aau').

Bread, 麵包 min'-ʻpaau, 麵頭 min'-t'au.

Breadth, 闊度 foot'-to'.

Break, 打爛 ʻta-laan'. 整爛 ʻching-laan', 破 p'oh', 折 chit', (off) 斷 ʻt'uen, (out) 發 faat', (the law) 犯法 faan'-faat', (bread) 擘餅 maak'-peng, (wind) 放屁 fong'-p'i'.

Breakfast, 早飯 ʻtso-faan'. 朝餐 chiu-ts'aan.

Bream, 扁魚 pin-*ne, 魴魚 fong-*ne.

Breast, 胸前 huung-ts'in. -

Breastplate, 護心鏡 oo'-sum-keng'.

Breasts, 奶 ʻnaai.

Breath, 口氣 ʻhau-hi', 氣息 hi'-sik.

Breathe, 抖氣 ʻtʻau-hiʼ, 呼吸 foo-kʻup.
Breathless, 氣都絕 hiʼ-too-tsuet.
Breech, the, 臀 tʻuen, (VULG.) 屄 tuuk, ʻshi-fut-ʻtun.
Breeches, 褲 fooʼ.
Breed, (to), 生產 shaang-ʻchʻaan, 生 shaang, 畜養 chʻuuk-ʻyeung.
Breeze, (a light) 風仔 fuung ʻtsai.
Brethren, 兄弟 hing-taiʼ.
Brew, 釀 yeungʼ.
Bribe, 賄賂 ʻfooi-loʼ, 買囑 ʻmaai-chuuk.
Bribery, 錢神用事 tsʻin-shan-yuungʼ-szeʼ.
Brick, 磚 chuen, (common) 青磚 tsʻing-chuen.
Brick-layer, 坭水匠 nai-ʻshui-*tseungʼ (ʻlo).
Bride, 新娘 san-*neung, 新抱 san-ʻpʻo, sum-ʻpʻo.
Bridegroom, 新郎 san-*long.
Bridge, 橋 kʻiu, (a) 一道橋 yat-toʼ-kʻiu, (of the nose) 鼻梁 piʼ-*leung.

Bridle, 韁 keung, 籠絡 luung-lokʼ.
Brief, 短 ʻtuen.
Brig, 兩枝桅船 ʻleung-chi-*wai-shuen.
Bright, 光明 kwong-ming.
Brilliant, 光朗 kwong-ʻlong.
Brim, 墘 kʻeng.
Brimful, 滿到墘 ʻmoon-toʼ-kʻeng.
Brimstone, 硫磺 lau-wong.
Brine, 鹹汁 haam-chup, 鹹水 haam-ʻshui.
Bring, 掉——來 ning——lai, 拈——來 nim——lai, 帶——來 taaiʼ——lai.
Brinjal, 茄 *kʻe, 矮瓜 ʻai-kwa.
Brink, 邊 pin, 變界 kaau-kaaiʼ, (on the) 將近呢睰 tseung-*kanʼ nē munʼ.
Brisket, 腜肉 mooi-yuuk.
Bristles, 猪鬃毛 chue-tsuung-mo, 箭毛 tsinʼmo.
Brittle, 脆 tsʻuiʼ.
Broad, 闊 footʼ, 廣闊 ʻkwong-footʼ.

Broad-cloth, 大呢 taai⁾-ni, 大絨 taai⁾-yuung.
Brocade, 花緞 fa-*tuen⁾, 局緞 kuuk-*tuen⁾.
Broccoli, 白菜 paak-tsʻoi⁾.
Brogue, 土談 tʻo-tʻaam.
Broil, 燒炙 shiu-chek⁾.
Broker, 經紀 king-ki.
Bronchocele, 鵝𠻦 ngoh-hau.
Bronze, 古銅色 ⸢koo-tʻuung-shik.
Brooch, (a) 襟頭針 kʻum-tʻau-chum, 心口針 sum-⸢hau-chum.
Brood, 伏卵 fuuk-⸢luun, 菢蛋 po⁾-*taan⁾.
Brook, 溪 kʻai, 溪澗 kʻai-kaan⁾, 山水坑 shaan-⸢shui-haang.
Broom, 把掃 ⸢pa-so⁾, 掃把 so⁾-⸢pa.
Brothel, 老舉寨 ⸢lo-⸢kue-*chaai⁾, 娼寮 chʻeung-*liu, 妓館 ki⁾-⸢koon.
Brother, (elder) 兄 hing, 哥 koh, 大佬 taai⁾-⸢lo, (younger) 弟 tai⁾, 細佬 sai⁾-⸢lo.

Brother-in-law, (a husband's) 妻舅 tsʻai-⸢kʻau, (a wife's) 大伯 taai⁾-paak⁾, 細叔 sai⁾-shuuk, (brother's or sister's) 姐夫 ⸢tse-foo, 妹夫 mooi⁾-foo.
Brow, 額 ngaak.
Brow-beat, 嚇薄 haak⁾-pok.
Brown, 棕色 tsuung-shik, 豬肝色 ⸢chue-⸢kohn-shik.
Bruise, (to powder) 研爛 ngaan-laan⁾, (with the foot) 踹 chʻaai⁾, ⸢naai, (hurt) 瘀傷 ue⁾-sheung, ⸢ue-⸢choh.
Brush, 擦 ⸢sʻaat⁾, 刷 shaat⁾, (a) 一個刷 yat-koh⁾-shaat⁾.
Brute, 禽獸 kʻum-shau⁾.
Brutish, 獸心 shau⁾-sum.
Bubble, 浮泡 fau-⸢pʻo, (up) 濆上 pʻun⁾-sheung.
Bubo, 魚口 ue-⸢hau.
Buck, 鹿公 luuk-kuung.
Bucket, 桶 ⸢tʻuung, 吊桶 tiu⁾-⸢tʻuung.
Buckle, 扣帶環 kʻau⁾-taai-*waan, 帶扣 taai⁾-⸢kʻau.
Buckwheat, 三角麥 saam-kok⁾-mak.

Bud, 芽 nga, 咪 *muuk* (flower) 啉 *lum*, (to) 發芽 *faat³-nga*, 爆咪 *paau³-muuk*, 出啉 *ch'uut-lum*.
Buddhism, 佛教 *Fut-kaau³*.
Buffalo, 水牛 ʻ*shui*-*ngau.
Buffoon, (male) 男丑 *naam-ʻch'au*, (female) 女丑 ʻ*nue-ʻch'au*.
Buffoonery, 雜脚 *tsaap-keuk³*.
Bug, 木虱 *muuk-shat*.
Build, 起 ʻ*hi*, 建造 *kin³-tso³*, 築 *chuuk*.
Bulb, 頭 *t'au*.
Bulk, (to break) 開艙 *hoi-ʻts'ong*.
Bulky, 太大 *t'aai³-taai³*, 大個 *taai³-koh³*.
Bull, 牛公 *ngau-kuung*.
Bullet, 彈子 *taan³-ʻtsze*, 碼 *ʻ*ma*.
Bullock, 騸牛 *shin³-ngau*.
Bullock's brains, 牛腦 *ngau-ʻno*.
Bully, 嚇 *ha*.
Bulwarks, 欄檻 *laan-laam³*, 欄圍 *laan-wai*, (of a city or fort) 城垣 *sheng-oon*.

Bum, 臀 *t'uen-tun*, 屁股 *p'i³-ʻkoo*, 尾后 ʻ*mi-tuuk*.
Bum-boat, 雜貨艇 *tsaap-foh³-ʻt'eng*.
Bump, (to) 捵着 *p'uung³-cheuk*, (down) 墩 *tun³*, *tuun³*.
Bumptious, 抗排 *k'ong-p'aai*.
Bunch, (a) 一把 *yat-ʻpa*, 一臺 *yat-k'uung*, 一球 *yat-k'au*, *yat-kau³*.
Bundle, 包 *paau*, 札 *chaat³*, 束 *ch'uuk*.
Bung, 榫 *suut*, 枳 *chat*.
Bungler, 劣工人 *luet³-kuung-yan*.
Buoy, 錨漂 *naau-p'iu*, 錨桶 *naau-ʻt'uung*, (to) 浮起 *fau-ʻhi*, 泡起 *p'o-ʻhi*.
Burden, 擔頭 *taam³-*ʻ*t'au*, 負任 *foo³-yum³*.
Burglary, 夜竊 *ye³-sit³*.
Burmah, 緬甸 ʻ*Min-tin³*.
Burn, (to) 燒 *shiu*, 燒壞 *shiu-waai³*, (with an iron) 鈉 *naat³*.

Burnish, 磨光 moh-kwong.
Burrow, 爬地籠 p'a-ti-luung.
Burst, 爆 paau', 炸 cha'.
Bursting. (to eat to) 喫到肚爆 yaak-to'-t'o-paau', (with rage) 揸頸 cha-ʿkeng.
Bury, 埋葬 maai-tsong', 葬山 tsong'-shaan.
Bush, 小樹 ʿsiu-shue', 密叢 mat-ts'uung, 枝葉 chi-ip.
Bushel, or peck, 斗 ʿtau, (English) 七斗 ts'at-ʿtau.
Business, 事幹 sze'-kohn', (trade) 生意 shang-i', (calling) 事業 sze'-ip, 頭路 t'au-lo'.
Business-like, 合事例 hop-sze'-lai'.
Bustle, 忙速 mong-ch'uuk, 頻嚟 p'un-lun.
Busy, 未閒 mi'-haan, 事忙 sze'-mong, 有事 ʿyau-sze', (diligent) 勤力 k'an-lik.

Busy-body, 好事之人 ʿho'-sze'-ʿke'-yan.
But, 但 taan', 但係 taan'-hai', 惟係 wai-hai', (except) 除嘵 ch'uc-hiu.
Butcher, 屠夫 t'o-foo, 屠戶 t'o-*oo', (to) 割 t'ony.
Butcher-bird, 伯鷯 paak'-liu.
Butler, 管家 ʿkoon-ka.
Butt, (to) 觸撞 chuuk-chong', 抵觸 ʿtai-chuuk.
Butter, 牛乳油 ngau-ʿue-yau.
Butter-fly, 蝴蝶 oo-*tip, 崩紗 pang-sha.
Buttock, 臋脧 t'uen-chue, 尾㞓 ʿmi-tuuk.
Button, 鈕 *ʿnau, (a) 一粒鈕 yat-nup-*ʿnau, (officer's) 粒頂 nup-ʿteng, 頂帶 ʿteng-taai', (1st & 2nd) 紅頂 huung-ʿteng, (3rd & 4th) 藍頂 laam-ʿteng, (5th & 6th) 白頂 paak-ʿteng, (7th, &c.) 金頂 kum-ʿteng.
Button-hole, 鈕口 *ʿnau ʿhau.

Buttress, 柱墩 ʻchʻue-ʻtun, 棨 ʻtoh.
Buy, 買 ʻmaai, 買入 ʻmaai-yup, 買來 ʻmaai-loi, 買到 ʻmaai-toʼ, 收買 shau-ʻmaai.
Buzz, 微響 mi-ʻheung, 孜孜聲 tsze-tsze-sheng, 甍甍 kwang-kwang.
Buzzing, ears, 耳鳴 ʻi-ming.
By, (with) 用 yuungʼ, (an agent) 被 piʼ, (through) 打 ʻta, 由 yau, (buy by the catty) 斷斤買 tuenʼ-kan-ʻmaai, (by himself) 另自 lingʼ-tszeʼ, (near) 近 kanʼ.
By-, (secluded) 背 pooiʼ.
By and bye, 慢慢 maanʼ-*maanʼ, 等一陣 ʻtang-yat-chanʼ.
By-word, 俗語 tsuuk-ʻue.

C

Cabal, 黨 ʻtong, 朋黨 pʻang-ʻtong.
Cabbage, 椰菜 ye-tsʻoiʼ.
Cabin, 房仔 fong-ʻtsai, (ship's) 船房 shuen-*fong (ʻtsʻong).
Cabinet, 匣 haap, (council) 內閣 noiʼ-kokʼ.
Cable, 纜 laamʼ.
Cackle, 晗晗 kuuk-kuuk, 朗託 kat-tʻok, kok-tok.
Cactus, 霸王 paʼ-wong.
Caddy, 箱仔 ʻseung-ʻtsai.
Cage, 籠 luung.
Caitiff, 奴才 no-tsʻoi, 小人 ʻsiu-yan.
Cajole, 挪然 noh-ʻnan.
Cake, 餅 ʻpeng, 糕 ko.
Calabash, 瓢 pʻiu, 葫蘆 oo-*loo.
Caladium, 茨菇 tsʻze-koo.
Calamity, 禍患 wohʼ-waanʼ, 災害 tsoi-hoiʼ.
Calculate, 算度 suenʼ-tok, 推測 chʻui-chʻaak.
Calculus, (stone) 石淋 shek-lum.
Calendar, 月份牌 uet-funʼ-pʻaai.
Calender, 碾 shinʼ.

Calends, 月朔 uet-*shok*ʼ, 朔日 *shok*ʼ-yat.
Calf, 牛仔 ngau-ʽ*tsai*.
Calico, (white) 白洋布 paak-yeung-*po*ʼ, (print) 印花布 *yan*ʼ-fa-*po*ʼ.
Calk, (to) 打掙 ʽ*ta*-chaangʼ.
Call, 叫 *kiu*ʼ, 呼 *foo*, 喊 *haam*ʼ, 嘥 *iu*, (name) 稱 ch‘ing, (invite) 請 ʽ*ts‘eng*, (on) 探 *t‘aam*ʼ.
Called, (named) 叫做 *kiu*ʼ-*tso*ʼ.
Calling, 事業 szeʼ-ip.
Callous, 硬 ngaangʼ, 不仁 *pat*-yan, 腍 ʽ*chum*.
Calm, 安靜 ohn-tsingʼ, 靜靜 tsingʼ-*tsing*ʼ, 無風無浪 ʽmo-*fuung*-ʽmo-longʼ.
Calomel, 輕粉 hing-ʽ*fun*.
Calumniate, 講壞 ʽkong-waaiʼ.
Calumny, 讒言 ts‘aam-in.
Calyx, 花托 fa-*t‘ok*ʼ.
Cambric, 袈裟布 ka-sha-*po*ʼ.
Camel, 駱駝 *lok*-t‘oh, 雙峰駝 sheung-*fuung*-t‘oh.
Cameleon, 蝘蜓 ʽin-t‘ing.
Camellia, 茶花 ch‘a-*fa*.
Camlet, 羽紗 ʽue-sha, 羽緞 ʽue-*tuen*ʼ.
Camomile, 甘菊 kom-kuuk.
Camp, 管盤 ying-p‘oon.
Campaign, 塲 ch‘eung.
Camp-stool, 馬极 ʽma-chaap.
Camphor, (tree) 樟木 cheung-muuk, (gum) 樟腦 cheung-ʽno.
Campoi-tea, 揀焙茶 ʽkaan-pooi-ch‘a.
Can, 得 tak, 做得 tsoʼ-tak.
Can, (a) 罐 ʽkoonʼ.
Canal, (the Great) 運河 wanʼ-hoh, (a) 水涌 ʽshui-ch‘uung.
Canary, 時辰雀 shi-shan-tseuk, 白燕 paak-ʽin.
Cancel, 删去 shaan-hueʼ.
Cancer, 癰疽 yuung-tsue, 巖疽 ngaam-tsue.
Candareen, 分 fun.
Candid, 明白 ming-paak, 正直 chingʼ-chik.
Candidate, 候選 hauʼ-suenʼ, 候缺 hauʼ-k‘uetʼ.

Candle, 燭 chuuk, (wax) 蠟燭 laap-chuuk.
Candle-stick, 燭臺 chuuk-*t'oi.
Candy, (to) 結冰 kit'-ping, (sugar) 冰糖 ping-t'ong.
Cane, (a) 枝鞭竿 chi-pin-kohn, (rattan) 籐 t'ang.
Cangue, 枷 ka, 木風領 muuk-fuung-ʻleng.
Canister, 鑵 koon'.
Canker, 熱毒 it-tuuk.
Cankered, 齩嫩 nau-nat.
Cannibals, 食人國 shik-yan-kwok'.
Cannon, 大炮 taai'-p'aau', 銃炮 ch'uung'-p'aau', (-ball) 炮碼 p'aau'-*ʻma.
Cannot, 不能 pat-nang, 'm-nang, 不得 pat-tak, 'm-tak.
Canon, 典 ʻtin.
Canopy, 上蓋 sheung'-k'oi', 栱篷 ʻkuung-*p'uung.
Canton, (province) 廣東 ʻKwong-tuung, (city) 羊城 Yeung-sheng, 省城 ʻshaang-sheng, *sheng.

Canvas, 帆布 faan-po'.
Canvass, (to make interest for) 吹噓 ch'ui-hue.
Cap, (a) 頂帽 ʻting-*mo', 冠 koon.
Capable, 能 nang, 會 ʻooi.
Capacity, 才質 ts'oi-chat, (containing) 度量 to'-leung'.
Cape, (of land) 山角 shaan-kok'.
Capers, 水瓜鈕 ʻshui-kwa-ʻnau.
Capital, (city) 京都 king-too, 京城 king-shing, (money) 本錢 ʻpoon-ts'in, (excellent) 妙 miu'.
Capon, 鐡雞 sin'-kai.
Capricious, 無定心 ʻmo-ting'-sum, 多心 toh-sum, 花花吓 fa-fa-fik.
Capsize, 覆轉 fuuk-ʻchuen, p'uuk-ʻchuen.
Capstan, 絞盆 ʻkaau-p'oon.
Captain, (ship-) 船主 shuen-ʻchue, (of a company) 把總 ʻpa-ʻtsuung.

Captain Superintendent of Police, 巡捕官 ts'uun-po'-koon.
Captive, (led-) 被虜 pi'-ʿlo
Capture, 拿獲 na-wok.
Carambola, 楊桃 yeung-*t'o.
Caraway, 細茴香 sai'-ooi-heung, 芫荽 uen-sai.
Carbuncle, (on the back) 發背 faat'-pooi', 背癰 pooi'-yuung.
Carcass, 遺骸 wai-hoi, 死屍 ʿsze-shi, (abusively) 死佬乾 ʿsze-ʿlo-kohn.
Card, (visiting) 拜帖 paai'-t'ip', 名帖 ming-*t'ip' (playing) 紙牌 ʿchi-*p'aai.
Card-case, 帖套 t'ip'-t'o.
Cardamom, 白荳蔻 paak-tau'-k'au'.
Cardinal points, 四方 sze'-fong.
Care, 掛慮 kwa'-lue', 蔽翳 pai'-ai', (to) 料理 liu'-ʿli, (don't) 不理 pat-ʿli.
Careful, 小心 ʿsiu-sum.

Carefully, look 睇仔細 ʿt'ai-ʿtsze-sai', 好聲 ʿho-ʿsheng.
Careless, 無小心 ʿmo-ʿsiu-sum, 無睇顧 ʿmo-ʿt'ai-koo', 苟且 ʿkau-ʿch'e.
Caress, 攬抱 ʿlaam-ʿp'o.
Cargo, 船貨 shuen-foh'.
Cargo-boat, 駁艇 pok'-ʿt'eng.
Carnation, (colour) 桃紅色 t'o-huung-shik.
Carnelian, 瑪瑙石 ʿma-ʿno-shek.
Carouse, 大飲一番 taai'-ʿyum-yat-faan, 閙酒 naau'-ʿtsau.
Carp, (a fish) 鯉魚 ʿli-*ue.
Carp, (to) 捉字失 chuuk'-tsze'-shat.
Carpenter, 木匠 muuk-*tseung'.
Carpet, 地氈 ti'-ʿchin.
Carriage, (a) 車 ch'e, 馬車 ʿma-ch'e.
Carrot, 紅蘿蔔 huung-loh-paak, 黃蘿蔔 wong-loh-paak, 金笋 kum-ʿsuun.

Carry, (on a pole) 擔 taam, (resting on one) 托 tʻokʼ, (between two) 抬 tʻoi, (about the person) 帶 taaiʼ, (on the back) 狽 me, (in the arms) 抱 ʻpʻo, (as a ship, &c.) 載 tsoiʼ.
Cart, 車 chʻe, (ox-) 牛車 ngau-chʻe.
Cartridge, 火藥筒 ʻfoh-yeuk-*tʻuung, 础碼 kipʼ-ʻma.
Cartridge-box, 九龍袋 ʻkau-luung-*toiʼ.
Carve, 雕刻 tiu-haakʼ, (ornament) 雕花 tiu-fa, (meat) 切 tsʻit.
Case, (holder) 套 tʻoʼ, 套匣 tʻoʼ-haap, (at law) 案件 ohnʼ-kinʼ.
Cash, 錢 *tsʻin, 文錢 mun-tsʻin, (ready) 現銀 inʼ-*ngan.
Cash-book, 進支簿 tsuunʼ-chi-ʻpo.
Cask, 桶 ʻtʻuung, 琵琶桶 pʻi-pʻa-ʻtʻuung.

Casket, 小匣 ʻsiu-haap, 寶匣 ʻpo-haap.
Cassia, 桂 kwaiʼ, (lignia) 桂皮 kwaiʼ-pʻi, (buds) 桂子 kwaiʼ-ʻtsze.
Cast, (throw) 投 tʻau, 丟 tiu, (to found) 鑄 chueʼ.
Cast-iron, 生鐵 shʻaang-tʻitʼ.
Castanets, 拍板 pʻaukʼ-ʻpaan.
Castellated, 有城人 ʻyau-sheng-*yan.
Castle, 城樓 sheng-*lau.
Castor oil, 瀉油 seʼ-yau, 萆蔴油 pi-ma-yau.
Castrate, 割勢 kohtʼ-shaiʼ, 閹 im, 鏾 sinʼ.
Casual, 無意中 mo-iʼ-ʻchuung.
Casuistry, 是非 shiʼ-fi.
Cat, 貓 ʻmaau, (a) 一隻貓 yat-chekʼ-ʻmaau.
Cat fish, 赤魚 chʻikʼ-*ue.
Catalogue, 號單 hoʼ-ʻtaan, 目錄 muuk-luuk.
Catamenia, 月水 uet-ʻshui.

Cataract, (water) 瀑布水 puuk-poʾ-ʿshui, (in the eye) 販睛 pʻaan-tsing, 睛珠變質不明 tsing-chue-pinʾ-chat-pat-ming.

Catch, 捉到 chuukʾ-ʿto, 捉獲 chuukʾ-wok (fasten) kʻekʾ.

Catechism, 問答書 munʾ-taapʾ-shue.

Catechu, 兒茶 i-chʻa.

Caterpillar, 螟蛉 ming-ling, 狗毛蟲 ʿkau-mo-*chʻuung, (silk-worm) 蠶蟲 tsʻaam-*chʻuung.

Caterwaul, 拗烏聲 aau-oo-sheng.

Cattle, 畜生 chʻuuk-shaang.

Catty, 斤 kan.

Caul, 大腸網膜 taaiʾ-chʻeung-ʿmong-mok.

Cauliflower, 花椰菜 fa-ye-tsʻoi.

Cause, 緣故 uen-kooʾ, 緣由 uen-yau, (to) 使 ʿshai, 令 lingʾ, 致 chiʾ.

Causeway, 逼石地 pik-shekʾ-tiʾ, 鵝卵石地 ngoh-ʿluun-shek-tiʾ.

Cauterize, 灸 kauʾ.

Cautious, 謹愼 ʿkan-shanʾ, 小心 ʿsiu-sum.

Cavalry, 馬兵 ʿma-ping.

Cave, 山籠 shaan-ʿluung, 巖穴 ngaam-uet.

Cavil, 捉字失 chuukʾ-tszeʾ-shat, 駁嘴 pokʾ-ʿtsui.

Cayenne, 辣椒 laat-tsiu.

Cease, 停息 tʻing-sik, 止 ʿchi, 歇 hitʾ.

Cedar, 柏香木 paakʾ-heung-muuk.

Ceiling, 天花板 tʻin-fa-ʿpaan.

Celandine, 知母 chi-ʿmo.

Celebrate, (a day) 造 tsoʾ, (midwinter) 造冬 tsoʾ-tuung.

Celebrity, 名聲 ming-shing, 出名 chʻuut-*meng.

Celery, 旱芹菜 ʿhohn-kʻan-tsʻoiʾ, 塘蒿 tʻong-ho.

Cell, 房仔 *fong-ʿtsai.

Cellar, 地窖 ti'-kaau', (wine) 酒房 ʻtsau-*fong.
Cement, 灰膠 fooi-kaau.
Cemetery, 陰山 yum-shaan.
Censer, 香爐 heung-lo.
Censor, 諫官 kaan'-koon, 御史 ue'-ʻsze.
Censure, 彈 tʻaan, 責 chaak'.
Census, 民籍 mnu-tsik, 口冊 ʻhau-chʻaak'.
Centipede, 百足 paak'-tsuuk.
Centre, 正中間 ching'-chuung-ʻkaan, 心 sum.
Centurion, 把總 ʻpa-ʻtsuung.
Century, 百年 paak'-nin.
Ceremony, 禮儀 ʻlai-i.
Certain, 的確 tik-kʻok,' 定 ting', ʻting.
Certainly, 斷斷 tuen'-tuen', 定然 ting'-in, 定喇 ʻting-la.
Certificate, (of character) 薦書 tsin'-shue, (of goods) 驗單 im'-ʻtaan.
Certify, 實證 shat-ching'.
Cess, 抽稅 chʻan-shui'.
Cess-pool, 水氹 ʻshui-ʻtʻum, 糞坑 fun'-haang.

Chafe, 擦壞 tsʻaat'-waai', (a person) 激氣 kik-hi'.
Chafer, 沙蟬 sha-shin.
Chaff, 粃糠 pʻi-hong, 糠 hong.
Chagrin, 鬱氣 wut-hi'.
Chain, 鍊 *lin', 鏈 lin, (a) 條鏈 tʻiu-*lin.
Chair, (a) 張椅 cheung-ʻi, sedan, 頂轎 ʻting-*kiu', coolie, 轎夫 *kiu'-foo.
Chalk, 火石粉 ʻfoh-shek-ʻfun.
Challenge, 惹敵 ʻye-tik.
Chamber, 房 *fong.
Chamber-pot, 便壺 pin'-*oo.
Chamois, 羚羊 ling-yeung.
Champion, 豪傑 ho-kit.
Chance, 偶然 ʻngau-in.
Chancellor, literary, 學台 hok-tʻoi.
Change, 改 ʻkoi, 更改 kang-ʻkoi, 更換 kang-oon', 換過 oon'-kwoh', 改變 ʻkoi pin'.
Changer, (money-) 找錢人 ʻchaau-*tsʻin-yan.

Channel, 條水 t'iu-ʻshui ʻshui-loʼ.
Chant prayers, 念經 nimʼ-king.
Chaos, 混沌 wunʼ-tuunʼ.
Chapel, 禮拜堂 ʻlai-paaiʼ-t'ong, 福音堂 fuuk-yum-t'ong.
Chapped, 坼口 ch'aakʼ-ʻhau.
Chapter, 章 cheung.
Char, 燒黑 shiu-hak.
Character, 品行 ʻpun-hangʼ, (or class) 脚色 keukʼ-shik, (a letter) 字 tszeʼ.
Charcoal, 柴炭 ch'aai-t'aanʼ.
Charge, (to give-) 付託 fooʼ-t'okʼ, (demand) 要取 iuʼ-ʻts'ue, (blame) 責罪 chaakʼ-tsuiʼ.
Chariot, 馬車 ʻma-ch'e.
Charity, 慈心 ts'ze-sum, (alms) 施舍 shi-ʻshe, 布施 poʼ-shiʼ.
Charm, (a) 符籙 foo-luuk.
Charming, 悅意 uet-iʼ.
Chart, 海沙圖 ʻhoi-sha-t'o.
Charter-party, 合同 hop-t'uung.

Chase, (to) 追趕 chui-ʻkohn.
Chasm, 缺陷 huetʼ-haamʼ.
Chaste, 清節 ts'ing-tsitʼ, 貞節 ching-tsitʼ.
Chastise, 責罰 chaakʼ-faat, 打 ʻta.
Chat, 談談 t'aam-t'aam.
Chattels, 什物 shap-mat.
Chatter, (to) 嘶嘶聲 si-si-sheng, wak-wak-sheng.
Chatter-box, 多嘴 toh-ʻtsui.
Cheap, 平 p'eng, 價錢低 kaʼ-ts'in-tai.
Cheat, 陋騙 nyaakʼ-p'inʼ 欺騙 hi-p'inʼ.
Check, 壓止 aatʼ-ʻchi, (in chess) 將軍 tseung-kwun.
Check-mate, 全勝局 ts'uen-shingʼ-kuuk, 贏棋 yeng-ʻk'i.
Cheek, 面脥 minʼ-ʻchue, 腮 soi.
Cheek-bones, 兩顴 ʻleung-k'uen.
Cheer (to) 喝采 hohtʼ-ʻts'oi.
Cheerful, 快活 faaiʼ-oot.
Cheese, 牛奶餅 ngau-ʻnaai-ʻpeng.

Chemise, 近身衣 kanʾ-ˌshan-i.
Chemistry, 化學 faʾ-hok.
Cheque, (a) 銀單 ngan-ˌtaan.
Cherish, 懷 waai.
Cherry, 李仔 ʿli-ˌtsai, 櫻 ying.
Chess, 象棋 tseungʾ-kʻi, (-board) 棋盤 kʻi-pʻoon, (-men) 棋子 kʻi-ˌtsze.
Chest, 箱 ˌseung, 槓 ˌluung, (strong) 夾萬 kaapʾ-maanʾ.
Chestnut, 風栗 fuung-*luut.
Chevaux-de-frise, 鹿角寨 luuk-kokʾ-*chaai.
Chew, 咬 ʿngaau, 嚼 tseukʾ.
Chicken, 鷄仔 kai-ˌtsai.
Chicken-pox, 水痘 ʿshui-*tauʾ.
Chicken-hearted, 小心小膽 ʿsiu-sum-ʿsiu-ʿtaam.
Chief, 頭一個 tʻau-yat-kohʾ, (man) 頭目 tʻau-muuk, 頭人 tʻau-yan, 主 ʿchue.
Chief Justice, 按察司 ohnʾ-chʻaatʾ-sze.

Chiefly, 大約 taaiʾ-yeukʾ, (most of all) 至緊要 chiʾ-ˌkan-iuʾ.
Chilblains, 生蘿蔔 shang-loh-paak, 寒瘡 hohn-ˌchʻong.
Child, 細蚊仔 saiʾ-mun-ˌtsai.
Child-bed, 分娩 funˋ-ʿmin.
Chill, 傷寒 sheung-hohn.
Chillies, 花椒 fa-tsiu.
Chimney, 烟通 in-tʻuung.
Chin, 下頷 haʾ-ʿhom, 下爬 haʾ-pʻa.
China, 中國 Chuung-kwokʾ, 唐山 Tʻong-shaan.
China-aster, 菊花 kuuk-fa.
China-root, 茯苓 fuuk-ling.
Chinese, (a) 唐人 Tʻong-yan, (language) 唐話 Tʻong-*wa.
Chink, (a) 罅 laʾ, 條罅 tʻiu-laʾ.
Chintz, 印花布 yanʾ-fa-poʾ.
Chip, (to) 斲 teukʾ, 削 seukʾ.
Chips, 斧口柴 ʿfoo-ʿhau-chʻaai, pʻekʾ-ʿhau-chʻaai.

Chirp, 吱啁 chi-chaau, 啁啁 chaau-chaau.
Chisel, 鑿 ʽtsok, 鑿刀 tsaam⸴-to.
Chit (a), 一塊字紙 yat-faai⸴-tsze⸴-ʽchi.
Chit-book, 信部 suun⸴-*po⸴.
Chloroform, 痲藥 ma-yeuk.
Choice } 揀擇的 ʽkaan-chaak-ke⸴.
Chosen
Choke, 骾 ʽkʽang, 壅塞 ʽyuung-sak, tsuuk.
Cholera, 攪腸沙 ʽkaau-chʽeung-sha, 霍亂吐瀉 fok⸴-luen⸴ tʽo⸴-se⸴.
Choose, 揀選 ʽkaan-ʽsuen.
Chop, (a mark), 字號 tsze⸴-ho⸴.
Chop (to) 切 tsʽit⸴.
Chop-boat, 西瓜扁 sai-kwa-ʽpin, (floating-house) 樓船 lau-*shuen.
Chopping block, 砧板 chum-ʽpaan.
Chopping-knife, 切菜刀 tsʽit⸴-tsʽoi⸴-to.
Chop-sticks 快子 faai⸴-ʽtsze.

Chops, (meat) 牌骨 pʽaai-kwut.
CHRIST, 基督 KI-TUUK.
Christian, 信耶穌人 suun⸴-YE-SOO-yan.
Christianity, 耶穌教 YE-SOO-kaau⸴.
Christmas, 耶穌生日 YE-SOO-shang-yat.
Chronic, 舊病 kau⸴-peng⸴.
Chrysalis, 繭虫 ʽkaan-chʽuung, 蛹 ʽyuung, 螵 pʽiu.
Chrysanthemum, 菊花 kuuk-fa.
Chub, (a fish) 鰱魚 lin-*ue.
Chunam, (to) 打灰沙 ʽta-fooi-sha.
Church, 教會 kaau⸴-ooi⸴.
Churlish 古毒 ʽkoo-tuuk.
Churn, (to) 扯 ʽchʽe, 攪 ʽkaau.
Cicada, 秋蟬 tsʽau-*shin.
Cigar, 呂宋烟 ʽLue-suung⸴-ˏin, (-ette) 孖姑烟 ˏma-ˏkoo-ˏin.
Cinders, 燒剩 shiu-shing⸴.

Cinnabar, 銀硃種 ngan-chue-ʻchuung, 硃砂 chue-sha.
Cinnamon, 肉桂 yuuk-kwaiʼ.
Circle, 圈 huen.
Circuit, 週 chau.
Circular, (a) 告白 koʼ-paak, 傳字 chʻuen-*tszeʼ.
Circulate, 循環 tsʻuun-waan.
Circumcision, 割禮 kohtʼ-ʻlai.
Circumference, 圈界 huen-kaaiʼ.
Circumstance, 事勢 szeʼ-shai, 境遇 ʻking-ue', 際遇 tsaiʼ-ueʼ.
Circumvent, 扭計 ʻnau-*kaiʼ.
Circumvented, 扭倒計 ʻnau-ʻto-(toʼ)-kaiʼ.
Circus, 圓戲場 uen-hiʼ-chʻeung.
Cistern, 蓄水缸 chʻuuk-ʻshui-kong, 石井 shek-ʻtseng.
Citron, 香櫞 heung-*uen, 佛手 fut-ʻshau.

City, 邑 yup, (walled) 城 sheng, *sheng.
Civet, 香狸 heung-*li.
Civil and military, 文武 mun-ʻmoo.
Civility, 禮 ʻlai, 禮數 ʻlai-shoʼ, (outward) 禮貌 ʻlai-maauʼ.
Civilize, 教化 kaauʼ-faʼ.
Clack, 剔撻聲 tʻik-tʻat-sheng.
Claim, 討 ʻtʻo, 問要 munʼ-iuʼ.
Clam, 沙蜆 sha-ʻhin.
Clammy, 黐泥 chʻi-ni'.
Clamour, 喧嘩 huen-wa, 巴閉 pa-paiʼ.
Clamp, (to) 碼住 ʻma-chueʼ.
Clan, 族 tsuuk, 姓 singʼ.
Clap, 拍 pʻaakʼ.
Claret, 紅酒 huung-ʻtsau.
Clash, 相撞 seung-chongʼ, 抵冱 ʻtai-ʻng.
Clasp, (a) 扣 kʻauʼ, (hands) 叉手 chʻa-ʻshau, (to mend) 碼 ʻma.
Clasp-knife, 摺刀 chipʼ-ʻto.

Class, (a) 等 ʻtang, (in school) 班 paan, (profession) 脚色 keukʼ-shik.
Classic, 經 king.
Clatter, 捆捆聲 kwaak-kwaak-sheng.
Clause, 句 kueʼ, (of a treaty) 欵 ʻfoon, 條 tʻiu.
Claw, 爪 ʻchaau.
Clay, 泥 nai.
Clean, 潔淨 kitʼ-tsengʼ, 乾淨 kohn-tsengʼ, ʻkʻi-ʻli.
Cleanse, 做乾淨 tsoʼ-kohn-tsengʼ.
Clear, 清 tsʻing, 明 ming, (sky) 晴 tsʻing.
Clearance, (port-) 紅牌 huung-*pʻaai.
Cleave, (split) 破開 pʻohʼ-hoi.
Clench, (the fist) 揸埋拳頭 cha-maai-kʻuen-tʻau.
Clepsydra, 滴漏 tik-lauʼ.
Clerk, 書辦 shue-*paanʼ, 寫字人 ʻse-tszeʼ-yan.
Clerodendrum, 龍船花 luung-shuen-fa.

Clever, 有本事 ʻyau-ʻpoon-szeʼ, 聰明 tsʻuung-ming, 精 tseng.
Click, 迪特聲 tik-tak-sheng.
Cliff, 企坡 ʻkʻi-poh, 巖 ngaam.
Climate, 水土 ʻshui-ʻtʻo.
Climb, 攀上 pʻaan-ʻsheung, 躝上 laan-ʻsheung.
Clinch, (nails) 打開釘尾 ʻta-hoi-ʻteng-ʻmi, 轉釘尾 ʻchuen-ʻteng-ʻmi.
Cling to, 膠漆 kaau-tsʻat.
Clip, 剪 ʻtsin, 裁剪 tsʻoi-ʻtsin.
Cloak, 大蓑 taaiʼ-ʻlau.
Clock, 時辰鐘 shi-shan-ʻchuung, (o'clock) 點鐘 ʻtim-ʻchuung.
Clock-tower (the), 大鐘樓 Taaiʼ chuung-*lau.
Clod, 偋坭 kauʼ-nai.
Clog, (to) 阻滯 ʻchoh-chaiʼ.
Clogs, 木屐 muuk-kʻek.
Close, (to) 閂埋 shaan-maai, 閤埋 hop-maai, (finish) 完結 uen-kitʼ.

Close, (ADJ.) 密 mat, (near) 近 kan⁾, ʽkʽan.
Close-fisted, 手指密 ʽshau-ʽchi-mat.
Clot, (to) 結 kit⁾, 擎 kʽing.
Cloth, 布 po⁾, (woollen) 絨 *yuung.
Clothe, 着衣服 cheuk⁾-i-fuuk, 衣⁾i⁾.
Clothes, 衣服 i-fuuk, 衣裳 i-sheung.
Clothes-brush, 衣擦 i-tsʽaat⁾.
Clothes-horse, 衣架 i-ʽka.
Cloud, 雲 wan.
Cloudy, 矇矓 muung-luung.
Clove, 丁香 ting-heung.
Clown, (actor) 白鼻哥 paak-piʾ-koh, (rustic) 鄉下佬 heung-haʾ-ʽlo.
Club, (stick) 棍 kwan⁾, 椎 *chʽui.
Club-footed, 胎生腳 ʽtoi-ʽshang-keuk⁾.
Club-house, 會館 ooi⁾-ʽkoon.
Cluck, 咯咯 kuuk-kuuk.
Clue, 毬線 kʽau-sin⁾, kauʾ-sin⁾, (winding of) 絮 ʽsue, 頭緒 tʽau-ʽsue.

Clumsy, 粗俗 tʽso-tsuuk.
Cluster, 球 kʽau, kauʾ.
Clyster, 灌穀道法 chok-kuuk-toʾ-faat⁾.
Coach, 馬車 ʽma-chʽe.
Coachman, 車夫 chʽe-foo.
Coagulate, 凝結 ying-kit⁾, 結埋 kit⁾-maai.
Coal, 煤炭 mooi-tʽaan⁾, (burning) 着炭 cheukʾ-tʽaan⁾.
Coalesce, 生埋 shaang-maai.
Coarse, 粗 tsʽo.
Coast, 海邊 ʽhoi-ʽpin.
Coat, 大衫 taaiʾ-shaam, (of paint) 浸 chumʾ.
Coax, 引誘 ʽyan-ʽyau.
Cob-web, 蜘蛛網 ʽchi-ʽchue-ʽmong.
Cobra, 破基峽 pʽohʾ-ki-haap, 扁頭蜂 ʽpin-tʽau-fuung.
Cochineal, 牙蘭米 nga-ʽlaan-ʽmai.
Cock, 雞公 ʽkai-ʽkuung.
Cock up, 叞起 hiuʾ-hi.

Cock, (of a gun) 朗鷄 kat-ˌkai, (to) 攪朗鷄 maan-kat-ˌkai.
Cockatoo, 白鸚鵡 paak-ying-ˋmoo.
Cockles, 蜊蚶 sze-ˌom.
Cockroach, 甴甲 kaat-tsaat.
Cocoa-nut, 椰子 ye-ˋtsze, (juice) 椰水 ye-ˋshui.
Cocoon, 繭 ˋkaan, 蠶繭 ts'aam-ˋkaan.
Cod-fish, 鰵魚 ˋmun-ue.
Coerce, 強逼 k'eung-pik.
Coffin, 棺材 koon-ts'oi.
Cog-wheel, 齒輪 ˋch'i-luun.
Cohabit, 狎居 haap-kue.
Cohere, 黐埋 ch'i-maai.
Coil, (to) 盤埋 p'oon-maai.
Coin, 錢 *ts'in.
Coincide, 符合 foo-hop, 啱 ˌngaam.
Coir, 椰衣 *ye-i, 椶 ˋsuung.
Cold, 冷 ˋlaang, 凍 tuungˋ, (indifferent) 薄情 pok-ts'ing, 冷面 ˋlaang-minˋ, 冷淡 ˋlaang-taamˋ, (a cold) 傷風 sheung-fuung, 感冒 ˋkom-moˋ.

Coleopterous, 甲蟲類 kaapˋ-ch'uung-lui.
Colewort, 黃牙白 wong-nga-paak.
Colic, 肚痛 ˋt'o-t'uungˋ.
Collapse, 崩敗 pang-paaiˋ, 凹曉 nup-hiu, 冚曉 nip-hiu.
Collar, 風領 fuung-ˋleng.
Collar-bone, 鎖匙骨 ˋsoh-shi-kwut.
Collate, 對過 tuiˋ-kwohˋ.
Collect, 聚埋 tsueˋ-maai.
Collision, 相撞 seung-p'uungˋ, 抵牫 ˋtai-ˋng.
Colloquial, 俗話 tsuuk-*wa.
Collusion, 同謀 t'uung-mau.
Colonel, 參將 ts'aam-tseung.
Colonial Secretary, 輔政司 fooˋ-chingˋ-sze.
Colonial Treasurer, 庫務司 fooˋ-mooˋ-sze.
Colony, 新疆 san-keung, 屬國 shuuk-kwokˋ.
Colour, 色 shik, 顏色 ngaan-shik, 色澤 shik chaak.

Column, (of letters) 行 hong, (pillar), 柱 ʻchʻue.
Coma, 昏睡病 fun-shuiʼ-pengʼ.
Comatose, 忘魂 mong-wan.
Comb, 梳 shoh, (a) 隻梳 chekʼ-ʻshoh, (fine) 鎞 *pi'.
Combative, 鬥氣 tauʼ-hiʼ.
Combine, 和合 woh-hop.
Come, 來 loi, (COL.) 嚟 lai.
Comedy, 作笑戲文 tsok-siuʼ-hiʼ-mun 劇 kʻek.
Comet, 掃把星 soʼ-ʻpa-sing, 攬擸星 laap-chʻa-ʻsing.
Comfits, 糖彈 tʻong-*taanʼ.
Comfort, 安慰 ohn-waiʼ, 勸解 huenʼ-ʻkaai.
Comfortable, 安樂 ohn-lok.
Comic, 好笑 ʻho-siuʼ.
Command, 吩咐 fun-fooʼ.
Commander, 兵頭 ping-*tʻau, 頭人 tʻau-yan.
Commandment, 誡命 kaaiʼ-mingʼ.
Commemorate, 表記 ʻpiu-kiʼ.
Commence, 開手 hoi-ʻshau, 埋手 maai-ʻshau, 開工 hoi-kuung, 起首 ʻhi-ʻshau.
Commencement, 起初 ʻhi-chʻoh, 興工 hing-kuung, 始初 ʻchʻi-chʻoh.
Commend, 褒獎 po-ʻtseung, 舉薦 ʻkue-tsinʼ.
Comment, 註解 chueʼ-ʻkaai.
Commerce, 貿易 mauʼ-yik, 交易 kaau-yik, 買賣 ʻmaai-maaiʼ, 生意 shang-iʼ.
Commiserate, 可憐 ʻhoh-lin.
Commission, (to) 差委 chʻaai-ʻwai 委托 ʻwai-tʻokʼ.
Commissioner, 欽差 yum-chʻaai.
Commit, (crime) 犯 faanʼ.
Committee, 值理人 chik-ʻli-yan.
Commode, 尿櫃 niuʼ-*kwaiʼ.
Common, (public) 公 kuung, (vulgar) 俗 tsuuk, (usual) 平常 pʻing-sheung.
Communicate, 交給 kaau-kʻup, (tell) 通知 tʻuung-chi.
Communion, 交通 kaau-tʻuung, (spiritual) 心交 sum-kaau.
Community, 人民 yan-manʼ, 百姓 paakʼ-singʼ.

Compact, 密實 mat-shat, (a) 合同 hop-t'uung.
Companion, 同班輩 t'uung-paan-pooi, 同伴 t'uung-poon'.
Company, (mercantile) 公司 kuung-sze.
Compare, 比較 ʻpi-kaauʼ, 對過 tuiʼ-kwohʼ.
Compartment, 間房 kaan-*fong.
Compass, 羅經 loh-ʻkaang, 羅盤 loh-pʻoon.
Compasses, 規 kʻwai.
Compassion, 慈悲 tsʻze-pi.
Compel, 強 ʻkʻeung, 監 kaam.
Compendious, 簡畧 ʻkaan-leuk.
Compensate, 補償 ʻpo-sheung, 賠補 pʻooi ʻpo.
Compete, 鬬 tauʼ.
Competent, 足用 tsuuk-yuungʼ, (man) 能事 nang-szeʼ, 稱職 chʻingʼ-chik.
Complain, 訴冤 soʼ-uen, 出怨言 chʻuut-uenʼ-in.
Complaisant, 婉轉 ʻuen-ʻchuen.

Complete, 周全 chau-tsʻuen, 十全 shap-tsʻuen, (to) 成 shing.
Completely, 嗮 saaiʼ.
Complexion, 面色 minʼ-shik.
Complicated) 深 shum, 深奧 shum-oʼ, 多故 toh-kooʼ.
Complex)
Complication, 多事整埋 toh-szeʼ-ʻching-maai.
Compliments, 問候 munʼ-hauʼ, (congratulations) 恭喜 kuung-ʻhi.
Comply, 依從 i-tsʻuung, 聽從 tʻengʼ-tsʻuung, 順從 shuunʼ-tsʻuung.
Compose, 安埋 ohn-maai, 砌埋 tsʻai-maai, (write) 作 tsokʼ.
Compositor, 執字人 chup-tszeʼ-yan, 排活板人 pʻaai-oot-ʻpaan-yan.
Compound, 攪勻 ʻkaau-wan, 摳勻 kʻau-wan.
Compound interest, 利上利 liʼ-sheungʼ-liʼ.
Comprador, 買辦 ʻmaai-*paanʼ.

Comprehend, 曉透 ʻhiu-tʻauʼ, (comprise) 包括 paau-kʻootʼ.
Compress, 壓 aatʼ, 責住 chaakʼ-chue, 挾 kip, 夾 kaapʼ, 搇 kum, 擘 maan.
Comprise, 包括 paau-kʻootʼ.
Compromise, 相饒省事 seung-iu-ʻshaang-szeʼ, (involve) 拖累 tʻoh-lui.
Compute, 算度 suenʼ-tok.
Comrade, 夥計 ʻfoh-kiʼ.
Concave, 中間凹 ʻchuung-ʻkaan-nup.
Conceal, 藏匿 tsʻong-nik, (one's self) 躲匿 ʻtoh-nik, 避 piʼ, 匿埋 nik-maai, ni-maai.
Concede, 許准 ʻhue-ʻchuun.
Conceited, 自高 tszeʼ-ko, 自大 tszeʼ-taaiʼ.
Conceive, 懷胎 waai-tʻoi, 有六甲 ʻyau-luuk-kaapʼ, (think) 想 ʻseung.
Concern, (to) 關涉 kwaan-shipʼ, 關屬 kwaan-shuuk, (a) 事幹 szeʼ-kohnʼ.

Concert, (in) 和諧 woh-haai, (a) 和奏樂音 woh-tsauʼ-ngok-yum.
Conciliate, 拍和 pʻaakʼ-woh, 和 woh, 勸和 huenʼ-woh, 勸息 huenʼ-sik.
Concise, 簡畧 ʻkaan-leuk, 簡捷 ʻkaan-tsit.
Conclude, 完了 uen-ʻliu, uen-hiu, (decide) 定意 tingʼ-iʼ.
Concord, 和 woh.
Concubine, 妾 tsʻipʼ, 妾氏 tsʻipʼ-shi.
Concur, 同意 tʻuung-iʼ, 同致 tʻuung-chiʼ.
Condemn, 定罪 tingʼ-tsuiʼ.
Condense, 收縮 shau-shuuk, 結埋 kitʼ-maai.
Condescend, 下顧 haʼ-kooʼ, 垂念 shui-nimʼ, 臨下 lum-haʼ.
Condiments, 醬料 tseungʼ-*liuʼ, 送 suungʼ.
Condition, 情勢 tsʻing-shaiʼ, 景地 ʻking-ti, (terms) 章程 cheung-chʻing.

Condole, 弔慰 tiu'-wai'.
Conduct, 行爲 hang-wai.
Conduct, 帶引 taai'-ʿyan.
Cone, 筍子樣 ʿsuun-ʿtsze-*yeung', 尖形 tsim-ying.
Confederate, 同盟 t'uung-mang.
Confer, (give) 賜 ts'ze', (consult) 斟酌 chum-cheuk'.
Confess, 認 ying', 招認 chiu-ying', (a mistake) 賠不是 p'ooi-pat-shi'.
Confide, 信托 suun'-t'ok'.
Confident, 確信 k'ok'-suun'.
Confine, (to) 收禁 shau-kum', 押住 aap'-chue'.
Confirm, 堅定 kin-ting', 批實 p'ai-shat.
Confiscate, 歸官 kwai-koon.
Conflict, 相撞 seung-chong', 反拗 ʿfaan-aau'.
Conform, 照依 chiu'-i, 按 ohn', 按准 ohn'-ʿchuun.
Confound, 打混 ʿta-wan', (by fear) 驚亂 king-luen', (mix) 混雜 wan'-tsaap, 撈亂 lo-luen', lo-lo-*luen'.

Confounded, 混賬 wan'-cheung'.
Confront, 對面企 tui'-*min'-ʿk'i, 質訊 chat-suun'.
Confucius, 孔夫子 ʿHuung-foo-ʿtsze.
Confute, 駁倒 pok'-ʿto͵.
Confused, 亂 luen'.
Congeal, 凝凍 k'ing-tuung'.
Congee, 粥 chuuk.
Congenial, 合心水 hop-sum-ʿshui.
Congenital, 胎生 t'oi-ʿshang.
Congestion, 內熱成積 noi'-it-shing-tsik.
Congo, 工夫茶 kuung-foo-ch'a.
Congratulate, 恭喜 kuung-ʿhi, 賀喜 hoh'-ʿhi.
Congregate, 聚會 tsue'-ooi'.
Congregation, 會衆 ooi'-chuung'.
Congruous, 符合 foo-hop, 啱 ʿngaam.
Conical, 筍子樣 ʿsuun-ʿtsze-*yeung', (COL.) tuet'.

Conjecture, 猜想 ch'aai-ʽseung, 猜摸 ch'aai-ʽmoh, 估摸 ʽkoo-mok².
Conjunction, 會合 ooi²-hop.
Connect, 接續 tsip²-tsuuk.
Connive, 詐不見 cha²-pat-kin², cha²-'m-kin².
Conquer, 勝敵 shing²-tik, 贏 yeng.
Consanguinity, 骨肉親 kwut-yuuk-ts'an.
Conscience, 良心 leung-sum.
Conscious, 自覺 tsze²-kok, 自知 tsze²-chi.
Consent, 允准 ʽwun-ʽchuun, 允肯 ʽwun-ʽhang.
Consequence, 關系 kwaan-hai².
Consequently, 所以 ʽshoh-ʽi.
Conservative, 守經 ʽshau-king.
Consider, 思想吓 sze-ʽseung-ha.
Considerably, 稍 ʽshaau, 畧畧 leuk-*leuk.
Considerate, 有細心 ʽyau-sai²-sum, 通情理 t'uung-ts'ing-ʽli.

Consignee, 承辦人 shing-paan²-yan.
Consist of, 內有 noi²-ʽyau.
Consistent, 前後相對 ts'in-hau²-seung-tui², (with) 合 hop.
Console, 安慰 ohn-wai².
Consipicuous, 特出 tak-ch'uut.
Conspire, 結盟 kit²-mang, (things) 湊埋來 ts'au²-maai-lai.
Constable, (local protector) 地保 ti²-ʽpo, (police) 捕役 po²-yik.
Constant, 耐久無變 noi²-ʽkau-ʽmo-pin², 不歇 pat-hit².
Constipation, 痞滿 ʽpi-ʽmoon, 大便不通 taai²-pin²-pat-t'uung, 結恭 kit²-kuung.
Constitute, 立 laap, 成 shing.
Constitution, 質地 chat-*ti², 資質 tsze-chat.
Constrain, 勉強 ʽmin-ʽk'eung, 強使 ʽk'eung-shai².

Construct, 建造 kin'-tso'.
Consul, 領事官 'ling-sze'-koon.
Consult, 斟酌 chum-cheuk' 商量 sheung-leung.
Consume, (spend) 費 fai'.
Consummate, 完全 uen-ts'uen, (to) 成 shing.
Consummately, 十分 shap-fun.
Consumption, (disease) 肺勞症 fai'-lo-ching'.
Contact, 鬥合 tau'-hop, 湊合 ts'au'-hop.
Contagious, 傳染 ch'uen-'im, 會傳染 'ooi-ch'uen-'im.
Contain, 裝載 chong-tsoi', 包涵 paau-haam.
Contemn, 鄙慢 'p'i-maan', 輕慊 hing-im', 鄙薄 'p'i-pok.
Contemplate, 默想 mak-'seung.
Contemptible, 可鄙 'hoh-'p'i.
Contend, } 爭 chaang.
Contest,

Content, 安分 ohn-fun', 見够 kin'-kau', 知足 chi-tsuuk, 自得 tsze'-tak.
Context, 上下文 sheung'-ha'-mun.
Continent, 大洲 taai'-chau.
Continually, 屢屢 lui'-lui', 一流 yat-*lau, 不留 pat-*lau, 不歇 pat-*hit'.
Continue, 耐久 noi'-'kau.
Continuous, 相連 seung-lin.
Contraband goods, 私貨 sze-foh'.
Contract, (a) 合同 hop-t'unng, (to) 立約 laap-yeuk', (for work) 拌工 p'oon' kuung, (lessen) 縮短 shuuk-'tuen, 縮細 shuuk-sai'.
Contradict, 辦駁 pin'-pok', 話不是 wa'-pat-shi', wa'-'m-hai', 翻轉話 faan-'chuen-wa'.
Contrary, 相反 seung-'faan, 逆 yik, ngaak.
Contribute, (money) 捐銀 kuen-*ngan.

Contrive, 計算 kai⁾-suen⁾, 想像 ˋseung-tseung⁾.
Control, 制 chai⁾.
Contumely, 凌辱 ling-yuuk.
Convalescent, 病將近好 peng⁾ tseung-*kan⁾-ˋho.
Convenient, 便當 pin⁾-tong⁾, 方便 fong-pin⁾, 便 pin⁾.
Convent, 庵堂 om-t'ong.
Converse, 談論 t'aam-luun⁾, 談談 t'aam-t'aam, 相交 seung-kaau.
Convert, (to) 感化 ˋkom-fu⁾, 變轉 pin⁾-ˋchuen.
Convert, (a) 進教 tsuun⁾-kaau⁾.
Convex, 中間凸 ˌchuung-ˌkaan-tut.
Convey, 搬運 poon-wan⁾, 搬帶 poon, taai⁾, 載 tsoi⁾.
Convict, (to) 定罪 ting⁾-tsui⁾.
Convict, (a) 犯人 faan⁾-yan.
Convince, 辯倒 pin⁾-ˋto, 令──知 ling⁾──chi.
Convolvulus, 纏籐花 ch'in-t'ang-fa, (the lilac) 五爪龍 ˋng-ˌchaau-*luung.
Convoy, 送行 suung⁾-hang.

Convulsions, 抽搐病 ch'au-ch'uuk-peng⁾.
Cook, 火頭 ˋfoh-*t'au, 廚人 ch'ue-yan, (female) 煮飯媽 ˋchue-faan⁾-ˋma (ma), (to) 煮 ˋchue, 煮熟 ˋchue-shuuk.
Cooked, 熟 shuuk, 煮熟 ˋchue-shuuk.
Cool, 涼 leung, (to) 整凍 ˋching-tuung⁾, 涼過 leung-kwoh⁾.
Coolie, 管店 ˋkoon-tim⁾, (strect-) 挑夫 ˌt'iu-foo.
Coolly, 坦然 ˋt'aan-in.
Cooper, 箍桶匠 foo-ˋt'uung-tseung⁾, foo-ˋt'uung-ˋlo.
Co-operate, 協力 hip-lik.
Copper, 銅 t'uung, 紅銅 huung-t'uung, 熟銅 shuuk-t'uung.
Copperas, 青礬 ts'ing-faan.
Coppersmith, 銅匠 t'uung-*tseung⁾, ˋta-t'uung-ke⁾.
Copulate, 交媾 kaau-kau⁾, 行房 hang-fong, 交合 kaau-hop, (said of animals) 打種 ˋta-ˋchuung.

Copy, (a) 稿 ‘ko, (to) 抄寫 ch‘aau-ʽse, (slips) 印字格 yan’-tsze-*kaak’.
Coral, 珊瑚 shaan-*oo.
Cord, 條繩 t‘iu-*shing, 繩仔 shing-ʽtsai.
Cordially, 熱中 it-chuung, 甘心 kom-sum.
Core, 心 sum.
Coriander, 芫荽 uen-ʽsai.
Cork, (a) 枳 chat, (to) 枳住 chat-chue’, 塞口 sak-ʽhau.
Cork-screw, 酒鑽 ʽtsau-tsuen’.
Cormorant, 鸕鷀 lo-*ts‘ze.
Corn, 禾 woh, 穀 kuuk’, (on the toe) 雞眼 kai-ʽngaan.
Cornelian, 瑪瑙 ʽma-ʽno.
Corner, 角 kok, 角頭 kok’-*t‘au, (of a room) 角落頭 kok’-lok-*t‘au.
Cornice, 牆頭線 ts‘eung-t‘au-*sin’.
Coroner, 驗屍官 im’-shi-koon.
Corpse, 死屍 ʽsze-shi, 屍首 shi-ʽshau.

Corpulent, 肥大 fi-taai’.
Correct, 無錯 ‘mo-ts‘oh’, 着 chenk, 端正 tuen-ching’, 端方 tuen-fong, (to) 改削 ʽkoi-seuk’, 改正 ʽkoi-ching’.
Correspond, 相應 seung-ying’, (by letter) 通信 t‘uung-suun’.
Corridor, 廊 long.
Corroborate, 證實 ching’-shat.
Corrode, 銹壞 sau’-waai’, 銹蝕 sau’-shik.
Corrupt, (morally) 邪 ts‘e, (putrid) 腐爛 foo’-laan’, (to) 滾壞 ʽkwun-waai’.
Cosey, (tea) 茶唅 ch‘a-ʽk‘am (see Cozy).
Cost, (the) 買價 ‘maai-ka’, (to) 抵 ʽtai.
Costiveness, 大便不通 taai’-pin’-pat-t‘uung.
Costly, 貴 kwai’.
Costume, 粧扮 chong-paan’.
Cottage, 小屋 ʽsiu-uuk, 屋仔 uuk-ʽtsai.

Cotton, (raw) 棉花 min-*fa*, (yarn) 棉紗 min-*sha*, (cloth) 布 *po*'.
Couch, 睡椅 shui'-'i, 匠床 k'ong'-ch'ong.
Cough, 咳嗽 k'at-sau'.
Council, 會 *ooi'.
Counsel, 勸 huen'.
Counsellor, (legal) 狀師 chong'-sze.
Count, (to) 算數 suen'-sho', 數 'sho.
Countenance, 面貌 min'-maau', (to) 照顧 chiu'-koo'.
Counter, (a shop-) 櫃圍 kwai'-*wai.
Counter-balance, 對抵 tui'-'tai.
Counteract, 禁制 kum'-chai', 擋住 'tong-chue', 抵住 'tai-chue'.
Counterfeit, 假做 'ka-tso'.
Counterpane, 被面 'p'i-*min'.
Country, 國 kwok', (the) 鄉下 heung-*ha'.
Couple, 偶 'ngau, 對 tui'.

Couplet, 對聯 'tui-*luen, 對 'tui.
Courage, 膽量 'taam-leung', 勇氣 'yuung-hi', (keep up) 揚起心肝 tik-'hi-sum-kohn.
Courageous, 大膽 taai'-'taam.
Course, 道路 to'-lo', (of course) 自然 tsze'-in, (at a meal) 一度 yat-to' 一味送 yat-*mi'-sung'.
Court, (the Imperial) 朝廷 ch'iu-t'ing, (of justice) 衙門 nga-*moon, (Supreme) 臬署 nip-'shue, (Police) 巡理府 ts'uun-'li-'foo, (to) 逑 k'au.
Court-yard, 天井 t'in-'tseng.
Courtesan, 老舉 'lo-'kue.
Courtesy, 禮文 'lai-mun, 禮體 'lai-'t'ai, 禮數 'lai-sho'.
Cousin, 堂兄弟 t'ong-*hing-tai', (of another surname) 表兄弟 'piu-hing-tai'.
Covenant, 約 yeuk', 盟約 mang-yeuk'.

Cover, 遮蓋 che-k'oi, 喼任 ʻk'um-chue, 笈 k'up, 蓋 k'oi, 掩 ʻim, ʻum, (to put a covering on) 捫 moon.
Coverlet, 被面 ʻp'i-*min.
Covet, 貪 t'aam.
Covetous, 貪心 t'aam-sum.
Cow, 牛母 ngau-ʻmoo, 牛乸 ngau-ʻna.
Coward, 無膽 ʻmo-ʻtaam, 膽怯 ʻtaam-hip, 泵堆 tum-tui.
Coxcomb, (flower) 雞冠花 ʻkai-ʻkoon-ʻfa, (a fop) 貪威 t'aam-wai.
Cozy, 安煖 ohn-ʻnuen (see Cosey).
Crab, 蟹 ʻhaai, (small) 蟚蜞 p'aang-*k'i.
Crack, 坼裂 ch'aak-lit, (to) 裂開 lit-hoi, 整裂 ʻching-lit, (the fingers) 整手卜 ʻching-ʻshau-puuk.
Cracked voice, 坼坼聲 ch'aak-ch'aak-sheng.
Crackers, 爆竹 p'aau-chuuk, 爆像 p'aau-*tseung.

Cracking, 逼迫聲 pik-paak-sheng, p'lik-p'lak.
Craft, 藝業 ngai-ip.
Crafty, 乖巧 kwaai-ʻhaau.
Cram, 插實 ch'aap-shat, 插滿 ch'aap-ʻmoon.
Cramp, 筋縮埋 kan-shuuk-maai.
Cramped, 困逼 k'wan-pik.
Crane, 鶴 hok, 天鵝 t'in-ngoh, 鶄鶬 ts'ong-k'oot, (a machine) 千斤絞架 ts'in-kan-ʻkaau-ʻka.
Crank, (a) 絞柄 ʻkaau-peng.
Crape, 縐綢 tsau-ch'au, 縐紗 tsau-sha.
Crash, 彭聲 p'aang-shing, 砰磅 ping-ʻpong.
Crave, 求 k'au.
Craving, (an artificial) 癮 ʻyan, (natural) 欲 yuuk.
Craw-fish, (sea) 龍蝦 luung-ʻha.
Crawl, 躝 laan, 爬行 p'a-hang, (as a worm) 縮吓 shuuk-ʻha, 哆哆吓 ʻmiu-ʻmiu-*ha.

Crazy, 戇 ngong⁾, 瘋癲 fuung-tin.
Creak, 齧聲 nget-sheng, kwit-sheng.
Cream, 牛奶皮 ngau-ˊnaai-p'i.
Crease, 縐 ch'aau, 整縐 ˊching-ch'aau. 捼縐 noh-ch'aau.
Create, 創造 ch'ong⁾-tso⁾.
Creator, 做化主 tso⁾-fa⁾-ˊchue, 創造主 ch'ong⁾-tso⁾-ˊchue.
Credit, 信 suun⁾, (buy or sell on) 賒 she, (give me) 過信 kwoh⁾-suun⁾.
Creditor, 債主 chaai⁾-ˊchue.
Credulous, 輕信 hing-suun⁾.
Creed, 信經 suun⁾-king.
Creek, 涌 ch'ung, 涌滘 ch'ung-kaau⁾.
Creep, 躝 laan.
Creeper, 躝籐 laan-t'ang.
Creeping sensation, 麻麻痹 ma-ma-pi⁾.
Crescent, 新月形 san-uet-ying.

Cress, 水芹菜 ˊshui-k'an-ts'oi⁾.
Crest, (of a cock) 雞冠 ˌkai-ˌkoon, ˌkai-ˌkwaan, (of other birds) 髻 kai⁾, ˊkai.
Crevice, 罅隙 la⁾-kwik.
Crib, 欄 laan; (a book for " cribbing ") ˊlam.
Cricket, 蟋蟀 sik-tsuut, 促織 ts'uuk-chik, tsuuk-tsit⁾.
Crime, 罪 tsui⁾.
Criminal, 罪人 tsui⁾-yan.
Crimp, (a) 拐帶佬 ˊkwaai-taai⁾-ˊlo.
Crimp, (to) 縐埋 tsau⁾-maai, ch'aau-maai.
Crimson, 大紅色 taai⁾-huung-shik.
Crinum, 脫衣換錦 t'uet-i-oon⁾-ˊkum.
Cripple, 跛腳 pai-keuk⁾.
Crisis, (come to a) 至極地 chi-kik-*ti⁾, 事到頭來 sze⁾-to⁾-t'au-loi (lai).
Crisp, 脆 ts'ui⁾.
Criticise, 批評 p'ai-p'ing.
Crockery, 磁器 ts'ze-hi⁾.

Crocodile, 鱷魚 ngok-ue.
Crooked, 彎曲 waan-k'uk, 攣曲 luen-k'uk.
Crop, 收穫 shau-wok, 造 tso', (a bird's) 觳胞 sui-,paau, 穀窩 sui-,wo.
Cross, (a) 十字架 shap-tsze-,ka, (-wise) 橫 waang, (make a) 交加 ,kaau-,ka, (irritate) 激嬲 kik-nau.
Cross, (peevish) 蠻 maan, 嬲嫐 nau-nat.
Cross-bar, 橫壓 wang-aat', 橫欄 waang-*luung.
Cross-examine, 橫詰 waang-kit, 橫間 waang-mun'.
Cross-grained, 橫紋 waang-*mun, 乖張 kwaai-cheung.
Crotchety, 奇橫 k'i-waang.
Crouch, 踡伏 ts'uen-fuuk, 屈氣 wut-hi', 瞾低 mau-tai.
Croup, 哮喘 haau-,ch'uen, 哮病 haau-peng'.
Crow, 老鴉 ,lo-,a, 烏鵲 ,oo-tseuk', (to) 啼 t'ai.
Crowbar, 鹹鏊 tuung'-,ts'iu.

Crowd, 擁集 ,yuung-tsaap, (to) 擠擁 tsai-,yuung, 偪 pik.
Crown, (top) 頂 ,ting, (ornamental) 冠冕 koon-,min.
Crucify, 釘 —— 十字架 teng —— shap-tsze-,ka, 釘死 teng-,sze.
Cruel, 殘忍 ts'aan-,yan.
Cruet-stand, 五味架 ,ng-mi'-,ka.
Cruiser, 巡船 ts'un-*shuen.
Crumb, 屑碎 sit'-sui, 咂碎 sap-,sui.
Crumble, 擣碎 ,to-sui'.
Crumple, 縐揞揞 ch'aun-mang-mang.
Crush, 壓壞 aat'-waai', 壓爛 aat'-laan', 搾 cha', (with the hand) 揸爛 cha-laan,' 搾 cha'.
Crust, 殼 hok', 硬皮 ngaang'-*p'i.
Crusty, 惡 ok'.
Crutch, 扠杖 ch'a-cheung', 扠枴 ch'a-,kwaai, 枴杖 ,kwaai-*cheung'.

Cry, 喊 haam², 叫聲 kiu²-sheng, 噲 aai², 嘍 iu.
Crystal, 水晶 ʻshui-ʻtsiny.
Cube, 立方 laap-fong, 立方形 laap-fong-ying, 色子樣 shik-ʻtsze-*yeung².
Cubit, 尺 chʻek².
Cuckold, 龜公 ʻkwai-kung.
Cuckoo, (Chinese) 催耕雀 tsʻui-kang-tseuk², 杜鵑 toʻ-ʻkuen.
Cucumber, 王瓜 wong-kwa.
Cud, (to chew) 翻草 faan-ʻtsʻo.
Cudgel, 木棒 muuk-ʻpʻaang.
Cue, 辮 ʻpin, 條辮 tʻiu-ʻpin.
Cuff, 袖口 tsau²-ʻhau, (to) 拳打 kʻuen-ʻta.
Culpable, 可責 ʻhoh-chaak².
Cultivate, 耕種 kang-chung², (plants) 恐 ʻnun.
Cumber, 阻滯 ʻchoh-chai², 滯 chai².
Cumbersome, 累贅 lui²-chui².
Cunning, 多計 toh-*kai², 詭譎 ʻkwai-kwut.
Cup, 盃 ʻpooi.

Cup-board, 碗櫃 ʻoon-*kwai².
Curb, 勒住 lak-chue², 管束 ʻkoon-chʻuk².
Curd, 乳結 ʻne-kit², (bean-) 荳腐 tau²-foo².
Curdle, 凝結 ying-kit².
Cure, 醫好 i-ʻho.
Curiosity, (of mind) 練見識 lin²-kin²-shik, 查查察察 chʻa-chʻa-chʻaat²-chʻaat².
Curiosities, 古董 ʻkoo-ʻtung, 奇珍 kʻi-chan.
Curl, 攣埋 luen-maai.
Curly hair, 捲髮 ʻkuen-faat².
Currants, 珠菩提 chue-pʻo-tʻai.
Current. (a) 水流 ʻshui-lau.
Current money, 通寶 tʻung-ʻpo.
Current price, 時價 shi-ka².
Curry-powder, 黃薑粉 wong-keung-ʻfun, (-stuff) 架厘材料 ka²-li-tsʻoi-liu².
Curse, 呪咀 chau²-choh², (to vow) 賭呪 ʻto-chau².
Curtain, 布簾 po²-*lim, (mosquito-) 蚊帳 mun-*cheung².

Curve, 彎曲 waan-kuuk.
Cushion, 褥仔 yuuk-ʽtsai, 椅墊 ʽi-tin' (tsin').
Cuspidor, 痰鑵 t'aam-koon'.
Custard-apple, 番荔枝 faan-lai'-ʽchi.
Custom, (common) 規矩 k'wai-ʽkue, 世俗 shai'-tsunk, 風俗 funng-tsunk, (tribute) 稅 shui', (house) 關口 kwaan-ʽhau, 稅館 shui'-ʽkoon.
Customer, 買客 ʽmaai-haak'.
Cut, 割 koht', 切 ts'it', (off) 斬 ʽchaam, (acquaintance) 不偢彩 'm-ts'au-ʽts'oi.
Cuttlefish, 張魚 cheung-ue, 墨魚 mak-ue.
Cycle of sixty, 花甲 fa-kaap'.
Cyclone, 旋風 suen-funng, 風颶 funng-kau'.
Cymbals, 鐃鈸 naau-poot, 鈔 ʽch'aau.
Cynical, 鼓氣 ʽkoo-hi'.
Cypress, 扁柏 ʽpin-paak'.

D

Dab, 搭 tap, 呩 tat, (to wet) 搭濕 tap-shup, tat-shup.
Dab, fish, 沙孟魚 sha-maang'-*ue.
Dabble in, 弄 luung'.
Dace, fish, 黃尾鱗 wong-ʽmi-luun.
Daddy, 爹爹 te-te.
Dagger, 短劍 ʽtuen-kim'.
Daggle, 拖惣 t'oh-ʽnun.
Dahlia, 芍藥 cheuk'-yeuk.
Daily, 日日 yat-yat, 每日 ʽmooi-yat, (use) 日用 yat-yunng'.
Dainties, 味 *mi'.
Dainty, 嬌貴 kiu-kwai'.
Dam, (mother) 嬭 ʽna.
Dam, (a water-) 基圍 ki-wai, 陂 pi, (to) 塞陂 sak-pi, 壅 ʽyunng.
Damage, 損壞 ʽsuen-waai'.
Damask, 大花緞 taai'-fa-*tuen'.
Damn, (to curse) 咒詛 chau'-choh'.

Damned, to be, 折墮 chit⁾-toh⁾, 墮落雞 toh⁾-lok-kai.
Damp, 濕 shap, (and soft) 腍 num, (to become) 潮濕 chʻiu-shup, (to) 整濕 ʻching-shup.
Damson, 小梅 ʻsiu-mooi.
Dance, 跳舞 tʻiu⁾-ʻmoo.
Dandelion, 蒲公英 pʻoo-ʻkuung-ʻying.
Dandle, 搖吓 iu-ʻha, 榴吓 ʻlau⁾-ʻha.
Dandruff, 頭坭 tʻau-nai.
Dandy, 裝腔 ʻchong-ʻhong, 紈褲子弟 uen-foo⁾-ʻtsze-tai⁾.
Danger, 危險 ngai-ʻhim.
Dangerous, 險 ʻhim.
Dangle, 調調佞 tiu⁾-*tiu⁾-fing⁾.
Dare, 敢 ʻkom, 膽敢 ʻtaam-ʻkom.
Daring, 大膽 taai⁾-ʻtaam.
Dark, 黑 hak, 黑暗 hak-om⁾.
Darling, 痛愛 tʻuung⁾-oi⁾, 掌上珠 ʻcheung-sheung⁾-ʻchue.

Darn, 織補 chik-ʻpo.
Dart, (to) 閃 ʻshim, (an arrow) 袖箭 tsau⁾-tsin⁾, 標 piu.
Dash, (to) 冲撞 chʻuung-chong⁾.
Date, (time) 年月號 nin-uet-ho⁾.
Dates, (dried) 蜜棗 mat-ʻtso, (jujube-tree) 棗樹 ʻtso-shue⁾, (palm) 波斯棗 poh-sze-ʻtso, 洋棗 yeung-ʻtso.
Datura, 鬧羊花 naau⁾-yeung-fa, 曼陀羅 maan⁾-tʻoh-loh.
Daub, 塗污 tʻo-oo, 搽 chʻa.
Daubed, 抹得粗 maat-tak-tʻso.
Daughter, 女 ʻnue, (your) 千金 tsʻin-ʻkum, (-in-law) 媳婦 sik-ʻfoo.
Daunted, 喪氣 song⁾-hi⁾.
Davits, 朗枅 kat-ʻkai.
Dawn, 天僅光 tʻin-ʻkan-kwong⁾, 懷亮 muung-leung⁾.
Day, 日 yat, 日子 yat-ʻtsze.

Day-light, 白晝 paak-chau⁾, 白日 paak-yat, (morning) 天光 tʻin-kwong.
Dazzle, 瞠花眼 chʻaang⁾-fa-ʻngaan, 瞠 chʻaang⁾.
Deacon, 執事 chap-sze⁾.
Dead, 死咀 ʿsze-ʿchoh, ʿsze-hiu, 身故 shan-koo⁾, 過身 kwoh⁾-shan.
Deaf, 聾 luung, 耳聾 ʻi-luung, (dull) 耳背 ʻi-pooi⁾.
Deal, (to) 交易 kaau-yik, (a good-) 好多 ʻho-toh.
Deal, (wood) 杉木 chʻaam⁾-muuk.
Dear, 貴 kwai⁾, (loved) 切愛 tsʻit⁾-oi⁾.
Death, 死 ʿsze, 死亡 ʿsze-mong.
Death-rattle, 扯氣 ʿchʻe-hi⁾.
Debase, 傾低銀水 kʻing-tai-ngan-ʿshui.
Debate, 鬥口角 tau⁾-ʿhau-kok⁾, 爭論 chaang-luun⁾.
Debauch, (to) 點污 ʿtim-oo, 玷汚 tim⁾-oo.
Debauchee, 酒色之徒 ʿtsau-shik-chi-tʻo.

Debauchery, 蹬脚 sang⁾-*keuk⁾.
Debilitate, 損元氣 ʿsuen-uen-hi⁾, 壞氣力 waai⁾-hi⁾-lik, 壞身 waai⁾-shan.
Debility, 軟弱 ʿuen-yeuk, 元氣傷 uen-hi⁾-sheung, 虛 hue.
Debit note 揭單 kʻit⁾-ʿtaan.
Debt, 欠債 him⁾-chaai⁾, 欠負 him⁾-foo⁾, (debts) 欠項 him⁾-hong⁾.
Debtor, 債仔 chaai⁾-ʿtsai, 欠債人 him⁾-chaai⁾-yan.
Decade, 旬 tsʻuun.
Decalogue, 十誡 shap-kaai⁾.
Decamp, 退避 tʻui⁾-pi⁾.
Decant, 捭 pi⁾.
Decapitate, 殺頭 shaat⁾*tʻau.
Decapitation, 正法 ching⁾-faat⁾.
Decayed, 衰壞 shui-waai⁾, 霉爛 mooi-laan⁾, 枯槁 foo-ʿko.
Deceit, 詭譎 ʿkwai-kwut.
Deceitful, 詐假 cha⁾-ʿka.
Deceive, 瞞騙 moon-pʻin⁾, 呃 ngaak, 噋 tʻum⁾.

December, 英十二月 ʻYing-shap-iʼ-uet.
Decency, 合禮 hop-ʻlai, 合式 hop-shik.
Decide, 決斷 kʻuetʼ-tuenʼ, 定 tingʼ.
Decision, 主意 ʻchue-i.
Deck, (the) 艙板 tsʻong-ʻpaan, (to) 裝整 chong-ʻching.
Declare, 話實 wa-shat, (shew) 表明 ʻpiu-ming.
Decline, (downwards) 墜落去 chuiʼ-lok-hueʼ, 向低去 heungʼ-tai-hueʼ, (refuse) 辭謝 tsʻze-tse, 推辭 tʻui-tsʻze, (seeing) 免見 ʻmin-kinʼ, 擋駕 ʻtong-kaʼ.
Declivity, 斜坂 tsʻeʼ-ʻpaan, 斜落 tsʻe-*tsʻe-lok, 坡 poh.
Decoct, 煎 tsin.
Decorate, 裝整 chong-ʻching.
Decorum, 禮所當然 ʻlai-ʻshoh-tong-in, 容儀 yuung-i, 儀注 i-chueʼ.
Decoy, (to) 引誘 ʻyan-ʻyau, (birds) 裝雀 chong-*tseukʼ, (to) 做媒 tsoʼ-*mooi.

Decrease, 減少 ʻkaam-ʻshiu, 縮減 shuuk-ʻkaam.
Decree, 命令 mingʼ-lingʼ.
Decrepit, 老邁 ʻlo-maaiʼ.
Dedicate, 供奉 kuungʼ-fuungʼ.
Deduct, 減 ʻkaam, 扣除 kʻauʼ-chʻue, 去 ʻhue.
Deed, 行爲 hang-wai, 事 szeʼ, (bond) 契 kʻaiʼ, (stamped-) 印契 yanʼ-kʻaiʼ.
Deep, 深 shum.
Deer, 鹿 *luuk, (moschus) 黃麇 wong-ʻkeng, 麞 ʻcheung.
Deer's horn, 鹿茸 luuk-yuung.
Defame, 壞——名聲 waaiʼ——ming-shing.
Defeat, 敗 paaiʼ, 打敗 ʻta-paaiʼ, 打贏 ʻta-yeng.
Defect, 虧缺 fai-kʻuetʼ.
Defend, 保護 ʻpo-ooʼ.
Defendant, 被告 piʼ-koʼ.
Defer, 改期 ʻkoi-kʻi, 展緩 ʻchin-oonʼ, (yield) 推讓 tʻui-yeungʼ, 寬限 foon-haanʼ.
Deficiency, 短欠 ʻtuen-himʼ, 欠缺 himʼ-kʻuetʼ.

Defile, 染汚 ʽim-oo, 玷汚 tim’-oo, (a) 山峽 shaan-haap.
Definite, 定 ting’, 定然 ting’-in.
Deflect, 轉邪 ʽchuen-tsʽe.
Deformed, 醜怪 ʽchʽau-kwaai’.
Defraud, 呃騙 ngaak-pʽin’.
Defy, 激鬥 kik-tau’, 惹敵 ʽye-tik, 輕敵 hing-tik, 撩打 ʽliu-ʽta.
Degenerate, 下流 ha’-lau, 入下流 yup-ha’-lau, 不肖 pat-tsʽiu’.
Degrade, (in rank) 降級 kong’-kʽup, 參革 tsʽaam-kaak’, (one's self) 丟面 tiu-*min’.
Degree, 等 ʽtang, 層 tsʽang, 級 kʽup, (measure) 度 to’.
Deign, 垂顧 shui-koo’.
Dejected, 愁默默 shau-mak-mak, 悶沉沉 moon’-chʽum-chʽum.
Delay, 擔擱 taam-kok’, 遲緩 chʽi-oon’.

Delegate, (to) 交托 kaau-tok’, (a) 委托之人 ʽwai-tʽok’-ke’-yan.
Deliberate, 斟酌 chum-cheuk’, 商量 sheung-leung’, (ADJ.) 澹定 taam’-ting’.
Delicate, 嬌嫩 kiu-nuen’, 柔弱 yau-yeuk, 幼細 yau’-sai’.
Delicacy, (a) 珍饈 chan-sau.
Delicious, 佳味 kaai-mi’, 美味 ʽmi-mi’.
Delight, 歡喜 foon-ʽhi.
Delineate, 畫出 waak-chʽuut.
Delirious, 發狂 faat’-kʽwong.
Delirium, 狂 kʽwong.
Deliver, (save) 救 kau’, (up) 交 kaau’, 遞 tai’, (over to) 解 kaai’.
Delude, 迷惑 mai-waak, 蠱惑 ʽhoo-waak.
Deluge, 洪水 huung-ʽshui.
Demand, (in) 時興 shi-hing.
Demand, (to) 問取 mun’-tsʽue, 要取 iu’-tsʽue, 必要 pit iu’, (with violence) 逼取 pik-ʽtsʽue.

Demolish, 拆嘥 ch'aak'-saai'.
Demon, 鬼 ‘kwai.
Demonstrate, 指明証據 ‘chi-ming-ching'-kue'.
Demoralized, (as troops) 潰 ‘fui, 盡覆 tsuun'-fuuk', (the mind) 壞心術 waai'-sum-shuut.
Demur, 不肯 pat-‘hang, 'm-‘hang, 推 t'ui, 推延 t'ui-in.
Den, 籠 ‚luung, 穴 uct, 竇口 tau'-‘hau.
Denomination, 名字 ming-tsze', 字號 tsze'-ho'.
Denote, 指實 ‘chi-shat.
Denounce, 控告 huung'-ko'.
Dense, 稠密 ch'au-mat.
Dentist, 牙科醫生 nga-‚foh-‚i-‚shang.
Deny, 不認 pat-ying', 'm-ying', 話唔係 wa'-'m-hai', (one's self) 克己 hak-‘ki, 捨己 ‘she-‘ki.
Depart, 別去 pit-hue', 行離 hang-li, 離去 li-hue'.

Department, 該管 koi-‘koon, 職守 chik-shau, 所屬 ‘shoh-shuuk, 部 po'.
Depend on, 倚賴 ‘i-laai', 倚靠 ‘i-k'aau'.
Deplorable, 可恨 ‘hoh-han' 堪悲 hom-pi.
Deplore, 悲哀 pi-oi.
Deport, 搬去 poon-hue'.
Deportment, 行爲 hang-wai, (correct) 容儀 yuung-i.
Depose, 革職 kaak'-chik.
Deposit, (a) 當頭 tong'-t'au, (to) 墜落 chui'-lok, (pawn) 按當 ohn'-tong', 押 aat'.
Deposition, (verbal) 口供 ‘hau-kuung, (from office) 廢 fai', 革職 kaak'-chik.
Depraved, 邪惡 ts'e-ok', 心壞 sum-waai'.
Depreciate, 看低 hohn'-tai, 睇輕 ‘t'ai-heng.
Depress, 壓落 aat'-lok.
Depressed, 困鬱 k'wun'-wut.
Deprive, 奪 tuet, 革去 kaak'-hue'.

Depute, 委託 ʻwai-tʻokʼ.
Deranged, 亂 luenʼ, 癲 tin.
Deride, 戲笑 hiʼ-siuʼ, 嬉笑 hi-siuʼ.
Derive, (obtain) 得倒 tak-ʻto.
Derogate, 損 ʻsuen.
Descend, 下降 ʻha-kong.
Descendants, 後裔 hauʼ-yui.
Describe, 指出 ʻchi-chʻuut, 歷歷表明 lik-lik-ʻpiu-ming, 講清楚 ʻkong-tsʻing-ʻchʻoh, (write) 寫出 ʻse-chʻuut.
Description, (every) 各色 kokʼ-shik.
Desecrate, 褻瀆 sitʼ-tuuk.
Desert, 野 ʻye, 野外 ʻye-ngoiʼ, 郊外 kaau-ngoiʼ.
Desert, (merit), 因果 yan-ʻkwoh, 功勞 kuung-lo.
Desert, (to) 逃脫 tʻo-tʻuetʼ, 走路 ʻtsau-lo, 拋離 pʻaau-li.
Deserve, 應係 ying-haiʼ, 該當 koi-tong, 應分 ying funʼ.

Design, (to) 計謀 kaiʼ-mau, (a) 意像 iʼ-tscungʼ, 謀畧 man-leuk, (intention) 主意 ʻchue-iʼ.
Designation, 字號 tszeʼ-hoʼ.
Designate, 稱呼 chʻing-foo.
Desire, 欲 yuuk, 願 uenʼ, 情願 tsʻing-uenʼ, (covet) 貪 tʻaam.
Desist, 止息 ʻchi-sik, 罷了 paʼ-liu, 歇手 hitʼ-ʻshau.
Desk, 寫字臺 ʻse-tszeʼ-*tʻoi, (portable) 寫字箱 ʻse-tszeʼ-seung.
Desolate, 孤寒 koo-hohn, 零落 ling-lok.
Despair, 絕望 tsuetʼ-mongʼ, 失望 shat-mongʼ.
Desperate, 無奈何 ʻmo-noiʼ-hoh.
Despise, 藐視 ʻmiu-shiʼ, 侮慢 ʻmoo-maanʼ, 輕忽 hing-fut, 睇不上眼 ʻtʻai-ʼm-sheungʼ-ngaan.
Despond, 失望 shat-mongʼ.
Despotic, (oppressive) 酷 hunk, (government) 全權政 tsʻuen-kʻuen-chingʼ.

Destination, 去向 ʿhue-heungʾ.
Destiny, (fate) 命 mengʾ, 數 shoʾ.
Destitute, 窮 kʻuung, 窮困 kʻuung-kʻwunʾ.
Destroy, 毀滅 ʿwai-mit, 毀爛 ʿwai-laanʾ, 敗壞 paaiʾ-waaiʾ.
Destruction, 滅亡 mit-mong.
Desultory, 撈雜 laap-tsaap, 無層次 ʿmo-tsʻang-tsʻze.
Detach, 分開 fun-hoi.
Detail, (in) 逐一 chuuk-yat, (to) 逐一逐二講 chuuk-yat-chuuk-*iʾ-ʿkong.
Detain, 留住 lau-chueʾ, 揩阻 kʻangʾ-ʿchoh.
Detect, 察出 chʻaatʾ-chʻuut, 訪出 ʿfong-chʻuut.
Deter, 攔阻 laan-ʿchoh.
Deteriorate, 舊壞 kauʾ-waaiʾ, 衰壞 shui-waaiʾ.
Determination, 決意 kʻuetʾ-iʾ
Determine, 定 tingʾ, 決 kʻuetʾ.
Detest, 恨惡 hanʾ-ooʾ, 厭惡 imʾ-ooʾ, 憎惡 tsang-ooʾ.

Detract, 講損 ʿkong-ʿsuen.
Devastation, 荒廢 fong-faiʾ.
Develope, 舒開 shue-hoi, 伸發 shan-faatʾ, 發開 faatʾ-hoi.
Deviate, 行差 hang-chʻa.
Device, 計 kaiʾ, *kaiʾ.
Devil, 魔鬼 moh-ʿkwai.
Devise, 計謀 kai-mau, 籌畫 chʻau-waak.
Devoid of, 無 ʿmo or moo.
Devolve, 交落 kaau-lok.
Devoted, 仰慕 ʿyeung-mooʾ, 心慕 sum-mooʾ, 深服 shum-fuuk.
Devotion, 誠敬之禮 shing-kingʾ-chi-ʿlai, 虔敬 kʻin-kingʾ.
Devour, 硬吞 ngaangʾ-tʻun.
Devout, 誠心 shing-sum, 虔敬 kʻin-kingʾ.
Dew, 露水 loʾ-ʿshui, 霧 moʾ.
Dexterous, 巧手 ʿhaau-ʿshau.
Diabetes, 尿淋 niuʾ-lum.
Diabolical, 惡妖 okʾ-iu, 兇惡 huung-okʾ.
Diagnose, 診 ʿchʻan.

Diagonal, 斜線 ts'e-*sin*, 對角線 tui*-kok*-*sin*.
Diagrams, (the eight) 八卦 paat*-kwa*.
Dial, 日晷 yat-ʿkwai, 日窺 yat-ʿkʻwai.
Dialect, 土話 ʿt'o-*wa*, 土談 ʿto-t'aam.
Dialogue, 問答 mun*-taap*, 相論 seung-luun*.
Diameter, 徑線 king*-*sin*.
Diamond, 金剛石 kum-kong-shek, 鑽石 tsuen*-shek.
Diarrhœa, 疴 oh, 水瀉 ʿshui-se*.
Diary, 日記 yat-ki*.
Dice, 色子 shik-ʿtsze.
Dice-playing, 擲色 chaak-shik.
Dictate, 囑咐 chuuk-foo*, 主張 ʿchue-cheung, (to a writer) 口授 ʿhau-shau*.
Dictionary, 字典 tsze*-ʿtin, 字彙 tsze*-ʿlui.
Dictum, 硬話 ngaang*-*wa*.

Die, (to) 死 ʿsze, (said of men) 過世 kwoh*-shai*, 身故 shan-koo*.
Diet, (to) 戒口 kaai*-ʿhau.
Differ, 爭 chaang, 有分別 ʿyau-ʃun-pit.
Difference, 差 chʻa, 分別 fun-pit, 爭 chaang.
Different, 不同 ʼm-tʻuung, (very) 差得遠 chʻa-tak-ʿuen.
Difficult, 難 naan, 惡做 ok*-tso*.
Difficulty, 艱難 kaan-naan.
Diffident, 信不過 suun*-ʼm-kwoh*.
Diffuse, 佈散 po*-saan*, 播揚 poh*-yeung.
Dig, 掘 kwut.
Digest, 消化 siu-fa*.
Dignified, 威嚴 wai-im.
Dignity, 威儀 wai-i, 威風 wai-fuung.
Digress, 支離 chi-li.
Dike, 基堢 ki-pok*.
Dilapidated, 頹壞 t'ui-waai*.

Dilate, 撐開 ch'aang-hoi, (expatiate) 講詳細 ʿkong-ts'cung-sai.

Dilatory, 遲慢 ch'i-maan', (*maan').

Dilemma, 兩難 ʿleung-naan.

Diligent, 勤力 k'an-lik, 勤 k'an.

Dilute, 攪水 ʿkaau-ʿshui, 摳稀 k'au-hi.

Dim, 矇矓 muung-luung, 矇 muung.

Dimensions, 長闊 ch'eung-foot', 度量 to'-leung'.

Diminish, 減少 ʿkaam-ʿshiu.

Diminutive, 細微 sai'-mi, sai'-mi.

Dimple, 酒凹 ʿtsau-nup.

Din, 嘈响 ts'o-ʿheung, 吧閉 pa-pai'.

Ding-dong, 玎璫 ʿting-ʿtong.

Dinner, 大餐 taai'-ts'aan.

Dip, 蘸 chaam', 沉下 ch'um-*ha', 浸下 yum'-ʿha, tsim'.

Direct, 正直 ching'-chik, (to) 指點 ʿchi-ʿtim, 指教 ʿchi-kaau, 管理 ʿkoon-li.

Direction, 去向 hue'-heung', 方向 fong-heung'.

Directly, 卽刻 tsik-haak, 卽時 tsik-shi.

Dirt, 泥土 nai-ʿt'o, (dung) 屎 ʿshi.

Dirty, 污糟 oo-tso, 鏪鮓 la'-cha, (to) 整污糟 ʿching-oo-tso.

Disabled, 無能 mo-nang.

Disabuse the mind, 開茅塞 hoi-maau-sak.

Disadvantage, 受虧 shau'-fai, 不直 pat-chik.

Disaffected, 不輸服 'm-shue-fuuk.

Disagree, 不對 'm-tui', 唔啱 'm-ʿngaam, 相爭 seung-chaang.

Disagreeable, 醜 ʿch'au, 掯 k'ang', 泌 sum'.

Disappear, 失去 shat-hue'.

Disappoint, 不遂願 pat-sui'-uen', 撞板 chong'-ʿpaan, 不趁願 'm-ch'an'-uen'.

Disapprove, 不中意 'm-chuung-i'.

Disaster, 凶事 huung-szeʾ.
Disavow, 不認 'm-yingʾ.
Disband, 散班 saanʾ-paan.
Disburse, 使費 ʿshai-faiʾ, 使 ʿshai, 支 chi, 出 chʻuut.
Discard, 除免 chʻue-ʿmin, 除出 chʻue-chʻuut.
Discern, 睇破 ʿtʻai-pʻohʾ.
Discernment, 聰明 tsʻuung-ming.
Discharge, 出 chʻuut, 放 fongʾ, (duty) 盡本分 tsuunʾ-ʿpoon-funʾ.
Disciple, 門生 moon-ʿshang, 學生 hok-ʿshaang.
Discipline, 教法 kaauʾ-faatʾ, (exercise) 練習 linʾ-tsaap.
Disclose, 敗露 paaiʾ-loʾ, 露出 loʾ-chʻuut.
Discomfit, 打敗 ʿta-paaiʾ.
Discomfort, 不爽快 'm-ʿshong-faaiʾ.
Discomposed, 淹悶 im-moonʾ.
Disconcerted, 失愕 shat-ngok.
Disconsolate, 憂憶 yau-yik, 憂鬱 yau-wat.

Discontented, 不滿意 pat-ʿmoon-iʾ, 不知足 pat-chi-tsuuk, 喬扭 kʻiuʾ-ʿnau.
Discontinue, 止了 ʿchi-ʿliu, 斷 tʻuenʾ, 間斷 kaanʾ-tʻuenʾ.
Discordant, 不和 pat-woh, 唔啱 'm-ʿngaam.
Discount, 扣頭銀 kʻauʾ-tʻau-*ngan, 扣銀水 kʻauʾ-ngan-ʿshui, 扣 kʻauʾ.
Discountenance, 免相與 ʿmin-seung-ʿue, 唔同埋 'm-tʻuung-maai.
Discourage, 丟── 駕 tiu ── kaʾ, 落── 臺 lok ── tʻoi, 勸止 huenʾ-ʿchi.
Discouraged, 喪氣 songʾ-hiʾ.
Discourse, 議論 ʿi-luunʾ, 論 luunʾ.
Discover, 尋見 tsʻum-kinʾ, 考明 ʿhaau-ming, 查出 chʻa-chʻuut.
Discredit, (disbelieve) 不信 'm-suunʾ, 思疑 sze-i.
Discreet, 仔細 ʿtsze-saiʾ.

Discrepancy, 不對之處 ⁽pat-tui⁾-chi-chʻue⁾, 不相對處 ʼm-seung-tui⁾-chʻue⁾.
Discrepant, 不對 pat-tui⁾, ʼm-tui⁾.
Discretion, 謹慎 ⁽kan-shan⁾, (at your) 隨你主意 tsʻue-⁽ni-⁽chue-i⁾.
Discretionary, 隨便 tsʻue-*pin⁾, 任意 yum⁾-i⁾.
Discriminate, 分明 fun-ming, 分別 fun-pit, 辯別 pin⁾-pit.
Discuss, 辯論 pin⁾-luun⁾.
Disdain, 藐視 ⁽miu-shi⁾.
Disease, 疾病 tsat-peng⁾, 病症 peng⁾-ching⁾.
Disengage, } 解出 ⁽kaai-chʻut, 解甩 ⁽kaai-lut.
Disentangle,
Disengaged, 得閒 tak-haan.
Disgrace, 污辱 oo-yuuk, 羞辱 sau-yuuk.
Disguise, 假扮 ⁽ka-paan⁾.
Disgust, 憎厭 tsang-im⁾.
Disgusting, 可惡 ⁽hoh-oo⁾.
Dishes, 碗碟 ⁽oon-tip.

Disheartened, 心恢 sum-fooi.
Dishevel, 散亂 ⁽saan-luen⁾.
Dishonest, 無眞誠 ⁽mo-chan-shing, 無眞實 ⁽mo-chan-shat.
Dishonour, (to), 辱 yuuk.
Dishonourable, 無體面 ⁽mo-⁽tʻai-min⁾.
Disinclined, 不想 ʼm-⁽seung, 不願 ʼm-nen⁾.
Disinherit, 出 chʻuut.
Disinterested, 無私心 ⁽mo-sze-sum.
Disjoint, 挫歪骨節 tsʻoh⁾-⁽me-kwut-tsit⁾, 整開骨節 ⁽ching-hoi-kwut-tsit⁾.
Disk, 輪 luun.
Dislike, 嫌 im.
Dismal, 深啉 shum-lum.
Dismay, 大驚 taai⁾-king.
Dismembering, (a punishment) 凌遲 ling-chʻi.
Dismiss, 使 ── 去 ⁽shai, ── hue⁾, 不用 pat-yuung⁾, 放 fong⁾, (clear out. ── I dismiss you) 落箱 lok-⁽seung.

Disobedient, 悖逆 pooi'-yik.
Disobey, 違背 wai-pooi', 不聽話 'm-t'eng-wa'.
Disobliging, 無照應 'mo-chiu'-ying', 啞情 ngaak-ts'ing.
Disordered, 亂 luen'.
Disorderly, 佬憆 'lo-'ts'o, 鹵莽 'lo-'mong, 妄 'mong, 立亂 laap-luen'.
Disown, 不認 'm-ying'.
Disparage, 講低 'kong-tai.
Disparity, 差 ch'a.
Dispatches, 文書 mun-shue.
Dispensary, 藥館 yeuk-'koon, (a shop) 藥材舖 yeuk-ts'oi-'p'o.
Dispense, 施 shi, (with) 免 'min.
Disperse, 離散 li-saan'.
Dispirit, 喪志 song'-chi'.
Displace, 搬亂 poon-luen'.
Displaced, 離位 li-*wai'.
Display, 顯見 'hin-in', 彰明 cheung-ming.
Displeased, 不歡喜 'm-foon-'hi.
Disposal, 管理 'koon-li.

Dispose, (arrange) 安排 ohn-p'aai.
Disposition of mind, 品格 'pun-kaak', 品性 'pun-sing', 皮氣 p'i-hi'.
Dispute, 辯駁 pin'-pok'.
Disquietude, 無平安 'mo-p'ing-ohn.
Disregard, 不顧 'm-koo'.
Disreputable, 失體 shat-'t'ai, 不好意思 'm-'ho-i'-sze', 下流 ha'-lau.
Disrepute, 無名聲 'mo-ming-shing, 不興 'm-hing.
Disrespectful, 不恭敬 'm-kuung-king'.
Dissatisfied, 不知足 'm-chi-tsuuk', 不滿意 'm-'moon-i'.
Dissemble, 詐造 cha'-tso', 詐成 cha'-shing, 詐假意 cha'-'ka-i', cha'-'ka-i'.
Disseminate, 佈散 po'-saan', 傳布 ch'uen-po', 散開 saan'-hoi.
Dissent, 懷異意 waai-i'-i', 唔信從 'm-suun'-ts'uung.

Dissimilar, 不似 'm-'ts'ze.
Dissipate, 散 saan'.
Dissipated, ⎱ 放肆 fong'-sze',
Dissolute, ⎰
放蕩 fong'-tong', 花消 fa-siu.
Dissolve, 化開 fa'-hoi, 消散 siu-saan'.
Dissuade, 勸戒 huen'-kaai'.
Distant, 遠 'uen, 隔遠 kaak-'uen.
Distaste, 見淡 kin'-t'aam.
Distend, 張開 cheung-hoi, 撐開 chaang-hoi.
Distil, 蒸 ching, 甑 tsang'.
Distinct, 分明 fun-ming, 明白 ming-paak.
Distinguish, 分別 fun-pit.
Distinguished, 出衆 ch'uut-chuung', 超羣 ch'iu-k'wun.
Distorted, 歪 waai, 'me.
Distract the mind, 分心 fun-sum, (crazed) 喪心 song'-sum.
Distress, 艱難 kaan-naan, 急逼 kup-pik, (want) 坳㘃 aau-ai'.

Distribute, 分派 fun-p'aai'.
District, 縣 uen'.
Distrust, 思疑 sze-i.
Disturb, 攪動 'kaau-tuung', 攪亂 'kaau-luen'.
Disturbance, (make) 生事 shang-sze'.
Ditch, 溝渠 kau-k'ue, 坑 haang.
Diuretic, 利水藥 li'-'shui-yeuk.
Dive, 寐水 mi'-'shui.
Diverge, 分支 fun-chi, 叉口 ch'a-hau.
Divers, 幾個 'ki-koh', 不止一個 'm-'chi-yat-koh', 不一 pat-yat.
Diverse, 幾樣 'ki-*yeung', 不同 'm-t'uung.
Divert, 引開 'yan-hoi, (the mind) 開心 hoi-sum.
Divide, 分開 fun-hoi.
Divination, 占卜 chim-puuk.
Divine, (of God) 上帝 (的) 嘅 Sheung'-tai'-ke'.
Divining blocks, 筊杯 kaau'-pui.

Division, (a) 一段 yat-tuen', 一分 yat-fun', 一股 yat-̒koo.
Divorce, 休棄 yau-hi', 出 ch'uut, 分妻 fun-ts'ai.
Divulge, 話人知 wa'-yan-chi.
Dizzy, 暈 wun', 頭暈 t'au-wun', t'au-wun, t'au-wun.
Do, 做 tso', 行 hang, 爲 wai, (don't) 不好 'm-̒ho, 咪 ̒mai.
Dock, (for ships) 船澳 shuen-o', 做船涌 tso'-shuen-ch'uung.
Doctor, 醫生 ̒i-̒shaang.
Doctrine, 教 kaau', 道理 to'-̒li.
Documents, 書契 shue-k'ai', 文書 mun-shue.
Dodder, 無葉籐 mo-ip-t'ang.
Dodge, 用計 yuung'-*kai'.
Doe, 麀 yau, 麋 mi.
Dog, 狗 ̒kau, 犬 ̒huen.
Dog fish, 跌倒沙 tit'-̒to-sha.
Dog-rose, 棠䕨花 t'ong-̒aang-fa.

Dogged, 古板 ̒koo-̒paan, 硬頸 ngaang'-̒keng.
Dogmatic, 執意 chup-i', 固執 koo'-chup.
Doleful, 贔屭 pai'-ai'.
Dolichos, 葛 koht'.
Doll, 公仔 ̒kuung-̒tsai.
Dollar, 銀錢 ngan-*ts'in, 大元 taai'-uen.
Dolt, 鸞仔 ngau'-̒tsai.
Domestic, 家 ka, (servants) 家人 ka-yan.
Dominate, 揸權柄 cha-k'uen-ping'.
Dominoes, 骨牌 kwut-*p'aai.
Done, 做完 tso'-uen, 完 uen.
Donkey, 驢 *lue.
Dooms-day, 歸結日子 kwai-kit'-yat-̒tsze, 審判日 ̒shum-p'oon'-yat.
Door, 門 moon, (-way) 門口 moon-̒hau.
Dose, (a) 劑 tsai.
Dot, 點 ̒tim.
Dotage, 老懵懂 ̒lo-̒muung-̒tuung.

Dote on, 溺愛 nik-oiʼ.
Dotted, 一點點 yat-ʽtim-ʽtim.
Double, 兩倍 ʽleung-ʽpʽooi, (ADJ.) 雙 sheung, 孖 ma, (meaning) 雙關話 ʽsheung-ʽkwaan-ʽwa, (to) 加一倍 ka-yat-ʽpʽooi, (to fold) 摺 chipʼ.
Double flower, 雙托花 sheung *tʽokʼ-fa.
Double-tongued, 三口兩脷 saam-ʽhau-ʽleung-li.
Doubt, 思疑 sze-i, 疑惑 i-waak.
Doubtful, 不定 ʼm-tingʼ.
Doubtless, 無錯 ʽmo-tsʽohʼ.
Dough, 發麵 faatʼ-min.
Dove, 鴿 kopʼ, 班鳩 ʽpaan-ʽkau.
Dove-tailed, 交指榫 kaau-ʽchiʼ-ʽsuun, 門筍 tauʼ-ʽsuun.
Down, (feathers) 毡毛 yuung-mo, (on the skin) 寒毛 hohn-mo, 幼毛 yauʼ-mo.
Down, (-ward) 下 haʼ, 落 lok.

Down stairs, 樓梯下 lau-tʽai-haʼ, (go) 落樓 lok-*lau.
Dowry, 妝奩 chong-lim.
Doze, (to) 恰瞓眼 hap-ʽngaan-funʼ.
Drab, (a colour) 栗色 luut-shik.
Drag, 拉 laai, 挴 mangʼ, ʽmang, 拖 tʽoh.
Dragon, 龍 luung, (a) 條龍 tʽiu-luung.
Dragon-fly, 螳蜢 tʽong-ʽmi.
Drain, (to, land) 開竇 hoi-tauʼ, (a) 暗渠 omʼ-kʽue, 陰溝 yum-kau.
Drake, 鴨公 aapʼ-ʽkuung.
Draught, (a drink) 一淡 yat-taamʼ.
Draught, a rough, 草稿 ʽtsʽo-ʽko, (wind) 通風處 tʽuung-fuung-shueʼ.
Draw, 拉 laai, 挴 mangʼ, (towards) 擯 ʽmaan, (pictures) 寫 ʽse, (water) 汲 kʽap, 打 ʽta, 拂 fut, (a sword) 拔 pat, 取出 ʽtsue-chʽuut, (to influence) 引 ʽyan.

Drawer, 櫃桶 kwai⁾-ᶜt'uung.
Drawing-room, 客廳 haak⁾-ᶜt'eng.
Drawl, 拉長聲講 laai-ch'eung-sheng-ᶜkong.
Dread, 畏懼 wai⁾-kue⁾, 慌怕 fong-p'a⁾.
Dreadful, 利害 li⁾-hoi⁾.
Dream, 夢 muung⁾, (to) 發夢 faat⁾-muung⁾.
Dreary, 蔽翳 pai⁾-ai⁾.
Dredge, (to) 撈 laau.
Dregs, 渣滓 cha-ᶜtsze, 脚 keuk⁾.
Drench, 濕透 shup-t'au⁾, 濕嗮 shup-saai⁾.
Dress, 裝扮 chong-paan⁾, (to) 着衣服 cheuk-i-fuuk⁾.
Dressing-case, 鏡奩 keng⁾-lim, 鏡粧 keng⁾-ᶜchong.
Dried up, 涸乾 k'ok⁾-kohn, 乾嗮 kohn-saai⁾.
Drift, to, 漂流 p'iu-lau.
Drifting, 蒲蒲泛 p'o-p'o-faan⁾ (p'aan⁾).
Drill, (to) 鑽 tsuen⁾, (a) 鑽子 tsuen⁾-ᶜtsze, (practice) 習鍊 tsaap-lin⁾, 操 ts'o.

Drink, 飲 ᶜyum.
Drip, 滴滴落來 tik-tik-lok-lai.
Drive, (away) 逐去 chuuk-hue⁾, 趕逐 ᶜkohn-chuuk, (push) 推 t'ui, (a horse) 駛 ᶜshai.
Drizzle, 落雨微 lok-ᶜue-ᶜmi.
Droll, 好趣 ᶜho-ts'ue⁾, (a laughing stock) 笑柄 siu⁾ peng⁾.
Drollery, 趣話 ts'ue⁾-ᶜwa.
Dromedary, 獨峰駝 tuuk-fuung-t'oh.
Droop, 垂 shui, (decay) 衰 shui.
Drop, (a) 滴 tik, (to stop) 放落 fong⁾-lok, (fall) 跌落 tit⁾-lok.
Dropsy, 水臌 ᶜshui-ᶜchuung, 蠱脹 ᶜkoo-cheung⁾.
Dross, 屎 ᶜshi, 渣滓 cha-ᶜtsze, (of silver) 密佗僧 mat-t'oh-sang.
Drought, 天旱 t'in-ᶜhohn.
Drown, 沉死 ch'um-sze, 溺死 nik-ᶜsze, 浸死 tsum⁾-sze.

Drowsy, 眼瞓 ʽngaan-ʽfun, 瞓瘟 fun⸴-wun, hap-ʽngaan.
Drub, 棒打 ʽpʽaang-ʽta.
Drudgery, 賤藝 tsin⸴-ngai⸴.
Drugs, 藥材 yeuk-tsʽoi.
Drum, 鼓 ʽkoo, (a) 一面鼓 yat-min⸴-ʽkoo.
Drum-stick, 鼓槌 ʽkoo-*chʽui.
Drunk, 醉酒 tsui⸴-ʽtsau.
Drunkard, 爛酒人 laan⸴-ʽtsau-yan.
Dry, 乾 kohn, 旱 ʽhohn, 爽 ʽshong, (to) 整乾 ʽching-kohn, (in the sun) 晒乾 shaai⸴-kohn, (at the fire) 焙 pooi⸴, (in the air) 晾乾 long⸴-kohn.
Duality, (the two modes of nature) 兩儀 ʽleung-i, 陰陽 yum-yeung.
Duck, 鴨 aap⸴, (wild) 水鴨 ʽshui-*aap⸴, (Muscovy) 番鴨 faan-aap⸴.
Duck-weed, 蒲蕎 pʽo*-kʽiu.
Due, 該當 koi-tong, 當還 tong-waan, (owing) 欠 him⸴.

Dug, (a) 奶頭 ʽnaai-tʽau.
Duke, 公爺 kuung-ye.
Dull, 鷔 ngau⸴, 鈍 tuun⸴, 鷔豆 ngau⸴-tau⸴, (gloomy) 陰陰沉沉 yum-yum-chʽum-chʽum, 陰翳 yum-ai⸴, (tint) 瘀 ʽue.
Duly, 依期 i-kʽi.
Dumb, 瘂口 ʽa-ʽhau.
Dumfound, 嚇親 haak⸴-tsʽan, 嚇到呆 haak⸴-to⸴-ngoi.
Dummy, 瘂口 ʽa-ʽhau, 瘂仔 ʽa-ʽtsai.
Dumpling, 水餃子 ʽshui-kaau⸴-ʽtsze, 餛飩 wun⸴-ʽtun.
Dun, (to) 催迫 tsʽooi-pik, 迫攞 pik-ʽloh.
Dunce, 鈍胎 tuun⸴-tʽoi.
Dung, 糞 fun⸴, 屎 ʽshi, (to) 落糞 lok-fun⸴.
Dungeon, 地牢 ti⸴-lo.
Dung-hill, 糞堆 fun⸴-ʽtui.
Duped, 上當 ʽsheung-tong, 中計 chuung⸴-kai⸴.
Duplicity, 二心 i⸴-sum, 三口兩脷 saam-ʽhau-ʽleung-li⸴.

Durable, 矜使 kʻum-ʻshai, 矜得耐 kʻum-tak-noiʾ.
During, ——之耐 —— chi-noiʾ, ——咁耐—— komʾ-noiʾ.
Dusk, 黃昏 wong-fun, 挨晚 aai-*ʻmaan.
Dust, 塵 chʻan, 塵埃 chʻan-oi, (to) 拂塵 fut-chʻan, faakʾ-chʻan, 抰 ʻyeung.
Duster, 拂塵布 faakʾ-chʻan-poʻ, (feather-) 毛掃 mo-ʻso.
Dutiful, 純良 shuun-leung, 順從 shuunʾ-tsʻuung.
Duty, 本分 ʻpoon-fun, (custom) 餉銀 ʻheung-*ngan.
Dwarf, 矮人 ʻai-yan, (to) 屈古樹 wut-ʻkoo-shueʾ.
Dwell, 居 kue, 居住 kue-chueʾ.
Dwelling house, 住家屋 chueʾ-ka-uuk.
Dwindle, 漸漸縮 tsimʾ-tsimʾ-shuuk.
Dye, 染色 ʻim-shikʾ.
Dynamite, 炸藥 chaʾ-yeuk.

Dynasty, 朝 chʻiu, 國朝 kwokʾ-chʻiu.
Dysentery, 紅痢 huung-liʾ, 紅白痢 huung-paak-liʾ.
Dyspepsia, 停食 tʻing-shik, 不消化 pat-siu-faʾ.
Dysury, 小便不通 ʻsiu-pinʾ-pat-tʻuung.

E

Each, 每 ʻmooi, 各 kokʾ, (each other) 相—— seung ——.
Eager, 懇切 ʻhan-tsʻitʾ, 嫩 nat.
Eagle, 神鷹 shan-ʻying.
Ear, 耳躲 ʻi-tö, 耳仔 ʻi-ʻtsai.
Ear of corn, 穗 suiʾ, 一芎穀 yat-kʻuung-kuuk.
Ear-ring, 耳環 ʻi-*waan.
Ear-wax, 耳屎 ʻi-ʻshi, 耳油 ʻi-yau.
Ear-wig, 蚰蜒 yau-in.
Earl, 伯 paakʾ.
Early, 早 ʻtso.

Earn, 賺 chaan’, *chaan’.
Earnest, 懇誠 ‘han-shing, 熱中 i̇t-chuung.
Earth, 地 ti’, (matter) 坭土 nai-‘t‘o.
Earthen-ware, 瓦器 ‘nga-hi’, 缸瓦 kong-‘nga, (fine) 磁器 ts‘ze-hi’.
Earthquake, 地震 ti’-chan’.
Earth-worm, 地龍 ti’-luung, 黃犬 wong-‘huen.
Ease, 安 ohn, 安樂 ohn-lok (with) 流利 lau-li’ (lai’), (to) 放鬆 fong’-suung, (nature) 出恭 ch‘uut-‹kuung, 大便 taai’-pin’.
East, 東 tuung, 東邊 tuung-pin, 東方 tuung-fong.
Easy, 容易 yuung-i’, (comfortable) 自在 tsze’-tsoi’.
Eat, 食 shik, 吃 yaak.
Eaves, 鬃口 yum-‘hau, 鬃頭 yum-*t‘au, 簷口 im-‘hau.
Eaves-dropping, 門外打聽 moon-ngoi’-‘ta-t‘eng’.
Ebb, 水乾 ‘shui-kohn.

Ebony, 烏梅木 oo-mooi-muuk, (Chinese) 酸枝 suen-‹chi.
Ebullition, 滾起 ‘kwun-‘hi.
Eccentric, 出規矩外 ch‘uut-k‘wai-‹kue-ngoi’, 不同人 pat-t‘uung-yan, ’m-t‘uung-yan-ti’.
Echo, 回响 ooi-‘heung, 應聲 ying’-sheng, 撞聲 chong’-sheng.
Eclipse, 蝕 shik.
Ecliptic 黃道 wong-to’.
Economical, 儉 kim’, 儉用 kim’-yuung’, 慳廉 haan-lim.
Economize, 儉用 kim’-yuung’, 惜 sik.
Ecstasy, 注神 chue’-shan, 神游極 shan-yau-kik.
Eddy, 回旋 ooi-suen, (water) 倒槽水 ‘to-ts‘o-‘shui, (wind) 轉頭風 ‘chuen-t‘au-fuung.
Edge, (of a knife) 口 ‘hau, 鋒 fuung, (side) 邊 pin, (near the) 吻 mun’.

Edict, 札諭 chaat⁾-ue⁾, 上諭 sheung⁽-ue⁾.
Edify, 輔德 foo⁾-tak, 建德 kin⁾-tak, 養心 ⁽yeung-sum.
Edit, 校訂 kaau⁾-ting⁾.
Educate, 教養 kaau⁾-⁽yeung.
Educated, 讀書 tuuk-shue, 學文 hok-mun.
Eel, 鱔魚 ⁽shin-ue, (congor) 海鰻 ⁽hoi-maan⁾.
Effect, 效驗 haau⁾-im⁾, 所致 ⁽shoh-chi⁾, 所成 ⁽shoh-shing, 所使然 ⁽shoh-⁽shai-in, 果 ⁽kwoh.
Effeminate, 女人形 ⁽nue-*yan-ying.
Effervesce, 發滾 faat⁾-⁽kwun.
Efficacious, 功效 kuung-haau⁾, 靈 leng.
Effluvia, 穢氣 wai⁾-hi⁾.
Effort, (make an) 奮力 ⁽fun-lik, 出力 ch'uut-lik.
Egg, 蛋 *taan⁾, 卵 ⁽luun, 鷇 ch'uun.
Egg-plant, 苦瓜 ⁽foo ⌐kwa, 矮瓜 ⁽ai-⌐kwa.
Egg-shell, 蛋殼 *taan⁾-hok⁾.

Egregiously, 太甚 t'aai⁾-shum⁾.
Egret, 白鷺 paak-lo⁾.
Eight, 八 paat⁾.
Eighth, 第八 tai⁾-paat⁾.
Either, 或 waak.
Eject, 趕出 ⁽kohn-ch'uut, 出 ch'uut.
Elaborate, 費心機 fai⁾-sum-ki.
Elapsed, 過了 kwoh⁾-⁽liu, kwoh⁾-hiu.
Elastic, 韌 ngan⁾, 有韌力 ⁽yau-ngan⁾-lik.
Elated, 志氣昂昂 chi⁾-hi⁾-ngong-ngong.
Elbow, 手睜 ⁽shau-chaang.
Elbow-chair, 圈手椅 huen-⁽shau-⁽i.
Elder than, 大於 taai⁾-ue, 老過 ⁽lo-kwoh⁾.
Elders, 長老 ⁽cheung-⁽lo.
Eldest son, 長子 ⁽cheung-⁽tsze, 大仔 taai⁾-⁽tsai.
Elect, 揀 ⁽kaan, 選 ⁽suen.
Electric eel, 火鱔 foh-⁽shin.
Electric telegraph, 電報 tin⁾-po⁾.

Electricity, 電氣 tin⁾-hi⁾.
Electro-plate, 電鍍（金） tin⁾-to⁾-(kum).
Elegant, 靚 leng⁾, 幽幽雅雅 yau-yau-ᶜnga-ᶜnga, 文雅 mun-ᶜnga.
Elements, 元質 uen-chat, (the five) 五行 ᶜng-hang, (of learning) 初學 ch'oh-hok, 學之始基 hok-chi-ᶜch'i-ki.
Elephant, 象 tseung⁾.
Elephantiasis, 大砂蹄 taai⁾-sha-t'ai, 赤瘋 ch'ik⁾-fuung.
Elevate, 舉 ᶜkue.
Elevated, 高昂 ko-ngong.
Eleven, 十一 shap-yat.
Eleventh, 第十一 tai⁾-shap-yat.
Elf, 妖怪 iu-kwaai⁾, 馬騮精 ᶜma-ᶜlau-tsing.
Eligible, 合用 hop-yuung⁾.
Ellipse, 長圓形 ch'eung-uen-ying, 橢圓 ᶜt'oh-uen.
Elliptical language, 省文 ᶜshaang-mun.
Elk, 麋鹿 mi-luuk.

Elm, 榆 ue.
Elope, 私跳 sze-t'o, 走路 ᶜtsau-lo⁾.
Eloquence, 口才 ᶜhau-ts'oi.
Eloquent, 好口角 ᶜho-ᶜhau-kok⁾.
Else, (besides) 另外 ling⁾-ngoi⁾, (if not) 若不是 yeuk-pat-shi⁾, 若唔係 yeuk-'m-hai⁾, (then) 就係 tsau⁾-hai⁾.
Elsewhere, 第二處 tai⁾-i⁾-shue⁾, tai⁾-shue⁾.
Elude, 逃脫 t'o-t'uet⁾, 逃甩 t'o-lut.
Elysium, 極樂世界 kik-lok-shai⁾-kaai⁾.
Emaciated, 瘦損 shau⁾-ᶜsuen.
Emancipate, 放 fong⁾, 釋放 shik-fong⁾.
Embankment, 基 ki, 基壆 ki-pok⁾.
Embargo, 禁止行船 kum⁾-ᶜchi-hang-shuen.
Embark, 落船 lok-shuen.
Embarrass, 掯阻 k'ang⁾-ᶜchoh, 桔据 kat-kue (k'ö), 累 lui⁾.

Embarrassment, 煩難 faan-naan.
Embassador, 欽差 yum-chʻaai.
Embellish, 修飾 sau-shik.
Embers, 火剩 ʻfoh-shing⁾.
Embezzle, 私取 sze-ʻtsʻue.
Emblem, 喻表 ue⁾-ʻpiu.
Embossed, 浮凸 fau-tut.
Embowel, 剖肚 tʻong-ʻtʻo.
Embrace, 懷抱 waai-ʻpʻo.
Embrasure, 埤堄 ʻpʻai-ʻngai, 城人 sheng-*yan.
Embroider, 繡花 sauʻ-ʻfa.
Embroil, 鬧亂 naauʻ-luenʻ.
Embryo, 胚 ʻpʻooi.
Emendation, 改正處 ʻkoi-ʻchingʻ-chʻue⁾.
Emerald, 呂宋綠 Luiʻ-suungʻ-luuk, 鸚鵡綠 ying-ʻmoo-luuk, (an) 綠玉 luuk-yuuk.
Emerge, 出來 chʻuut-lai, 出現 chʻuut-inʻ.
Emergency, 急切時候 kup-tsʻitʻ-shi-hauʻ.
Emetic, 發嘔藥 faatʻ-ʻau-yeuk.

Emeu, 食火鷄 shik-ʻfoh-ʻkai.
Emigrate, 出外方住 chʻuut-ngoiʻ-ʻfong-chue⁾.
Eminent, 高 ko, 尊 tsuen.
Emolument, 俸祿 ʻfuung-luuk.
Emotion, 情 tsʻing, 情動 tsʻing-tuung⁾.
Emperor, 皇帝 wong-taiʻ.
Emphatic, 懇聲 ʻhan-sheng.
Empire, (the world) 天下 tʻin-haʻ.
Empiric practice, 斷估工夫 tuenʻ-ʻkoo-kuung-foo, 估吓試吓 ʻkoo-ʻha-shiʻ-ʻha.
Employ, 任用 yumʻ-yuungʻ, 使 ʻshai.
Employer, 事頭 szeʻ-*tʻau.
Employment, 事業 szeʻ-ip.
Empower, 俾權 ʻpi-kʻuen.
Empress, 皇后 wong-hauʻ.
Empty, 空虛 huung-hue, 空 huung, 吉 kat (a euphemism for huung), (to) 整空 ʻching-huung.
Emulate, 賽勝 tsʻoiʻ-shingʻ, 賽贏 tsʻoiʻ-yeng, 鬥效 tauʻ-hauʻ.

Enable, 令――能 ling²――nang.
Enact, 設 ch'it², 作 tsok².
Enamel, 磁器油 ts'ze-hi²-yau, (COL.) 哴油 ʻlong-*yau.
Encamp, 劄營 chaap²-ying.
Enchantment, 迷魂陣 mai-wan-chan².
Encircle, } 圍埋 wai-maai,
Enclose, } 圍住 wai-chue².
Encoffin, 收殮 shau-ʻlim.
Encompass, 圍住 wai-chue².
Encore, 再演 tsoi²-ʻin.
Encounter, 遇 ue².
Encourage, 勉勵 ʻmin-lai², 勸勉 huen²-ʻmin, 鼓舞 ʻkoo-ʻmoo.
Encroach, 侵佔 ts'um-chim².
Encumber, 累贅 lui²-chui².
Encyclopedia, 類書 lui²-shue.
End, 收尾 shau-ʻmi (ʻmi), 終 chuung, (either) 頭 t'au.
Endanger, 累――險 lui²――ʻhim.
Endeavour, 出力 ch'uut-lik, 試 shi².

Endless, 無窮 mo-k'uung, 無盡 mo-tsuun².
Endowments, 品質 ʻpun-chat, 才 ts'oi, (property) 營業 sheung-ip.
Endure, (last) 存 ts'uen, 衿 k'um, (bear) 忍耐 ʻyan-noi², 耐得 noi²-tak.
Enemy, 仇敵 ch'au-tik, 對敵 tui²-tik.
Energy, 力 lik, 勢力 shai²-lik.
Enervated, } 衰弱 shui-yeuk.
Enfeebled, }
Enforce, 勒令 lak-ling², 使 ʻshai, 必使 pit-ʻshai.
Engage, 任用 yum²-yuung², (to marry) 定親 ting²-ts'an.
Engaged, (occupied) 有事 ʻyau-sze², 不得閒 ʻm-tak-haan.
Engagement, (agreement) 約 yeuk², 約信 yeuk²-suun², (business) 事幹 sze²-kohn².
Engine, 機器 ki-hi².
Engineer, chief, 大計 taai²-*kai², second, 二計 i-*kai².

England, 英吉利國 Ying-kat-li'-kwok', 英倫 Ying-lun.
English, 英 Ying.
Engraft, 劗樹 ts'im-shue', 接枝 tsip'-chi.
Engrave, 雕刻 tiu-hak.
Engross, 攬埋 'laam-maai.
Enigma, 啞謎 'a-*mooi, 背語 pooi'-'ue.
Enjoin, 叮篤 teng-tuuk.
Enjoy, 享 'heung.
Enlarge, 發大 faat'-taai', 整大 'ching-taai'.
Enlighten, 照光 chiu'-kwong.
Enlist, 招 chiu.
Enmity, 仇怨 ch'au-uen'.
Ennui, 懶倦 haai'-kuen'.
Enormous, (great) 甚大 shum'-taai'.
Enough, 够 kau', 足 tsuuk.
Enquire, 訪問 'fong-mun'.
Enrage, 激怒 kik-no', 激嬲 kik-nau.
Enraptured, 了不得歡喜 'liu-pat-tak-foon-'hi.
Enrich, 令──富 ling'──foo'.

Ensign, 旗 k'i.
Ensure, 保領 'po-'ling.
Entangle, 揹任 k'ang'-chue', k'waang'-chue', 絞亂 'kaau-luen'.
Enter, 入 yup, 進入 tsuun'-yup, (on life) 出身 ch'uut-shan.
Enterprising, 好逞奇 ho'-'ch'ing-k'i, 肯作肯為 'haang-tsok'-'haang-wai.
Entertain, 招接 chiu-tsip', 看待 hohn-toi'.
Enthusiasm, 苦志 'foo-chi', 烈熱之氣 lit-it-chi-hi'.
Entice, 引誘 'yan-'yau, (or urge to) 摟 lau.
Entire, 十全 shap-ts'uen.
Entirely, 齊嗮 ts'ai-saai', 一槩 yat-k'oi', 盡地 tsuun-*ti'.
Entitled to 應得 ying-tak.
Entrails, 臟腑 tsong'-'foo, (ox's) 牛雜 ngau-tsaap.
Entranced, 入幻境 yup-waan'-'king.
Entrapped, 入圈套 yup-huen-t'o'.

Entreat, 懇求 ʻhan-kʻau.
Entry, 入路 yup-loʾ.
Enunciate, 講出 ʻkong-chʻut.
Envelop, 包住 paau-chue'.
Envelope, (of a letter) 信函 suun'-haam, 信套 suun'-tòʾ, 信封 suunʾ-fuung.
Envy, 嫉妒 tsat-toʾ, 妒忌 toʾ-kiʾ, 眼紅 ʻngaan-huung.
Epicure, 膏粱子弟 ko-leung-ʻtsze-taiʾ.
Epidemic, 時症 shi-chingʾ.
Epidendrum, 吊蘭 tiuʾ-*laan.
Epilepsy, 發羊吊 faatʾ-yeung-tiuʾ.
Epistle, 信札 suunʾ-chaatʾ.
Epitaph, 墓誌 mooʾ-chiʾ.
Epithet, 別號 pit-hoʾ.
Epitome, 大畧 taaiʾ-*leuk.
Equal, 等 ʻtang, 相等 seung-ʻtang, 均平 kwan-ping.
Equally, 均 kwan, 平 pʻing.
Equanimity, 心定 sum-tingʾ.
Equator, 赤道 chʻikʾ-toʾ.

Equinox, 日夜平分 yat-yeʾ-ping-fun, (vernal) 春分 chʻuun-fun, (autumnal) 秋分 tsʻau-fun.
Equipped, (dressed out) 全身披掛 tsʻuen-shan-pʻi-kwaʾ.
Equitable, 公平 kuung-ping.
Equivalent, 值咁多錢嘅 chik-komʾ-toh-*tsʻin-keʾ.
Equivocate, 講雙關話 ʻkong-ʻsheung-ʻkwaan-*waʾ.
Erase, 刮去 kwaatʾ-hueʾ, 搽去 *chʻa-hueʾ.
Erect, 立直 laap-chik, 豎起 shueʾ-ʻhi, (to build) 起 ʻhi, (upright) 企 kʻi.
Err, 差失 chʻa-shat, 失誤 shat-ʻng, 致誤 chiʾ-ʻng.
Error, 錯 tsʻohʾ.
Eruption, (on the skin) 出疹 chʻut-ʻchʻan, 癍疹 paan-ʻchʻan.
Erysipelas, 癉疽 ʻtaan-tsue.
Escape, 走得甩 ʻtsau-takʾ-lut, 脫離 tʻuetʾ-li, (a way of) 去路 hueʾ-loʾ.
Escort, 護送 ooʾ-suungʾ.

Especially, 特要 tak-iu῾, 更係 ῾kang-hai῾, 至緊要 chi῾-῾kan-iu.

Essay, (an) 文章 mun-cheung.

Essence, 精華 tsing-wa, 精髓 tsing-῾sui.

Essential, 必須 pit-sue.

Establish, 建立 kin῾-laap, 立定 laap-ting῾.

Estate, 基業 ki-ip.

Esteem, (consider) 以爲 ῾i-wai, (respect) 尊重 tsuen-chuung῾.

Estimate, 筭度 suen῾-tok, 量度 leung-tok.

Et cetera, 又有添 yau῾-῾yau-t῾im.

Eternal, 永遠 ῾wing-῾uen.

Etiquette, 小禮 ῾siu-῾lai, 小節 ῾siu-tsit, 儀注 i-chue῾.

Eunuchs of the palace, 太監 t῾aai῾-kaam῾.

Euphemism, 吉祥話 kat-ts῾eung-*wa, 雅緻話 ῾nga-chi῾-*wa.

Europe, 歐羅巴 Au-loh-pa.

Evacuate, 搬空 poon-hung, (bowels) 解手 ῾kaai-῾shau, 出恭 ch῾uut-kung.

Evade, 推甩 t῾ui-lut.

Evaporate, 升散 shing-saan῾.

Evasive, 旁敲側擊 p῾ong-haau-chak-kik, 閃縮 ῾shim-shuuk.

Even, 平 p῾ing, (number) 雙數 ῾sheung-sho῾, (also) 亦 yik, 都 too.

Evening, 晚 ῾maan, (towards) 挨晚 aai-*῾maan, (dark) 晚黑 ῾maan-hak.

Evening-star, 長庚星 ch῾eung-kang-῾sing.

Event, 事情 sze῾-ts῾ing, (important) 大事 taai῾-sze῾.

Eventually, 收尾 shau-῾mi.

Ever, 不歇 pat-hit, (eternally) 永遠 ῾wing-῾uen, (any time) 幾時 ῾ki-shi.

Ever-green, 週年青 chau-nin-ts῾ing.

Everlasting, 永 ῾wing, 永世 ῾wing-shai῾.

Every, 個個 koh'-koh', (N.B.—*Every* is expressed by repeating the noun), 每 ʿmooi.
Everything, 樣樣野 yeung' yeung' ye, (-is) 乜野都係 mat-ʿye-too-hai.
Everywhere, 到處 to'-ch'ue', 周圍 chau-wai.
Evidence, 證據 ching'-kue', 憑 p'ang, (verbal) 口供 ʿhau-kuung.
Evident, 明白 ming-paak.
Evil, 惡 ok'.
Ewe, 羊母 yeung-ʿmoo.
Ewer, 水瓶 ʿshui-p'eng.
Exact, 合 hop, 正 ching', (COL.) 啱啱 ʿngaam-ʿngaam.
Exact, (to) 抽剝 ch'au-mok, (extort) 勒索 lak-sok', 逼勒 pik-lak.
Exaggerate, 講得太過 ʿkong-tak-t'aai'-kwoh', 極言 kik-in.
Exaggeration, 太過 t'aai'-kwoh'.
Exalt, 舉高 ʿkue-ko.

Examination, (literary) 考試 ʿhaau-shi'.
Examine, 考究 ʿhaau-kau', (judicially) 審問 ʿshum-mun', 盤問 p'oon-mun'.
Example, 樣子 yeung'-ʿtsze, (effect of) 風化 fuung-fa'.
Exasperate, 抄爆 ch'aau-paau'.
Exceed, 勝過 shing'-kwok'.
Exceedingly, 太過 t'aai'-kwoh', 太甚 t'aai'-shum'.
Excel, 贏 yeng, 勝過 shing'-kwoh'.
Excellency, (a title) 大人 taai'-yan, 憲臺 Hin'-t'oi.
Excellent, 極好 kik-ʿho.
Except, (to) 除去 ch'ue-hue', 不計 pat-kai', (unless) 苟不 ʿkau-pat, 倘若不 ʿt'ong-yeuk-'m.
Excess, 過當 kwoh'-tong, 過度 kwoh'-to'.
Excessively, 過頭 *kwoh'-t'au.
Exchange, 兌換 tui'-oon'.

Excite, 撩惹 ʻliu-ʻye, 慫慂 ʻsuung-ʻyuung, 聳起 ʻsuung-ʻhi, 驚動 king-tuung'.
Exclaim, 呼喊 foo-haam'.
Exclude, 除出 chʻue-chʻuut.
Excrement, 屎 ʻshi.
Excrescence, 疣贅 yau-chui', 贅瘤 chui'-*lau.
Excruciating, 慘 ʻtsʻaam.
Exculpate, 表白 ʻpiu-paak.
Exculpation, 解說 ʻkaai-shuet', 推諉 tʻui-ʻwai.
Excuse, (to) 見諒 kin'-leung', (make an) 托辭 tʻok'-tsʻze, 倘塞 tʻong-sak.
Execute, 做成 tso'-shing, 辦成 paan'-shing.
Execution, 正法 ching'-faat', (ground) 法場 faat'-chʻeung.
Executioner, 殺手 shaat'-ʻshau.
Executive council, 議政局 ʻi-ching'-*kuuk.
Executor, 受托之人 shau'-tʻok'-chi (keʼ)-yan, 承辦人 shing-paan'-yan.

Exempt, 免 ʻmin.
Exercise, (motion) 行動 hang-tuung', (practice) 習練 tsaap-lin'.
Exert, 奮 ʻfun, 發奮 faat'-ʻfun, (strength), 奮力 ʻfun-lik.
Exhalation, 所出之氣 ʻshoh-chʻuut-chi-hiʼ.
Exhaust, 盡 tsuun', 使盡 ʻshai-tsuun'.
Exhibit, 發現 faat'-in', 顯示 ʻhin-shiʼ.
Exhilarated, 爽神 ʻshong-shan.
Exhort, 勸 huen'.
Exigency, 緊急 ʻkan-kup.
Exist, 在 tsoi', 有 ʻyau, 存 tsʻuen.
Exit, (way) 去路 hue'-lo', 出處 chʻuut-chʻue'.
Exorbitant, 太過 tʻaai'-kwoh', 多得嚌 toh-tak tsai'.
Exorcise, 逐鬼 chuuk-ʻkwai.
Expand, 張開 cheung-hoi.
Expanse, 浩蕩 ho'-tong', 廣闊處 ʻkwong-foot'-shue'.

Expect, 望 mongʾ, 待 toiʾ, 料 liuʾ, 料必 liuʾ-pit.
Expedient, (convenient) 便宜 pinʾ-i, (an) 計 kaiʾ.
Expel, 趕出 ʿkohn-chʿuut.
Expend, 使費 ʿshai-fuiʾ.
Expense, 使用銀 ʿshai-yuungʾ-*ngan.
Experienced, 老練 ʿlo-*linʾ, 慣熟 kwaanʾ-shuuk, (hand) 老手 ʿlo-ʿshau.
Experiment, 試驗 shiʾ-imʾ, 比併 ʿpi-pʿing.
Expert, (hand) 巧手 ʿhauu-ʿshau, (at) 善精 shinʾ-tsing.
Expiate, 贖 shuuk.
Expire, 呼 foo, 噴氣 pʿunʾ-hiʾ, (die) 絶氣 tsuet-hiʾ, 斷氣 ʿtʿuen-hiʾ, 盡 tsuunʾ, (time) 滿 ʿmoon.
Explain, 解 ʿkaai.
Explanation, 解說 ʿkaai-shuetʾ, 解法 ʿkaai-faatʾ.
Expletive, 虛字 hue-tszeʾ.
Explicity, 明明白白 ming-ming-paak-paak.

Explode, 炸 chaʾ, 爆出 paauʾ-chʿuut.
Explore, 遊觀 yau-koon, 探索 tʿaamʾ-shaakʾ, 巡查 tsʿuun-chʿa.
Explosion, 嘭 paang, paang.
Export, 裝(貨)出口 chongʾ-(fohʾ) chʿuut-ʿhau.
Expose, 顯露 ʿhin-loʾ, 攻詰 kuung-kʿitʾ.
Expostulate, 諫 kaanʾ, 勸諫 huenʾ-kaanʾ.
Expound, 講解 ʿkong-ʿkaai.
Express, (to) 講出 ʿkong-chʿuut, (an) 千里馬 tsʿin-ʿli-ma.
Expression, 詞語 tsʿze-ʿue, (of face) 氣色 hiʾ-shik.
Expressive, (open as the face) 淺露 ʿtsʿin-loʾ.
Expressly, 特登 tak-ʿtang.
Expunge, 擦去 *chʿa-hueʾ.
Exquisite, 妙 miuʾ, 妙極 miuʾ-kik.
Extant, 所存 ʿshoh-tsʿuen.
Extempore, to speak, 順口講 shuunʾ-ʿhau-ʿkong.

Extend, 伸開 shan-hoi, (widen) 伸闊 shan-foot', (lengthen) 伸長 shan-ch'eung.
Extensive, 廣闊 ʻkwong-foot'.
Extenuate, 減輕 ʻkaam-heng.
Exterior, 外面 ngoi'-min'.
Exterminate, 剿滅 ʻtsiu-mit.
External, 外 ngoi'.
Extinguish, 滅 mit, 熄 sik, (by blowing) 吹滅 ch'ui-mit.
Extort, 勒索 lak-sok'.
Extract, 脫出 t'uet'-ch'uut, 拔出 pat-ch'uut.
Extraordinary, 格外 kaak'-ngoi'.
Extravagant, 奢 ch'e, 無節制 mo-tsit'-chai', (expense) 花費 fa-fai', (price) 太貴 t'aai'-kwai'.
Extreme, 極 kik.
Extremely, 至極 chi'-kik, 甚 shum'.
Extricate, 脫甩 t'uet'-lut.
Exult, 歡喜到跳 ʻfoon-ʻhi-to'-t'iu'.

Eye, 眼 ʻngaan, 眼目 ʻngaan-muuk.
Eye-ball, 眼珠 ʻngaan-ʻchue, 眼核 ʻngaan-wat.
Eye-brow, 眼眉 ʻngaan-mi.
Eye-lash, 眼盦毛 ʻngaan-yup-*mo.
Eyelid, 眼蓋 ʻngaan-koi'.
Eye-service, 裝米面工夫 chong-*mai-*min'-kuung-foo, 光面工夫 kwong-*min'-kuung-foo.

F

Fable, 寓言 ue'-in, 小說 ʻsiu-*shuet'.
Fabric, (texture) 織做之物 chik-tso'-chi-mat, chik-tso'-ke'-ʻye.
Fabricate, 杜撰 to'-chaan'.
Fabulous, 虛誕 hue-taan'.
Face, 面 min', (to) 對面 tooi'-min', 當面對 tong-min'-tooi', (to see) 覿面 tik-min', 見面 kin'-min'.

Face to face, 面晤 min²-'ng², 兩面相向 ʻleung-min²-seung-heung².
Facile, 容易 yuung-i².
Facility, 順便 shuun²-*pin².
Fac-simile, 摹成似眞 mo-shing-tsʻze-chan.
Fact, 實事 shat-sze².
Faction, 黨 ʻtong, 黨羽 ʻtong-ʻue.
Factory, 行 *hong.
Faculty, 能幹 nang-kohn².
Fade, 殘毀 tsʻaan-ʻwai, (as colour) 轉色 ʻchuen-shik.
Faded, 殘嘵 tsʻaan-hiu.
Fagged, 困倦 kʻwun²-kuen², 夠倦 kau²-kuen², kooi².
Faggot, (a) 一把柴 yat-ʻpa-chʻaai.
Fail, 廢 fai², (become bankrupt) 倒行 ʻto-*hong, 倒灶 ʻto-tso².
Faint, (to) 昏迷 fun-mai, 失魂 shat-wun, (feeble) 軟弱 ʻnen-yeuk, 力盡 lik-tsuun².

Fair, (clear) 清 tsʻing, 晴 tsʻing, (pretty) 清秀 tsʻing-sau², (just) 公道 ʻkuung-to², (-wind) 順風 shuun²-fuung, (tide) 順水 shuun²-shui.
Fairy, 仙 ʻsin, 神仙 shan-ʻsin, 野仙 ʻye-ʻsin, (female) 仙女 sin²-ʻnue.
Fairy-land, 蓬萊仙境 pʻuung-loi-sin-ʻking.
Faith, 信德 suun²-tak.
Faithful, 忠心 chuung-sum.
Falcon, 獵鷹 lip-ying, 鸇 ʻchuun.
Fall, 跌 tit², 慣倒 kwaan²-ʻto, (COL.) tap.
False, 假 ʻka.
Falschood, 大話 taai²-wa², 謊言 ʻfong-in.
Falsify, 詐假意 cha²-ʻka-i (ʻka-i) 整假 ʻching-ʻka.
Fame, 名聲 ming-shing, 名 ming.
Familiar, 狎習 haap-tsaap, 啱橋 ʻngaam-*kʻin, (too) 藝狎 sit²-haap.

Family, 家 ka, 家眷 ka-kuen', 家口 ka-'hau, (how is your?) 寶眷平安呀 'po-kuen'-p'ing-ohn-a? (well, thank you) 家小都托賴 ka-'siu-'too-t'ok-laai'.
Famine, 飢荒 ki-fong.
Famishing, 餓到死嗽 ngoh'-to'-'sze-'kom, 餓得急 ngoh'-tak-kup.
Fan (a) 把扇 'pa-shin', (to) 打扇 'ta-shin', 撥 p'oot'.
Fanatic, 信到狂 sunn'-to'-k'wong, 信到癲 sunn'-to'-tin.
Fancy, 幻想 waan'-'seung, 夢想 mung'-'seung, (suit the) 如意 ue-i', (rare) 玩 oon'.
Fanners, 風櫃 fuung-kwai'.
Far, 遠 'uen.
Farce, (a) 弄戲一出 lunng'-hi'-yat-ch'uut'.
Fare, (money) 水脚 'shui-keuk', 脚錢 keuk'-*ts'in.
Farewell, 望你平安 mong'-'ni-p'ing-ohn.

Farm, 田庄 t'in-chong, (to) 耕田 kang-t'in.
Farmer, 農夫 nunng-foo.
Fascinating, 有引 'yau-'yan.
Fashion, (the) 時欵 shi-foon, (a) 樣 *yeung'.
Fashionable, 依時欵 i-shi-foon, 時興 shi-hing.
Fast, (to) 禁食 kum'-shik, 食齋 shik-chaai.
Fast, (quick) 快 faai'. 趕快 'kohn-faai', (firm) 堅實 kin-shat.
Fasten, 綁緊 'pong-'kan, 整實 'ching-shat, (a door) 閂 shaan.
Fastidious, 難悅 naan-uet, 俺尖 im-tsim.
Fat, 肥 fi, (SUB.) 油 yau, 膏油 ko-yau.
Fate, 天命 t'in-ming', 定數 ting'-sho'.
Father, 父 foo', 父親 foo'-ts'an, (COL.) 'lo-tau', 老子 'lo-'tsze.
Father-in-law, 外父 ngoi'-*foo', 岳丈 ngok-*cheung', (wife's) 家翁 ka-yung.

Fathom, (10 feet) 丈 cheung⁾, (to) 測度 ch'ak-tok.
Fatigue, 困倦 k'wan⁾-kuen⁾.
Fatten, 養肥 ⸢yeung-fi.
Fault, 不是處 pat-shi⸢-ch'ue⁾, 毛病 mo-peng⁾, 弊病 pai⸢-peng⁾, 過失 kwoh⁾-shat.
Favour, 恩 yan, 人情 yan-ts'ing, (to) 幫襯 pong-ch'an⁾.
Favourable, 順 shuun⁾.
Favourite, 寵愛 ⸢ch'uung-oi⁾.
Fawn, (to) 挪撚 noh-⸢nun, 撥馬尾 p'oot⸢-ma-⸢mi.
Fear, 怕 p'a⁾, 恐怕 ⸢huung-p'a⁾.
Feasible, 可以 ⸢hoh-⸢i.
Feast, 筵席 in-tsik, 酒席 ⸢tsau-tsik.
Feather, 羽毛 ⸢ue-mo, 雀毛 tseuk⁾-mo.
February, 英二月 Ying-i⸢-uet.
Feces, 屎 ⸢shi, (refuse) 渣滓 cha-⸢tsze.
Fee, 規銀 k'wai-*ngan, (secret) 規 k'wai.

Feeble, 軟弱 ⸢uen-yeuk.
Feed, 養 ⸢yeung, 養口 ⸢yeung-⸢hau, (give food to) 喂 wai⁾, 餼 hi⁾, (fatten) 養肥 ⸢yeung-fi.
Feel, 覺 kok⁾, 見 kin⁾, (with the hand) 摸 ⸢moh.
Feeling, 情 ts'ing.
Feign, 詐 cha⁾, 佯為 yeung-wai.
Felicity, 福 fuuk.
Fell, 斬 ⸢chaam, 倒──落來 ⸢to──lok-lai.
Fellow, 同伴 t'uung-poon⁾, (common) 佬 ⸢lo.
Fellowship, 相交 seung-kaau.
Fellow-townsman, 鄉親 heung-ts'an.
Felony, 死罪 ⸢sze-tsui⁾, 大罪 taai⸢-tsui⁾.
Felt, 毛氈 mo-⸢chin, 鞋氈 haai-⸢chin.
Female, 母 ⸢mo, 嫲 ⸢na, (woman) 女 ⸢nue, (gender) 陰類 yum-lui⁾.
Fence, 籬笆 li-pa, 圍 *wai.
Fence (to) 舞劍 ⸢moo-kim⁾.
Fencing, 劍術 kim⁾-shuut.

Fender, 圍 *wai, (ship's) 唥 ‚leng.
Ferment, 發酵 faat‚-kaau’, (spoil) 發 faat’.
Fern, 黃狗毛 wong-‚kau-‚mo, 井底荽 ‚tseng-‚tai-‚sai, 賞萁 long-ki, (edible) 蕨 k‘uet’.
Ferocious, 勢兇 shai’-huung.
Ferocity, 殘殺之性 ts‘aan-shaat’-chi-sing’.
Ferret, 白獴獩 paak-muung-kwai’.
Ferry, 渡頭 to’-t‘au.
Ferry-boat, 橫水渡 waang-‚shui-*to’.
Fertile, 沃 yuuk, 肥 fi.
Fervent, 熱 it.
Fester, 生瘡 shang-‚ch‘ong.
Festival, 節期 tsit’-k‘i.
Fetch, 拎——來 ning——lai.
Fetid, 臭 ch‘au’.
Fetters, 柽梏 chat-kuuk’, (hand-) 手繚 ‚shau-liu, (feet-) 脚繚 keuk’-liu.
Fetus, 胚 p‘ooi, 胚胎 p‘ooi-t‘oi.

Fever, 發熱 faat’-it, (intermittent) 打擺子 ‚ta-‚paai-‚tsze.
Feverish, 殷 heng’.
Few, 少 ‚shiu, 些少 se-‚shiu.
Fib, 詐偽呆 cha’-‚ngi-‚ngoi.
Fibres, 紋 mun, 絲 sze.
Fickle, 無定性 mo-ting’-sing’, (COL.) fa-fik.
Fiction, 小說 ‚siu-*shuet’.
Fictitious, 假 ‚ka.
Fiddle, (two stringed) 二絃 i’-*in, (to) 研二絃 ngaan-i’-*in.
Fidelity, 忠心 chuung-sum.
Fidgety, 瑣碎 ‚soh-sui’.
Fie! 咄 ts‘oi! ch‘ö!
Field, 田 t‘in.
Fiend, 惡鬼 ok’-‚kwai.
Fierce, 猛烈 ‚mang-lit.
Fife, 橫笛 waang-*tek.
Fifth, 第五 tai’-‚ng.
Fig, 無花菓 mo-fa-‚kwoh.
Fight, 打架 ‚ta-ka’, (in war) 打仗 ‚ta-cheung’ (cheung’), 交戰 kaau-chin’.
Figurative, 比喻 ‚pi-ue’.

Figure, 形像 ying-tseung⁾, (of speech) 譬喻 p'i⁽-ue⁾.
File, (a tool) 把銼 ⁽pa-ts'oh⁾, (to) 銼卟 ts'oh⁾-⁽ha, (papers) 疊埋 tip-maai.
File fish, 剝皮洋 mok⁾-p'i yeung.
Filial, 孝順 haau⁾-shuun⁾.
Fill, 放滿 fong⁾-⁽moon, 打滿 ⁽ta-⁽moon.
Fillet of beef, 牛柳 ngau-⁽lau.
Film, 膜 mok, 衣膜 i-mok.
Filter, 隔清 kaak⁾-ts'ing, 濾 lue⁾, (a) 砂漏 sha-*lau⁾.
Filth, 穢物 wai⁾-mat.
Filthy, 污穢 oo-wai⁾, 污糟 oo-tso.
Fin, 翅 ch'i⁾.
Final, 結尾 kit⁾-⁽mi (⁽mi), 收尾 shau-⁽mi.
Finally, 終然 chuung-in, 究竟 kau⁾-⁽king.
Find, 揾着 ⁽wan-cheuk, (by accident) 遇着 ue⁾-cheuk, (-out) 查出 ch'a-ch'uut.

Fine, 幼細 yau⁾-sai⁾, (elegant) 靚 leng⁾, 妙 miu⁾, 講究 ⁽kong-kau⁾.
Fine, (to) 罰銀 faat-*ngan.
Finery, 浮華之物 fau-wa-chi-mat.
Finger, 手指 ⁽shau-⁽chi.
Finger-glass, 手盅 ⁽shau-⁽chuung.
Finger-ring, 戒指 kaai⁾-⁽chi.
Finical, 小家種 ⁽siu-⁽ka-⁽chuung.
Finish, 做完 tso⁾-uen.
Finite, 有限 ⁽yau-haan⁾.
Fir, 杉 ch'aam⁾, 松 ts'uung.
Fire, 火 ⁽foh, (to) 燒 shiu, (a gun) 鈉炮 naat⁾-*p'aau⁾.
Fire-arms, 火炮 ⁽foh-p'aau⁾, (foreign muskets) 洋鎗 yeung-⁽ts'eung.
Fire-crackers, 炮像 p'aau⁾-*tseung⁾.
Fire-engine, 水車 ⁽shui-ch'e.
Fire-fly, 螢火 ying-⁽foh.
Fire-wood, 柴 ch'aai.
Fire-works, 烟花 in-fa, (to burn) 燒烟火 shiu-in-⁽foh.

Firm, 主固 ‘chue koo’, 堅定 kin-ting’, 堅硬 kin-ngaang’.
Firm, (a) 公司 ˳kuung-˳sze, 行 *hong.
Firmament, 穹蒼 k‘uung-ts‘ong.
First, 第一 tai’-yat.
First-born, 頭長 t‘au-‘cheung.
First-rate, 頂好 ‘ting-‘ho.
Fish, 魚 ue, *ue, (a) 一條魚 yat-t‘iu-*ue, (to) 打魚 ‘ta-*ue, 羅魚 ‘loh-*ue, 拗魚 ‘aau-*ue, (angle) 釣魚 tiu’-*ue.
Fisherman, 羅魚人 ‘loh-ue-yan.
Fishy smell, 魚腥 ue-seng.
Fissure, 罅隙 la’-kwik.
Fist, 拳頭 k‘uen-t‘au.
Fistula, 生穿 shang-ch‘uen.
Fit, 着 cheuk, (a) 一塲 yat-ch‘eung, (fainting) 昏迷一塲 fun-mai-yat-ch‘eung.
Fitch, 小荳 ‘siu-*tau’.
Five, 五 ‘ng.
Fix, 定實 ting’-shat.

Fixed number, 額數 ngaak-sho’.
Flabby, 鬆呸 suung-p‘au.
Flag, (a) 旗 k‘i, (to) 衰頹 shui-t‘ui.
Flag-staff, 旗杆 k‘i-kohn.
Flag-stone, 石板 shek-‘paan.
Flagitious, 兇悍 huung-hohn’.
Flagrant, 明妄 ming-‘mong, 當面 tong-min’.
Flail, 打禾棒 ‘ta-woh-‘p‘aang.
Flake, 片 p‘in’.
Flame, 火尾 ‘foh-‘mi, 火熖 ‘foh-im’.
Flank, 軟脅 ‘uen-hip.
Flannel, 小絨 ‘siu-*yuung.
Flap, 揜 ’im, 蓋揜 koi’-‘im.
Flapping, 拍拍吓 p‘aak-p‘aak-*ha’.
Flash, (to) 閃 ‘shim, 爗 ship’.
Flask, 罇 ˳tsuun.
Flat, 平正 p‘ing-ching’, (thin) 扁 ‘pin, (ground) 低地 tai-ti’, (insipid) 淡淡地 ‘t‘aam-*t‘aam-*ti’.

Flatter, 阿媚奉承 oh-miʼ-fuungʼ-shing.
Flattery, 諂媚 ʽchʽim-mi ʼ.
Flatulent, 食滯發氣 shik-chaiʼ-faatʼ-hiʼ.
Flaunt, 映轉處 ʽyeung-ʽchuen-shueʼ.
Flavour, 氣味 hiʼ-miʼ.
Flaw, 瑕疵 ha-tsʽze.
Flax, 麻 ma.
Flay, 剝皮 mok-pʽi.
Flea, 狗虱 ʽkau-shat, 跳虱 tʽiuʼ-shat.
Flee, 逃走 tʽo-ʽtsau, 走去 ʽtsau-hueʼ.
Fleet, 跑得快 ʽpʽaau-tak-faaiʼ, 速 tsʽuuk, (a) 一幫 yat-pong.
Fleeting, 飛咁快 fi-komʼ-faaiʼ.
Flesh, 肉 yuuk.
Fleur-de-lis, 蝴蝶花 oo-*tip-fa.
Flexible, 柔軟 yau-ʽuen, 屈得 wat-tak.
Flighty, 兩頭跳 ʽleung-tʽau-tʽiuʼ, 桃撻 tʽiu-tʽaatʼ.
Flinch, 畏縮 waiʼ-shuuk.

Fling, 投 tʽau, 抹 wing.
Flint, 火石 ʽfoh-shek.
Flippant, 油嘴 yau-ʽtsui, 下爬輕輕 haʼ-pʽa-heng-heng.
Float, 浮 fau, 蒲 pʽo.
Flock, 羣 kʽwun.
Flog, 鞭打 pin-ʼta, (bamboo) 打板子 ʽta-ʽpaan-ʽtsze.
Flood, (the) 洪水 huung-ʽshui.
Flood-tide, 水大 ʽshui-taaiʼ.
Flooding, 血崩 huetʼ-pang, 血山崩 huetʼ-shan-pang.
Floor, 樓板 *lau-ʽpaan, (ground-) 地臺 tiʼ-tʽoi.
Floss-silk, 絲絨 sze-yuung.
Flounder, 左口魚 ʽtsoh-ʽhau-*ue, 鰜閉魚 tsangʼ-paiʼ-ue.
Flour, 麵粉 minʼ-ʽfun, (1st) 澄麵 tangʼ-minʼ, (2nd) 標麵 piu-minʼ, (3rd) 灰麵 fooi-minʼ.
Flourishing, 茂盛 mauʼ-shingʼ.
Flow, 流 lau.

Flower, 花 fa, (a) 一朵花 yat-ʻtoh-fa.
Fluctuating, 不定得 ’m-tingʼ-tak, 兩頭流 ʻleung-tʻau-lau.
Fluent, 流利 lau-liʼ (laiʼ).
Fluid, 水啖樣 ʻshui-ʻkom-ʻyeung.
Flurry, 慌忙 fong-mong.
Flush, 發紅 faatʼ-huung.
Flute, 簫 siu, 橫笛 waang-*tek.
Flutter, (to) 撲翼 pʻokʼ-yik, (in a) 心亂 sum-luenʼ, 着急 cheuk-kup, 頻撲 pʻan-pʻokʼ.
Fly, (to) 飛 fi, (a) 烏蠅 ʻoo-ʻying, (blue bottle) 青蠅 tsʻing-ying, 金烏蠅 ʻkam-ʻoo-ʻying.
Foam, 浮漚 fau-au, (at the mouth) 吐沫 tʻoʼ-mootʼ.
Foe, 敵 tik.
Fog, 朦霧 muung-moʼ, 迷霧 mai-moʼ.
Foist in, 亂入 luenʼ-yap, 搵入 wanʼ-yap.

Fold (for sheep) 羊欄 yeung-laan, (to) 摺 chipʼ, (one) 單 ʻtaan, (two or more) 倍 ʻpʻooi.
Foliage, 葉茂 ip-mauʼ.
Follow, 跟從 kan-tsʻuung, 隨後 tsʻui-hauʼ.
Folly, 戇氣 ngongʼ-hiʼ, 呆事 ngoi-szeʼ.
Foment, 熱淋 it-lum.
Fond of, 痛愛 tʻuungʼ-oiʼ.
Fondle, 懷撫 waai-ʻfoo, 撫抱 ʻfoo-ʻpʻo.
Food, 食物 shik-mat, 伙食 ʻfoh-shik, 野食 ʻye-shik.
Fool, 呆人 ngoi-yan, 蠢子 ʻchʻuun-ʻtsze.
Foolish, 蠢鈍 ʻchʻuun-tuunʼ.
Foolishly, 莽 ʻmong.
Foolhardy, 冒險 moʼ-ʻhim.
Foot, 脚 keukʼ, 足 tsuuk, (measure) 尺 chʻekʼ.
Footprint, 脚印 keukʼ-yanʼ.
Footstep, 脚跡 keukʼ-tsik.
Foot-stool, 脚踏凳 keukʼ-taap-tangʼ.

Fop, 裝腔 ₍chong-₎hong.
For, (ADV.) 因 yan, 因爲 yan-wai, (PREP.) 代 toi⁾, 替 t'ai⁾, 爲 wai⁾.
Forbear, 縮手 shuuk-⸲shau, 忍住 ⸲yan-chue⁾.
Forbearance, 忍耐 ⸲yan-noi⁾.
Forbid, 禁止 kum⁾-⸲chi.
Force, 力 lik, (to) 強 ⸲k'eung, 逼 pik.
Forced, 勉強 ⸲min-⸲k'eung.
Forceps, 鐵鉗 t'it⁾-⁎k'im, 鉗仔 ⁎k'im-⸲tsai.
Ford, (to) 步涉 po⁾-ship⁾, kaang⁾.
Fore, 前 ts'in, 先 sin.
Forearm, 手肘 ⸲shau-⸲chaau.
Forefinger, 二指 i⁾-⸲chi, 點鹽指 ⸲tim-im-⸲chi.
Forego, 丟開 tiu-hoi, 放下 fong⁾-ha.
Forehead, 額頭 ngaak-t'au.
Foreign goods, 來路貨 loi-⁎lo⁾-foh⁾.
Foreign nation, 外國 ngoi⁾-kwok⁾.

Foreigner, 外國人 ngoi⁾-kwok⁾-yan, (European) 洋人 yeung-yan, (the Chinese call foreigners) 番人 faan-yan, (with a little more respect) 老番 ⸲lo-₎faan, (and in contempt) 番鬼 faan-⸲kwai.
Foreknow, 預先知到 ue⁾-sin-chi-to⁾.
Foreman, 頭人 t'au-yan, 亞總 a⁾-⸲tsuung, 攬頭 ⸲laam-⁎t'au.
Forenoon, 上晝 sheung⁾-chau⁾.
Forerunner, 先驅 sin-k'ue, 先鋒 sin-₎fuung.
Foresee, 先見 sin-kin⁾, 早知 ⸲tso-chi, 大早知到 taai⁾-⸲tso-chi-to⁾.
Forest, 樹林 shue⁾-lum.
Forethink, 預先估 ue⁾-sin-⸲koo, 預料 ue⁾-liu⁾.
Forfeit, 抵填 ⸲tai-t'in.
Forge, (a) 打鐵爐 ⸲ta-t'it⁾-lo.
Forge, (to) 假冒 ⸲ka-mo⁾.

Forgery, 託名僞書 t'ok'-ming-ngai'-shue.
Forget, 忘記 mong-ki'.
Forgetful, 不上心 'm-ʻsheung-sum, 無記性 ʻmo-ki'-sing'.
Forgive, 赦免 she'-ʻmin.
Fork, (a) 枝叉 chi-ch'a.
Forked, 了叉 ʻa-ch'a.
Forlorn, 孤獨 koo-tuuk.
Form, (shape) 模式 moo-shik, 式 shik, (body) 形 ying, 像 tseung'.
Formality, mere, 虛禮 hue-ʻlai.
Formosa, 臺灣 T'oi-waan.
Former, (time) 在先 tsoi'-sin.
Formerly, 從前 ts'uung-ts'in, 起先 ʻhi-sin, 舊時 kau'-shi.
Fornication, 私情 sze-ts'ing, 苟合 ʻkau-hop.
Forsake, 遺棄 wai-hi', 棄 hi', 拋離 p'aau-li.
Forsooth, 眞个 chan-koh'.
Fort, 炮臺 p'aau'-*t'oi.
Forth, 出 ch'uut.

Fortify, 築城 chuuk-sheng, 築營壘 chuuk-ying-ʻlui, 起炮臺 ʻhi-p'aau'-*t'oi.
Fortitude, 堅忍 kin-ʻyan, 堅心 kin-sum, 剛強 kong-k'eung.
Fortunate, 吉 kat, 好命 ʻho-meng'.
Fortunately, 好彩 ʻho-ʻts'oi.
Fortune, 造化 tso'-fa, 命 meng', 運數 wan'-sho'.
Fortune-teller, 算命人 suen'-meng'-yan.
Forward, (go) 上前 ʻsheung-ts'in, (bold) 大胆 taai'-ʻtaam.
Foster, 養 ʻyeung.
Foul, 汚穢 oo-wai', 汚糟 oo-tso, (wind) 逆風 ngaak-fuung.
Found, (metals) 鑄 chue', (establish) 鼎建 ʻting-kin'.
Foundation, 基址 ki-ʻchi, 基 ki, 墻脚 ts'eung-keuk', (stones) 地牛碪 ti'-ngau-ʻchum.
Foundling, 執倒嘅仔 chup-to-ke'-ʻtsai.

Fountain, 泉源 ts'uen-uen, 源頭 uen-t'au, (artificial) 噴水景 p'un'-'shui-'king.
Four, 四 sze'.
Four-square, 四方 sze'-fong-ke'.
Fourth, 第四 tai'-sze', (a) 四分一 sze'-fun'-yat.
Fowl, 鷄 kai, (generally) 雀鳥 tseuk-'niu.
Fowling-piece, 鳥鎗 'niu-ts'eung.
Fox, 狐狸 oo-*li.
Fractious, 嬲嫐 nau-nat.
Fragment, 碎片 sui'-p'in'.
Fragrant, 馨香 hing-heung.
Frail, 脆弱 ts'ui'-yeuk.
Frame, (a) 架 ka'.
France, 法蘭西 Faat'-,laan-,sai, 法國 Faat'-kwok'.
Frank, 坦易 't'aan-i', 直白 chik-paak.
Frankincense, 乳香 'ue-heung.
Frantic, 癲狂 tin-k'wong.
Fraternity, 結義兄弟 kit'-i'-hing-tai'.
Fraud, 騙局 p'in'-kuuk.

Freak, 出奇事 ch'uut-k'i-sze', 新樣 san-*yeung'.
Freckled, 斑點 paan-'tim, paan-'tim-ke'.
Free, 自由 tsze'-yau, 自主 tsze'-,chue, 無拘管 mo-k'ue-'koon.
Free, (to) 放甩 fong'-lat.
Freely, 隨便 ts'ui-*pin', (gratuitously) 白白 paak-paak, (willingly) 甘心 kom-sum.
Freeze, 結冰 kit'-ping, 冷硬 'laang-ngaang', 凍 tuung'.
Freight, 水脚 'shui-keuk'.
Frequent, (to) 常時來往 sheung-shi-loi-'wong.
Frequently, 屢次 lue'-ts'ze', 多賬 toh-cheung'.
Fresh, 新鮮 san-sin, (water) 淡 't'aam, taam'.
Fretful, 焦積 tsiu-tsik.
Friction, 相磨 seung-moh.
Friday, 禮拜五 'lai-paai'-'ng.
Friend, 朋友 p'ang-'yau.
Friendly, 相好 seung-'ho.

Frighten, 嚇怕 haak'-p'a'.
Frightful, 可怕 'hoh-p'a'.
Fringe, 絮 *sue, 纓 ,ying.
Frisk, (to) 跳轉處 t'iu-'chuen-shue'.
Frith, 河口 hoh-'hau.
Frivolous, 輕浮 hing-fau.
Frog, 蛤姆 kop'-'na, 田雞 t'in-,kai.
Frolic, 戲耍 hi'-'sha, 反斗 'faan-'tau.
From, 由 yau, 從 ts'uung, 自 tsze, (distant) 去 hue', 離 li.
Front, 前頭 ts'in-t'au, 前邊 ts'in-pin (pin'), (to) 面向 min'-heung'.
Frontier, 境界 'king-kaai'.
Frost, 霜降 seung-kong'.
Froth, 泡 'p'o.
Frown, 縐埋眉頭 tsau'-maai-mi-t'au.
Frugal, 省儉 'shaang-kim'.
Fruit, 菓子 'kwoh-'tsze, 菓實 'kwoh-shat.
Fruitful, 豐盛 fuung-shing'.
Fruit-tree, 菓木 'kwoh-muuk.

Frustrate, 破敗 p'oh'-paai', (good) 孤負 koo-foo'.
Fry, 煎炒 tsin-'ch'aau, 蓏 ch'aau'.
Frying-pan, 鑊 wok.
Fuel, 柴 ch'aai, 柴火 ch'aai-foh.
Fulfil, 成就 shing-tsau', 踐 tsin', 應驗 ying'-im'.
Fulfilment, 應驗 ying'-im'.
Full, 滿 'moon, 盈 ying.
Fully, 嘥 saai', 盡地 tsuun'-*ti'.
Fume, (rage) 鬧 naau', 生氣 shang hi'.
Fumigate, 燻 fan.
Fun, 頑笑 waan-siu', 戲耍 hi'-'sha.
Function, (office,) 職 chik, (use) 用處 yuung'-ch'ue'.
Fund, 嘗銀 sheung-*ngan, 嘗項 sheung-hong'.
Fundamental, 根本 kan-'poon.
Funeral, 送葬 suung'-tsong', 喪事 song-sze'.
Fungus, 香信 heung-suun', 菌 'k'wun, 'k'an, (on trees) 木耳 muuk-'i.

Funnel, 漏斗 lau⁾-poot⁾, (chimney) 煙通 in-t'uung.
Fur-dress, 裘 k'au, 皮衣 p'i-i, (sable) 貂鼠皮 tiu-˚shue-p'i.
Furbish, 擦光 ts'aat⁾-kwong.
Furious, 暴 po⁾, 兇暴 huung-po⁾.
Furl, 捲埋 ˚kuen-maai.
Furlough, 假 ka⁾, (to ask) 告假 ko⁾-ka⁾, (to give) 放假 fong⁾-ka⁾.
Furnace, 爐 lo, 灶 tso⁾, (portable) 風爐 fuung-*lo.
Furnish, 給 k'up, 備辦 pi-paan⁾, 齊備傢伙 ts'ai-pi⁾-ka-˚foh.
Furniture, 傢伙 ka-˚foh.
Furrow, 犂路 lai-lo⁾, 田溝 t'in-kau.
Further, 更遠 kang⁾-˚uen, 再進 tsoi⁾-tsuun⁾.
Furthermore, 而且 i-˚ch'e.
Fury, 怒狂 no⁾-k'wong.
Fuse, 燒鎔 shiu-yuung.
Fussy, 浮躁 fau-ts'o⁾.
Fusty, 宿宿地 suuk-suuk-*ti⁾, yik.

Futile, 虛徒 hue-t'o.
Future, 將來 tseung-loi, 來 loi, 後 hau⁾.

G

Gabble, 嘮嘈 lo-ts'o.
Gable, 金髻 kum-kai⁾, 墻髻 ts'eung-kai⁾.
Gad about, 開逛 haan-k'waang⁾.
Gad-fly, 牛蝱 ngau-mong.
Gag, 鉗口 k'im-˚hau, 塞口 sak-˚hau.
Gage, (a) 準則 ˚chuun-tsak.
Gaiety, 繁華 faan-wa.
Gain, 利 li⁾, 利息 li⁾-sik, (to) 賺 chaan⁾, 贏 yeng, 獲 wok.
Gait, 舉動 ˚kue-tuung⁾.
Galangal, 艮薑 leung-keung.
Gale, 大風 taai⁾-fuung.
Gall, 膽 ˚taam, 膽汁 ˚taam-chup.
Gall-nut, 五倍子 ˚,ng-˚p'ooi-˚tsze, 沒石 moot-shek.

Gallant, (heroic) 英雄 ying-huung.
Gallery, 樓臺 lau-t'oi, 樓 ˏlau.
Gallipot, 冚盅 hom⁾-ˏchuung.
Gallon, (a) 一斗 yat-ˋtau.
Gallop, 跑 ˋp'aau.
Gallows, 縊架 ai⁾-*ka⁾.
Gambier, 薯茛 shue-leung.
Gamble, 賭錢 ˋto-*ts'in.
Gambler, 賭棍 ˋto-kwun⁾.
Gambling-house, 番攤館 ˏfaan-ˏt'aan-ˋkoon.
Gamboge, 籐黃 t'ang-wong.
Gambol, 隨處跳 ts'ui-ch'ue⁾-t'iu⁾.
Game, (a) 博局 pok⁾-kuuk, 博戲 pok⁾-hi⁾, (to play) 戲耍 hi⁾-ˋsha, (make, of) 舞弄 ˋmoo-luung⁾.
Game, (meat) 野味 ˋye-*mi⁾.
Gammon, 嘴滑 ˋtsui-waat, (to) 噋 t'um⁾.
Gammon, (ham) 火腿 ˋfoh-ˋt'ui.
Gander, 鵝公 ngoh-ˏkuung.
Gang, 隊 tui⁾.

Gangrene, 肉死 yuuk-ˋsze.
Gaol, 監房 kaam-fong.— Superindendent of, 司獄官 sze-yuuk-koon.
Gaoler, 司獄 sze-yuuk, 禁子 kum⁾-ˋtsze, 看監 hohn-ˏkaam.
Gap, 山口 shaan-ˋhau, 一個口 yat-koh⁾-ˋhau.
Gape, 擘大個口 maak⁾-taai⁾-koh⁾-ˋhau, (and stare) 擘口定眼 maak⁾-ˋhau-ting⁾-ˋngaan.
Garble, 講歪 ˋkong-ˋme, 半吞半吐 poon⁾-t'un-poon⁾-t'o⁾.
Garden, 園 uen, *uen.
Gardener, 園丁 uen-ˏting.
Gardenia florida, 白蟾花 paak-shim-fa, 黃梔 wong-chi.
Gargle, 漱口 sau⁾-ˋhau, ˋlong-ˋhau.
Garland, 花冠 fa-koon.
Garlic, 青蒜 ts'ing-*suen⁾, 大蒜 taai⁾-*suen⁾, 蒜頭 suen⁾-t'au.

Garment, 衣服 i-fuuk, 衣裳 i-sheung.
Garoupa, 石班 shek-ˏpaan.
Garret, 貼脊頂樓 tʻipˊ-tsekˊ-ˋting-lau, 樓仔 *lau-ˋtsai, 閣仔 kokˊ-ˋtsai.
Garrison, 兵 ping, 屯兵 tʻuen-ˏping.
Garrulous, 沉贅 chʻum-chuiˊ.
Garter, 襪帶 mat-taaiˊ.
Gas, (coal-) 煤氣 mooi-hiˊ.
Gas-light, 煤燈 mooi-ˏtang.
Gash, 傷口 sheung-ˋhau.
Gasp, 喘氣 ˋchʻuen-hiˊ, 抽氣 chʻau-hiˊ.
Gate, 門 moon, (with bars) 閘門 chaap-moon, (rolling) 走櫳 ˋtsau-*luung.
Gate-keeper, 看門公 hohn-moon-ˏkuung.
Gather, 積埋 tsik-maai, 收拾 shau-shup, 聚埋 tsueˊ-maai.
Gaudy, 排塲 pʻaai-chʻeung.
Gauze, 紗 sha, 機紗 ki-sha, 亮紗 leungˊ-sha.
Gay, 奢華 chʻe-wa, (person) 好奢華 hoˊ-cʻhe-wa.

Gaze, 睇定眼 ʻtʻai-ting-ˋngaan, (at) 定眼睇住 tingˊ-ˋngaan-tʻai-chueˊ.
Gazelle, 羚羊 ling-yeung.
Gazette, 通報 tʻuung-poˊ, (Peking-) 京報 ˏKing-poˊ 京抄 King-ˏchʻaau.
Gecko, 蛤蚧 kop-*kaaiˊ, 雷公蛇 lui-ˏkuung-*she.
Gelatine, 膠 kaau.
Geld, 閹 im, 割勢 kohtˊ-shaiˊ.
Gem, 玉 *yuuk, 寶石 ˋpo-shek.
Gender, (to) 生 shaang.
Genealogy, 族譜 tsuuk-ˋpʻo, 世系 shaiˊ-haiˊ.
General, 總共 ˋtsuung-kuungˊ, 通 tʻuung.
General, (a) 將軍 tseung-kwun.
Generally, 大凡 taaiˊ-faan, 大約 taaiˊ-*yeukˊ.
Generate, (as animals) 傳種 chʻuen-ˋchuung, (produce) 生 shaang.
Generation, 世代 shaiˊ-toi

Generous, 慷慨 ʻkʻong-kʻoiʼ, 大量 taaiʼ-leungʼ, 四海 szeʼ-ʻhoi.
Genial, 溫和 wan-woh.
Genii, 神仙 shan-ˌsin.
Genius, 英才 ying-tsʻoi.
Genteel, 斯文 sze-mun.
Gentian, 黃連 wong-lin.
Gentle, 溫柔 wan-yau.
Gentleman, (in character) 君子 kwun-ˈtsze, (a teacher) 先生 sin-shang, 老師 ʻlo-sze, (an old) 老爺 ʻlo-ye, (young) 相公 seungʼ-kuung.
Gentlemen! 列公 lit-ˌkuung.
Gently, (lightly) 輕輕地 heng-heng-*tiʼ (slowly) 慢慢地 maanʼ-maanʼ-*tiʼ.
Gentry, 紳襟 shan-kʻum, 紳士 shan-szeʼ.
Genuine, 眞 chan.
Geography, 地理 tiʼ-ˈli.
Geomancy, 風水 fuung-ˈshui.
Geometry, 幾何 ʻki-hoh, 丈量 cheungʼ-leung.
Geranium, 香葉 heung-ip.

Germ, 芽 nga, (seed) 仁 yan, ngan.
German-silver, 白銅 paak-tʻuung.
Germany, 德國 Tak-kwokʼ.
Germinate, 發芽 faatʼ-nga, 爆咪 paauʼ-muuk.
Get, 得到 tak-ʻto, 攞到 ʻloh-ʻto, 攞得 ʻloh-tak, 得 tak.
Ghost, 鬼 ʻkwai.
Giant, 偉丈夫 ʻwai-cheungʼ-foo, 長人 chʻeung-yan.
Giblets, 蒲肶 pʻo-cʻhiʼ.
Giddy, 頭暈 tʻau-wanʼ (wan), (light) 佻橽 tʻiu-tʻaatʼ.
Gift, (a) 送俾 suungʼ-ˈpi, suungʼ-ˈpi-keʼ 送禮 suungʼ-ˈlai, (from a superior) 賜 tsʻzeʼ.
Giggle, 笑嬉嬉 siuʼ-hi-hi.
Gild, (to) 鍍金 toʼ-ˌkum, 黐金 cʻhi-ˌkum.
Gills, 鰓 soi.
Gimlet, 手鑽 ʻshau-tsuenʼ.
Gin, (snare) 圈套 huen-tʻoʼ.

Ginger, 薑 keung, (preserved) 糖薑 t'ong-ˌkeung, (stem) 子薑 ˈtsze-ˌkeung.
Ginseng, 人參 yan-shum.
Gipsies, (Chinese) 三姑六婆 saam-koo-luuk-p'oh.
Gird, (to) 束住 ch'uuk-chue', 箍住 k'oo-chue'.
Girdle, 腰帶 iu-*taai', 褲頭帶 foo'-t'au-*taai'.
Girl, 女仔 ˈnue-ˈtsai, (servant) 妹仔 mooi-ˈtsai.
Girth, 肚帶 ˈt'o-*taai'.
Give, 俾 ˈpi, (present) 送俾 suung'-ˈpi.
Gizzard, 腎 ˈshan, (skin of the) 脆腟 p'i-c'hi.
Glad, 歡喜 foon-ˈhi.
Glance, (to) 閃 ˈshim, (at) 睇一吓 ˈt'ai-yat-ˈha 一睇 yat-ˈt'ai.
Glands, 津液之核 tsuun-yik-chi-wat.
Glare, 光猛 kwong-ˈmang.
Glaring, 明明 ming-ming.
Glass, 玻璃 ˌpoh-ˌli, (a tumbler) 玻璃杯 ˌpoh-ˌli-ˌpooi.
Glass-grinding, 車料 ch'e-*liu'.
Glass-melting, 燒料 shiu-*liu'.
Glauber-salts, 玄明粉 uen-ming-ˈfun.
Glazed, 光滑 kwong-waat, 玻璃光 ˌpoh-ˌli-kwong, (glass put in) 鑲玻璃 seung-ˌpoh-ˌli.
Glib, 利口 li'-ˈhau, (slippery) 滑 waat.
Glide, 流 lau, 慢流 maan'-lau.
Glimmer, 微光閃 mi-kwong-ˈshim.
Glitter, 發光 faat'-kwong, (show) 光華 kwong-wa.
Globe, 球 k'au, (the) 地球 ti'-k'au.
Gloomy, 晦氣 fooi'-hi', (weather) 天色暗 t'in-shik-om', 烏雲 oo-wan.
Glorify, 歸榮 kwai-wing.
Glory, 榮 wing, 榮光 wing-kwong.
Glossy, 閃靚 ˈshim-leng'.
Gloves, 手笠 ˈshau-lup.

Glow-worm, 放光蟲 fong²-kwong-*ch'uung.
Glue, 牛皮膠 ngau-p'i-kaau.
Glutton, 大食王 taai²-shik-wong, (VULG.) 大食鬼 taai²-shik-'kwai.
Gluttonous, 貪喫 t'aam-yaak.
Gnash, (the teeth) 咬牙 'ngaau-nga, 切齒 ts'it²-'ch'i.
Gnat, 蚊蟲 mong-ch'uung, 蚊 ₍mun.
Gnaw, 齧 nget, 咽 luun.
Go, 去 hue², 往 'wong, 行 hang, (be off) 扯 'ch'e.
Goal, 準頭 'chuun-t'au.
Goat, 山羊 shaan-*yeung, 草羊 ₍ts'o-*yeung, 羊咩 yeung-₍me.
Gobble, 吞 t'un, 捋聲吞 luet-sheng-t'un, 'ts'uun.
Go-between, 中人 chuung-*yan, 媒 mooi, (female) 媒婆 mooi-*p'oh.
Goblet, 壺 *oo, 鍾 chuung.

GOD, 上帝 SHEUNG²-TAI², (the gods) 諸上帝 chue-sheung²-tai², 鬼神 'kwai-shan.
Godown, 貨倉 foh²-ts'ong.
Goitre, 大頸疱 taai²-'keng-₍p'aau.
Gold, 金 kum, 黃金 wong-₍kum.
Gold-leaf, 金薄 ₍kum-pok.
Gone, 去了 hue²-'liu, hue²-hiu, 無咯 'mo-lok².
Gong, 鑼 *loh, (a) 一面鑼 yat-min²-*loh.
Gonorrhea, 白濁 paak-chuuk.
Good, 好 'ho, 善 shin².
Good-bye, (to the remaining) 坐了 *tsoh²-a, (to the going) 好行 'ho-haang.
Goose, 草鵝 ₍ts'o-*ngoh, (wild) 鴈鵝 ngaan²-*ngoh.
Gore, (to) 觸傷 ch'uuk-sheung, 抄 ch'aau.
Gorgeous, 榮華 wing-wa.
Gormandize, 食太過 shik-t'aai²-kwoh².
Gospel, 福音 fuuk-yum.

Gossamer, 草蛛網 ‵ts‵o-ᵨchue-﹡moug, 遊絲 yau-sze.
Gossip, 閒談 haan-t'aam, 是非 shi'-fi, (to) 聞風捉影 mun-fuung-chuuk-ᵨying, (a) 巷婆 hong'-﹡p'oh.
Gouge, (a) 啉鑿 lum-tsok.
Gouge (to), 鑿 tsok, 挖 waat'.
Gourd, 匏瓜 p'aau-ᵨkwa, 葫蘆 oo-﹡loo, (snake-) 絲瓜 ᵨsze ᵨkwa.
Gout, 脚風 keuk'-fuung.
Govern, 管理 ‵koon-‵li, 治 chi'.
Government, 國家 kwok'-ka, 皇家 wong-ka, 國政 kwok-ching', 治 chi', —Offices 督憲署 ‵tuuk-hin'-‵shue.
Governor General, 督憲 tuuk-hin', 總督 ‵tsuung-tuuk, 制台 chai'-t'oi, (the Supreme) 主宰 ‵Chue-‵tsoi.
Gown, 長衫 ch'eung-ᵨshaam, 袍 ﹡p'o.

Grace, (mercy) 恩典 yan-‵tin.
Graceful, 斯文 sze-mun, 雅ᵨnga.
Gracious, 恩 yan.
Grackle, 了哥 ᵨliu-ᵨkoh.
Gradation, 次等 ts'ze'-‵tang.
Grade, 脚色 keuk'-shik.
Gradually, 漸漸 tsim'-﹡tsim', 漸次 tsim'-ts'ze'.
Graduate, (of 1st deg.) 秀才 sau'-﹡ts'oi, (of 2nd) 舉人 ‵kue-yan, (of 3rd) 進士 tsuun'-sze', (of 4th) 翰林 hohn'-lum, (to) 登科 tang-foh, (1st) 入學 yup-hok, (2nd) 扳桂 p'aan-kwai'.
Graft, (to) 劗 ts'im, (to slip) 駁 pok'.
Grain, 穀 kuuk, (a) 粒 nup, (of wood) 紋 mun.
Grammar, 作文法 tsok'-mun-faat'.
Grampus, 鯨魚 k'ing-ue.
Granary, 穀倉 kuuk-ts'ong.
Grand, 高大 ko-taai', 大 taai', 巍巍 ngai-ngai.

Grand-father, 祖父 ʽtso-fooʼ, 公爺 kuung-ye, 亞公 aʼ-kuung, (mother) 祖母 ʽtso-ʽmo, 亞婆 aʼ-pʽoh, (child) 孫 suen, ʽsuen.
Granite, 青石 tsʽing-shek, 花剛青 fa-ʽkong-ʽtsʽeng, 白石 paak-shek.
Grant, 許准 ʽhue-ʽchuun.
Grapes, 葡提子 pʽo-tʽai-ʽtsze.
Graphic, 形容得出 ying-yuung-tak-chʽuut.
Grasp, 揸 cha.
Grass, 草 ʽtsʽo.
Grass-cloth, 蔴布 ma-poʼ, 夏布 haʼ-poʼ.
Grass-hopper, 蚱蜢 chaʼ-ʽmang, 草蜢 ʽtsʽo-ʽ*mang.
Grate, (a) 鐵火爐 tʽitʼ-ʽfoh-lo, (to) 刮 kwaatʼ, 擦 tsʽaatʼ, 刮沙 kwaatʼ-sha.
Grateful, 感恩 ʽkom-yan, 感謝 ʽkom-tseʼ.
Grater, 磨 mohʼ, *mohʼ.
Gratified, 快悅 faaiʼ-uet.
Gratify, 悅 uet.

Grating, (noise) 刮刮聲 kwit-kwit-sheng, (an iron) 鐵柱 tʽitʼ-ʽchʽue.
Gratis, 白白 paak-paak.
Gratitude, 感心 ʽkom-sum.
Gratuity of money, 贈銀 tsangʼ-*ngan.
Grave, (a) 墳墓 fun-mooʼ, 塚墓 ʽchʽuung-mooʼ.
Grave, (sedate) 莊敬 chong-kingʼ, 嚴肅 im-suuk, (heavy) 重 ʽchʽuung.
Gravestone, 墓碑 mooʼ-pi.
Graveclothes, 壽衣 shau-i.
Gravel, 砂 sha, 砂石 sha-shek, (a disease) 砂痳 sha-lum.
Graving-tool, 鏨刀 tsaamʼ-to.
Gravitation, 相汲力 seung-kʽup-lik.
Gravy, 醬 tseungʼ, 汁 chup.
Gray, 褐色 hohtʼ-shik, 灰色 fooi-shik, (hair) 白髮 paak-faaiʼ.
Grease, 膏油 ko-yau.

Greasy, 肥膩 fi-ni', 油膩 yau-ni'.
Great, 大 taai'.
Great-grand-father, 曾祖 tsang-ʿtso, (-son) sak.
Greedy, 貪心 tʻaam-sum, (of food) 爲食 wai'-shik.
Greek, 希利尼 Hi-li-ni.
Green, 綠色 luuk-shik, 青綠 tsʻing-luuk.
Greenhorn, 不入世 'm-yup-shai'.
Greens, 青菜 tsʻing-tsʻoi', 波菜 poh-tsʻoi'.
Greet, 問候 mun'-hau'.
Gridiron, 鐵鈀 tʻit'-*pʻa.
Grief, 憂悶 yau-moon'.
Grievance, 委曲 ʿwai-huuk.
Grievous, (heavy) 重 ʿchʻuung, (lamentable) 可哀 ʿhoh-oi.
Grievously, 交關 kaau-kwaan.
Griffin, or unicorn, 麒麟 kʻi-*luun.
Grill, 炒 ʿchʻaau.
Grimace, 歪面 ʿme-min'.

Grin, 噬起牀牙 shai'-ʿhi-chʻong-nga.
Grind, 磨 moh.
Grinding, (noise) 啥啥聲 ngum'-ngum'-sheng.
Grindstone, 磨刀石 moh-to-shek.
Gripes, 扭痛 ʿnau-tʻuung'.
Gristle, 脆骨 tsʻui'-kwut.
Grits, 麥頭 mak-tʻau, 麥碎 mak-sui.
Gritty, 帶沙 taai'-sha.
Groan, 嘆氣 tʻaan'-hi', 哷哷聲 'ny-'ng-sheng, 硬硬聲 ngang-ngang-sheng.
Grocery, (a) 雜貨舖 tsaap-foh'-pʻo.
Groin, 髀摺 ʿpi-chip'.
Groom, 馬夫 ʿma-foo.
Groove, (a) 一條坑 yat-tʻiu-haang, (to) 入柳 yup-ʿlau.
Grope, 摩探 moh-tʻaam', 摸 ʿmoh.
Gross, 粗 tsʻo, (large) 粗大 tsʻo-taai'.
Grotesque, 古怪 ʿkoo-kwaai'.
Ground, 地 ti', 土 ʿtʻo.

Ground-nut, 花生 fa-ʿshang, 地豆 tiʾ-*tauʾ.
Groundless, 無根無本 mo-kan-mo-ʿpoon.
Grounds, (dregs) 渣滓 cha-ʿtsze.
Group, 隊 tuiʾ, 堆 tui, (to) 成隊 shing-tuiʾ.
Grovelling, 下作 haʾ-tsokʾ, 卑陋 pi-lauʾ.
Grow, 生長 shaang-ʿcheung, 長大 ʿcheung-taaiʾ, 生 shaang.
Growl, 胡胡聲 oo-oo-sheng.
Grub, 蟛蟮 tsʻai-tsʻo, 地底蟲 tiʾ-ʿtai-chʻuung.
Grudge, 吝惜 luunʾ-sik, (a) 私怨 sze-uenʾ.
Gruel, 粥 chuuk.
Gruff, 粗魯 tsʻo-ʿlo.
Grumble, 哈沈 ngum-chʻum.
Grunt, 嚙齧聲 nguet-nguet-sheng.
Guano, 鳥糞 ʿniu-funʾ.
Guarantee, (to) 包 paau.
Guard, 守 ʿshau, 護衞 ooʾ-waiʾ, (against) 防 fong.

Guard-boat, 巡船 tsʻuun-*shuen.
Guardian, 養主 ʿyeung-ʿchue.
Guava, 番石榴 faan-shek-*lau.
Gudgeon, 白鴿魚 paak-kopʾ-*ne.
Guess, 猜 chʻaai, 試猜 shiʾ-chʻaai, 猜度 chʻaai-tok, haaiʾ.
Guest, 人客 yan-haakʾ.
Guide, 引路 ʿyan-loʾ.
Guild, 行 hong, 會館 ooiʾ-ʿkoon.
Guile, 詭譎 ʿkwai-kwut, 詭計 ʿkwai-kaiʾ.
Guilt, 罪辜 tsuiʾ-koo.
Guilty, 有罪 ʿyau tsuiʾ.
Guise, 貌 maauʾ, 裝扮 chong-paanʾ.
Guitar, 琵琶 pʻi-*pʻa.
Gulf, 大灣 taaiʾ-waan, (an abyss) 深淵 shum-uen.
Gull, (a) 鷗 au (to) 欺騙 hi-pʻinʾ, 欺弄 hi-luungʾ.
Gullet, 咽喉 in-hau, 喉嚨 hau-luung.

Gully, 坎坑 ʻhaang-ʻhom.
Gulp, 硬吞 ngaangʼ-tʻun.
Gum, 樹膠 shueʼ-kaau.
Gum-benjamin, 安息香 ohn-sik-ʻheung.
Gums, 牙齦肉 nga-kan-yuuk.
Gun, (fowling-piece) 鳥鎗 ʻniu-ʻtsʻeung, (cannon) 炮 pʻauʼ.
Gun-cap, 銅帽子 tʻuung-moʼ-ʻtsze.
Gun-powder, 火藥 ʻfoh-yeuk.
Gun-powder-tea, 小珠茶 ʻsiu-chue-chʻa.
Gush, 噴溢 pʻunʼ-yat.
Gust, 陣風 chanʼ-fuung, 口風 ʻhau-fuung, 閃山風 ʻshim-shaan-fuung.
Gut, 腸 chʻeung.
Gutta-percha, 硬樹膠 ngaangʼ-shueʼ-kaau.
Gutter, 溝渠 kau-kʻue.
Gymnastics, 打把寶 ʻta-ʻpa-shat, 練工夫 linʼ-kuung-foo.
Gypsum, 石膏 shek-ʻko.
Gyves, 脚鐐 keukʼ-liu.

H

Ha! 喺 ʻhai!
Habit, 慣例 kwaanʼ-laiʼ, (in the) 慣習 kwaanʼ-tsaap, 做慣 tsoʼ-kwaanʼ.
Habitable, 住得 chueʼ-tak, chueʼ-tak-keʼ.
Hack, (to) 斲 teuk, 削 seukʼ.
Haddock, 黃畫 wong-*waak.
Hades, 陰間 yum-kaan, 陰府 yum-ʻfoo.
Haft, 柄 pingʼ, pengʼ.
Haggard, 瘦壞 shauʼ-waaiʼ, 醜樣 ʻchʻau-*yeungʼ.
Haggle, 疾口 tsat-ʻhau.
Hail, 雹 pok, (a fall of) 落雹 lok-pok.
Hail, (to) 遠遠叫 ʻuen-ʻuen-kiuʼ, 招 chiu.
Hair, 毛 mo, (of the head) 頭髮 tʻan-faatʼ.
Hair-breadth, 一毫 yat-ho, 絲毫 sze-ho.(-escape) 啱啱得甩 ʻngaam-ʻngaam-tak-lut.

Hair-cloth, 毛布 mo-poʼ.
Hair-gum, (used by women) 鉋花 pʻaau-ˏfa.
Hair-pin, 髻頭針 kaiʼ-*tʻau-ˏchum, (clasp) 簪 ˏtsaam.
Halberd, 斧鉞 ˈfoo-uct.
Hale, (to) 拉 laai, 拖 tʻoh.
Hale, (healthy) 壯健 chongʼ-kinʼ.
Half, 半 poonʼ.
Halibut, 將軍甲 tseung-kwun-kaapʼ.
Hall, 廳 ˏtʻeng, 堂 tʻong, 館 ˈkoon.
Halo, 氶 huungʼ, 暈 wanʼ.
Halt, (to) 停脚 tʻing-keukʼ, (limp) 趷脚 kat-keukʼ.
Halter, 馬籠頭 ˈma-luung-tʻau, (noose) 老鼠結 ˈlo-ˈshue-litʼ, 生結 shaang-litʼ.
Ham, 火腿 ˈfoh-ˈtʻui.
Hamlet, 村 ˏtsʻuen.
Hammer, 鐵鎚 tʻitʼ-*chʻui, (to) 槌 chʻui, 打 ˈta, 𢱡 ˈtum.
Hammock, 吊牀 tiuʼ-chʻong.

Hamper, (a) 籠 luung, 簍 ˈlau, (to) 逼窄 pik-chaakʼ, 窒手脚 chatʼ-ˈshau-keukʼ.
Hand, 手 ˈshau.
Hand-bill, 招帖 chiu-tʻipʼ, 街招 ˏkaai-ˏchiu.
Hand-cuffs, 手鐐 ˈshau-liu.
Handful, (a) 一揸 yat-chu.
Handicraft, 手作 ˈshau-tsokʼ, 手藝 ˈshau-ngaiʼ.
Hand-kerchief, 手巾 ˈshau-ˏkan, 汗巾 hohnʼ-ˏkan.
Hand-writing, 筆跡 pat-tsik.
Handle, (to) 抖 tauʼ, 摩 moh, ˈmoh.
Handle, (a) 條柄 tʻiu-pengʼ.
Handmaid, 婢 ˈpʻi.
Handsome, 精緻 tsing-chiʼ.
Handy, 抵手 ˈtai-ˈshau, (convenient) 便當 pinʼ-tongʼ.
Hang, 吊 tiuʼ, 懸掛 uen-kwaʼ, (up) 掛起 kwaʼ-ˈhi, (down the head) 嗒低頭 tap-tai-*tʻau, (by the neck) 吊頸 tiuʼ-ˈkeng.

Hanger-on, 黃脚鷄 wong-keukʼ-ˌkai.
Hanker after, 貪 tʻaam, 戀 luenʼ.
Happen, 遇有 ueʼ-ˌyau, 遇着 ueʼ-cheuk.
Happily, 幸 hangʼ, 好彩 ˈho-ˈtsʻoi.
Happiness, 福 fuuk.
Happy, 有福 ˈyau-fuuk.
Harass, 難爲 naan-wai.
Harbour, (a) 港口 ˈkong-ˈhau, (to) 窩藏 wohtsʻong, 隱藏 yan-tsʻong.
Harbour Master, 船政廳 shuen-chingʼ-ˌtʻeng.
Hard, 堅硬 kin-ngaangʼ, 硬 ngaangʼ, (difficult) 難 naan, (hearted) 忍心 ˈyan-sum.
Harden, 整硬 ˈching-ngaangʼ.
Hardship, 艱難 kaan-naan.
Hardly, 爭的 ˌchaang-ˌti, 難 naan, 僅 ˈkan.
Hardy, 強健 kʻeung-kinʼ.
Hare, 野兎 ˈye-tʻoʼ.
Harelip, 崩口 pang-ˈhau.

Harlot, 娼妓 chʻeung-kiʼ.
Harm, 害 hoiʼ, 傷 sheung.
Harmony, 和 woh.
Harness, 器具 hiʼ-kueʼ, (to a horse) 配置 pʻooiʼ-chiʼ.
Harp, 箏 chang.
Harpoon, 鏢 piu.
Harrow, 耙 pʻa, 犂耙 lai-pʻa.
Harsh, 倔 kwut, 齳 haai, 刻薄 haakʼ-pok.
Hart, 鹿公 luuk-ˌkuung.
Harts-horn, 鹿茸 luuk-yuung.
Harvest, 收割時候 shaukohtʼ-shi-hauʼ, 秋收 tsʻau-shau, 收成 shau-shing.
Hash, 斬傷 ˈchaam-sheung, 切爛 tsʻitʼ-laanʼ.
Hasp, (hook) 鈎 ngau, (for a padlock) 鎖牌 ˈsoh-pʻaai.
Haste, 急切 kup-tsʻitʼ.
Hasten, 趕快 ˈkohn-faaiʼ.
Hasty, 急 kup.
Hat, 帽 *moʼ, (put on) 戴帽 taaiʼ-*moʼ.
Hatch, (a) 艙門 tsʻong-moon, (to) 苞 poʼ, (artificially) 焙 pooi.

Hatch-way, 艙口 ⸢ts'ong-⸢hau.
Hatchet, 斧頭 ⸢foo-*t'au.
Hate, 恨怒 han'-no', 怨恨 uen'-han', 憎 tsang.
Hateful, 可惡 ⸢koh-oo'.
Haughty, 大腔 taai'-⸢hong, 驕傲 kiu-ngo'.
Haul, 扯 ⸢ch'e.
Have, 有 ⸢yan.
Havoc, 殘害 ts'aan-hoi'.
Hawk, 鷹 ⸢ying.
Hawker, 販仔 faan'-⸢tsai, 小販 ⸢siu-*faan'.
Hawthorn, 枳 ⸢chi.
Hazard, 危險 ngai-⸢him, (to) 敢 ⸢kom, 冒 mo', 拚 p'oon', 冒險 mo'-⸢him.
Haze, 雲霧 wan-moo'.
Hazel-nut, 榛 ⸢yui.
He, 佢 ⸢k'ue.
Head, 頭 t'au, 首 ⸢shau.
Headache, 頭痛 t'au-t'uung', 頭瘌 t'au-ts'ek'.
Headstrong, 硬頸 ngaang'-⸢keng.
Heal, 醫 i, 醫好 i-⸢ho.

Healthy, 爽神 ⸢shony-shan, 強壯 k'eung-chong', 壯 chong'.
Heap, 堆 tui, (up) 堆埋 tui-maai, 堆起 tui-⸢hi, 重重疊疊 ch'nung-ch'nung-tip-tip.
Hear, 聽 t'eng, 聽聞 t'eng-mun, 聽見 t'eng-kin'.
Hearken, 俾耳聽 ⸢pi-⸢i-t'eng.
Hearsay, 風聞 fuung-mun.
Hearse, 喪車 song-kue.
Heart, 心 sum.
Heart-burn, 心酸 sum-suen, 發瘌酸 faat'-laak'-suen, 煩口 fuan-k'au'.
Hearth, 火爐底 ⸢foh-lo-⸢tai.
Heartily, (willing) 甘心 kom-sum.
Hearty, 爽快 ⸢shong-faai', 眞心 chan-sum.
Heat, 熱 it, 熱氣 it-hi', (to) 燒熱 shiu-it, 整熱 ⸢ching-it.
Heathen, 教外異民 kaau'-ngoi'-i'-mun.

Heave, (pull) 扯 ‘ch'e, (throw) 投 t'au, (swell) 冲起來 ch'uung-‘hi-lai.
Heaven, 天 t'in. (the abode) 天堂 t'in-t'ong.
Heavy, 重 ‘ch'uung.
Hebrew, 希伯來 Hi-paak'-loi.
Hedge, 籬笆 li-pa, 笏籬 lak-li.
Hedge-hog, 蝟 wai', 箭猪 tsin'-chue.
Heed, 顧住 koo'-chue'.
Heedless, 不留心 ‘m-lau-sum.
Heel, 脚踭 keuk'-chaang.
Heifer, 牛母仔 ngau-‘moo-‘tsai.
Heighten, 起高 ‘hi-ko, 整高 ‘ching-ko.
Heir, 嗣子 tsze'-‘tsze, 冢子 ‘ch'uung-‘tsze, (to) 承業 shing-ip.
Hell, 地獄 ti'-yuuk.
Hellebore, 藜蘆 lai-lo.
Helm, 舵 t'oh, 舵 ‘t'aai, 舵筒 ‘t'aai-t'uung.

Helmsman, 梢公 shaau-kuung.
Helmet, 頭盔 t'au-k'wai.
Help, 幫助 pong-choh', 照顧 chiu'-koo', (no) 無奈何 ‘mo-noi'-hoh.
Helping-hand, 幫手 pong-‘shau.
Hem, 邊骨 pin-kwut, (to) 挑邊骨 t'iu-pin-kwut.
Hem and ha, e-e-a'-a'.
Hemp, 麻 ma.
Hen, 雞母 kai-‘moo, 雞姆 kai-‘na.
Hence, 故此 koo'-‘tsze, (away) 離此 li-‘tsze, 離呢處 li-ni-shue'.
Henceforth, 自今以後 tsze'-kum-‘i-hau'.
Her, 個女人 koh'-‘nue-*yan, 佢 ‘k'ue, (POSS.) 佢嘅 ‘k'ue-ke'.
Herald, 宣令官 suen-ling'-koon, 宣報 suen-po'.
Herb, 草菜 ‘ts'o-ts'oi'.
Herbalist, 採藥先生 ‘ts'oi-yeuk-sin-shang.
Herd, 羣 k'wun.

Herdsman, 牧人 muuk-yan, (of cows) 牧牛人 munk-ngau-yan.
Here, 呢處 ni-ch'ue', ni-shue'.
Hereafter, 此後 'ts'ze-hau', 嗣後 tsze'-hau'.
Heresy, 異端 i'-tuen, 邪教 ts'e-kaau'.
Heretofore, 從來 ts'uung-loi, 向來 heung'-loi.
Hermit, 離世獨居之人 li-shai'-tuuk-kue-ke'-yan, 山人 shaan-yan.
Hernia, 小腸氣 'siu-ch'eung-hi'.
Hero, 英雄 ying-huung, 豪傑 ho-kit.
Heron, 白鷺 paak-lo'.
Herring, 鱠魚 ts'o-*ue, 鯽魚 ch'i-*ue, 黃魚 wong-*ue.
Herring-bone (in sewing) 隔骨 kaak'-kwut.
Hesitate, 踟躇 ch'i-ch'ue, 思疑 sze-i, (in speaking) 呢喃 luun-chuun, 劫喀 lak-k'ak.

Heterodoxy, 異教 i'-kaau'.
Hew, (to) 斷 teuk', 削 seuk', 劈 p'ek'.
Hibernate, 潛藏 ts'im-ts'ong.
Hibiscus, (rosa) 紅花 huung-fa, (mutab) 芙蓉 foo-yuung, (manihot) 黃蜀葵 wong-shuuk-k'wai, (Syriaca) 佛桑 fut-song.
Hiccough, 打嘶嗌 'ta-sze-yik.
Hide, (to) 匿埋 nik-maai, 匿埋 ni-maai, 藏埋 ts'ong-maai.
Hide, (a) 皮張 p'i-cheung, 隻皮 chek'-p'i.
Hideous, 醜貌 'ch'au-maau', 醜惡 'ch'au-ok'.
High, 高 ko, (on high) 上高 sheung'-ko, 在上 tsoi'-sheung'.
High-water, 水大定 'shui-taai'-ting'.
Hill, 山 shaan, 陵 ling.
Hilly, 崎嶇 k'i-k'ue, 多山 toh-shaan.

Hilt, 條柄 t'iu-*peng*ʾ, 柯 oh.

Him, 佢 ʿk'ue.

Himself, 佢自己 ʿk'ue-tsze²-ʿki.

Hinder, 阻 ʿchoh, 欄阻 laan-ʿchoh.

Hindermost, 末後 moot-hauʾ, 收尾 shau-mi.

Hinge, 鉸 kaauʾ.

Hint, 謎語 mai-ʿne; (to) 打暗號 ʿta-omʾ-*hoʾ, (at) 暗指 omʾ-ʿchi.

Hip, 大腿 taaiʾ-ʿt'ui, 大髀 taaiʾ-ʿpi.

Hippocampus, 海馬 ʿhoi-ʿma.

Hippopotamus, 河馬 hoh-ʿma.

Hire, (house, &c.) 租 tso, 賃 yumʾ, (men) 任用人工 yumʾ-yuungʾ, (wages) 工銀 yan-kuung, 工銀 kuung-*ngan.

His, 佢嘅 ʿk'ue-keʾ.

Hiss, 嘶嘶 sze-sze, 嚌臺 ch'aai-t'oi.

Historian, 修史人 sau-ʿsze-yan.

History, 史記 ʿsze-kiʾ, (national) 綱鑑 kong-kaamʾ.

Hit, 打着 ʿta-cheuk, 揰親 p'uung-ts'an, (with a stone) 掟親 tengʾ-ts'an.

Hither, 到呢處 toʾ-ʿni-shueʾ.

Hitherto, 向來 heungʾ-loi, 至到今 chiʾ-toʾ-kum, 平素 p'ing-soʾ.

Hive, 蜜蜂籠 mat-fuung-*luung.

Hoard, (to) 積蓄 tsik-ch'uuk.

Hoarseness, 沙聲 sha-sheng.

Hoax, 戲弄 hiʾ-luungʾ.

Hobgoblin, 妖怪 ʿiu-kwaiʾ, 馬騮精 ʿma-*lau-tsing.

Hoe, (to) 鎊 pong, (a) 張鎊 cheung-pong, 鋤頭 ch'oh-t'au.

Hog, 猪 ʿchue.

Hog's lard, 猪油 chue-yauʾ.

Hoist, 扯 ʿch'e, 扯起 ʿch'e-ʿhi, 上 ʿsheung, 扯上 ʿch'e-ʿsheung.

Hold, (to) 把守 ˏpaˊ-ˋshau, 把持 ˏpaˊ-chʻi, 執 chup, 揸住 cha-chueˋ, (contain) 裝 chong, 藏得 tsʻong-tak, 入得 yup-tak, (fast) 定實 tingˊ-shat.
Hold, (ship's) 艙 ˏtsʻong.
Hole, 孔 ˋhuung, 寵 ˏluung.
Holiday, (to give) 放假 fongˊ-kaˊ, (a gala day) 高興日子 ko-hing-yat-ˋtsze.
Hollow, 空壟 huung-ˋluung, 凹 nup.
Hollyhock, 葵花 kʻwai-fa.
Holy, 聖 shingˊ.
Home, 家 ka, (at) 在家 tsoiˊ-ka, (go) 歸 kwai, 翻歸 fuan-kwai, 囬家 ooi-ka.
Home-made, 家欄 ka-*laan, ka-*laan-keˊ.
Hone, 潮石 chʻiu-shek.
Honest, 老實 ˋlo-shat.
Honey, 蜜糖 mat-tʻong.
Honey-comb, 蜜房 mat-fong, 蜜竇 mat-tauˊ.
Honey-suckle, 金銀花 kum-ngan-ˏfa.

Hongkong, 香港 Heung-ˋkong.
Honour, 尊貴 tsuen-kwaiˊ, (to) 敬重 kingˊ-chuungˊ.
Hood, 雪帽 suetˊ *moˊ, 頭蓋 tʻau-kʻoiˊ.
Hoof, 蹄 tʻai.
Hook, 鈎 kau, ngau.
Hoop, (to) 箍 foo, kʻoo, (a) 條篾 tʻiu-mit, (iron-) 鐵箍 tʻitˊ-foo (kʻoo).
Hoot, 喝 hoht, 喝聲 hoht-sheng.
Hop, 單脚跳 taan-keukˊ-tʻiuˊ.
Hope, 望 mongˊ, 指望 ˋchi-mongˊ.
Hoppo, 關部 kwaan-pooˊ, 海關 ˋhoi-ˏkwaan.
Horizon, 地平 tiˊ-pʻing, (visible) 天脚 tʻin-keukˊ.
Horn, 角 kokˊ, (edible deer's) 鹿茸 luuk-yuung.
Hornet, 鶯蜂 ˏang-ˏfuung, 木蜂 muuk-ˏfuung.
Horrible, 淒慘 tsʻai-ˋtsʻaam.
Horror, 嗀嫌 huuk-tsʻuuk.

Horse, 馬 ʻma, (a) 一隻馬 yat-chekʼ-ʻma.
Horse-racing, 跑馬 pʻaau-ʻma, 鬥馬 tauʼ-ʻma.
Horse-radish, 辣根 laat-kan.
Horse-shoe, 馬夾 ʻma-kaapʼ.
Horse-whip, 馬鞭 ʻma-pin.
Hose, 襪 mat, (of a fire engine) 牛喉 ngau-hau.
Hospitable, 喜客 ʻhi-haakʼ, ʻhi-haakʼ-keʼ.
Hospital, 醫館 i-ʻkoon.
Host, 主家 ʻchue-ka, (troop) 軍 kwun.
Hostages, 質 chiʼ, (to exchange) 交質 kaau-chiʼ.
Hot, 熱 it, (feverish) 燰 hingʼ.
Hotel, 客寓 haak-ueʼ, 酒店 ʻtsau-timʼ.
Hound, 獵狗 lip-ʻkau.
Hour, 點鐘 ʻtim-ʻchuung, (quarter of an) 刻 haakʼ.
House, 屋 uuk, 屋企 uuk-ʻkʻi, (a) 一間屋 yat-kaan-uuk, (mercantile) 行 *hong.
Household, 家室 ka-shat, (domestics) 家人 ka-yan.

Hovel, 寮 *liu.
Hover about, 徘徊 (pʻooi-ooi) 行吓望吓 hang-ʻha-mongʼ-ʻha, (as a bird) 飛飛吓 fi-fi-ʻha.
How, 點 ʻtim, 點樣 ʻtim-*yeungʼ, 何 hoh.
How many? 幾多 ʻki-toh, 多少 toh-ʻshiu.
However, 雖然 sui-in.
Howl, 嘷嘷聲 ho-ho-sheng, 叫 kiuʼ.
Hubbub, 喧鬧 huen-naauʼ, 吧閉 pa-paiʼ.
Huddled, 拉雜埋 lai-tsaap-maai.
Huff, (in a) 生氣 shaang-hiʼ.
Hull, (of a ship) 船身 shuen-ʻshan.
Hull rice, 舂米 chuung-ʻmai.
Hum, 宏宏聲 wang-wang-sheng, 轟轟聲 kwaang-kwaang-sheng.
Human, 人類 yan-luiʼ, yan-luiʼ-keʼ, (relations) 人倫 yan-luun.

Humane, 慈心 ts'ze-*sum*, 腹心 *fuuk-sum*.
Humanity, (benevolence) 仁 yan.
Humble, 謙遜 *him-suun*', (to) 令—— 謙卑 *ling*'——*him-pi*, (one's self) 自謙 *tsze*'-*him*.
Humbly, 伏 *fuuk*, 匐伏 *p'o-fuuk*.
Humbug, (a) 下馬威 *ha*'-*ma-wai*, (to) 噤 *t'um*'.
Humility, 謙遜 *him-suun*', 謙遜之心 *him-suun*'-*ke*'-*sum*.
Humorous, 好調笑 '*ho*-*t'iu-siu*', 好講笑 '*ho*-*kong-siu*'.
Hump-back, 陀背 *t'oh-pooi*'.
Hump, bullock's, 牛肩 *ngau-kin*.
Hundred, 百 *paak*'.
Hundredth, 第百 *tai*'-*paak*'.
Hunger, 饑餓 *ki-ngoh*'.
Hungry, 肚餓 '*t'o-ngoh*'.
Hunt, 打獵 '*ta-lip*.
Hurrah! 好 '*ho*!

Hurricane, 風颶 *fuung*-*kue*', *fuung*-*kau*'.
Hurry, (to) 催逼 *ts'ui-pik*, (in a) 忙迫 *mong-pik*, 緊急 '*kan-kup*.
Hurt, 傷 *sheung*, (by a knock) 坎親 '*hom-ts'an*.
Husband, 丈夫 *cheung*'-*foo*, (COL.) 老公 '*lo-kuung*.
Husbandman, 農夫 *nuung-foo*, 耕田人 *kang-t'in-yan*.
Hush, 禁默 *kum*'-*mak*, (hush!) 咪聲 '*mai-sheng*.
Hush-money, 揞焙手 '*om*'-*pooi*'-'*shau*.
Husks, 糠 *hong*, 糠粃 *hong-p'i*.
Husky voice, 沙聲 *sha-sheng*.
Hut, 茅屋 *maau-uuk*.
Hyacinth, (stone) 赤瑪瑙 *ch'ik*-'*ma*-'*no*.
Hymn, 神詩 *shan*-'*shi*, 聖詩 *shing*'-'*shi*.
Hyper, 太過 *t'aai*'-*kwoh*'.
Hypocrite, 偽善 *ngai*'-*shin*', 假善 '*ka-shin*'.
Hyson-tea, 熙春茶 *hi*-*ch'uun*-*ch'a*.

Hyssop, 牛膝草 ngau-sat-ʽtsʽo.

I

I, 我 ʽngoh.
Ice, 冰 ping, 冰凍 ping-tuungʼ, (commonly called in Canton) 雪 suetʼ (snow).
Idea, 意 iʼ, 意思 iʼ-szeʼ, 想頭 ʽseung-tʽau, 想像 ʽseung-tseungʼ.
Identical, 相同 seung-tʽuung, 同一個 tʽuung-yat-kohʼ.
Idiom, 講法 ʽkong-faatʼ.
Idiomatic, 講得去 ʽkong-tak-hueʼ, 依講法 i-ʽkong-faatʼ.
Idiot, 呆人 ngoi-yan.
Idiotic, 痴呆 chʽi-ngoi.
Idle, 閒 haan, (to) 偷閒 tʽau-haan.
Idol, 菩薩 pʽoo-saatʼ.
If, 若 yeuk, 倘若 ʽtʽong-yeuk, 若係 yeuk-hai.
Ignis fatuus, 鬼火 ʽkwai-ʽfoh.
Ignite, 着火 cheuk-ʽfoh.

Ignorant, 無知 mo-chi, 無見識 mo-kinʼ-shik.
Iguana, 蛤蚧 kopʼ-ʽkaai.
Ill, (sick) 有病 ʽyau-pengʼ, (bad) 不好 ʼm-ʽho.
Illegal, 犯法 faanʼ-faatʼ, 不合法 ʼm-hop-faatʼ.
Illegitimate, } 私 sze, 不法 pat-faatʼ.
Illicit,
Illiberal, 窄心 chaakʼ-sum.
Ill-natured, 猛性 ʽmang-singʼ, 嬲㷀 nau-nat.
Illness, 病 pengʼ.
Illuminate, (with lamps) 張燈 cheung-tang, (enlighten) 照光 chiuʼ-kwong.
Illustrate, 表明 ʽpiu-ming.
Illustrious, 顯達 ʽhin-taat.
Ill-will, 恨 hanʼ.
Image, 偶像 ʽngau-tseungʼ.
Imagine, 懸想 uen-ʽseung, 想 ʽseung.
Imbecile, 懦弱 nohʼ-yeuk.
Imbue, 沾 chim, 洽 haap.
Imitate, 學效 hok-haauʼ.
Immaculate, 無瑕疵 ʽmo-ha-tsʽze.

Immaterial, 無形無像 mo-ying-mo-tseung', (unimportant) 無相干 'mo-*seung*-kohn.
Immediately, 卽時 *tsik*-shi, 登時 *tang*-shi.
Immense, 極大 kik-taai'.
Immerse, 沉 chum', 浸 *tsum*'.
Imminent, the matter is, 事在旦夕 sze'-tsoi'-taan'-tsik.
Immoderate, 過頭 'kwoh-t'au, 過當 kwoh'-tong'.
Immodest, 無禮 'mo-'lai, 失禮 shat-'lai, 無廉恥 'mo-lim-'ch'i.
Immoral, 不端正 'm-tuen-ching'.
Immortality, 永生 'wing-shang.
Immutable, 不易 pat-yik.
Imp, 鬼仔 'kwai-'tsai.
Impair, 損 'suen.
Impart, 傳 ch'uen, 傳俾 ch'uen-'pi.
Impartial, 公平 kuung-p'ing.
Impatient, 着急 cheuk-kup, 無忍耐 'mo-'yan-noi'.

Impeach, 告 ko', 告狀 ko'-*chong', 醴 'lai.
Impede, 眈誤 taam-'ng', 阻住 'choh-chue'.
Impediment, 防碍 fong-ngoi'.
Impel, 推 t'ui, 催逼 ts'ui-pik, 擁去 'uung-hue'.
Impending, 臨近 lum-'k'an.
Imperative, 少不得 'shiu-pat-tak.
Imperfect, 不周全 pat-chau-ts'uen, 有缺 'yau-k'uet'.
Imperfection, 缺乏 k'uet'-faat.
Imperial, 御 ue', 欽 yum, 皇家 wong-ka.
Imperious, 霸氣 pa'-hi'.
Impertinent, 犯分 faan'-fun', 越禮犯分 uet-'lai-faan'-fun', 僭分 ts'im'-fun', (not concerned) 不關涉 'm-kwaan-ship'.
Impetuous, (disposition) 性急 sing'-kup.
Impervious, 不得透 'm-tak-t'au'.

Implacable, 硬不和 ngaang⁻-'m-woh.
Implement, 器 hi⁾, 器具 hi⁾-kue⁾.
Implicate, 拖累 t'oh-lui⁾, 株連 chue-lin, 干連 kohn-lin.
Implicitly, 無二心 mo-i⁻sum, 硬係 ngaang⁾-hai⁾.
Implied meaning, 意在言外 i⁾-tsoi⁾-in-ngoi⁾, 內意 noi⁾-i⁾.
Implore, 懇求 ʿhan-k'au.
Imply, 暗指 om⁾-ʿchi.
Import, (goods) 載——入口 tsoi⁾——yup-ʿhau.
Important, 緊要 ʿkan-iu⁾.
Importune, 嗌 ngai, 不歇求 pat-hit⁾-k'au.
Impose, 加 ka, (upon) 欺騙 hi-p'in⁾.
Impossible, 斷無 tuen⁾-ʿmo, tuen⁾-ʿmo-ke⁾, 勢不得 shai⁾-'m-tak.
Impostor, 光棍 kwong-ʿkwun⁾.
Imposts, 稅鈔 shui⁾-ch'aau⁾.

Impotence, 無能 ʿmo-nang.
Impracticable, 不做得 'm-tso⁾-tak.
Impress, 打印 ʿta-yan⁾, (the mind) 打動 ʿta-tuung⁾, 激 kik.
Imprison, 困入監 k'wun⁾-yup-ʿkaam, 收監 shau-ʿkaam.
Imprisoned, 坐監 ʿts'oh-ʿkaam.
Improbable, 難信 ʿnaan-suin⁾, 難有 naan-ʿyau, 不似真 'm-ʿts'ze-chan.
Improper, 不着 'm-cheuk.
Improve, 越好 uet-ʿho, 做更好 tso⁾-ʿkang⁻-ʿho, (the time) 愛惜光陰 oi⁾-sik-kwong-yum.
Imprudent, 無思量 ʿmo-sze-leung.
Impudent, 不識避忌 'm-shik-pi⁾-ki⁾, 放肆 fong⁾-sze⁾, 無忌憚 ʿmo-ki⁾-taan⁾.
Impure, 不潔淨 'm-kit⁾-tsing⁾.

In, (to be) 在 tsoi’, 喺 ‘hai, 喺處 ‘hai-shue’, 向處 ‘heung-shue’, (into) 入 yup.
Inaccurate, 有錯 ‘yau-ts‘oh’.
Inadequate, 不夠 ’m-kau’.
Inadmissible, 不歸得埋 ’m-kwai-tak-maai.
Inadvertence, 錯誤 ts‘oh’-’ng’, 失覺 shat-kok’.
Inadvertently, 不覺 ’m-kok’.
Inattentive, 不用心 ’m-yuung’-sum.
Inauspicious, 不吉 pat-kat, 不利市 ’m-li’-shi’.
Inborn ⎫ 生在內 shaang-’tsoi’-noi’,
In-bred ⎭ 天然 t‘in-in, 生成 shaang-sheng.
Incalculable, 不可勝數 pat-‘hoh-shing-‘sho, 無窮 mo-k‘uung.
Incapable, 不能 ’m-nang, 不會 ’m-‘ooi.
Incarnation, 降生 kong’-shang.
Incense, (to) 激怒 kik-no’.
In’cense, 香 ‚heung, (sticks) 線香 sin’-‚heung, 脚香 keuk’-‚heung.

Incessant, 不歇 pat-hit’.
Incest, 親屬相姦 ts‘an-shuuk-seung-kaan.
Inch, 寸 ts‘uen’.
Incident, 事情 sze’-ts‘ing, 偶然事 ‘ngau-in-sze’.
Incidental, 偶然 ‘ngau-in, 額外 ngaak-*ngoi’.
Incision, 刀傷 to-sheung, 刀路 to-lo’.
Incite, 勉勵 ‘min-lai’.
Incivility, 無禮 mo-‘lai.
Inclined, 偏歪 p‘in-‘me, 側的 chak-‚ti, (the mind) 心向 sum-heung’, 肯 ‘hang.
Inclose, (in a letter) 加封 ka-fuung, (by a fence) 圍埋 wai-maai.
Include, 包在內 paau-tsoi’-noi’, 包括 paau-k‘oot’.
Incoherent talk, 譖話 ngaam’-wa’.
Income, 入息 yup-sik.
Incomparable, 無雙 mo-sheung, 無比併 ‘mo-‘pi-p‘ing’.
Incompatible, 不共得埋 ’m-kuung’-tak-maai.

Incompetent, 不勝任 'm-shing-yum'.
Incomplete, 不齊 'm-ts'ai.
Incomprehensible, 不可測識 pat-'hoh-ch'ak-shik.
Incongruous } 不對 pat-tui', 唔啱 'm-'ngaam.
Inconsistent }
Inconstant, 無常 mo-sheung, 不定 pat-ting'.
Incontinent, 不自制 'm-tsze'-chai'.
Inconvenient, 不方便 'm-fong-pin'.
Incorrect, 錯 ts'oh'.
Incorrigible, 頑梗不化 waan-'kang-pat-fa'.
Incorruptible, 不壞得 'm-waai'-tak, 不買囑得 'm-'maai-chuuk-tak.
Increase, 加多 ka-toh, 加增 ka-tsang, 添 t'im.
Incredible, 不可信 pat-'hoh-suun', 不入信 'm-yup-suun'.
Incubate, 菢蛋 po'-*taan'.
Incumbent, 本分 'poon-fun', 'poon-fun'-ke'.

Incur, 致 chi', 致到 chi'-to', 招 chiu, 招惹 chiu-'ye.
Incurable, 唔醫得 'm-i-tak, 無法 'mo-faat'.
Indebted, 欠 him', 欠債 him'-chaai'.
Indecent, 非禮 fi-'lai, 粗 ts'o.
Indecision, 無決意 'mo-k'uet'-i'.
Indeed, 眞正 chan-ching', 實 shat, 委實 'wai-shat. 實在 shat-tsoi'.
Indefatigable, 無倦 'mo-kuen'.
Indefinite, 不限定 'm-haan-ting'.
Indelible, 不用得 'm-lut-tak.
Indemnify, 賠翻 p'ooi-faan.
Independent, 自立 tsze'-laap, 不靠 pat-k'aau', 另自 ling'-tsze'.
Index, 目錄 muuk-luuk.
India, 印度國 Yan'-to'-kwok'.
Indian corn, 粟米 suuk-'mai, 包粟 paau-suuk.

Indian ink, 墨 mak.
India-rubber, 象皮 tseungʾ-pʻi, 印度樹膠 Yanʾ-toʾ-shueʾ-kaau.
Indicate, 指示 ʻchi-shiʾ.
Indict, 告狀 koʾ-*chongʾ.
Indifferent, 薄情 pok-tsʻing, 冷淡 ʻlaang-taamʾ, (any way) 隨隨便便 tsʻui-tsʻui-pinʾ-pinʾ (*pinʾ).
Indigestion, 食滯 shik-chaiʾ.
Indignant, 憾恨 homʾ-hanʾ.
Indignation, 惱恨 nau-hanʾ.
Indigo, 藍靛 laam-tinʾ, (the tree) 藍樹 laam shueʾ.
Indirect, 非直頭 fi-chik-tʻau, ʾm-haiʾ-chik-tʻau.
Indiscreet, 不仔細 pat-ʻtsze-saiʾ.
Indiscriminately, 無分彼此 ʻmo-fun-ʻpi-ʻtsʻze.
Indispensable, 必需 pit-sue, pit-sue-keʾ, 少不得 ʻshiu-pat-tak.
Indisposed, 欠安 himʾ-ohn, 不自在 ʾm-tszeʾ-tsoiʾ, 唔 nup, (disinclined) 不想 ʾm-ʻseung.

Indissoluble, 不化得開 ʾm-faʾ-tak-hoi, 不離得開 ʾm-li-tak-hoi.
Indistinct, 不明白 ʾm-ming-paak, 未清楚 miʾ-tsʻing-ʻchʻoh.
Individual, 位 waiʾ, (an) 一個人 yat-kohʾ-yan, (thing) 件 kinʾ, (See A.), (by itself) 另自 lingʾ-tszeʾ.
Indivisible, 不分得 ʾm-fun-tak.
Indolent, 躲懶 ʻtoh-ʻlaan.
Indomitable, 不認輸 put-yingʾ-shue.
Induce, 誘 ʻyau, 招引 chiu-ʻyan.
Indulge, 姑息 koo-sik, 縱慣 tsuungʾ-kwaanʾ, 放縱 fongʾ-tsuungʾ.
Indulgent, 寬大 foon-taaiʾ, (self) 自暇 tszeʾ-haʾ, 自縱 tszeʾ-tsuungʾ.
Industrious, 勤工 kʻan-kuung.
Inefficacious, 不靈 pat-leng, ʾm-leng, 不應 ʾm-yingʾ.

Inert, 懶 ʻlaan, 不會郁 'm-ʻooi-yuuk.

Inestimable, 無價寶 ʻmo-kaʼ-ʻpo.

Inevitable, 不免得 'm-ʻmin-tak, 無奈何 ʻmo-noiʼ-hoh.

Inexcusable, 無可推諉 ʻmo-ʻhoh-tʻui-ʻwai, 無可恕 ʻmo-ʻhoh-shuʼ.

Inexhaustible, 無窮盡 ʻmo-kʻuung-tsuunʼ.

Inexpedient, 不便宜 'm-pinʼ-i.

Inexperienced, 生手 shaang-ʻshau.

Inexplicable, 無可解 ʻmo-ʻhoh-ʻkaai.

Inexpressible, 言不能盡 in-pat-nang-tsuunʼ, 講不了 ʻkong-'m-ʻliu.

Inextricable, 解不出 ʻkaai-pat-chʻuut, ʻkaai-'m-lut.

Infamous, 臭 chʻauʼ, 醜 ʻchʻau.

Infant, 嬰兒 ying-i, 亞蘇仔 aʼ-ʻso-ʻtsai.

Infantry, 步兵 pooʼ-ping.

Infatuated, 瘋癲 fuung-tin, 入迷魂陣 yup-mai-wan-chanʼ.

Infect, 染 ʻim, 感染 ʻkom-ʻim.

Infectious, 會染 ʻooi-ʻim, 感染 ʻkom-ʻim, ʻkom-ʻim-keʼ.

Infer, 推度 tʻui-tok, 類推 ʻlui-tʻui.

Inferior, 下等 haʼ-ʻtang, 呤 yai, (goods) 呤貨 yai-fohʼ.

Infernal, 地獄噉 tiʼ-yuuk-ʻkom.

Infest, 紛擾 fun-ʻiu.

Infinite, 無窮 mo-kʻuung, 無限 mo-haanʼ.

Infirm, 衰弱 shui-yeuk.

Inflame, 憂猛火氣 pʻootʼ-ʻmang-foh-hiʼ.

Inflammation, 結熱 kitʼ-it.

Inflate, 鼓起 ʻkoo-ʻhi, (magnify) 張大 cheung-taaiʼ.

Inflexible, 堅硬 kin-ngaangʼ.

Inflict, 加 ka.

Influence, 勢子 shai⁰-ʿtsze, (example) 風化 fuung-fa⁰, (to) 感動 ʿkom-tuung⁰, 化 fa⁰.
Infold, 包裹 paau-ʿkwoh.
Inform, 話——知 wa⁰——chi, 通知 tʻuung-chi.
Infuriated, 嬲嬲爆 nau-nau-paau⁰.
Infuse, (tea) 冲茶 chʻuung-chʻa, (METAPH.) 浸入去 tsum⁰-yup-hue⁰.
Ingenious, 精乖 tseng-kwaai, 精巧 tsing-ʿhaau.
Ingenuous, 無私心 ʿmo-sze-sum, 直白 chik-paak, 慷慨 ʿkʻong-kʻoi⁰, 光明正大 kwong-ming-chingʿ-taai⁰.
Ingot, 錠 ting⁰, 元寶錠 uen-ʿpo-ting⁰.
Ingratitude, 忘恩 mong-yan.
Ingulf, 吞陷 tʻun-haam⁰.
Inhabit, 居 kue.
Inhabitant, 居民 kue-mun.
Inhale, 吸 kʻup, 嗊入 shok⁰-yup.

Inherent, 生在內 shang-tsoi⁰-noi⁰, 自內有 tsze⁰-noi⁰-yau.
Inherit, 承 shing, 嗣 tszeʿ.
Inheritance, 家業 ka-ip.
Inhuman, 無人性 ʿmo-yan-sing⁰, 狼心 long-sum.
Inimitable, 不及得 ʼm-kʻaap-tak.
Iniquitous, 無道 ʿmo-to⁰.
Initiate, 開例 hoi-lai⁰, (introduce) 引進 ʿyan-tsuun⁰, 引入 ʿyan-yup.
Injure, 害 hoi⁰, 損害 ʿsuen-hoi⁰, 傷害 sheung-hoi⁰.
Injurious, 利害 liʿ-hoi⁰.
Ink, 墨 mak, (liquid) 墨水 mak-ʿshui.
Ink-stand, 墨水池 mak-ʿshui-chʻi.
Ink-stone, 墨硯 mak-in (*in⁰).
Inland, 內地 noi⁰-tiʿ.
Inlay, 鑲 seung.
Inlet, 入處 yup-chʻue⁰.
Inmost, 至深 chiʿ-shum, (heart) 深心 shum-sum.

Inn, 歇店 hitʼ-timʼ, 客館 haakʼ-ʿkoon.
Innate, 天然 tʻin-in, 生在內 shang-tsoiʼ-noiʼ.
Inner, 內 noiʼ.
Innocent, 無罪 ʿmo-tsuiʼ.
Innocuous, 無毒 ʿmo-tuuk.
Innovate, 新入 san-yup.
Innovation, 新冲之事 san-chʻuung-chi-szeʼ.
Innuendo, 暗剌 omʼ-tsʻzeʼ.
Innumerable, 不可勝數 patʼ-ʿhoh-shing-ʿsho, 了不得 ʿliu-pat-tak-komʼ, 吥多 ʿtoh.
Inoculate, 種痘 chuungʼ-*tauʼ.
Inordinate, 無節制 ʿmo-tsitʼ-chaiʼ, 濫 laamʼ.
Inquest, 驗屍 imʼ-shi.
Inquire, 訪問 ʿfong-munʼ.
Inquisitive, 好查問 hoʼ-chʻa-munʼ.
Insane, 發癲 faatʼ-tin.
Insatiable, 無厭 ʿmo-imʼ, 不知足 ʼm-chi-tsuuk.
Inscription, 碑文 pi-mun, 扁額 ʿpin-ngaak.

Inscrutable, 不可測 patʼ-ʿhoh-chʻak.
Insect, 蟲 chʻuung, 細腰蟲 saiʼ-iu-chʻuung.
Insecure, 不穩 ʼm-ʿwan.
Insensible, 無知覺 ʿmo-chi-kokʼ, 痲痳 ma-muuk, 不省人事 ʼm-ʿsing-yan-szeʼ.
Inseparable, 解不開 ʿkaai-ʼm-hoi, 不分得 ʼm-fun-tak.
Insert, 插入 chʻaapʼ-yup, 入 yup, 鑲 seung.
Inside, 裏頭 ʿlue-tʻau, 裏面 ʿlue-minʼ, 內 noiʼ.
Insidious, 多變 toh-pinʼ, 奸猾 kaan-waat.
Insignificant, 微毫 mi-ho, 微末 mi-moot, 虛 hue.
Insincere, 不至誠 ʼm-chiʼ-shing.
Insinuate, 讒佞 tsʻaam-ningʼ, 偷偷入 ʿtʻau-ʿtʻau-yup.
Insipid, 淡 taamʼ, ʻtʻaam, 無味道 ʿmo-miʼ-toʼ.

Insist, 勒令 lak-ling', 必要 pit-iu'.
Insnare, 陷害 haam'-hoi', 籠絡 luung-lok'.
Insolent, 傲慢 ngo'-maan', 侮慢人嘅 'moo-maan'-yan-ke'.
Insoluble, 不化得 'm-fa'-tak, 不解得 'm-ˋkaai-tak.
Insolvent, 債墩 chaai'-ˋtun.
Insomuch, 致于 chi'-ue, 致到 chi'-to', 甚至 shum'-chi'.
Inspect, 查察 ch'a-ch'aat', 監 kaam, 督 tuuk.
Inspector, 監督 kaam-tuuk.
Inspire, 吸氣 k'up-hi', (divinely) 默牖 mak-ˋyau.
Inspirit, 悚起 ˋsuung-ˋhi, 聳動 ˋsuung-tuung'.
Instable, 不穩 'm-ˋwan.
Instance, (for) 比如 ˋpi-ue.
Instant, 片刻 p'in'-haak'.
Instead, (of) 替代 t'ai'-toi'.
Instep, 脚背彎 keuk'-pooi'-waan.
Instigate, 唆悚 soh-ˋsuung.

Instil, 浸入去 tsum'-yup-hue'.
Instinct, 性情 sing'-ts'ing, 本性 ˋpoon-sing'.
Institute, 設 ch'it'.
Instruct, 教 kaau'.
Instruction, 教訓 kaau'-fun', 教令 kaau'-ling'.
Instrument, 器具 hi'-kue'.
Insubordination, 違逆 wai-yik.
Insufferable, 不忍得 'm-ˋyan-tak, 'm-ˋyan-tak-ke'.
Insufficient, 不够 'm-kau'.
Insult, 欺負 hi-foo', 凌辱 ling-yuuk, 侮慢 ˋmoo-maan'.
Insuperable, 過不得 kwoh'-pat-tak, kwoh'-'m-tak-ke', 不過得去 'm-kwoh'-tak-hue'.
Insupportable, 當不起 tong-pat-ˋhi, tong-'m-ˋhi-ke'.
Insurance, 保險 ˋpo-ˋhim.
Insure, 買保險 ˋmaai-ˋpo-ˋhim.
Insurrection, 作亂 tsok'-luen'.

Integrity, 純厚 shuun-hau', 剛正 kong-ching'.
Intelligence, 見識 kin'-shik, (news) 聲氣 sheng-hi'.
Intelligent, 聰明 ts'uung-ming.
Intelligible, 明白 ming-paak.
Intemperance, 放恣 fong'-ts'ze', 縱恣 tsuung'-ts'ze', 無度 mo-to'.
Intend, 意欲 i'-yuuk, 欲 yuuk, 想 ʻseung.
Intense, 極甚 kik-shum'.
Intention, 意思 i'-sze', 意 i'.
Intentioned, 有意 ʻyau-i', 故意 koo'-i'.
Intentness, 專心 chuen-sum.
Inter, 葬埋 tsong'-maai.
Intercalary, 閏 yuun'.
Intercede, 代求 toi'-kʻau.
Intercept, 攔截 laan-tsit.
Interchange, 相換 seung-oon', 交易 kaau-yik.
Intercourse, 交接 haau-tsip', 往來 ʻwong-loi.
Interdict, 禁戒 kum'-kaai'.
Interest, 利息 li'-sik, 利錢 li'-tsʻin.

Interest, (to move) 打動 ʻta-tuung', (concern) 關 kwaan.
Interesting, 引動个心 ʻyan-tuung'-koh'-sum.
Interfere, 涉 ship', 理 ʻli, 打理 ʻta-ʻli, (meddle) 插手 chʻaap'-ʻshau, 插嘴 chʻaap'-ʻtsui.
Interim, 時間 shi-kaan.
Interior, 內地 noi'-ti', 裏頭 ʻluc-tʻau.
Interlace, 變加 ʻkaau-ʻka.
Interleave, 隔紙 kaak'-ʻchi.
Intermediate, 中間 ʻchuung-ʻkaan.
Intermission, 停息之間 tʻing-sik-chi-kaan.
Intermit, 間歇 kaan'-hit'.
Internal, 內 noi'.
International law, 萬國公法 maan'-kwok'-kuung-faat'.
Interpolate, 混入字句 wan'-yup-tsze'-kue'.
Interpose, 入中間 yup-ʻchuung-ʻkaan, 入其中 yup-kʻi-chuung.

Interpret, 傳話 ch'uen-*wa’, 解 ʿkaai.
Interpreter, 通事 t'uung-*sze’, 傳供 ch'uen-kuung, (official) 繙譯官 faan-yik-koon.
Interrogate, 盤問 p'oon-mun’.
Interrupt, 阻斷 ʿchoh-ʿt'uen, 阻定 ʿchoh-ting’, 攪轉處 ʿkaau-ʿchuen-shue’.
Intersect, 相交 seung-kaau.
Interstice, 疏罅 shoh-la’.
Interval, 間 kaan.
Intervene, 入中間 yup-ʿchuung-ʿkaan.
Interview, 面見 min’-kin’.
Intestines, 腸 ch'eung, *ch'eung.
Intimate, 相熟 seung-shuuk, 親 ts'an, 親近 ts'an-kan’, (to) 告知 ko’-chi.
Intimidate, 恐嚇 ʿhuung-haak’, 嚇壓 ha-aat’, (in order to extort) 嚇霸 ha-pa’.
Into, 入 yup, 入內 yup-noi’.

Intolerable, 難容 naan-yuung, 不容得 ’m-yuung-tak, 不抵得 ’m-ʿtai-tak.
Intoxicated, 醉酒 tsui’-ʿtsau.
Intoxicating, 會醉人 ʿooi-tsui’-yan, ʿooi-tsui’-ke’.
Intractable, 不受教 ’m-shau’-kaau’.
Intrenchment, 營壘 ying-ʿlui.
Intrepid, 膽生毛 ʿtaam-shaang-mo.
Intricate, 錯雜 ts'ok’-tsaap.
Intrigue, 詭詐 ʿkwai-cha’, (to) 挑唆 t'iu-soh, 奸計 kaan-kai’.
Introduce, 引入 ʿyan-yup, 引進 ʿyan-tsuun’, 引見 ʿyan-kin’, (a subject) 提起 t'ai-ʿhi, 挈 k'it’.
Introduction, (to a book) 小引 ʿsiu-ʿyan, (recommendation) 荐書 tsin’-shue.
Intrude, 搪揬 t'ong-tat, 插入 ch'aap’-yup, 撞入去 chong’-yup-hue’.
Intrusive, 躁暴 ts'o’-po’.

Intrust, 托 t'ok', 交托 kaau-t'ok'.
Intuitively, (to know) 生而知之 shang-i-chi-chi.
Inundate, 水漲 'shui-cheung', 水浸 'shui-tsum', 水浸哂 'shui-tsum'-saai'.
Inundation, 潦水 'lo-'shui.
Invade, 侵入去 ts'um-yup-hue'.
Invalid, 病壞 peng'-waai'.
Invaluable, 無價寶 mo-ka'-'po.
Invariable, 不易 pat-yik.
Inveigh, 鬧 naau'.
Inveigle, 鈎引 kau-'yan.
Invent, 製造 chai'-tso'.
Inventory, 物業單 mat-ip-,taan.
Invert, 倒轉 'to-'chuen.
Inverted, 顛倒 tin-'to.
Invest, with, 加 ka, (money for profit) 出息 ch'uut-sik, (in property) 置實業 chi'-shat-ip.
Investigate, 查察 ch'a-ch'aat', 追究 chui-kau'.

Inveterate, 舊無改 kan'-'mo-'koi, 根深柢固 kan-shum-'tai-koo', 久病難醫 'kau-peng'-naan-i.
Invidious, 招妒忌 chiu-to'-ki'.
Invigorate, 補力 'po-lik.
Invincible, 無敵 'mo-tik.
Inviolable, 不傷犯得 'm-sheung-faan'-tak.
Invisible, 無形可見 'mo-ying-'hoh-kin'.
Invitation-card, 請帖 'ts'eng-'t'ip.
Invite, 請 'ts'eng.
Invoice, 貨單 foh'-,taan.
Invoke, 呼籲 foo-yeuk'.
Involve, 拖累 t'oh-lui', 連累 lin-lui'.
Involuntary, 不做得主 'm-tso'-tak-'chue.
Inward, 內 noi'.
Ipomœa, 錦屏風 'kum-p'ing-,fuung, (reptans) 甕菜 ung'-ts'oi'.
Iris, 眼睛 'ngaan-,tsing, 烏睛 oo-,tsing, (flower) 亡憂花 mong-yau-,fa.

Iron, 鐵 t'it', (for clothes) 熨斗 t'ong'-ʿtau, (to) 熨 t'ong'.
Ironically, to speak, 鑿人 tsok-yan, 反倒轉講 ʿfaan-ʿto-ʿchuen-ʿkong.
Irony, 杯獎話 pooi-ʿtseung-*wa'.
Irrational, 無情理 ʿmo-tsʿing-ʿli.
Irrecoverable, 不得翻 'm-tak-faan.
Irregular, 亂 luen', 無法度 ʿmo-faat'-to', 不齊 'm-tsʿai.
Irrelevent, 丫丫開 a-a-hoi, nga-nga-hoi.
Irremediable, 無奈何 ʿmo-noi'-hoh, 無法可救 ʿmo-faat'-ʿhoh-kau'.
Irresistible, 無人敵得住 ʿmo-yan-tik-tak-chue'.
Irresolute, 無主意 ʿmo-ʿchue-i', 無定性 ʿmo-ting'-sing'.
Irrigate, 灌溉 koon'-k'oi', 淋瀨 lum-laai'.

Irritable, 嬲嫩 nau-nat, 火頸 ʿfoh-ʿkeng.
Irritate, 激嬲 kik-nau, 撩起 ʿliu-ʿhi.
Irritated, 谷氣 kuuk-hi'.
Is, 係 hai', 是 shi', (there is) 有 ʿyau.
Isinglass, 魚膠 ue-kaau.
Island, 海島 ʿhoi-ʿto, 海洲 ʿhoi-chau.
Isolated, 另自 ling'-tsze'.
Issue, (to) 發 faat', 出 chʿuut.
Isthmus, 山腰 shaan-iu.
It, 佢 ʿkʿue.
Itch, 癩 laai'.
Itching, 痕 han, 痕癢 han-ʿyeung.
Itinerary, 路程 lo'-chʿing.
Ivory, 象牙 tseung'-nga.
Ivy, 藤 t'ang, 長春藤 chʿeung-chʿuun-t'ang.

J

Jabber, 孜孜咁咁 tsze-tsze-tsa-tsa.
Jacana, 白勝雞 paak-shing'-kai.

Jacinth, 赤玉 ch'ik-yuuk.	Jargon, 譖話 ngaam'-wa'.
Jack-fruit, 波羅蜜 poh-loh-mat.	Jasper, 碧玉 pik-yuuk.
Jackal, 野狗 'ye-'kau, 狗獾 'kau-foon.	Jatropha, 桐樹 t'uung-shue'.
	Jaundice, 黃疸 wong-'t'aan.
Jack-daw, 烏雀 oo-tseuk'.	Jaunt, 出遊 ch'uut-yau.
Jacket, 短衫 'tuen-,shaam.	Java-sparrow, 和鵠 ·woh-kuuk.
Jadestone, 璧 pik, 玉石 yuuk-shek.	Javelin, 手箭 'shau-tsin', 標 piu.
Jagged, 狗牙樣 'kau-nga-*yeung'.	Jaw, 牙牀 nga-ch'ong.
	Jaw-bone, 牙關骨 nga-kwaan-kwut.
Jail, 監房 kaam-fong.	
Jailer, 司獄 sze-yuuk, 看監 ,hohn-,kaam, 禁子 kum'-'tsze.	Jay, 鵲 ts'euk.
	Jealous, 妒忌 to'-ki'.
	Jealousy, 嫉妒 tsat-to'.
Jam, 糖菓 t'ong-'kwoh, (to) 逼 pik, 逼實 pik-shat, 逼緊 pik-'kan.	Jeer, 戲弄 hi'-luung', 欺笑 hi-siu', 譏誚 ki-ts'iu'.
	JEHOVAH, 耶和華 YE-WOH-WA.
Jangle, 吵鬧 'ch'aau-naau'.	
January, 英正月 Ying-ching-uet.	Jelly, 菓汁 'kwoh-chup, (animal) 糕 ,ko, (generally) 凍 'tuung.
Japan, 日本國 Yat-'poon-kwok'.	
	Jeopardy, 危險 ngai-'him.
Jar, (a) 埕 ch'ing, 塔 t'aap', 甖 ,aang, 瓶 *p'eng, 甕缸 uung'-kong, (to) 相摐 seung-p'uung', 爭拗 chaang-aau'.	Jerk, 力逼 lik-pik, 扭 'nau.
	Jessamine, 茉莉花 moot-li'-fa.
	Jest, 講笑 'kong-siu'.
	Jesting, 笑話 siu'-*wa'.

JESUS, 耶穌 YE-*SOO*.
Jet, (fossil) 黑玉 *hak*-yuuk,
(of water) 射水 she'-'shui,
浙水線 chit-'shui-sin'.
Jetty, 馬頭 'ma-*t'au.
Jew, 猶太人 Yau-t'aai'-yan.
Jewel, 珍寶 chan-'po, 寶玉 'po-yuuk.
Jigger, 沙虱 sha-shat.
Jingall, 銃 ch'uung'.
Jingle, 响動聲 'heung-tuung'-sheng, (COL.) kwing-kwang, kwang-lang.
Job, (a) 一件工夫 yat-kin'-kuung-foo.
Job-work, 散工 'saan-'kuung.
Jog, 揰 p'uung', (along) 躊躊吓 'ch'au-'ch'au-'ha.
Joggle, 謷 ngo.
Join, 連 lin, 合埋 hop-maai, 附貼 foo'-t'ip'.
Joint, 節 tsit', (ginglymus) 骨計 kwat-*kai'.
Joint-stock, 合本 hop-'poon.
Joist, 樓陣 *lau-chan', 桁 *haang.

Joke, (to) 講笑 'kong-siu', 調笑 t'iu-siu', 打諢 'ta-wun'.
Jolly, 福相 fuuk-seung', 寬容 foon-yuung, 爽快 'shong-faai'.
Jolt, 嘌蕩 p'iu-tong', 移移郁 i-i-yuuk.
Jonquil, 水仙花 'shui-'sin-fa.
Jostle, 搒郁 p'uung'-yuuk.
Jot, 點 'tim.
Journal, 日記 yat-ki'.
Journey, 路程 lo'-ch'ing, 程 ch'ing.
Jovial, 快活 faai'-oot.
Joy, 喜樂 'hi-lok.
Jubilee, 禧年 hi-nin.
Judea, 猶太國 Yau-t'aai-kwok'.
Judge, 按察司 ohn'-ch'aat'-sze, 審事官 'shum-sze-koon, (to) 審判 'shum-p'oon'.
Judgment-day, 審判日子 'shum-p'oon'-yat-'tsze.
Judicious, 好打算 'ho-'ta-suen'.

Jug, 耳瓶 ʻi-*pʻeng.
Jugglery, 斥法 chʻik-faatʼ.
Juice, 汁 chup, 汁漿 chup-tseung.
Jujube, 棗 ʻtso.
July, 英七月 Ying-tsʻat-uet.
Jumble, 打混 ʻta-wunʼ, 混亂 wunʼ-luenʼ.
Jump, 跳 tʻiuʼ, up and down, 噏噏吓 ngup-ngup-*haʼ.
Junction, 相交處 seung-kaau-chʻueʼ.
June, 英六月 Ying-luuk-uet.
Jungle, 叢林 tsʻuung-lum.
Junior, 少年 shiuʼ-nin, 少 shiuʼ, 後生 hauʼ-ʻshaang.
Juniper, 扁柏 ʻpin-pʻaakʼ.
Junk, 船 shuen, 大眼雞 taaiʼ-ʻngaan-ʻkai.
Jupiter, (planet) 木星 muuk-ʻsing.
Jury, 秉公之人 ʻping-kuung-chi-yan, 陪審官 pʻooi-ʻshum-koon.

Just, 公平 kuung-pʻing, 公道 kuung-toʼ, (ADV.) 僅 ʻkan, 啱啱 ʻngaam-ʻngaam, 剛啱 ʻkong-ʻngaam.
Justice, 公道 kuung-toʼ, 公義 kuung-iʼ, (to do) 秉公 ʻping-kuung, Chief 按察司 ohnʼ-chʻaat-sze,—of peace 紳士 shan-szeʼ.
Justify, 以爲義 ʻi-wai-iʼ.
Jut-out, 凸出來 tut-chʻuut-lai.
Juvenile, 嫩 nuenʼ.

K

Kaleidoscope, 萬花筒 maanʼ-fa-tʻuung.
Kalpa, 刼 kipʼ.
Keel, 艣 ngo.
Keen, 快利 faaiʼ-liʼ, 爽利 ʻshong-liʼ, 關係 kwaan-haiʼ.
Keep, 守 ʻshau, 留 lau, 收埋 shau-maai, 常有 sheung-ʻyau, 存 tsʻuen.

Keeper, 看守人 hohn-ʻshau-yan.
Keepsake, 表記 ʻpiu-kiʼ.
Kerchief, 巾 kan.
Kernel, 核 wat, 仁 yan, ngan, 粒 nup.
Kerosine, 煤油 mooi-yau, 火水 ʻfoh-ʻshui.
Ketchup, 豉油 shiʼ-yau.
Kettle, 提壺 tʻai-*oo, 煲 ₍po.
Key, 鎖匙 ʻsoh-shi.
Key-hole, 鎖匙眼 ʻsoh-shi-ʻngaan.
Khan, 可汗 ʻhoh-hohnʼ.
Kick, 踢 tʻekʼ.
Kid, 山羊仔 shaan-*yeung-ʻtsai.
Kidnap, 拐帶 ʻkwaai-taaiʼ.
Kidnapper, 拐帶佬 ʻkwaai-taaiʼ-ʻlo, 拐子佬 ʻkwaai-ʻtsze-ʻlo.
Kidney, 內腎 noiʼ-shanʼ, (of beasts) 腰子 iu-ʻtsze.
Kill, 殺 shaatʼ, 殺死 shaatʼ-ʻsze, 打死 ʻta-ʻsze, 整死 ʻching-ʻsze, (animals) 劏 tʻong.

Kiln, 窰 iu, 燒窰 shiu-iu.
Kind, (sort) 類 luiʼ, 樣 yeungʼ, *yeungʼ, 種 ʻchuung.
Kind, (good) 好心田 ʻho-sum-tʻin, 腹心 fuuk-sum.
Kindle, 起火 ʻhi-ʻfoh, 着火 cheuk-ʻfoh, 透火 tʻauʼ-ʻfoh.
Kindness, 惠愛 waiʼ-oiʼ.
Kindred, 親戚 tsʻan-tsʻik.
King, 王 wong.
King-crab, 鱟 hauʼ.
Kingdom, 國 kwokʼ.
Kingfisher, 釣魚郎 tiuʼ-ue-long, (feathers of) 翠毛 tsʻuiʼ-mo.
Kiss, 啜面脥 chuet-minʼ-chue, 親嘴 tsʻan-ʻtsui.
Kitchen, 廚房 chʻue-*fong, (opsonium) 送 suungʼ.
Kite, (bird) 鳶 uen, (paper) 紙鷂 ʻchi-*iu, (to fly) 放紙鷂 fongʼ-ʻchi-*iu.
Knapsack, 背袋 pooiʼ-*toiʼ.
Knave, 光棍 kwong-kwunʼ.
Knead, 搓 chʻaai (COL.) nuuk.
Knee, 膝 sat, 膝頭哥 sat-tʻau-koh.

Knee-pan, 膝頭骨 sat-tʻau-kwut.
Kneel, 屈膝 wat-sat, 跪下 kwaiʼ-haʼ.
Knife, 刀 to, (a) 一張刀 yat-ˍcheung-ˍto, 一把刀 yat-ˈpa-ˍto.
Knight, 巴圖魯 pa-tʻo-ˈlo.
Knit, 挑織 tʻiu-chik, (the brows) 皺眉頭 tsauʼ-mi-tʻau.
Knob, 粒珠 nup-ˍchue, 粒凸 nup-tuet, 粒頂 nup-ˈteng, 鈕 ˈnau.
Knock, 打 ˈta, 拍 pʻaakʼ, 揿 ˈhom.
Knocking, (COL.) pop-pop.
Knot, (to) 打結 ˈta-kitʼ, ˈta-litʼ, (a) 結頭 kitʼ-tʻau, litʼ-tʻau, (in wood) 罌 ˍang, (any thing small) 粒 nup.
Know, 知 chi, 知到 chi-toʼ, 識 shik, 識得 shih-tak.
Knowledge, 見識 kinʼ-shik.
Knuckle, 拳頭骨 kʻuen-tʻau-kwut.
Kohl rabi, 芥蘭頭 kaaiʼ-*laan-tʻau.

L

Label, 號標 hoʼ-ˍpiu, 號頭紙 hoʼ-tʻau-ˈchi.
Laborious, 辛苦 san-ˈfoo, 勤苦 kʻan-ˈfoo.
Labour, 工夫 kuung-foo, (to) 做工夫 tsoʼ-kuung-foo, 勞力 lo-lik, (in-) 臨產 lum-ˈchʻaan.
Labourer, 工人 kuung-yan.
Labyrinth, 曲折 huuk-chitʼ.
Labrus, 黃花魚 wong-fa-*ue.
Lac, 紫梗 ˈtsze-ˈkang.
Lace, 織線衣邊 chik-sinʼ-i-ˍpin, 花邊 fa-ˍpin, 線帶 sinʼ-*taaiʼ.
Lacerate, 抓爛 ˈchaau-laanʼ.
Lack, 少 ˈshiu, 欠 himʼ, 無 ˈmo.
Lacker, 漆 tsʻat, (ware) 漆器 tsʻat-hiʼ.
Lad, 細蚊仔 saiʼ-ˍmun-ˈtsai, 童 tʻuung, 後生 hauʼ-ˍshaang.

Ladder, 梯 t'ai, (a hand-) 手梯 ʻshau-t'ai.
Lade, (to load) 落貨 lok-foh’, (to lift) 扃 foo’, 舀 ʻiu, 拂 fut.
Ladle, 杓 sheuk’, 勺 cheuk’, 殼 hok’.
Lady, 娘 neung, 師奶 sze-ʻnaai, 奶奶 ʻnaai-ʻnaai, 夫人 foo-yan.
Lady's maid, 梳頭媽 shoh-t'au-*ʻma.
Lag, 落後便 lok-hau’-pin’.
Lake, 湖 oo.
Lamb, 綿羊仔 min-*yeung-ʻtsai, 羔 ko.
Lame, 跛脚 pai-keuk’.
Lament, 嘆惜 t'aan’-sik, 哭訴 huuk-so’.
Lamentable, 可哀 ʻhoh-oi.
Lamp, 燈 tang, 盞燈 ʻchaan-ʻtang, 枝燈 chi-ʻtang, 眼燈 *ʻngaan-ʻtang.
Lamp-chimney, 燈筒 tang-*t'uung.
Lamp-shade, 燈罩 ʻtang-chaau’.

Lamp-wick, 燈心 tang-sum.
Lamp-black, 烏烟 oo-in.
Lampoon, 白抄 paak-ch'aau.
Lance, 鎗矛 ts'eung-maau.
Lancet, 開瘡刀 hoi-ch'ong-to.
Land, 地 ti’, (cultivated) 田 t'in, (by) 旱路 ʻhohn-lo’, (to) 上岸 ʻsheung-ngohn’.
Landing-place, 步頭 po’-t'au, 馬頭 ʻma-t'au.
Landlord, 屋主 uuk-ʻchue, 地主 ti’-ʻchue, (of an inn) 店主 tim’-ʻchue.
Landscape, 光景 kwong-ʻking, 山水景 shaan-ʻshui-ʻking.
Lane, 巷 *hong’, 冷巷 ʻlaang-*hong’.
Language, 話 *wa’, (speech) 口音 ʻhau-yum.
Languid, 神倦 shan-kuen’, 懶倦 p'aai’-kuen’.
Lank, 凹 nup, 凹 nep’.
Lantern, 燈籠 tang-luung.
Lap, 膝頭處 sat-t'au-shue’, 衫被 shaam-p'i, (to) 舐 ʻlim, (COL.) ʻlaai.

Lapel, 衽 ʻyum.
Lapse, 過 kwohʼ.
Larboard, 船左 shuen-ʻtsoh.
Lard, 猪油 chue-yau.
Large, 大 taaiʼ.
Lark, 百鴿 paakʼ-ling, 山麻雀 shaan-ma-tseukʼ.
Larkspur, 彩雀花 ʻtsʻoi-tseuk-fa.
Larva, 蠐螬 tsʻai-tsʻo, 蟲 chʻuung.
Lascivious, 淫亂 yum-luenʼ.
Lash, 鞭 pin.
Last, 末 moot, 尾 ʻmi, 收尾 shau-ʻmi, (year, &c.) 昨 tsok, 舊 kauʼ, (to) 久存 ʻkau-tsʻuen, 留 lau, 賡 kʻum.
Last, (a) 鞋楦 haai-huenʼ.
Latch, (a door-) 門軌 moon-ʻkwai.
Late, 遲 chʻi, 慢 maanʼ, (in the day) 晏 aanʼ, 挨晚 ʻaai-ʻmaan, aai-*ʻmaan, (at night) 夜 yeʼ.
Lately, 近來 kanʼ-loi, 就先 tsauʼ-sin.

Latest, 至後 chiʼ-hauʼ, 至新 chiʼ-san.
Lath, 木片 muuk-pʻinʼ, 桷 kokʼ.
Lath and plaster wall, 假墻 ʻka-tsʻeung.
Lathe, 車牀 chʻe-chʻong.
Latitude, 地緯度 tiʼ-ʻwai-toʼ.
Lattice, 欖核格 ʻlaam-wat-kaakʼ, 象眼籬 tseungʼ-ʻngaan-li.
Laudable, 讚得過 tsaanʼ-tak-kwohʼ.
Laudanum, 鴉片酒 a-pʻinʼ-ʻtsau.
Laugh, 笑 siuʼ.
Laughable, 好笑 ʻho-siuʼ.
Laughing stock, 笑柄 siuʼ-pengʼ, 酸梅 suen-*mooi.
Laurel, 桂 kwaiʼ, 丹桂 taan-kwaiʼ.
Lavish, 破費 pʻohʼ-faiʼ.
Law, 法律 faatʼ-luut, 律例 luut-laiʼ, (to go to) 打官司 ʻta-koon-sze.
Lawyer, 狀師 chongʼ-ʻsze.

Law-suit, 官訟 koon-tsuung'. 案件 ohn'-*kin'.
Lawsonia, 指甲花 'chi-kaap'-fa.
Lax, 鬆 suung, (morally) 心鬆 sum-suung.
Laxative, 微利藥 mi-li'-yeuk.
Lay, (to) 放下 fong'-'ha, (up) 藏 ts'ong, 藏埋 ts'ong-maai, 擠埋 chai-maai.
Layer, 層 ts'ang.
Lazy, 懶惰 'laan-toh'.
Lead, 鉛 uen, 黑鉛 hak-uen, (the) 泵鉈 tum'-*t'oh.
Lead, (to) 引 'yan, 引導 'yan-to', 帶 taai', (by the hand) 拖 t'oh, 拖住 t'oh-chue'.
Leader, 頭目 t'au-muuk.
Leaf, 葉 ip, (of a book) 篇 p'in.
Leaf-fan, 葵扇 k'wai-shin'.
League, (combine) 聯合 luen-hop.

League, (10 'li) 塘汛 t'ong-suun', 甫路 'p'o-lo'.
Leak, 漏水 lau'-'shui, 滲漏 shum'-lau'.
Lean, 瘦 shau', (to) 极側 chaap-chak, (upon) 倚着 'i-cheuk, 挨埋 aai-maai.
Leap, 跳 t'iu', (over) 颶 naam'.
Leap-frog, 跳猪肉臺 t'iu'-chue-yuuk-*t'oi.
Learn, 學 hok, (and practice) 學習 hok-tsaap, (begin to) 上學 'sheung-hok.
Learned, 博學 pok'-hok.
Lease, 批 p'ai, (to) 租賃 tso-yum'.
Least, 至小 chi'-'siu, (the least quantity) 的咁多 tik-kom'-toh, (not the) 無的 'mo-tik.
Leather, 熟皮 shuuk-p'i.
Leave, (to) 離別 li-pit, 離 li, (things) 漏 lau', 嚫 laai', (alone) 由得 yau-tak, (to take) 告別 ko'-pit, (to ask for) 請假 'ts'eng-ka', (permission) 許准 'hue-'chuun.

Leaven, 酵 kaau ͑, 酒餅 ʿtsau-ʿpeng, (to) 發酵 faat ͑-ʿkaau.
Lecherous, 好嫖 hoʾ-pʻiu.
Lecture, 講書 ʿkong-shue.
Ledge, (on a wall) 級 ngap ͑, (of rocks) 石檯 shek-tʻoi.
Ledger, 登記簿 tang-kiʾ-*po ͑.
Lee, 下風便 ha ͑-ʿfuung-*pin ͑.
Leech, 牛蜞 ngau-kʻi, 蜞姆 kʻi-ʿna.
Leek, 韭菜 ʿkau-tsʻoi ͑.
Leer, 丟眼角 tiu-ʿngaan-*kok ͑.
Lees, 渣 cha, 肒 ngan ͑.
Left, the 左 ʿtsoh, (what is) 餘剩 ue-shing ͑.
Left handed 使左唒 ʿshai-ʿtsoh-ʿyaau.
Leg, 脚 keuk ͑, 小腿 ʿsiu-ʿtʻui, (calf) 脚瓜 keuk ͑-ʿkwa, 脚囊 keuk ͑-ʿnong.
Leg of mutton, 羊髀 yeung-ʿpi.
Legacy, 遺囑財物 wai-chuuk-tsʻoi-mat.
Legal, 依例 i-lai ͑.

Legation, 欽差衙門 yum-chʻaai-nga-*moon.
Legend, 古語 ʿkoo-ʿue.
Leggings, 套褲 tʻo ͑-fooʾ.
Legislate, 設例 chʻit ͑-lai ͑.
Legislative council, 定例局 ting ͑-lai ͑-kuuk.
Legitimate, (proper) 正 ching ͑, 着 cheuk.
Leisure, 閒 haan, 閒暇 haan-ha ͑, (at) 得閒 tak-haan.
Leisurely, 慢慢 maan ͑-*maan ͑.
Lemon, 檸檬 ning-ʿmuung.
Lemonade, 檸檬水 ning-ʿmuung-ʿshui.
Lemur, 幽嫺 yau-aat ͑.
Lend, 借去 tseʾ-hueʾ, 借過 tseʾ-kwoh ͑.
Lengthwise, 從長 tsʻuung-chʻeung, 長便 chʻeung-pin ͑, 掂 tim ͑.
Lenient, 寬恕 foon-shue ͑.
Lens, 玻璃鑒 poh-li-sui ͑.
Lentil, 扁豆 ʿpin-*tau ͑.
Leopard, 金錢豹 kum-tsʻin-pʻaau ͑.

Leprosy, 痲瘋 ma-ʃuung.
Leprous, 發瘋 faatʼ-ʃuung.
Less, 小 ʻsiu, 更小 kangʼ-ʻsiu, 少 ʻshiu.
Lessen, 減少 ʻkaam-ʻshiu.
Lesson, 課 fohʼ, (daily-) 日課 yat-fohʼ.
Lest, 恐怕 ʻhuung-pʻaʼ, 免致 ʻmin-chiʼ.
Let, 由得 yau-tak, 任 yumʼ, 俾 ʻpi, (go) 放 fongʼ, (loose) 鬆 suung, (alone) 咪鬥 ʻmai-tauʼ, (rent) 出賃 chʻuut-yumʼ.
Lethargy, 沈瘖 chʻum-kooiʼ.
Letter, (character) 字 tszeʼ, (epistle) 封信 fuung-suunʼ, 書信 shue-suunʼ, (rigid following of the) 解死 ʻkaai-ʻsze.
Lettuce, 生菜 shang-tsʻoiʼ.
Levee, 坐朝 tsohʼ-chʻiu, ʻtsʻoh-chʻiu.
Level, 平 pʻing, 平正 pʻing-chingʼ, (to find the) 打平水 ʻta-pʻing-ʻshui.
Lever, 千斤柝 tsʻin-kan-tak, 撬柝 kiuʼ-tak.

Lever-watch, 騎馬鏢 kʻe-ʻma-ʻpiu.
Levity, 輕薄 hing-pok.
Lewdness, 嫖 pʻiu.
Liable, (for) 是問 shiʼ-munʼ, (to) 有——險 ʻyau——ʻhim.
Liar, 講大話嘅 ʻkong-taaiʼ-waʼ-keʼ.
Libel, 壞名 waaiʼ-ming.
Liberal, 仁厚 yan-hauʼ, 四海嘅 szeʼ-ʻhoi-keʼ, (in politics) 達權 taat-kʻuen.
Liberate, 釋放 shik-fongʼ.
Liberty, 自由 tszeʼ-yau.
Library, (the room) 書房 shue-*fong, (the books) 書籍 shue-tsik.
License, (a) 執照 chup-chiuʼ, (to) 任從 yumʼ-tsʻuungʼ.
Licentious, 放縱 fongʼ-tsuungʼ, 淫泆 yum-yat.
Lichen, 苔 tʻoi, 石耳 shek-ʻi.
Li-chi, 荔枝 laiʼ-ʻchi, (best sorts) 糯米柿 nohʼ-ʻmai-tsʻze, 黑葉 hak-*ip.

Lick, (to) 舐 ʻlim, 舐 shaai, (the fingers) 吮手指 ʻshuen-ʻshau-ʻchi.

Lid, 蓋 koiʼ, (put on a) 冚住 homʼ-chueʼ.

Lie, (down) 眠下 min-haʼ, 瞓倒處 funʼ-ʻto-shue, (to tell) 講大話 ʻkong-taaiʼ-waʼ, (a) 謊言 ʻfong-in, 大話 taaiʼ-waʼ.

Lieutenant, 副 fooʼ.

Life, 生 shaang, 生命 shaang-mengʼ, 性命 singʼ-mingʼ.

Lift, 抽起 chʻau-ʻhi, 舉起 ʻkue-ʻhi, (off or up) 撳 ʻkʻin, 揭 kʻitʼ.

Light, (not heavy) 輕 ʻheng, (in colour) 淺 ʻtsʻin, (the light) 光 kwong, (bring a) 點火來 ʻtim-ʻfoh-lai, (to light) 點 ʻtʻim, 透 tʻauʼ, (alight) 落 lok.

Lighthouse, 燈塔 ʻtang-tʻaapʼ.

Lightning, 電光 tinʼ-kwong, 閃電 ʻshim-tinʼ, 靚火 lengʼ-ʻfoh.

Like, (resembling) 好似 ʻho-ʻtsʻze, (to) 中意 chuungʼ-iʼ.

Likely, 大概 taaiʼ-kʻoiʼ, 怕係嘟 pʻaʼ-haiʼ-kwaʼ.

Likeness, 真 ʻchan, 相 *seungʼ, 像 *tseungʼ.

Likewise, 亦 yik, 又 yauʼ.

Lilac, 青蓮色 tsʻing-*lin-shik.

Lily, 百合花 paakʼ-hop-fa, (water-) 蓮花 lin-fa.

Limb, 肢體 chi-ʻtʻai.

Lime, 灰 fooi, 殼灰 hokʼ-fooi, 石灰 shek-fooi, (fruit) 檸檬 ning-ʻmuung.

Lime-stone, 灰石 fooi-shek.

Limit, 界限 kaaiʼ-haanʼ, 限 haanʼ.

Limited, 有限 yau-haanʼ.

Limp, (a) 趌脚 kat-keukʼ.

Limpet, 扁螺 ʻpin-*loh.

Line, 線 sinʼ, (stroke) 畫 waak.

Linen, 麻布 ma-poʼ.

Linger, 逗遛 tauʼ-lau.

Linguist, 通事 tʻuung-*szeʼ.

Lining, 裡布 ʻli-poʼ, 裏 ʻli.

Link, (a) 連環 lin-waan, (to) 扣連 kʻau⸢-lin.
Linseed, 胡麻子 oo-ma-⸢tsze, (oil) 胡子油 oo-⸢tsze-yau.
Lint, (cloth) 揿絨布 ⸢wa-*yuung-poʼ.
Lintel, 條楣 tʻiu-mi.
Lion, 獅子 sze-⸢tsze.
Lip, 口唇 ⸢hau-shuun.
Liquid, 水類 ⸢shui-luiʼ.
Liquidate, (accounts) 清數 tsʻing-shoʼ.
Liquor, (spirits) 酒 ⸢tsau.
Liquorice, 甘草 kom-⸢tʻso.
List, 條目 tʻiu-muuk.
Listen, 細聽 sai⸣-tʻeng, 靜聽 tsingʼ-tʻing, 聽下 tʻeng-⸢ha, 打聽 ⸢ta-tʻengʼ.
Listless, 無心聽 ⸢mo-sum-tʻeng.
Literally, 正講 chingʼ-⸢kong, 字面 tszeʼ-*minʼ, 正面 chingʼ-*minʼ.
Literary, 學文 hok-mun, 斯文 sze-mun.
Literati, 讀書人 tuuk-shue-yau, 紳士 shan-*szeʼ.

Literature, 文墨 muu-mak.
Litharge, 陀僧 tʻoh-⸢sang.
Litigation, 爭訟 chaang-tsuungʼ.
Little, 細 saiʼ, 小 ⸢siu, (a) 的 tik, (a very) 的咁多 tik-komʼ-toh.
Live, 生 shaang, 活 oot, (dwell) 住 chueʼ.
Live stock, 畜牲 chuuk-shang, 生口 shaang-⸢hau.
Livelihood, 過日 kwohʼ-yat, (seeking a) 搵頭路 ⸢wan-tʻau-loʼ, 搵計 ⸢wan-kaiʼ.
Lively, 活潑 oot-pʻootʼ.
Liver, 肝 kohn, (COL.) ⸢yuun.
Livid, 青黑 tsʻeng-hak.
Lizard, 蚺蛇 im-*she.
Lo! 睇嗱 tʻai-na!
Loach, 烏魚 oo-ue.
Load, (a) 擔 taam, 擔子 taamʼ-⸢tsze, 載 tsoiʼ, (to) 裝貨 chong-fohʼ.
Load-stone, 攝石 shipʼ-shek.
Loaf, 麵頭 minʼ-tʻau, 麵包 minʼ-⸢paau.
Loafer, 掘脚 lo-*keukʼ.

Loan, 借債 tse²-chaai², (put out to) 出借 chʻuut-tse².
Loathe, 憎憾 tsang-im².
Loathsome, 可惡 ʿhoh-oo.
Lobby, 門口廳 moon-ʿhau-ₑtʻeng.
Lobe, (ear-) 耳朵 ʿi-ʿtoh, 耳尖 ʿi-ₑtsim, ʿi-ₑteung.
Lobster, 龍蝦 luung-ₑha.
Local, 一方 yat-fong, yat-fong-ke², (of this place) 土 ʿtʻo, 本地 ʿpoon-*tiʾ.
Lock, (a) 把鎖 ʿpa-ʿsoh, (with a latch or bolt) 軌鎖 ʿkwai-ʿsoh, (of a canal) 水閘 ʿshui-chaap, (to) 鎖埋 ʿsoh-maai.
Locust, 蝗蟲 wong-chʻuung.
Lodge, (to) 歇宿 hitʾ-suuk, 住 chueʾ, (house) 歇店 hitʾ-tim², 寓 ueʾ.
Lodger, 歇客 hitʾ-haakʾ.
Lofty, 高 ko.
Log, 木頭 muuk-tʻau.
Logic, 辯論之理 pinʾ-ʿluunʾ-chi-ʿli, 辯論法 pinʾ-luunʾ-faatʾ.

LOGOS, 道 TOʾ.
Loins, 腰 iu, 小腌 ʿsiu-ʿim.
Loiter, 逗遛 tauʾ-lauʾ, 囉囉鑽 loh-loh-tsuenʾ.
Lonely, 冷落 ʿlaang-lok, 孤獨 koo-tuuk.
Long, (in space) 長 chʻeung, (in time) 長久 chʻeung-ʿkau, 久 ʿkau, 耐 *noiʾ, noiʾ, (to) 戀慕 luenʾ-mooʾ, 渴想 hohtʾ-ʿseung.
Long-ells, 嗶機 putʾ-ₑki.
Longevity, 長壽 chʻeung-shauʾ.
Longitude, 地經度 tiʾ-king-toʾ.
Longsuffering, 忍耐 ʿyan-noiʾ.
Look, 看 hohnʾ, 睇 ʿtʻai, (carefully) 關顧吓 kwaanʾ-kooʾ-ʿha, (down upon) 睥睨 ʿpʻai-ʿngai.
Looking-glass, 面鏡 minʾ-kengʾ.
Look-out, (place) 望樓 mongʾ-lau.
Loom, (a) 一架機 yat-kaʾ ₑki.

Loop, 紐圈 ʻnau-huen, 紐眼 ʻnau-ʻngaan.
Loop-hole, 狗竇 ʻkau-tauʼ, 墻口 tsʻeung-ʻhau, 漏罅 lauʼ-laʼ.
Loose, 鬆 suung, 散 ʻsaan, (to) 鬆開 suung-hoi, 解用 ʻkaai-lut.
Lop off, 割去 kohtʼ-hueʼ.
Loquacious, 多口 toh-ʻhau.
Loquat, 櫨橘 lo-kwut, 枇杷菓 pʻi-pʻa-ʻkwoh.
Lord, 主 ʻchue.
Lose, 失 shat, 遺失 wai-shat, (in trade) 貼本 shitʼ-ʻpoon, (in a game) 輸 shue.
Loss, 傷壞 sheung-waaiʼ, 虧缺 fai-kʻuetʼ.
Lost, 不見 ʼm-kinʼ, 失了 shatʼ-liu, shat-hiu, 亡 mong.
Lots, (cast) 抽籤 chʻau-ʻtsʻim, 拈鬮 nim-*chʻau.
Lotion, 洗藥 ʻsai-yeuk.
Lottery, 白鴿票 paak-kopʼ-ʻpiu, 賭票 ʻto-ʻpiu, (to open a) 開票 hoi-ʻpiu.
Lotus, 蓮花 lin-fa.
Loud, 大聲 taaiʼ-sheng.

Lounge, (to) 散逸 ʻsaan-yat, 閒散 haan-ʻsaan.
Louse, 虱 shat, 虱嫲 shat-ʻna.
Lout, 懶佬 ʻlaan-ʻlo.
Love, 愛 oiʼ, (tenderly) 愛惜 oiʼ-sik, (reverently) 敬愛 kingʼ-oiʼ.
Love-apple, 金錢桔 kum-tsʻin-kat.
Low, 低 tai, 矮 ʻai, 卑 pi, (water) 水乾慢 ʻshui-kohn-maanʼ.
Low, (to) 牛叫 ngau-kiuʼ.
Loyal, 忠信 chuung-suunʼ.
Lubber, 劣弱人 luetʼ-yeuk-yan, 大冬瓜 taaiʼ-tuung-kwa.
Lubberly, 生沙虱 shang-sha-shat, 大不用 taaiʼ-patʼ-yuungʼ.
Lubricate, 潤滑 yuunʼ-waat, 整滑 ʻching-waat.
Lucid, 明亮 ming-leungʼ, 明朗 ming-ʻlong.
Lucifer-match, 自來火 tszeʼ-loi-ʻfoh.

Luck, 造化 tso⁾-fa⁾, 命運 ming⁾-wan⁾, (good) 好彩數 ʿho-ʿtsʻoi-sho⁾.
Luckily, 好彩 ʿho-ʿtsʻoi.
Lucky, 吉 kat, 幸 hang⁾, 有彩 ʿyau-ʿtsʻoi.
Lucrative, 發財 faat⁾-tsʻoi-ke⁾.
Lucubration, 靜夜作文 tsing⁾-ye⁾-tsokʻ-mun.
Ludicrous, 好笑 ʿho-siu⁾.
Luff, 扳舵 pʻaan-ʻtʻoh, maan-tʻaai.
Luggage, 行李 hang-ʿli.
Lugubrious, 愁苦 shau-ʿfoo, 晦氣 fooi⁾-hi⁾.
Lukewarm, 半冷半熱 poon⁾-ʿlaang-poon⁾-it, 冷煖間 ʿlaang-ʿnuen-kaan.
Lull, 畧息 leuk-sik.
Lumbago, 腰骨痛 iu-kwut-tʻuung⁾.
Luminaries, (the 3) 三光 saam-kwong.
Luminous, 光明 kwong-ming.
Lump, 塊 faai⁾, 俲 kau⁾, (to) 擸埋 laap⁾-maai.

Lunatic, 發癲 faat⁾-tin.
Lungs, 肺家 fai⁾-ka, 肺腑 fai⁾-ʿfoo.
Lurch, 打側 ʿta-chak.
Lurk, 埋伏 maai-fuuk.
Luscious, 甘味 kom-mi⁾, 甜念念 tʻim-num-num.
Lust, 慾火 yuuk-ʿfoh, (after) 貪饕 tʻaam-tʻo.
Lustre, 光 kwong, 光滑 kwong-waat.
Lustring, 絹 kuen⁾.
Luxuriant, 婆婆莎莎 poh⁾-poh⁾-sohʻ-sohʻ.
Luxurious, 好歎 ho⁾-tʻaan⁾, 嬌樂 kiu-lok, 奢侈 chʻe-chʻi.
Lychnis, 虞美人 ue-ʿmi-*yan.
Lycopodium, 卷柏 ʿkuen-pʻaakʻ.
Lye, 䂝水 ʿkaan-ʿshui, (sediment) 䂝沙 ʿkaan-sha.
Lyre, 三絃 saam-*in, (to play) 彈三絃 tʻaan-saam-*in.
Lyrics, 詞曲 tʻsze-kʻuuk.

M

Macao, 澳門 *O'*-*moon.
Macaroni, 通心粉 *t'uung-sum-'fun*, 粉條 *'fan-**t'iu*.
Mace, (one) 一錢 *yat-ts'in*. (of nutmegs) 荳蔻花 *tau'-k'au'-fa*.
Macerate, 漚 *au'*.
Machination, 機謀 *ki-mau*.
Machine, 機器 *ki-hi'*.
Mackerel, 鮎魚 *ch'i-**ue*.
Macroura, 蝦 *,ha*.
Maculate, 染污 *'im-oo*, 玷 *tim'*.
Mad, 狂 *k'wong*, 發狂 *faat'-k'wong*.
Madam, (respectfully) 奶奶 *naai-**naai*.
Madder, 茜草 *sin'-'ts'o*.
Made, 做了 *tso'-'liu*, *tso'-hiu*, *tso'-ke'*.
Maggots, (to breed) 生蛆 *shang-ts'ue*, 生蟲 *shang-ch'uung*.
Magic, 巫術 *moo-shuut*.

Magistrates, 官府 *koon-'foo*, —Police, 巡理府 *ts'uun-'li-'foo*.
Magnanimous, 豪俠 *ho-haap*.
Magnates, 大人家 *taai'-yan-ka*.
Magnet, 攝石 *ship'-shek*, 南針 *naam-,chum*.
Magnificent, 浩大 *ho'-taai'*, 華麗 *wa-lai'*.
Magnify, 影大 *'ying-taai'*, 整大 *'ching-taai'*.
Magnitude, 若干大 *yeuk-kohn-taai'*.
Magnolia, (fuscata) 含笑花 *hom-siu'-fa*, (conspicua) 玉蘭 *yuuk-laan*, (pumila) 夜合 *ye'-**hop*.
Magpie, 喜鵲 *'hi-ts'euk'*.
Mahogany, (Chinese) 森木 *,shum-muuk*, (flower—pride of India) 苦楝花 *'foo-lin-fa*.
Mahommedanism, 回回教 *Ooi-**ooi-kaau'*.
Maid, (servant) 使妹 *'shai-,mooi*, (old) 老女 *lo-**nue*.

Maiden, 童女 t'uung-ʻnue.
Mail, (armour) 甲冑 kaap'-chau'.
Mail, (letter carrying) 驛 yik, 帶信 taai'-suun'.
Maim, 殘缺 ts'aan-k'uet'.
Main, (principal) 大 taai', 正 ching', (the bulk) 大體 taai'-ʻt'ai, (most important) 最要 tsui'-iu'.
Main-spring, 法條 faat'-*t'iu.
Maintain, 固守 koo'-ʻshau, 保存 ʻpo-ts'uen, 保住 ʻpo-chue'.
Maize, 包粟 paau-suuk.
Majestic, 威嚴 wai-im.
Majority, (of age) 成丁 shing-tiny.
Make, 做 tso', 整 ʻching, 作 tsok', (a story) 安是安非 ohn-shi'-ohn-fi, (trouble) 生事 shaang-sze', (away with) 收拾 shau-shup.
Maker, 造者 tso'-ʻche.
Malaria, 山嵐瘴氣 shaan-laam-cheung'-hi'.

Male, 男 naam, 男人 naam-*yan, (of beasts) 公 ʻkuung, (generally) 陽類 yeung-lui'.
Malevolent, 黑心 hak-sum.
Malicious, 兇惡 huung-ok'.
Malignant, 惡毒 ok'-tuuk.
Malleable iron, 熟鐵 shuuk-t'it'.
Mallet, 木椎 muuk-*ch'ui.
Mallows, 葵 k'wai.
Mamma, 媽媽 ma-ʻma.
Man, 人 yan, *yan.
Man-of-war, 兵船 ping-shuen.
Manacles, 手鐐 ʻshau-liu.
Manage, 辦理 paan'-ʻli.
Manager, 總理 ʻtsuung-li, 揸品 cha-ʻpun, 揸大旗 cha-taai'-k'i.
Manchu, 滿洲 ʻMoon-ʻchau.
Mandarin, 官府 koon-ʻfoo, (dialect) 官話 koon-*wa'.
Mane, (horse's) 馬鬃 ʻma-ʻtsuung.
Mange, 生蟻 shaang-tsze.
Mangle, (a) 碾布具 shin'-po'-kue', (to spoil) 殘 ts'aan.

Mango, 楒菓 mony-ʻkwoh.
Mangosteen, 山竹菓 shaan-chuuk-ʻkwoh.
Manhood, 成人 shing-yan.
Maniac, 狂 kʻwong.
Manifest, 明白 ming-paak, (to) 顯明 ʻhin-ming, (a) 貨單 fohʼ-ʻtaan.
Manila, 小呂宋 ʻSiu-ʻlue-suungʼ.
Manis, 穿山甲 chʻuen-shaan-kaapʼ.
Mankind, 人類 yan-luiʼ.
Manly, 君子 kwan-ʻtsze, kwun-ʻtsze-keʼ.
Manner, 樣 yeungʼ, *yeungʼ.
Manners, 禮 ʻlai.
Mansion, 宅 chaak, 府 ʻfoo.
Mantis, 馬郎蚣 ʻma-long-*kʻong.
Mantle, 大蔞 taaiʼ-ʻlau.
Mantlepiece, 火爐額 ʻfoh-lo-ngaak.
Manual labour, 手作 ʻshau-tsokʼ.
Manufacture, 製做 chaiʼ-tsoʼ.

Manure, 糞 funʼ, (to) 落糞 lok-funʼ.
Manuscript, 手抄 ʻshau-ʻchʻaau, 寫嘅 ʻse-keʼ.
Many, 多 toh.
Map, 圖 tʻo, 地圖 tiʼ-tʻo.
Maple, 楓樹 fuung-shueʼ.
Mar, 損壞 ʻsuen-waaiʼ, ʻte.
Marble, 花粉石 fa-ʻfun-*shek, 雲石 wun-*shek, (white) 白粉石 paak-ʻfun-*shek.
March, 英三月 Ying-saam-uet, (to) 步師 poʼ-sze, 齊步行 tsʻai-poʼ-hang.
Mare, 馬母 ʻma-ʻmo.
Margarite, 珍珠 chan-chue.
Margin, 邊 pin.
Marines, 水師 ʻshui-sze.
Mariners, 水手 ʻshui-ʻshau.
Mark, 記號 kiʼ-hoʼ, 畫 waak, (to) 打印 ʻta-yanʼ, 打號 ʻta-hoʼ, (observe) 睇眞 ʻtʻai-chan.
Market, 市 ʻshi.
Market-place, 市頭 ʻshi-*tʻau, 欄 ʻlaan (town) 墟 hue.

Marking-line, 墨斗 mak-ʻtau.
Marquis, 侯 hau.
Marriage, 婚姻 fun-yan.
Marrow, 髓 sui.
Marry, (a wife) 娶 tsʻueʾ, 取心抱 ʻtsʻue-sum-ʻpʻo, (a husband) 嫁 kaʾ, (a couple) 成親 shing-tsʻan.
Mars, (planet) 火星 ʻFoh-sing, (the god of war) 武帝 ʻmoo-taiʾ, (Chinese) 關帝 Kʻwaan-taiʾ.
Marsh, 下沙 haʾ-sha, 沙灘 sha-ʻtʻaan, 澤 chaak.
Mart, 埠頭 fanʾ-tʻan.
Marten, 貂鼠 tiu-ʻshue.
Martial, 武 ʻmoo.
Martyrdom, 守死善道 ʻshau-ʻsze-shin-toʾ.
Marvel, 奇事 kʻi-szeʾ, (to) 詫異 chʻaʾ-iʾ.
Marvel of Peru, 胭脂花 in-chi-fa.
Masculine gender, 陽類 yeung-luiʾ.
Mash, 搓爛 chʻaai-laanʾ.

Mask, 笑面殼 siuʾ-minʾ-hokʾ.
Mason, 泥水人 nai-ʻshui-yan, (stone-) 石匠 shek-*tseungʾ.
Mass, 團 tʻuen, 俗 kauʾ, (people) 下民 haʾ-mun, 庶民 shueʾ-mun.
Massacre, 屠戮 tʻo-luuk, 殺戮 shaatʾ-luuk.
Massive, 厚大 hauʾ-taaiʾ.
Mast, 枝桅 chi-wai.
Master, 事頭 szeʾ-*tʻau, 主人公 ʻchue-yan-kung, 主 ʻchue, (teacher) 先生 sin-shang, 師傅 sze-*fooʾ.
Masticate, 嚼 tseukʾ, tsiuʾ.
Mat, 席 tsek, (of bamboo) 笪 taatʾ, (cushion) 墊 tinʾ.
Mat-shed, 棚廠 pʻaang-ʻchʻong.
Match, 火紙 ʻfoh-ʻchi, (Lucifer) 火柴 ʻfoh-chʻaai.
Match, (a mate) 偶 ʻngau.
Match-maker, 媒婆 mooi-*pʻoh.

Mate, (chief) 伙長 ʻfoh-ʻcheung, (2nd) 二伙 iʼ-ʻfoh, (generally) 伙計 ʻfoh-kiʼ.

Materials, 材料 tsʻoi-liuʼ, 物料 mat-liuʼ.

Matrix, (for type) 銅板模 tʻuung-ʻpaan-moo.

Matter, 質 chat, (affair) 事幹 szeʼ-kohnʼ, (no) 無乜緊要 ʻmo-mat-ʻkan-iuʼ, (from a boil) 膿 nuung.

Matter of fact, 事實 szeʼ-shat.

Mattress, 牀褥 chʻong-*yuuk.

Mature, 成熟 shing-shuuk.

Maxim, 箴規 chʻum-kʻwai.

May, (can) 得 tak, 可以 ʻhoh-ʻi. (I, or we, wish) 願 uenʼ.

Maze, 紛紛 fun-fun.

Meadow, 草塲 ʻtsʻo-chʻeung.

Meal, (a) 餐 tsʻaan, (flour) 粉 ʻfun.

Mealy-mouthed, 口恥 ʻhau-ʻchʻi.

Mean, (base) 鄙陋 ʻpʻi-lauʼ, 賤 tsinʼ, (to hit the) 得中 tak-chuung, (to) 意係 iʼ-haiʼ, (the doctrine of the) 中庸 chuung-yuung.

Meaning, 意思 iʼ-szeʼ.

Means, 資本 tsze-ʻpoon, (method) 法 faatʼ.

Means, (by no) 斷唔係 tuenʼ-ʼm-haiʼ.

Meanwhile, 同時 tʻuung-shi.

Measles, 痲症 *ma-chingʼ, 出痲 chʻut-*ma.

Measure, (to) 度 tok, 量度 leungʼ-tok, (a) 量 leungʼ, 度量 toʼ-leungʼ, (foot-) 尺 chʻekʼ.

Meat, 肉 yuuk.

Mechanic, 工匠 kuung-tseungʼ.

Mechanism, 機器 ki-hiʼ.

Meddle, 壽事 tsʻum-szeʼ, 打理 ʻta-ʻli.

Mediator, 中保 chuung-ʻpo.

Medicine, 藥材 yeuk-tsʻoi, (science of) 醫學 i-hok.

Meditate, 默想 mak-‘seung.
Medusa, 水母 ‘shui-‘mo.
Meek, 謙和 him-woh.
Meet, (to) 遇着 ue⁾-cheuk, 接着 tsip⁾-cheuk, (by appointment) 聚會 tsue⁾-ooi⁾.
Meeting, 會 ooi⁾. 聚集 tsue⁾-tsaap.
Melancholy, 悶悶 moon⁾-moon⁾.
Mellow, 熟腍 shuk-nam.
Melody, 佳音 kaai-yam.
Melon, 瓜 ‘kwa.
Melt, 鎔化 yuung-fa⁾.
Member, 股 ‘koo, (church-) 兄弟 hing-tai⁾.
Members, 百體 paak⁾-‘t‘ai.
Membrane, 衣膜 i-mok.
Memoir, 行狀 hang-chong⁾.
Memorial, 奏本 tsau⁾-‘poon.
Memory, 記性 ki⁾-sing⁾.
Mencius, 孟子 Mang⁾-‘tsze.
Mend, 補 ‘po, 修整 sau-‘ching.
Menial, 下役 ha⁾-yik.
Menses, 月經 uet-king.
Mental, 心内 sum-noi⁾.

Mention, 講及 ‘kong-k‘aap.
Mercantile, 生意 shang-i⁾, 買賣 ‘maai-maai⁾.
Mercenary, 求利 k‘au-li⁾.
Merchant, 商人 sheung-yan.
Merciful, 哀憐 oi-lin, 慈 ts‘ze, 慈心 ts‘ze-sum.
Merciless, 狠心 long-sum.
Mercury, 水銀 ‘shui-ngan, (planet) 水星 ‘Shui-‘sing.
Mercy, 慈悲 ts‘ze-pi, 憐憫 lin-‘mun.
Merely, 不過 pat-kwoh⁾, 獨係 tunk-hai⁾,——吤——chek.
Merge, 褪埋 t‘an⁾-maai.
Meridian, 子午線 ‘tsze-‘ng-sin⁾, (-lines) 經線 king-sin⁾.
Merino, 羽斜 ‘ue-ts‘e.
Merit, 功勞 kung-lo, 功 kung, (to) 應得 ying-tak, 功勞應得 kung-lo-ying-tak.
Merry, 喜笑 ‘hi-siu⁾, 好趣 ‘ho-ts‘ue⁾.
Merry-andrew, 雜脚 tsaap-keuk⁾, 丑 ‘ch‘au.

Mesh, 網眼 ʻmong-ʻngaan.
Mess, (medley) 攙雜 laap-tsaap.
Mess together, 同囊 tʻnung-tsʻuen'.
Message, 報信 poʼ-sum'.
Messenger, 差人 chʻaai-yan, (official) 委員 ʻwai-uen.
Metal, 金類 kum-lui'.
Metaphor, 借語 tseʼ-ʻue, 借意 tseʼ-i'.
Metempsychosis, 輪回 luun-ooi.
Meteor, 流星 lau-ʻsing, 墜星 chui'-ʻsing.
Method, 方法 fong-faat', 法子 faat'-tsze.
Metonomy, 借講 tseʼ-ʻkong.
Metropolis, 京城 king-sheng, 京都 king-too'.
Mettle, 精氣 tsing-hiʼ.
Mew, }
Mewl, } 坳聲 ngaau-sheng.
Miasma, 瘴氣 cheungʼ-hiʼ, (damp) 濕氣 shap-hiʼ, 濕瘴 shap-cheungʼ.
Mica, 千層紙 tsʻin-tsʻang-ʻchi.

Microcosm, 小天地 ʻsiu-tʻin-ti'.
Microscope, 顯微鏡 ʻhin-mi-keng'.
Mid, 中 chuung.
Mid-day, 晏晝 aan'-chau'.
Middle, 中間 ʻchuung-ʻkaan.
Middle-man, 媒人 mooi-*yan.
Middle-woman, 媒婆 mooi-*pʻoh.
Middling, 嘛嘛吔 ma-*ma-ti'.
Midnight, 半夜 poon'-ye'.
Mid-summer, 夏至 haʼ-chiʼ, 端陽 tuen-yeung.
Mid-way, 半路 poon'-lo'.
Midwife, 接生婆 tsipʼ-ʻshang-*pʻoh, 穩婆 ʻwan-*pʻoh, 執媽 chup-ʻma.
Might, 能 nang.
Mighty, 大能 taai'-nang.
Migratory, 依時來往 i-shi-loi-ʻwong.
Mild, 溫良 wan-leung.
Mildew, 霉 mooi, 漚霉 au'-mooi.

MIN 159 MIS

Mile, (36/100 of an English) 里 ‘li.
Military, 武 ‘moo.
Milk, 乳 ‘ue, 嬭 ‘naai, (COL.) ‚nin.
Mill, 磨 moh’, *moh’.
Millet, 小米 ‘siu-‘mai, 粟 suuk.
Million, 百萬 paak’-maan’.
Mimic, 學 hok.
Mince, 切細 ts‘it’-sai’.
Mincing, 嬭娜 ‚nia-‘noh.
Mind, 心 ‚sum, (to) 顧住 koo’-chue’.
Mindful, 有細心 ‚yau-sai’-‚sum, (you are) 有心 ‚yau-‚sum.
Mine, (to) 掘 (金) 礦 kwat- (‚kum-) ‚lung, (a) 礦 k‘wong’.
Minister, (to) 執事 chup-sze’, 司事 sze-sze’, (a) 臣 ‚shan, (prime) 宰相 ‘tsoi-seung’.
Mint, 香花茶 ‚heung-fa-ts‘ai’, (a) 錢局 ts‘in-kuuk.
Minus, 減 ‘kaam.

Minute, 細微 sai’-mi, (of time) 分時 ‚fun-shi.
Miracle, 異跡 i’-tsik.
Mire, 泥淜 ‚nai-paan’.
Mirror, 面鏡 min’-keng’.
Mirth, 快樂 faai’-lok.
Miscarriage, 小產 ‘siu-‘ch‘aan.
Miscellaneous, 零星 ‚ling-‚sing, 雜 tsaap, 拾碎 shup-sui’, 啞碎 sup-sui’.
Mischief, 故傷 koo’-‚sheung, 損害 ‘suen-hoi’.
Miser, 慳財人 ‚haan-ts‘oi-‚yan, 慳壞 ‚haan-waai’.
Miserable, (as a miser) 自賤 tsze’-tsin’, (poor) 拗戻 ‚aau-ai’.
Misery, 苦楚 ‘foo-‘ch‘oh, 悽涼 ts‘ai-‚leung.
Misfortune, 不幸 pat-hang’, 苦命 ‘foo-meng’, 凶事 ‚hung-sze’.
Misinterpret, 解錯 ‘kaai-ts‘oh’.
Mislead, 引錯 ‘yan-ts‘oh’.
Misprint, 印錯 yan’-ts‘oh’.

Misrepresent, 講歪 ‘kong-‘me.

Miss, (young lady) 姑娘 koo-neung, (to) 失 shat, 唔中 ‘m-chuung’.

Missionary, 傳教人 ch‘uen-kaau’-yan, (society) 傳教會 ch‘uen-kaau’-ooi’.

Misspend, 浪費 long’-fai’.

Mist, 烟霧 in-moo’, 霞霧 ha-moo’, 雲霧 wan-moo’.

Mistake, 估錯 ‘koo-ts‘oh’, (a) 錯 ts‘oh’, *ts‘oh’, 錯過 ts‘oh’-kwoh’.

Mister, (Mr) 先生 sin-shaang, ——公——kuung.

Mistress, (Mrs) 奶奶 naai-*naai, (of a household) 事頭娘 sze’-t‘au-neung, 主人娘 ‘chue-yan-neung, 主母 ‘chue-‘moo, (of a school) 女師 ‘nue-sze, (a kept) 老契 ‘lo-k‘ai.

Misunderstand, 不會意 ‘m-ooi’-i’, 聽錯 t‘eng-ts‘oh’.

Mix, 攪勻 ‘kaau-wan, 調和 t‘iu-woh, 摳勻 k‘au-wan.

Moan, 嗟嘆 tse-t‘aan’, 嘆氣 t‘aan’-hi’.

Mob, 百姓鬧亂 paak’-sing’-naau-luen’.

Mock, 戲弄 hi’-luung’, 訕笑 shaan’-siu’.

Model, 模樣 moo-yeung’, moo-*yeung’.

Moderate, 不多不少 pat’-toh-pat’-‘shiu, 適中 shik-chuung, 中和 chuung-woh, (to) 調勻 t‘iu-wan.

Modern, 今 kum, 新 san, (times) 近世 kan’-shai’.

Modest, 有廉恥 ‘yau-lim-‘ch‘i, 知羞 chi-sau, 謙退 him-t‘ui’.

Modify, 改削 ‘koi-seuk’.

Moist, 濕 shup, 腍 num.

Moisten, 潤 yuun’.

Mole, 田鼠 t‘im-‘shue, (on the skin) 黑疵 hak-ts‘ze-hak-chi’, 黑痣

Mole-cricket, 土狗 ‘t‘o-‘kau.

Molest, 難爲 naau-wai.

Moment, 片刻 p‘in’-hak, 頃刻 ‘king-hak.

Monastery, (Tau.) 觀 ʻkoonʼ, (Bud.) 寺 tszeʼ, (Rom.) 修道院 sau-toʼ-*uenʼ.
Monday, 禮拜一 ʻlai-paaiʼ-yat.
Money, 錢 tsʻin, *tsʻin, 銀錢 ngan-*tsʻin, *ngan.
Mongol, 蒙古 Muung-ʻkoo.
Mongrel, 雜種 tsaap-chuung.
Monkey, 馬騮 ʻma-ʻlau.
Monomania, 心病狂 sum-pengʼ-kʻwong, 因事病狂 yan-szeʼ-pengʼ-kʻwong.
Monopolist, 蠹家 ʻtuun-ʻka.
Monopolize, 蠹貨 ʻtuun-fohʼ.
Monstrous, 怪祟 kwaaiʼ-suiʼ.
Month, 月 uet.
Monument, 牌坊 pʻaai-fong, 碑記 pi-kiʼ.
Mood, 心情 sum-tsʻing, 情景 tsʻing-ʻking.
Moody, 鼓氣 ʻkoo-hiʼ.
Moon, 月 uet, (light) 月光 uet-ʻkwong.
Moor, (to) 灣泊 waan-pok, 灣劖 waan-chaapʼ.
Mop, 布拂 poʼ-fut.

Mope, 發悶 faatʼ-moonʼ.
Morally, 依情理 i-tsʻing-ʻli.
Morals, 行為 hang-wai, 德行 tak-hang, (good) 善德 shinʼ-tak.
More, 添 tʻim, 多 toh, (COMP. DEG.) 更 kangʼ, 重 chuungʼ.
Moreover, 更兼 kangʼ-kim, 況且 fongʼ-chʻe, 而且 i-ʻchʻe.
Morning, 早 ʻtso, 朝 chiu, (good) 早晨 ʻtso-shan, (-star) 啓明星 ʻkʻai-ming-ʻsing.
Morose, 陰沉 yum-chʻum.
Morra, 猜梅 chʻaai-mooi.
Mortal, 會死 ʻooi-ʻsze.
Mortally, 致死 chiʼ-ʻsze.
Mortar, 泥 nai, (a) 舂坎 chuung-ʻhom.
Mortgage, (a house) 典屋 ʻtin-uuk, 當屋 tongʼ-uuk.
Mortgagee, 典主 ʻtin-ʻchue.
Mortification, 枯廢 foo-faiʼ, 腐 fooʼ, (gangrene) 肉死 yuuk-ʻsze, (of spirit) 憔悴 tsʻiu-sui.

Mortise, 榫眼 ʿsuun-ʿngaan.
Mosquito, 蚊 ₍mun.
Mosquito-curtain, (a) 一堂蚊帳 yat-tʻong-₍mun-cheungʾ.
Moss, 苔蘚 tʻoi-ʿsin, 莓苔 mooi-tʻoi, 青苔 tsʻeng-tʻoi.
Most, (of quality) 至 chiʾ, 十分 shap-fun, (of quantity) 至多 chiʾ-toh.
Mostly, 大概 taaiʾ-*kʻoi, 大約 taaiʾ-*yeukʾ, 大體 taaiʾ-ʿtʻai.
Moth, 蛾 ngoh, 燈蛾 tang-*ngoh.
Mother, 老母 ʿlo-*ʿmoo, (respectfully) 母親 ʿmoo-tsʻan.
Mother-in-law, 外母 ngoiʾ-*ʿmoo.
Mother-of-pearl, 雲母殼 wan-ʿmoo-hokʾ.
Mother-wort, 益母草 yik-ʿmoo-ʿtsʻo.
Motion, 動 tuungʾ.
Motive, 起見 ʿhi-kinʾ, 念頭 nimʾ-tʻau.
Motto, 題句 tʻai-kueʾ.

Mould, (a) 模式 moo-shik.
Mouldy, 發毛 faatʾ-mo.
Mound, 土堆 ʿtʻo-₍tui, 封土 fuung-ʿtʻo.
Mount, (to) 上 ʿsheung, 升上去 shing-ʿsheung-hueʾ.
Mountain, 山 shaan.
Mourn, 吊喪 tiuʾ-song, 哀哭 oi-huuk.
Mourning, 喪服 song-fuuk, (put on) 着服 cheukʾ-fuuk.
Mouse, 鼠仔 ʿshue-ʿtsai, 石鼠 shek-ʿshue.
Mouth, 口 ʿhau.
Mouthful, (a) 一口 yat-ʿhau, 一啖 yat-taamʾ.
Move, 郁動 yuuk-tuungʾ, (remove) 搬 poon.
Mow, 鏟 ʿchʻaan.
Moxa, 艾茸 ngaaiʾ-yuung.
Much, 多 toh.
Mud, 坭 nai.
Muddy, 濁 chuuk, 泥潭 nai-paanʾ, 漚淖 auʾ-nau, (style) 拖泥帶水 tʻoh-nai-taaiʾ-ʿshui.
Muff, 拱手套 ʿkuung-ʿshau-tʻoʾ.

Mug, 水筒 ʿshui-*tʾuung.
Mulberry, (tree) 桑樹 song-shueʾ.
Mule, 騾馬 loh-ʿma.
Mullet, 黃尾鯊 wong-ʿmi-ʿtsʾai, 白尾鯊 paak-ʿmi-ʿtsʾai.
Multiply, 乘 shing, (increase) 生多 shaang-toh.
Multitude, 眾 chuungʾ, (the) 庶民 shueʾ-mun, 大眾百姓 taaiʾ-chuungʾ-paakʾ-singʾ.
Mumble, 唅沈 ngum-chʾum.
Mummery, 詭馬事 ʿkwai-ʿma-szeʾ.
Mumps, 生痄腮 shang-chaʾ-ʿsoi.
Munificent, 厚重 hauʾ-chuungʾ, 四海嘅 szeʾ-ʿhoi-keʾ.
Murder, 兇殺 huung-shaatʾ.
Murderer, 兇手 huung-ʿshau.
Murex, 刺螺 tsʿzeʾ-*loh.
Murmur, 論蠢 luunʾ-chuunʾ, (at) 怨嘆 uenʾ-tʾaanʾ.
Muscle, (of the body) 肌膚 ki-foo, 瘦肉 shauʾ-*yuuk.

Mushroom, 菌 ʿkʾwun, ʿkʾan.
Music, 樂音 ngok-yum.
Musicians, 吹打佬 chʾui-ʿta-ʿlo, (respectfully) 樂師 ngok-sze.
Musk, 麝香 sheʾ-heung.
Musk-melon, 香瓜 ʿheung-ʿkwa.
Musket, 鳥鎗 ʿniu-ʿtsʾeung.
Muslin, 棉紗 min-sha.
Mussel, (shell fish) 黃沙蜆 wong-ʿsha-ʿhin, 蜆 ʿhin.
Mussulman, (Moor) 摩囉人 ʿMoh-ʿloh-ʿyan, (Mohammedan) 回子 Ooi-ʿtsze.
Must, 必 pit, 必定 pit-tingʾ, 必要 pit-iuʾ, 是必 shiʾ-pit.
Mustaches, 髭 tsze, 八字鬚 paatʾ-tsze-so.
Mustard, 芥末 kaaiʾ-moot, 芥辣 kaaiʾ-laat, (seed) 芥子 kaaiʾ-ʿtsze.
Muster, 板 ʿpaan.
Musty, 糠隨 ʿhong-tsʾue 洽壞 upʾ-waaiʾ.
Mute, 唔聲 ʾm-sheng, 啞口 ʿa-ʿhau.
Mutilate, 殘害 tsʾaan-hoiʾ.

Mutiny, 叛逆 poon'-yik.
Mutter, (COL.) ʻkong-nge-nge-sheng, tʻup-tʻup-sheng.
Mutton, 羊肉 yeung-yuuk.
Mutual, 相 seung, 交相 kaau-seung-keʼ. 彼此 ʻpi-ʻtsʻze.
Muzzle, 口 ʻhau, 嘴 ʻtsui, (to) 笠住口 lup-chuc'-ʻhau.
My, mine, 我嘅 ʻngoh-keʼ.
Myriad, 萬 maan'.
Myrrh, 沒藥 moot-yeuk.
Myself, 我自己 ʻngoh-tszeʼ-ʻki, 本身 ʻpoon-shan, (I feed myself) 我食自己 ʻngoh-shik-tszeʼ-ʻki.
Mysterious, 奧妙 oʼ-miuʼ, 離明 naan-ming.
Myth, 古語 ʻkoo-ʻue.

N

Nail, 釘 ʻteng, (a) 一口釘 yat-ʻhau-ʻteng, (finger-, &c.) 甲 kaapʼ, 爪 ʻchaau.
Naked, 赤 chʻik, 光 kwong, (stark) 脫赤肋 tʻuetʼ-chʻikʼ-lak.
Nakedness, (destitution) 赤貧 chʻek-pʻun.
Name, 名 ming, *meng, (to) 改名 ʻkoi-*meng.
Namely, 卽 tsik.
Nankeen, cloth, 紫花布 ʻtsze-fa-poʼ, 赤布 chʻik-poʼ.
Nanking, 南京 Naam-king.
Nap, 毛 mo, 絨頭 yuung-tʻau, (sleep) 哈吓 hap-ʻha.
Napkin, 布仔 poʼ-ʻtsai, (table-) 茶巾 chʻa-ʻkan.
Narcissus, 水仙花 ʻshui-sin-fa.
Narcotic, 迷藥 mai-yeuk.
Narrate, 述出來 shuut-chʻuut-lai.
Narrow, 窄 chaakʼ, (tight) 挾 kip.
Nasturtium, 荷葉蓮 hoh-ip-lin.
Nasty, 臭 chʻauʼ.
Nation, 邦 pong, 國 kwokʼ.
Native, 本地 ʻpoon-*tiʼ, 土 ʻtʻo.

Natural, 天生 t'in-shang, t'in-shang-ke', 本性 ˻poon-sing'.
Naturally, 自然 tsze'-in, 天然 t'in-in.
Nature, 性 sing'.
Naughty, 頑皮 waan-p'i, 不好 'm-˻ho, k'waai'.
Nausea, 會嘔 ˻ooi-˻au, 想嘔 ˻seung-˻au.
Nautilus, 浮水螺 fau-˻shui-*loh.
Naval, (troops) 水師 ˻shui-˻sze, (officer) 水師官 ˻shui-˻sze-koon.
Nave, 輪心 luun-sum.
Navel, 肚臍 ˻t'o-ts'ze, (string) 臍帶 ts'ze-˻taai.
Navigate, 駛船 ˻shai-shuen.
Nay, 唔係 'm-hai', 不是 pat-shi'.
Near, 近 kan', ˻k'an, 附近 foo'-kan'.
Near-sighted, 近視眼 kan'-*shi'-˻ngaan.
Nearly, 差不多 ˻ch'a-pat-˻toh, 將近 tseung-kan'.

Neat, 齊整 ts'ai-˻ching, (clean) 乾淨 kohn-tseng'.
Necessary, 必要 pit-iu', 定必 ting'-pit, 無唔得 mo-'m-tak.
Neck, 頸 ˻keng.
Neck-lace, 頸鍊 ˻keng-*lin'.
Necktie, 頸領 ˻keng-˻leng.
Necrosis, 死骨 ˻sze-kwut.
Need, 須 sue, 須要 sue-iu'.
Needle, 眼針 ˻ngaan-chum, (magnetic) 南針 naam-˻chum.
Needle-woman, 補聯婆 ˻po-luen-*p'oh.
Needless, 不使 'm-˻shai, 不要 'm-iu'.
Needy, 窮乏 k'uung-fat.
Nefarious, 醜惡 ˻ch'au-ok'.
Negative, 對面話頭 tui'-min'-wa'-t'au, (positive &—) 有無 ˻yau-mo.
Neglect, 忘却 mong-k'euk', 失記 shat-ki', 失覺 shat-kok', 不顧 'm-koo'.
Negligent, 忽畧 fut-leuk.
Negotiate, 辦理 paan'-˻li.

Neigh, (嘶風 sze-fuung), 馬叫 ʿma-kiuʾ.
Neighbour, 隣人 luun-yan, 街坊 kaai-ˏfong.
Neighbours, 隣里 luun-ʿli, 四隣 szeʾ-luun.
Neighbouring, 隣近 luun-kanʾ, 隔離 kaakʾ-li.
Neighbourly, 好相與 ʿho-seung-ʿue.
Neither——nor, 不是—— 又不是 pat-shiʾ yauʾ-pat-shiʾ, 唔係—— 又唔係 ʾm-haiʾ——yauʾ-ʾm-haiʾ,—— 都唔係 too-ʾm-haiʾ.
Nephew, 姪子 chat-ʿtsze.
Neptune, 龍王 Luung-wong.
Nerve, 腦氣筋 ʿno-hiʾ-kan.
Nervous, (timid) 無志氣 ʿmo-chiʾ-hiʾ, (irritable) 內傷頸 noiʾ-sheung-ʿkeng.
Nest, 巢窩 chʾaau-woh, 竇 tauʾ.
Net, 網 ʿmong, 張網 cheung-ʿmong, (lifting) 罾 tsang.

Nettle rash, 風𤺥 fuung-naanʾ.
Neutral, 兩不相涉 ʿleung-pat-seung-shipʾ.
Neutralize, (medicine) 解藥 ʿkaai-yeukʾ, (poison) 解毒 ʿkaai-tuuk.
Never, (past) 未有 miʾ-ʿyau, 原來無 uen-loi-ʿmo, 總無 ʿtsuung-ʿmo, (to come) 終不 chuung-pat, 永遠無 ʿwing-ʿuen-ʿmo.
Nevertheless, 雖然 sui-in.
New, 新 san.
News, 新聞 san-*mun, 聲氣 sheng-hiʾ.
Newspaper, 新聞紙 san-mun-ʿchi.
Next, 第二 taiʾ-iʾ, 次 tsʿzeʾ, 對下 tuiʾ-haʾ, (day, &c.) 明日 ming-yat, &c., (near to) 近住 kanʾ-chueʾ.
Nice, 好 ʿho, 好樣 ʿho-*yeungʾ, 雅潔 ʿnga-kitʾ, (particular) 仔細 ʿtsze-saiʾ, (too) 俺尖 im-tsim.
Nickname, 花名 fa-*meng, 混名 wanʾ-*meng.

Niece, 姪女 chat-ʿnue.
Niggardly, 慳 haan, 鄙吝 ʿpʻi-luun⁾.
Night, 夜晚 ye⁾-ʿmaan.
Night-mare, 夢壓 muung⁾-aat⁾, 鬼責 ʿkwai-chaak⁾.
Night-dress, 䎞衫 fun⁾-ʿshaam.
Nimble, 輕快 hing-faai⁾, 快捷 faai⁾-tsit.
Nine, 九 ʿkau.
Nineteen, 十九 shap-ʿkau.
Ninety, 九十 ʿkau-shap.
Ninth, 第九 tai⁾-ʿkau.
Nip, 揑 nip, 鉗 kʻim, 械 mit.
Nippers, 鉗 *kʻim.
Nipple, 奶頭 ʿnaai-tʻau.
Nirvana, 涅盤 nip-pʻoon.
Nit, 虱乸嬈 shat-ʿna-chʻuun.
Nitre, 鹹硝 haam-siu, 硝 siu.
No, 不是 pat-shi⁾, 唔係 ʼm-hai⁾, 無 ʿmo.
Nobility, 爵 tseuk⁾.
Noble, 尊貴 tsuen-kwai⁾, (minded) 慷慨 ʿkʻong-kʻoi⁾, 光明正大 kwong-ming-ching⁾-taai⁾.

Nod, 點頭 ʿtim-tʻau, 低頭 tai-tʻau, 噏頭 ngup-*tʻau.
Noise, 聲響 sheng-ʿheung.
Noisome, 毒 tuuk.
Noisy, 嘈鬧 tsʻo-naau⁾.
Nominal, (merely) 有名無實 ʿyau-meng-mo-shat, 掛名 kwa⁾-*meng.
Nominate, 題名 tʻai-meng.
None, 無 ʿmo.
Nonsense, 讕話 ngaam⁾-wa⁾, 糊說 oo-shuet⁾.
Noon, 晏晝 aan⁾-chau⁾, 正午 ching⁾-ʿng.
Noose, 生結 shang-lit⁾, 老鼠耳 ʿlo-ʿshue-ʿi, 老鼠挾 ʿlo-ʿshue-kʻek⁾, (to) 挾住 kʻek⁾-chue⁾.
Nor, (see Neither).
North, 北 pak, (N. E., &c.) 東北 tuung-pak, &c.
Nose, 鼻 piʾ, 鼻哥 piʾ-koh.
Nosegay, 鮮花球 sin-fa-*kʻau.
Nostril, 鼻孔 piʾ-ʿhuung, 鼻籠 piʾ-ʿluung.
Not, 不 pat, 非 fi, 唔 ʼm.

Notable, 出衆 ch'uut-chuung, 非常 fi-sheung.
Notch, 割口 koht'-'hau, (a) 缺 k'uet', 崩口 pang-'hau.
Note, (to) 記 ki', 記住 ki'-chue', (sound) 音 yum, (a paper) 一張字 yat-cheung-tsze', (money) 銀紙 ngan-'chi.
Notepaper, 箋 ,tsin.
Nothing, 無乜野 'mo-mat-'ye, 無物 'mo-mat, 無野 'mo-'ye.
Notice, (to) 覺 kok', 顧 koo', 知見 chi-kin', 見得 kin'-tak, 睇見 't'ai-kin'.
Notification, 報單 po'-,tuan.
Notify, 報知 po'-,chi.
Notion, 想頭 'seung-t'au.
Notoriety, 起名 'hi-*meng.
Notwithstanding, 雖然 sui-in.
Noun, 實字 shat-tsze'.
Nourish, 養 'yeung, 養育 'yeung-yuuk.

Novel, (a) 小說 'siu-*shuet'.
Novelty, 新樣 san-*yeung', 新事 san-sze', (a) 新出物 san-ch'uut-mat.
November, 英十一月 Ying-shap-yat-uet.
Novice, 亞初 a'-,ch'oh.
Now, 如今 ue-kum, 家下 ka-'ha, 而家 i-ka.
Noxious, 惡 ok', 毒 tuuk.
Nozzle, 嘴 'tsui.
Nudity, 脫赤肋 t'uet'-ch'ik'-lak'.
Nugatory, 虛徒 hue-t'o.
Nugget, 金頭 kum-t'au.
Nuisance, 污糟 oo-tso, 臭物 ch'au'-mat.
Null and void, 廢字紙 fai'-tsze'-'chi.
Numbed, 痲痹 ma-muuk, 痲痺 ma-pi'.
Number, 數 sho', (No.) 第 tai'.
Numeral, 數目字 'sho-muuk-tsze'.
Numerically, 照數 chiu'-sho'.

Nun, (3 kinds) 三姑 saam-koo, (viz.) 尼姑 ni-koo, 道姑 to'-koo, 齋姑 chaai-koo, (Rom. Cath.) 修道女 sau-to'-ʻnue.
Nunnery, 庵堂 om-t'ong.
Nurse, 亞媽 a'-*ma, (wet) 奶媽 ʻnaai-ma, 濕媽 shup-ma, (dry) 乾媽 kohn-ma, (to) 餵奶 wai'-ʻnaai, (carry) 抱 p'o.
Nursery-garden, 怨樹園 ʻnun-shue'-*uen.
Nut, 核子 hat-ʻtsze.
Nut-crackers, 核子鉗 hat-ʻtsze-k'im.
Nutmeg, 荳蔻 tau'-k'au'.
Nutshell, 菓子殼 ʻkwoh-ʻtsze-hok'.
Nux-vomica, 馬前 ʻma-ts'in.

O

Oak, 橡 tseung', 櫟 lik.
Oakum, 碎纜料 sui'-laam'-*liu', 麻根 ma-kan, (used by Chinese) 竹絲 chuuk-ʻsze.

Oar, 枝槳 chi-ʻtseung.
Oath, 誓願 shai'-uen', 盟誓 mang-shai'.
Oatmeal, 粗麥粉 t'so-mak-ʻfun.
Obedient, 聽話 t'eng'-wa', t'eng'-wa'-ke'.
Obeisance, 拜跪 paai'-kwai'.
Obey, 遵 tsuun, 聽話 t'eng'-wa'.
Object, 物件 mat-kin', (of a verb) 所 —— ʻshoh ——, (aim) 意向 i'-heung', 志向 chi'-heung'.
Object, (to) 頂駁 ʻting-pok', (as an inferior) 駁嘴 pok'-ʻtsui.
Obligation, 本分 ʻpoon-fun', (a debt) 賬 cheung'.
Oblige, (force) 監 kaam, 強 ʻk'eung.
Obliged, (much) 多得 toh-tak, 足領 tsuuk-ʻling.
Obliging, 順情 shuun'-ts'ing.
Oblique, 斜 ts'e, ts'e'.
Obliterate, 滅去 mit-hue'.

Oblivion, 忘沒 mong-moot.
Oblong, 長方 ch'eung-fong, 日字樣 yat-tsze'-*yeung'.
Obloquy, 凌辱 ling-yuuk.
Obscene, 粗口 ts'o-ʿhau.
Obscure, 幽杳 yau-ʿmiu.
Obsequies, 喪禮 song-ʿlai.
Obsequious, 伏順 fuuk-shuun', 謙讓 him-yeung', 陰柔 yum-yau, (to the rich) 白鴿眼 paak-kop'-ʿngaan.
Observe, 睇 ʿt'ai, 觀 koon, (keep) 守 ʿshau.
Obstinate, 皮氣硬 p'i-hi'-ngaang', 固執 koo'-chup, 拗頸 aau'-ʿkeng.
Obstruct, 阻住 ʿchoh-chue', 壅滯 ʿyuung-chai', 塞住 sak-chue'.
Obstruction, 防碍 fong-ngoi', 阻塞 ʿchoh-sak.
Obtain, 得到 tak-ʿto.
Obtrusively, 自擅 tsze'-shin', 擅權 shin'-k'uen.
Obtuse, 鈍 tuun'.

Obviate, 免 ʿmin, 免得 ʿmin-tak.
Obviously, 當面 tong-min'.
Occasion, 機會 ki-ooi', (time) 排 *p'aai, (no) 不使 'm-shai, (to) 使 ʿshai.
Occasional, 或時 waak-shi.
Occult, 秘密 pi'-mat.
Occupation, 事業 sze'-ip, 工夫 kuung-foo.
Occupy, (take possession of) 據 kue', 住 chue'.
Occur, 遇有 —ue'-ʿyau—
Occurrence, 事 sze'.
Ocean, 洋海 yeung-ʿhoi.
Ochre, 石黃 shek-wong, 赭石 ʿche-shek, 雌黃 ts'ze-wong.
October, 英十月 Ying-shap-uet.
Ocular, 眼見 ʿngaan-kin'.
Oculist, 眼醫 ʿngaan-i, 眼科醫生 ʿngaan-foh-ʿi-ʿshang.
Odd, (single) 奇 ki, 單 taan, 零 leng, (strange) 古怪 ʿkoo-kwaai', 奇 k'i.

Ode, 詩 shi.
Odious, 可惡 ʻhoh-ooʼ.
Odium, (incur) 得人恨 tak-ɪan-hanʼ.
Odour, 香氣 heung-hiʼ, (bad) 臭氣 chʻauʼ-hiʼ.
Of, —— 之 —— chi, —— 嘅 —— keʼ, (course) 自然 tszeʼ-in, (made of) 俾 —— 做 ʻpi —— tsoʼ.
Off, 去 hueʼ, 離 li, (distant) 遠 ʻuen, (off the stage) 過造 kwohʼ-tsoʼ, (be off) 踍喇 liu-la.
Offence, 罪 tsuiʼ, (to take) 見怪 kinʼ-kwaaiʼ.
Offend, 干犯 kohn-faanʼ.
Offer, 許 ʻhue, 許口 ʻhue-ʻhau, (a price) 出 chʻuutʼ, 還 waan, (present) 送 suungʼ, 獻 hinʼ, (promise) 應承 ying-shing.
Office, (building) 寫字樓 ʻse-tszeʼ-*lau, 館 ʻkoon, 房 *fong, (situation) 職 chik.
Officer, 官府 koon-ʻfoo.
Official, 官 koon.

Officious, 多事 toh-szeʼ, toh-szeʼ-keʼ.
Often, 多次 toh-tsʻzeʼ, 屢次 lueʼ-tsʻzeʼ.
Ogle, 丟眼角 tiu-ʻngaan-*kokʼ.
Oh! 唉呀 ai-ya!
Oil, 油 yau.
Oiled cloth, 油布 yau-poʼ.
Oiled paper, 油紙 yau-ʻchi.
Ointment, 膏藥 ko-yeuk.
Old, 老年 ʻlo-nin, 老 ʻlo, (things) 舊 kauʼ.
Olea fragrans, 桂花 kwaiʼ-fa.
Oleander, 夾竹桃 kaap-chuuk-tʻo.
Olibanum, 乳香 ʻue-heung, 桃乳 tʻo-ʻue.
Olive, 橄欖 ʻkom-ʻlaam, (foreign) 水翁子 ʻshui-ʻyuung-ʻtsze.
Omelet, 鷄蛋餅 kai-taanʼ-ʻpeng.
Omen, 兆頭 chiuʼ-tʻau.
Omit, 漏 lauʼ, 嘞 laaiʼ, 遺失 wai-shat.

Omnipotent, 無所不能 mo-ʽshoh-pat-nang, 全能 tsʽuen-nang.

Omnipresent, 無所不在 mo-ʽshoh-pat-tsoiʼ.

Omniscient, 無所不知 mo-ʽshoh-pat-chi.

On, 上 sheungʼ, (to be) 在 — 上 tsoiʼ — shcungʼ, 喺 ʽhai.

Once, 一囘 yat-ooi, 一賬 yat-ʽheung, 一排 yat-*pʽaai, (at) 即時 tsik-shi.

One, 一 yat, 一個 yat-kohʼ, (single-) 單 taan.

One sided, 偏 pʽin, 一偏 yat-pʽin.

Onion, 葱頭 ʽtsʽuung-tʽau.

Only, 單 taan, 獨 tuuk, 但 taanʼ, 獨係 tuuk-haiʼ, 祇 ʽchi.

Onset } 力攻 lik-kuung.
Onslaught

Onward, 向前 heuungʼ-tsʽin.

Ooze, 滲漏 shumʼ-lau.

Opaque, 不透光 ʼm-tʽauʼ-kwong.

Open, 開 hoi, (fix open) 撐 chʽaangʼ, (out) 敷開 foo-hoi, (-faced) 率眞 suut-chan, (-handed) 手指疏 ʽshau-ʽchi-shoh, (wide apart) 疏 shoh.

Operation, 作爲 tsokʼ-wai, 工夫 kuung-foo, (surgical) 割症 kohtʼ-chingʼ.

Ophthalmia, 眼症 ʽngaan-chingʼ.

Opiate, 致睡藥 chiʼ-shuiʼ-yeuk.

Opinion, 意見 iʼ-kinʼ.

Opium, 鴉片 a-pʽinʼ.

Opium-shop, 烟館 in-ʽkoon, 鴉片館 a-pʽinʼ-ʽkoon.

Opopanax, 獨活糕 tuuk-oot-ko.

Opponent, 對頭 tuiʼ-*tʽau, 敵手 tik-ʽshau.

Opportunely, 恰好 hap-ʽho, 啱 ʽngaam.

Opportunity, 機會 ki-ooiʼ.

Oppose, 對 tuiʼ, 拒 ʽkʽue, 抗拒 kʽongʼ-ʽkʽue, 擋住 ʽtong-chueʼ, 對住 tuiʼ-chueʼ.

Opposite, 對面 tui⁾-min⁾, (contrary) 相反 seung-⸌fuan.
Oppress, 強壓 k‘eung-aat⁾, 困逐 k‘wun⁾-chuuk.
Opprobrious, 鄙薄 ⸌p‘i-pok.
Optional, 隨便 ts‘ui-*pin⁾, (for) 隨在 ts‘ui-tsoi⁾, 隨得 ts‘ui-tak.
Opulent, 豐富 fuung-foo⁾.
Or, 或 waak, 抑或 yik-waak, (-else) 定係 ting⁾-hai⁾.
Orach, 萊草 loi-⸌ts‘o (?).
Oral, 口講 ⸌hau-⸌kong, ⸌hau-⸌kong-ke⁾.
Orange, 橙 *ch‘aang, (loose skinned) 柑 ⸌kom, (small smooth) 桔 kat, (red) 砵砂桔 chue-sha-kat.
Orang-outang, 猩猩 ⸌sing-⸌sing.
Orator, 高談士 ⸌ko-t‘aam-sze⁾.
Orb, 輪 luun, 球 k‘au.
Orbit, 週道 chau-to⁾.
Orchard, 菓園 ⸌kwoh-uen.
Orchis, 蘭花 laan-fa, 石仙桃 shek-sin-t‘o.

Order, (arrangement) 次第 ts‘ze⁾-tai⁾, 次序 ts‘ze⁾-tsue⁾, 層次 ts‘ang-ts‘ze⁾, (to) 吩咐 fun-foo⁾.
Orderly, 停當 t‘ing-tong⁾.
Ordinary, 平常 p‘ing-sheung.
Ordure, 糞 fun⁾.
Ore, 礦 k‘waang⁾.
Organ, (musical) 大風琴 taai⁾-fuung-k‘um, (any) 器 hi⁾.
Orifice, 口 ⸌hau, 竅 k‘iu⁾, 籠 ⸌luung, 眼 ⸌ngaan.
Origin, 原頭 uen-t‘au, 原本 uen-⸌poon.
Originally, 原本 uen-⸌poon, 原來 uen-loi.
Originate, 創做 chong⁾-tso⁾, 初起 ch‘oh-⸌hi.
Oriole, 黃鳥 wong-⸌niu, 黃鶯 wong-⸌ang.
Ornament, 文飾 mun-shik, (to) 粧飾 chong-shik.
Ornamental, 好睇 ⸌ho-⸌t‘ai, 花 fa.
Orphan, 孤哀子 koo-oi-⸌tsze, 哀仔 oi-⸌tsai.
Orpiment, 雄黃 huung-wong.

Orthodox, 正教 chingʼ-kaauʼ.
Oscillate, 搖擺 iu-ʽpaai.
Osprey, 鶚 ngok.
Os-pubis, 交骨 kaau-kwut.
Ostensible, 名爲 ming-wai.
Ostentatious, 賣弄 maaiʼ-luungʼ, 弄巧 luungʼ-ʽhaau, 揮霍 fai-fokʼ.
Ostracion, 牛魚 ngau-ue.
Ostrich, 鴕鳥 tʼoh-ʽniu.
Other, 第二 taiʼ-iʼ, 別個 pit-kohʼ, 別 pit, 他 tʼa, (provinces) 外江 ngoiʼ-ʽkong.
Otherwise, 別樣 pit-yeungʼ, 若唔係 yeuk-ʼm-haiʼ.
Otter, 山獺 shaan-chʽaatʼ, (sea-) 海獺 ʽhoi-chʽaatʼ.
Ought, 應當 ying-tong, 應該 ying-koi, (not) 不可 pat-ʽhoh, 不好 ʼm-ʽho.
Ounce, (Chinese) 兩 ʽleung, (Eng.) 七錢五 tsʽat-tsʽin-ʽng.
Our, 我地嘅 ʽngoh-tiʼ-keʼ.
Out, 出 chʽuut, 外 ngoiʼ.
Outcry, 喊苦 haamʼ-ʽfoo.

Out-house, 外廠 ngoiʼ-ʽchʽong, 外屋 ngoiʼ-uuk, (built on) 狽仔屋 me-ʽtsai-uuk.
Out-let, 去路 hueʼ-loʼ.
Outrage, 橫暴 waang-poʼ.
Outrageous, 無度 ʽmo-toʼ.
Outside, 外 ngoiʼ, 外頭 ngoiʼ-tʽau, 外面 ngoiʼ-minʼ, 外便 ngoiʼ-pinʼ.
Outward, 向外 heungʼ-ngoiʼ, (appearance) 外貌 ngoiʼ-maauʼ.
Oval, 鵝蘂樣 ngoh-ʽchʽuun-*yeungʼ.
Oven, 焗爐 kuuk-lo.
Over, 過 kwohʼ, (above) 上 sheungʼ, (something over) 有剩 ʽyau-shingʼ.
Overbearing, 霸氣 paʼ-hiʼ.
Overcast, 起雲 ʽhi-wan.
Overcome, (to) 克制 haak-chaiʼ, 制服 chaiʼ-fuuk, 尅 haak.
Overflow, 水滿過 ʽshui-ʽmoon-kwohʼ.
Overgrown, 生滿 shang-ʽmoon.

Overhear, 旁聽 p'ong-t'eng.
Overlay, 鋪 p'o, 鍍 to'.
Overlook, 旁視 p'ong-shi', (not see) 唔睇 'm-'t'ai, (see Oversee).
Overmuch, 太多 t'aai'-toh, 多過頭 toh-'kwoh-t'au.
Overpass, 越 uet, 蹴過 naam'-kwoh'.
Overrun, (as types) 褪 t'un'.
Oversee, 督理 tuuk-'li, 照管 chiu'-'koon.
Overseer, 監督 kaam-tuuk.
Overspread, 遮蔽 che-pai', 遮蓋 che-k'oi'.
Overthrow, } 打倒 'ta-'to.
Overturn,
Overweening, 過傲 kwoh'-ngo'.
Overwhelm, 沉沒 ch'um-moot.
Overwhelming, 極甚 kik-shum'.
Oviparous, 蛋生 taan'-shang, 卵生 'luun-shang.
Owe, 欠 him'.
Owl, 貓兒頭鷹 ,maau-i-t'au-,ying.

Own, 自已嘅 tsze'-'ki-ke', 親 ts'an, (confess) 認 ying'.
Owner, 本主 'poon-'chue, 原主 uen-'chue.
Ox, 牛 ngau, (common) 黃牛 wong-ngau, (steer) 騸牛 shin'-ngau.
Oyster, 蠔 ho.
Oyster-shell windows, 明瓦 ming-'nga.

P

Pace, 步 po'.
Pacific Ocean, 太平洋 T'aai'-p'ing-yeung, 南洋 Naam-yeung.
Pacify, 開解 hoi-'kaai, 勸息 huen'-sik, 息 sik.
Pack, 收拾 shau-shup, 包好 paau-'ho, 裝好 chong-'ho, (off) 落箱 lok-seung.
Paddle, 扒 p'a, (a) 枝橈 chi-*iu.
Paddle-wheel, 火船車 'foh-shuen-ch'e.

Paddy, 禾 woh, (grain) 穀 kuuk.
Padlock, 荷包鎖 hoh-ʻpaau-ʻsoh.
Page, (leaf) 篇 pʻin, (one side of a leaf) 版 ʻpaan.
Pageant, 擺儀仗 ʻpaai-i-cheungʼ.
Pagoda, 塔 tʻaapʼ, (a) 枝塔 chi-tʻaapʼ.
Pail, (water-) 水桶 ʻshui-ʻtʻuung.
Pain, 痛 tʻuungʼ.
Pains-taking, 用心 yuungʼ-sum, 心機 sum-ki.
Paint, 油色 yau-shik, (water colours) 顏色 ngaan-shik.
Painter, 油漆師傅 yau-tsʻat-sze-*fooʼ, 油漆佬 yau-tsʻat-ʻlo, (picture-) 畫工 *waʼ-kuung.
Pair, 對 tuiʼ, 雙 sheung, (to) 配合 pʻooiʼ-hop.
Palace, 宮殿 kuung-tinʼ.
Palate, 腭 ngok, 上腭 sheungʼ-ngok.
Palaver, 虛話 hue-*waʼ.
Pale, 土色 ʻtʻo-shik, 白 paak.

Paling, 欄杆 laan-ʻkohn.
Palisade, 欄檻 laan-laamʼ.
Pall, (for a coffin) 棺罩 koon-chaauʼ.
Pall, (to) 失味 shat-miʼ.
Palliate, 減輕 ʻkaam-heng, 文飾 munʼ-shik.
Palm, 棕樹 tsuung-shueʼ, 桄榔 kwong-long, (cocoanut) 椰樹 ye-shueʼ, (date) 波斯棗 Poh-sze-ʻtso, (fan-) 葵 kʻwai.
Palm of the hand, 手版膛 ʻshau-ʻpaan-tʻong, 掌 ʻcheung.
Palpable, 明明白白 ming-ming-paak-paak.
Palpitate, 跳 tʻiuʼ, (col.) pop-pop-tʻiuʼ.
Palsy, 瘋癱 fuung-ʻtʻaan, 癱瘓 ʻtʻaan-oonʼ.
Paltry, 微賤 mi-tsinʼ.
Pamper, 縱慣口腹 tsuungʼ-kwaanʼ-ʻhau-fuuk.
Pamphlet, 小書 ʻsiu-shue.
Pan, 鐵鑊 tʻit-wok.
Pan-pipe, 笙 shang.

Pan-cake, 油煎餅 yau-tsin-ₑpeng.
Pancreas, 甜肉 t'im-yuuk.
Pander, 窩娼 woh-ch'eung.
Pane, 塊 faai⁾, 片 *p'in⁾.
Panelled, 瓜樣 ₑkwa-*yeung⁾, 凸朏 tat-ᶜkoo, (door) 瓜門 ₑkwa-*moon.
Pang, 暴痛 po⁾-t'uung⁾, 陣痛 chan⁾-t'uung⁾.
Pangolin, 穿山甲 ch'uen-shaan-kaap⁾.
Panic, 嚇殺 haak⁾-shaat⁾, 嚇死人 haak⁾-ᶜsze-yan.
Pansy, 堇菜 ᶜkan-ts'oi⁾.
Pant, 喘 ᶜch'uen.
Panther, 豹 p'aau⁾.
Pantomime, 戲舞 hi⁾-ᶜmoo.
Pantry, 管事房 ᶜkoon-sze⁾-*fong.
Papa, 爸爸 pa-pa.
Papaya, 乳瓜 ᶜue-ₑkwa, 木瓜 muuk-ₑkwa, 萬壽菓 maan⁾-shau⁾-ᶜkwoh.
Paper, 紙 ᶜchi.
Paper-money, 銀紙 ngan-ᶜchi, (for worship) 元寶 uen-ᶜpo, 紙錢 ᶜchi-ts'in.

Paper-mulberry, 楮 ᶜch'ue.
Papist, 天主教徒 T'in-ᶜchue-kaau⁾-t'o.
Parable, 譬喻 p'i⁾-ue⁾.
Parade-ground, 較塲 kaau⁾-*ch'eung.
Paradise, 樂園 lok-uen, (bird of) 雀皇 tseuk⁾-wong.
Paradoxical, 似相反 ᶜts'ze-seung-ᶜfaan.
Paraffine, 煤油 mooi-yau.
Paragraph, 段 tuen⁾, 條 t'iu.
Parallel, 平排 p'ing-p'aai, 平行 p'ing-hang.
Paralysis, 癱 ᶜt'aan.
Parapet, 欄圍 laan-wai, 圍墻 wai-ts'eung.
Paraphernalia, 嫁粧 ka⁾-chong.
Parasite, 寄生 ki⁾-ₑshang.
Parasol, 小綢遮 ᶜsiu-ch'au-ₑche.
Parboil, 煮半熟 ᶜchue-poon⁾-shuuk.
Parcel, 包野 paau-ᶜye.
Parched, 乾燥 kohn-ts'o⁾.
Parchment, 羊皮紙 yeung-p'i-ᶜchi.

Pardon, 赦 she', 赦免 she'-min, (beg-) 不該 'm-koi.
Parc, 剜削 p'ai-seuk', (scoop) 挖 waat'.
Paregoric, 止痛 ‘chi-t‘uung'.
Parents, 父母 foo'-‘moo, 兩親 ‘leung-ts‘an.
Park, 苑 ‘uen, (an enclosure) 圍 *wai.
Parliament, 上下議院 sheung'-ha'-‘i-*uen'.
Parlour, 客廳 haak'-‘t‘eng.
Parody, 改作笑話 ‘koi-tsok'-siu'-*wa'.
Paroquet, 鸚哥 ‘ang-‘koh.
Paroxysm, 抽搐 ch‘au-ch‘uuk', 忽然痛 fut-in-t‘uung'.
Parrot, 鸚鵡 ying-‘moo, 鶯哥 ‘ang-‘koh.
Parrot fish, 鷄公魚 ‘kai-‘kuung-*ue.
Parry, 擋格 ‘tong-kaak'.
Parsee, 白頭人 Paak-t‘au-yan, 波斯人 Poh-sze-yan.
Parsimonious, 慳吝 haan-luun'.

Parsley, 芫荽 uen-‘sai.
Parsnip, 葫蘿蔔 oo-loh-paak.
Part, 分 fun', (to) 分開 fun-hoi, (with) 捨 ‘she.
Partake, 有分 ‘yau-*fun'.
Partial, 一偏 yat-p‘in, yat-p‘in-ke'.
Participate, 有分 ‘yau-*fun'.
Particle, (word) 虛字眼 hue-tsze'-‘ngaan, (small) 微末 mi-moot.
Particular, (special) 特 tak, (important) 要緊 iu'-‘kan, (each) 一一 yat-yat, (careful) 仔細 ‘tsze-sai'.
Particularize, 逐一逐二 chuuk-yat-chuuk-i'.
Particularly, 特要 tak-iu', 專爲 chuen-wai.
Partition, 隔壁 kaak' pik, 間牆 kaan'-ts‘eung, (to) 間隔 kaan'-kaak'.
Partly, 有的係 ‘yau-‘ti-hai'.
Partner, 夥計 ‘foh-ki', 夥伴 ‘foh-poon'.

Partridge, 鷓鴣 che⁾-₍koo, 竹絲雞 chuuk-₍sze-₍kai.
Party, 羣黨 k'wan-⸌tong, 班 paan, 幫 pong.
Pass, (to) 過去 kwoh⁾-hue⁾, 行過 hang-kwoh⁾, (a) 關 kwaan, (a street-) 街紙 kaai-⸌chi, (night-) 夜紙 ye⁾-⸌chi, (mountain) 峽 haap⁾.
Pass a law, 設例 ch'it-lai⁾, (a time, or place) 過 kwoh⁾.
Passage, 路 lo⁾, 門 moon, 冷巷 ⸌laang-*hong⁾.
Passage-boat, 渡船 to⁾-shuen, *to⁾.
Passenger, 搭客 taap⁾-haak⁾.
Passion, (anger) 怒 no⁾, (desire) 情慾 ts'ing-yuuk, (generally) 烈氣 lit-hi⁾, (the seven passions) 七情 ts'at-ts'ing.
Passion-flower, 風車花 ₍fuung-₍ch'e-₍fa.
Passionate, 火性 ⸌foh-sing⁾-ke⁾.

Passive, (not moving) 不郁 'm-yuuk, (N.B. signs of the passive, as, 受 shau⁾, 被 pi⁾, 見 kin⁾, &c., should be used sparingly and in each case according to example of natives).
Passover, (the) 踰越節 ue-uet-tsit⁾.
Passport, 路票 lo⁾-p'iu⁾.
Pass-word, 暗號 om⁾-*ho⁾.
Past, 過了 kwoh⁾-⸌liu, kwoh⁾-hiu.
Paste, 漿糊 tseung-oo, (to) 裱 ⸌piu, 粘 nim.
Pasteboard, 裱紙皮 ⸌piu-⸌chi-p'i.
Paster, 裱匠 ⸌piu-tseung⁾.
Pastor, 牧 muuk, (minister) 牧師 muuk-sze.
Pastry, 點心 ⸌tim-⸌sum, 麵食 min⁾-shik, (covered dishes) 麵龜 min⁾-₍kwai.
Pasture, 牧草 muuk-⸌ts'o.
Pat, (to) 拍 p'aak⁾.
Patch, 補拈 ⸌po-⸌im, (to) 釘 補拈 teng-⸌po-⸌im, 補 po.
Patch-work, 摒 p'ing.

Patent, (to grant a) 批准 專做 *p'ai-ᶜchuun-chuen-tso'*, (a) 執照 *chup-chiu'*.
Path, 小路 *ᶜsiu-lo'*.
Pathetic, 傷心話 *sheung-sum-*wa'*, 動情 *tuung'-ts'ing*.
Patience, 忍耐 *ᶜyan-noi'*.
Patrimony, 基業 *ki-ip*.
Patron, 幫顧主 *pong-koo'-ᶜchue*, 主顧 *ᶜchue-*koo'*, 恩主 *yan-ᶜchue*.
Patronize, 照顧 *chiu'-koo'*, 幫襯 *pong-ch'an'*.
Patter, 滴滴達達 *tik-tik-taat-taat*.
Pattern, 樣子 *yeung'-ᶜtsze*.
Patty, 角仔 *kok'-ᶜtsai*, 餃子 *kaau-ᶜtsze*.
Pauper, 無倚賴 *ᶜmo-ᶜi-laai'*.
Pause, 歇吓 *hit'-ᶜha*.
Pave, 砌平石 *ts'ai'-p'ing-shek*.
Pavement, 石路 *shek-lo'*, 鋪石路 *p'o-shek-lo'*, (of bricks) 街磚地 *ᶜkaai-ᶜchuen-ti'*.

Pavilion, 凉亭 *leung-*t'ing*, 亭 *t'ing*.
Paw, (踏 faan), 掌 *ᶜcheung*, 爪 *ᶜchaau*.
Pawn, (to) 當 *tong'*, 當押 *tong'-aat'*, (a pledge) 當頭 *tong'-t'au*, (in chess) 卒 *tsuut*.
Pawn-broker, 當主 *tong'-ᶜchue*.
Pawn-shop, 當舖 *tong'-ᶜp'o*.
Pawn-ticket, 當票 *tong'-ᶜp'iu*.
Pay, 交(銀) *kaau (ngan)*, 還 *waan*.
Pay-day, 支銀日期 *chi-*ngan-yat-k'i*.
Payments, 支(銀) *chi, (ngan)*.
Peas, (green) 青荳 *ts'eng-*tau'*, 荷蘭荳 *Hoh-ᶜlaan-*tau'*.
Peace, 平安 *p'ing-ohn*, (international) 和 *woh*, (general) 太平 *t'aai'-p'ing*, (keep the) 守分 *ᶜshau-fun'*, 守和 *ᶜshau-woh*, (break the) 失和 *shat-woh*.

Peach, 桃 *t'o, (best kind) 鸚嘴桃 ying-⸌tsui-*t'o.
Peacock, 孔雀 ⸌huung-tseuk⸍.
Peacock's feather, 翎 ling, (superior double eyed) 雙眼花翎 sheung-⸌ngaan-fa-ling, (next order) 花翎 fa-ling, (inferior) 藍翎 laam-ling.
Peak, 山頂 shaan-⸌teng, 嶺頭 ⸌ling-t'au, 山峰 shaan-fuung.
Pear, 沙梨 sha-*li, (from the north) 雪梨 suet⸍-*li.
Pearl, 珍珠 chan-chue.
Pearl barley, 苡米 ⸌i-⸌mai.
Pearl-oyster, 珠蚌 chue-⸌p'ong.
Peasant, 村佬 ⸌ts'uen-⸌lo, 村夫 ⸌ts'uen-foo.
Peat, 地面炭 ti⸍-min⸍-t'aan⸍.
Pebble, 石䃯 shek-ch'uun.
Peck, (to) 啄 teuk⸍, teung; (a) 斗 ⸌tau.
Pecul, 擔 taam⸍.
Peculiar, 自己 tsze⸍-⸌ki, tsze-⸌ki-ke⸍, 另自 ling⸍-tsze⸍, 奇特 k'i-tak.

Pedant, 丟書包 tiu-⸌shue-⸌paau.
Pedler, 販仔 faan⸍-⸌tsai, 担頭仔 taam⸍-*t'au-⸌tsai.
Peel, (to) 剝皮 mok-p'i.
Peep, 窺探 k'wai-t'aam⸍, 覷 chong, 偷睇 t'au-⸌t'ai.
Peevish, 嬲嫩 nau-nat.
Peg, 釘杙 teng-tak.
Peking, 北京 Pak-king.
Pekoe-tea, 白毫茶 paak-ho-ch'a.
Pelican, 塘鵝 t'ong-*ngoh.
Pelt, (to) 揼 teng⸍.
Pelvis, 尻骨盤 haau-kwut-p'oon.
Pen, pencil, 支筆 chi-put, (lead-) 鉛筆 uen-put, (coop) 欄 laan.
Penalty, 刑罰 ying-fat.
Penang, 新埠 San-fau⸍.
Pending, 未定 mi⸍-ting⸍.
Pendulum, 擺 ⸌paai.
Penetrate, 透入 t'au⸍-yup, 深入 shum-yup.
Penguin, 企鵝 ⸌k'i-*ngoh.
Penis, 陽物 yeung-mat, (VULG.) ts'at.

Penitence, 悔心 fooi⌐-sum.
Pennant, 旆 p‘ooi⌐, 旗帶 k‘i-taai⌐.
Pension, 養老銀 ⌐yeung-⌐lo-*ngan, 太平糧 t‘ai-p‘ing-leung.
Pensive, 心思思 sum-sze-sze.
Penurious, 慳吝 haan-luun⌐.
Peony, 牡丹花 ⌐maau-taan-fa.
People, 民 mun, 百姓 paak⌐-sing⌐.
Pepper, 胡椒 oo-tsiu, 椒末 tsiu-moot, (red) 花椒 fa-tsiu.
Peppermint, 薄荷 pok-hoh.
Perambulate, 巡行 ts‘uun-hang.
Perceive, 覺得 kok⌐-tak, 見 kin⌐.
Per cent, 每一百 ⌐mooi-yat-paak⌐, (discount three) 九七扣 ⌐kau-ts‘at-k‘au⌐.
Perceptible, 睇得 ⌐t‘ai-tak, ⌐t‘ai-tak-ke⌐.
Perch, 栖 ts‘ai, (to) 踎 mau, (a fish) 鱸魚 lo-*ue, 鰂頭 waak-t‘au.

Percolate, 滲漏 shum⌐-lau.
Percussion cap, 銅帽子 t‘uung-mo⌐-tsze.
Peremptory, 緊緊 ⌐kan-⌐kan.
Perennial, 週年 chau-nin, chau-nin-ke⌐.
Perfect, 成全 shing-ts‘uen, 齊 ts‘ai.
Perfectly, 十分 shap-fun.
Perfidious, 奸詐 kaan-cha⌐.
Perforate, 鑽通 tsuen⌐-t‘uung, 穿 ch‘uen.
Perform, 行 hang, 做 tso⌐.
Perfume, 香 heung, 香料 heung-*liu⌐.
Pergularia, 夜蘭香 ye⌐-laan-⌐heung.
Perhaps, 或者 waak-⌐che, (it is) 係都唔定 hai⌐-⌐too-’m-ting⌐.
Peril, 危險 ngai-⌐him, 危險處 ngai-⌐him-shue⌐.
Period, (time) 時候 shi-hau⌐, (in writing) 斷句圈 ⌐t‘uen-kue⌐-⌐huen.
Periodic, 循還 ts‘uun-waan, 輪時 lnuu-shi.

Perish, 滅亡 mit-mong, 沈淪 ch'um-luun.
Perishable, 易壞 i'-waai'.
Perjure, 枉誓 'wong-shai', 發枉誓 faat'-'wong-shai'.
Perjury, 誓枉願 shai'-'wong-uen'.
Permanent, 恆久 hang-'kau.
Permeate, 通透 t'uung-t'au'.
Permit, 准 'chuun, 俾 'pi, 許准 'hue-'chuun, 由得 yau-tak.
Permit, (a) 人情紙 yan-ts'ing-'chi.
Pernicious, 利害 li'-hoi'.
Perpendicular, 豎直 shue'-chik, 企直 'k'i-chik, 棟企 tuung'-'k'e.
Perpetual, 永 'wing.
Perpetuate, 常存 sheung-ts'uen.
Perplex, 煩擾 faan-'iu.
Perplexity, 紛紛 fun-fun, 曲折 k'uuk-chit'.
Persecute, 困逐 'k'wun'-chuuk.

Perseverance, 始終如一 'c'hi-chuung-ue-yat, 恆心 hang-suin.
Persimmon, 柿 *ts'ze, (soft) 腍柿 num-*ts'ze.
Persist, 硬要 *ngaang'-iu', 不歇要 pat-hit'-iu, 固執 koo'-chup.
Person, 位 wai', 人 yan, (body) 身 shan, (in) 親身 ts'an-shan.
Perspicacious, 聰明 ts'uung-ming.
Perspicuous, 明白 ming-paak.
Perspiration, 汗 hohn'.
Perspire, 出汗 ch'uut-hohn'.
Persuade, 勸服 huen'-fuuk.
Pert, 傏突 t'ong-tat.
Pertinacious, 固執 koo'-chup, 執硬 chup-ngaang'.
Perturb, 擾亂 'iu-luen'.
Perturbed, 着忙 cheuk-mong.
Peruvian-bark, 金雞勒 kum-kai-lak.
Pervade, 通暢 t'uung-ch'eung, 暢達 ch'eung'-taat.

Perverse, 乖僻 kwaai-p'ik, 剛戾 kong-lui', 扭頸 'nau-'keng.
Pervert, 弄壞 luung'-waai'.
Pervious, 透得 t'au'-tak, t'au'-tak-ke'.
Pestilence, 瘟疫 wan-yik.
Pestle, 舂杵 chuung-'ch'ue, (for rice) 碓 tui'.
Pet, (child) 寵愛仔 'chuung-oi'-'tsai.
Petal, 花瓣 fa-faan'.
Petition, 禀 'pun.
Petroleum, 石油 shek-yau.
Petted, 縱慣 tsuung'-kwaan'.
Petticoat, 中裙 chuung-k'wun, 內裙 noi'-k'wun.
Pettish } 小嫌 'siu-im, 俺尖 im-tsim.
Petulant }
Petuntsze, 白不子 paak-'tuun-'tsze.
Pewter, 鑞錫 laap-sek'.
Phantom, 幻景 waan'-'king.

Pheasant, 山鷄 shaan-kai, (golden) 錦鷄 'kum-kai, (argus) 鸞鷄 luen-kai, (peacock-) 金錢鷄 kum-ts'in-kai.
Phenix, 鳳凰 fuung'-wong.
Phenomenon, 象 tseung'.
Philosopher, 博士 pok'-sze'.
Phlegm, 痰涎 t'aam-in, t'aam-shin.
Phlegmatic, 性慢 sing'-maan', 閒八 haan-paat', 慢閒 maan'-haan.
Phonography, (representing sounds merely) 寫白字 'se-paak-tsze'.
Photograph, 影相 'ying-*seung'.
Phrase, 句話 kue'-wa'.
Phthisis, 癆病 lo-peng'.
Physical, 有形 'yau-ying.
Physician, 醫生 i-'shang.
Physiognomy, 相 seung', (science) 相學 seung'-hok.
Piano, 洋琴 yeung-k'um.

Pick, up, 拈起 nim-ʻhi, 拾起 shap-ʻhi, 執 chup, (the teeth) 剌牙 tsʻzeʼ-nga, (flowers, &c.) 摘 chaak, (choose) 揀 ʻkaan, (tease) 搣 mit, (nibble) 咽 luun, (pierce) 啄 teung.

Pick-axe, 雞嘴斧 kaiʻ-ʻtsui-ʻfoo, 番釘 faan-ʻteng.

Picket, (a stake) 樁 chong.

Pickled, 鹹 haam.

Pickles, 酸菓 suen-ʻkwoh.

Pick-pocket, 剪綹 ʻtsin-ʻlau, ʻtsin-ʻnau-ʻlo, 插手佬 chʻaapʼ-ʻshau-ʻlo.

Picnic, 遊燕 yau-inʼ.

Picture, 畫 waʼ, *waʼ, (-frame) 畫架 waʼ-kaʼ.

Picul, 擔 taamʼ.

Pie, (bird) 喜鵲 ʻhi-tsʻeukʼ, (pastry) 麵龜 minʼ-kwai.

Pic-bald, 斑駁 paan-pokʼ.

Piece, 塊 faaiʼ, 件 kinʼ, (of cloth) 疋 pʻut.

Piece-work, 斷件工夫 tuenʼ-*kinʼ-kuung-foo.

Pier, 馬頭 ʻma-tʻau.

Pierce, 劖 tsʻim, 刮 kat, 刮穿 kat-chʻuen.

Piety, (filial) 孝 haauʼ, (religion) 虔敬 kʻin-kingʼ.

Pig, 猪 ʻchue, (a) 隻猪 chekʼ-ʻchue.

Pigeon, 白鴿 paak-kopʼ.

Pigment, 顏料 ngaan-liuʼ.

Pigmy, 矮佬仔 ʻai-ʻlo-ʻtsai.

Pigtail, 條辮 tʻiu-ʻpin.

Pike, (a) 一枝鎗 yat-chi-ʻtsʻeung.

Pike, fish, 班魚 paan-ue.

Pile up, 壘起 tip-ʻhi, 揪起 lumʼ-ʻhi, 疊 ʻlui, (drive piles) 打樁 ʻta-chong.

Piles, (disease) 痔瘡 chiʼ-ʻchʻong, (wooden) 樁 chong.

Pilfer, 鼠摩 ʻshue-ʻmoh, 鼠竊 ʻshue-sitʼ.

Pilferer, 三隻手 saam-chekʼ-ʻshau.

Pilgrim, 遊客 yau-haakʼ.

Pill, 藥丸 yeuk-*uen.

Pillage, 搶掠 ʻtsʻeung-leuk, 劫掠 kipʼ-leuk.

Pillar, 條柱 t'iu-ᶜch'ue, 柱墩 ᶜch'ue-ᶜtun, (monument) 碑 pi.
Pillow, 枕頭 ᶜchum-t'au.
Pilot, 引水人 ᶜyan-ᶜshui-yan, 帶水佬 taai²-ᶜshui-ᶜlo, naai²-shui-ᶜlo.
Piloting, 帶船 taai²-shuen, naai²-shuen.
Pimp, 做龜 tso²-ᶜkwai.
Pimple, 粉刺 ᶜfun-ts'ze².
Pin, 頭針 t'au-chum, 釘 teng.
Pinafore, 圍裙 wai-*k'wun.
Pincers, 鉗 *k'im.
Pinch, (to) 鑷 nip, 搣 mit.
Pine, (wood) 杉 ch'aam².
Pine, (to) 失志 shat-chi², 喪氣 song²-hi², 消瘦 siu-shau².
Pine-apple, 波羅菓 poh-loh-ᶜkwoh.
Pink, 剪邊羅 ᶜtsin-pin-loh.
Pin-money, 針黹銀 chum-ᶜchi-*ngan.
Pinnacle, 頂 ᶜteng.
Pint, (a) 半斤 poon²-kan.

Pioneer, 開路先鋒 hoi-lo²-ᶜsin-ᶜfuung.
Pious, 虔心 k'in-sum.
Pip, (of fowls) 鷄髁 kai-ᶜk'ang, (seed) 核 wat.
Pipe, 筒 *t'uung, (opium-) 鎗 ᶜts'eung.
Pirate, 海賊 ᶜhoi-ts'aak.
Pistil, 花蕊 fa-ᶜyui.
Pistol, 手鎗 ᶜshau-ᶜts'eung.
Piston, (牡 ᶜmau), 榫 suut.
Pit, 阱 ᶜtseng, 潭 t'aam, ᶜt'um.
Pitch, 吧碼油 ᶜpa-ᶜma-yau.
Pitcher, 水埕 ᶜshui-ch'ing.
Pitcher-plant, 猪籠草 chue-luung-ᶜts'o.
Pitch-fork, 禾杈 woh-ᶜch'a.
Pith, 樹心 shue²-sum.
Pith-paper, 通紙 ᶜt'uung-ᶜchi, 紙通 ᶜchi-t'uung.
Pithy, 有力 ᶜyau-lik, ᶜyau-lik-ke².
Pitted, (pock-) 痘皮 tau²-p'i.
Pity, 可憐 ᶜhoh-lin, 憐恤 lin-suut, 哀憐 oi-lin.

Pivot, 轉樖 ᶜchuen-suut.
Placable, 會和翻 ᶜooi-woh-faan.
Placard, 帖 t'ip², 揭帖 k'it-t'ip², (anonymous) 白帖 paak-*t'ip², (with a name) 長紅 ch'eung-huung.
Place, 處 ch'ue², 地方 ti-fong, 定 *teng², (to) 安置 ohn-chi², 擠 chai, (one) 一笪 yat-taat².
Placenta, 胎衣 ᶜt'oi-i, 後人 hau²-*yan.
Placid, 和氣 woh-hi².
Plagiarism, 抄襲 ch'aau-tsaap.
Plague, 瘟疫 wan-yik, 黃瘟病 wong-wan-peng², (to) 難爲 naan-wai.
Plaice, 甑閉魚 tsang-pai²-ue.
Plain, 明白 ming-paak, (even) 平 p'ing, (unadorned) 樸素 p'ok²-so², (a) 平原 p'ing-uen.
Plaintiff, 原告 uen-ko².
Plait, 橎埋 pun²-maai, (fold) 蹙埋 ts'uuk-maai.

Plan, 方法 fong-faat², (to) 謀 mau, 謀度 mau-tok.
Plane, (tool) 刨 *p'aau, (to) 刨 p'aau.
Planet, 行星 hang-ᶜsing.
Plank, 橋板 k'iu-ᶜpaan, 厚木板 hau²-muuk-ᶜpaan.
Plant, (a) 草 ᶜts'o, (to) 種 chuung², (rice) 蒔禾 shi²-woh.
Plantago, 車前草 ch'e-ts'in-ᶜts'o.
Plantain, 蕉 ᶜtsiu, (fragrant) 香牙蕉 heung-nga-ᶜtsiu, (long) 龍牙蕉 luung-nga-ᶜtsiu.
Plaster, (to) 抆灰 ᶜmun-fooi, 盪 tong², (medical) 膏藥 ko-yeuk.
Plat, (to) 搒 pun², (the cue) 搒辮 pun²-ᶜpin.
Plate, (a) 碟 *tip, 隻碟 chek²-*tip, (to) 鍍 to².
Platform, 棚 p'aang, 臺 t'oi, *t'oi.
Platina, 白金 paak-ᶜkum.
Plausible, 好似眞 ᶜho-ᶜts'ze-chan.

Play, 反斗 ʻfaan-ʻtau, 頑耍 waan-ʻsha, (TRANS. VERB) 打 ʻta, 弄 luung’, (as a guitar) 彈 tʻaan, (as a violin) 研 ngaan, (as a fife) 吹 chʻui.
Play-acting, 做戲 tso’-hi’.
Play-day, 放假日 fong’-ka’-yat.
Player, 戲子 hi’-ʻtsze.
Plea, 解訴 ʻkaai-so’, 供狀 kuung-chong’.
Pleasant, 爽快 ʻshong-faai’, 得意 tak-i’.
Please, 悅 uet, 樂 lok, (if you) 請 ʻtsʻeng, (as you) 隨便 tsʻui-*pin’.
Pleased, 歡喜 foon-ʻhi.
Pleasure, 快樂 faai’-lok, (— excursion) 遊嬉 yau-hi.
Plebeian, 俗 tsuuk.
Pledge, 當頭 tong-tʻau, (to) 按當 ohn’-tong’, 拚 pʻoon’, (in drinking) 酬酢 chʻau-tsok, 敬酒 king’-ʻtsau, 勸酒 huen’-ʻtsau.

Plenipotentiary, 全權 tsʻuen-kʻuen.
Plentiful, 豐阜 fuung-fau’, 豐足 fuung-tsuuk.
Plethora, 血實 huet’-shat, 壯實 chong’-shat.
Pleurisy, 肺胞膜炎 fai-paau-mok-im.
Pliable, 柔軟 yau-ʻuen, 循良 tsʻuun-leung, 易轉 i’-ʻchuen.
Plight, (state) 地位 ti’-wai’.
Plod, 勞勞 lo-lo.
Plot, 計策 kai’-chʻaak’, (lot) 塊 faai’.
Plough, (to) 犂 lai, 使 ʻshai, 耕 kang, (a) 把犂 ʻpa-lai.
Ploughshare, 犂頭嘴 lai-tʻau-ʻtsui.
Pluck, 摘 chaak, (out) 拔 pat, 猛出來 mang’-chʻuut-lai, (up courage) 揚起心肝 tik-ʻhi-sum-kohn.
Plug, (塞子 sak-ʻtsze), 榫 suut.
Plum, 梅 *mooi, 李 ʻli.
Plumb-line, 吊鉈 tiu’-tʻoh, 準繩 ʻchuun-shing.

Plume, 翎 ʻling.
Plump, 好肉耳 ʻho-yuuk-ʻi, 肥粒粒 fi-nup-nup.
Plunder, 打刼 ʻta-kip', 搶刼 ts'eung-kip'.
Plunge, 沈下 chum'-ha, 投水聲 t'au-shui, (noise) 泵聲 tum'-sheng.
Pluto, 閻羅王 Im-loh-wong.
Ply, 趕緊 ʻkohn-ʻkan, 勤 k'an, 趕起 ʻkohn-ʻhi.
Pocket, 衫袋 shaam-*toi', 袋 *toi'.
Pock-marked, 痘皮 tau'-p'i.
Pod, 荳荚 tau'-kaap'.
Poem, 首詩 ʻshau-ʻshi.
Poet, 詩人 shi-yan.
Poignant, 辣 laat.
Point, 尖 tsim, 尖處 tsim-shue', 尖嘴 tsim-ʻtsui, (dot) 點 ʻtim, (point out) 指出 ʻchi-ch'uut, 指點 ʻchi-ʻtim, (to plaster) 批灰 ʻp'ai-fooi.
Poise, 戥正 tang'-cheng'.
Poison, 毒 tuuk, 毒物 tuuk-mat, (to) 毒死 tuuk-ʻsze.

Poisoned, 服毒 fuuk-tuuk.
Poke, (to) 刺 ts'ze', (stir) 撩起 ʻliu-ʻhi.
Poker, 火棒 ʻfoh-ʻp'aang.
Poke-weed, 蕌 fuuk.
Pole, 竿 kohn, 杠 kong', (north) 北極 pak-kik, (south) 南極 naam-kik.
Pole a boat, 撐船 ch'aang-shuen.
Pole-cat, 臭貓 ch'au'-ʻmaan.
Polianthes, 玉簪花 yuuk-ʻtsaam-ʻfa.
Police, 差役 ch'aai-yik, (in Hongkong) 綠衣 luuk-ʻi.
Police Court, 巡理府 ts'uun-ʻli-ʻfoo.
Police-office, 巡捕廳 ts'uun-po'-ʻt'eng.
Polish, 磨擦 moh-ts'aat', 擦光 ts'aat'-kwong, 磨光 moh-kwong.
Polite, 有禮貌 ʻyau-ʻlai-maau', (you are) 好話 ʻho-wa'.
Politics, 國事 kwok'-sze'.
Pollen, 花粉 fa-ʻfun.

Pollute, 污衊 oo-mit, 整污 ʽching-oo.
Polypus, (in the nose) (鼻菌 piʼ-ʽkʽwun), 鼻蛇 piʼ-she.
Pomatum, 頭髮油 tʽau-faatʼ-yau, 香油 heung-yau.
Pomegranate, 石榴 shek-*lau.
Pommel, (to) 槌泵 chʽui-ʽtum.
Pomp, 繁華 faan-wa.
Pomphret, 鱠魚 ʽtsʽong-*ue.
Pompous, 駕子大 kaʼ-ʽtsze-taaiʼ.
Pond, 池塘 chʽi-tʽong.
Ponder, 默想 mak-ʽseung, 深想 shum-ʽseung, 細想 saiʼ-ʽseung.
Ponderous, 重 ʽchʽuung.
Pond-weed, 藻 tso.
Pongee, 綢 *chʽau.
Pool, 池 chʽi, 水氹 ʽshui-ʽtʽum.
Poop, 船尾樓 shuen-ʽmi-lau.
Poor, 貧窮 pʽun-kʽuung, 貧寒 pʽun-hohn.

Poor health, 不受用 ʼm-shauʼ-yuungʼ.
Pop, (a sound) (COL.) pop-sheng.
Pope, 教王 kaau-wongʼ.
Poppy, 罌粟 ang-suuk, 阿芙蓉 oh-foo-yuung.
Popular, 民愛 mun-oiʼ.
Population, 戶口 ooʼ-ʽhau.
Porcelain, 瓷 tsʽze, (ware) 瓷器 tsʽze-hiʼ.
Porch, 頭門拱 tʽau-moon-ʽkuung.
Porcupine, 箭豬 tsinʼ-chue.
Pores, 毛孔 mo-ʽhuung, 竅 kʽiuʼ.
Pork, 猪肉 chue-yuuk.
Porpoise, 猪魚 chue-ue.
Porridge, 麥粉羹 mak-ʽfun-kang, 煮熟麥粉 ʽchue-shuuk-mak-ʽfun.
Port, (a) 港口 ʽkong-ʽhau, 埠頭 *fauʼ-tʽau, (-side) 船左 shuen-ʽtsoh.
Port-clearance, 紅牌 huung-pʽaai.
Portent, 凶兆 huung-chiuʼ.

Porter, (at a gate) 看門公 hohn-moon-kuung, (carrier) 桃夫 tʻiu-foo, (to be a) 擔擔 taam-taamʼ.
Portfolio, 書夾 shue-kaapʼ.
Portion, 分子 funʼ-ʻtsze, 分 funʼ, 分額 funʼ-ngaak.
Portland cement, 英坭 ying-*nai.
Portly, 肥壯 fi-chongʼ.
Portmanteau, 背包 pooiʼ-paau.
Portrait, 眞 ʻchan, 像 *tseungʼ, 相 seungʼ.
Portray, 寫眞 ʻse-ʻchan.
Portugal, 西洋國 Sai-yeung-kwokʼ.
Pose, (to) 難 naan.
Position, 地位 tiʼ-waiʼ.
Positively, 一定 yat-tingʼ, 偏偏 ʻpʻin-ʻpʻin.
Possess, 有 ʻyau, 常有 sheung-ʻyau.
Possessed, (by a demon) 鬼迷 ʻkwai-mai.
Possessions, 所有 ʻshoh-ʻyau.
Possible, 做得 tsoʼ-tak, tsoʼ-tak-keʼ, 能 nang, 得 tak.

Post, (a pillar) 支柱 chi-ʻchʻue, (letter-) 通書信 tʻuung-shue-suunʼ, 驛 yik.
Postage, 酒資 ʻtsau-ʻtsze, 信資 suunʼ-ʻtsze.
Poster, 街招 ʻkaai-ʻchiu.
Postman, 千里馬 tsʻin-ʻli-ʻma, (-horse) 快馬 faaiʼ-ʻma.
Postmaster General, 驛務司 Yik-mooʼ-ʻsze.
Post-office, 書信館 shue-suunʼ-ʻkoon.
Postpone, 展緩 ʻchin-oonʼ, 推遲 tʻui-chʻi.
Postscript, 再筆 tsoiʼ-put.
Posture, 形勢 ying-shaiʼ.
Pot, 壺 oo, *oo, (chamber-) 便壺 pinʼ-*oo, (to boil in) 煲 ʻpo, (COL.) tup, (flower-) 花盤 fa-pʻoon.
Potash, 鹻 ʻkaan.
Potatoe, 荷蘭薯 Hoh-ʻlaan-*shue, 薯仔 shue-ʻtsai, (sweet) 番薯 faan-*shue.
Pot-belly, 肥肚腩 fi-ʻtʻo-ʻnaam.

Potency, 勢力 ʿshai³-lik, 功力 kuung-lik.
Pottage, (to make) 煮熟麥粉 ʿchue-shuuk-mak-ʿfun.
Pottery, 瓦器 ʿnga-hi³, 缸瓦 kong-ʿnga, (-kiln) 瓦窰 ʿnga-iu.
Pouch, 囊 nong, 袋 *toi³.
Poultice, 洽瘡材料 up-ʿchʻong-tsʻoi-liu³, (put on, of rice) 俾爛飯洽 ʿpi-laan³-faan³-up.
Poultry, 雞鴨 kai-aap³.
Pounce upon, 搶 ʿtsʻeung.
Pound, (to) 摏 chuung, (rub and grind) 擂 lui, (weight) 磅 pʻong, 十二兩 shap-i³-ʿleung.
Pour out, 斟 chum, 倒出 ʿto-chʻuut, (in) 潞 lo³, 灌入去 koon³-yup-hue³.
Pout, 櫻脣 ʿying-shuun.
Powder, 粉 ʿfun, 末 *moot, (gun-) 火藥 ʿfoh-yeuk, (medicine) 藥散 yeuk-ʿsaan.

Power, 才能 tsʻoi-nang, 勢力 ʿshai³-lik, 權柄 kʻuen-ping³.
Pox, (syphilis) 生疔病 shang-teng-peng³, 疳瘡 kom-ʿchʻong.
Practicable, 可用 ʿhoh-yuung³, 使得 ʿshai-tak, 可以做得 ʿhoh-ʿi-tso³-tak.
Practical joke, 整頓人 ʿching-tun³-yan-ke³.
Practice, 習練 tsaap-lin³.
Praise, 讚美 tsaan³-ʿmi, 讚美 tsaan³-sin³, 褒獎 po-ʿtseung.
Prance, 跳 tʻiu³, 跑來跑去 ʿpʻaau-loi-ʿpʻaau-hue³.
Prate, 支支咋咋 chi-chi-chaʾ-chaʾ.
Prattle, (COL.) i-i-a-a, ti-ti-te-te, (嘔啞 ʿau-a).
Prawns, 明蝦 ming-ha.
Pray, 祈禱 kʻi-ʿtʻo, 祈求 kʻi-kʻau, (I pray you) 請 ʿtsʻeng.

Preach, 宣傳 ꜀suen-ch'uen, 講書 ꜂kong-shue, 講道 ꜂kong-to꜄.
Precarious, 險險地 ꜂him-꜂him-*ti꜄.
Precaution, 預防 ue꜄-fong.
Precede, 在先 tsoi꜄-sin, (go first) 先行 sin-hang.
Precedent, 先起例 sin-꜂hi-lai꜄.
Precept, 教訓 kaau꜄-fun꜄, 規條 k'wai-t'iu, 箴規 chum-k'wai.
Precession of the equinoxes, 歲差 sui꜄-ch'a.
Precincts, 境界 ꜂king-kaai꜄.
Precious, 寶貝 ꜂po-pooi, 珍寶 chan-꜂po.
Precipice, 危巖 ngai-ngaam, 山崖 shaan-ngaai.
Precipitate, 忙速 mong-ts'uuk, (to) 傾跌 k'ing-tit꜄.
Precipitous, 危聳 ngai-꜂suung.
Precise, 端方 tuen-fong, 端正 tuen-ching꜄, 正經 ching꜄-king.

Precisely, 正 ching꜄, 啱啱 ꜀ngaam-꜀ngaam.
Preclude, 阻隔 ꜂choh-kaak꜄, 免致 ꜂min-chi꜄, 不俾 ꜀'m-꜂pi.
Precocious, 老辣 ꜂lo-laat.
Preconceive, 預估 ue꜄-꜂koo.
Predecessor, 先任 sin-yum꜄.
Predetermine, 預定 ue꜄-ting꜄.
Predict, 預言 ue꜄-in, 預先話 ue꜄-sin-wa꜄.
Predisposed, 先向 sin-heung꜄.
Predominate, 嬴過 yeng-kwoh꜄.
Pre-eminent, 出類 ch'uut-lui꜄, 出衆 ch'uut-chuung꜄.
Pre-engaged, 先應 sin-ying.
Preface, 書序 shue-tsue꜄.
Prefect, 知府 chi-꜂foo.
Prefecture, 府 ꜂foo.
Prefer, 寧愛 ning-oi꜄, 寧願 ning-uen꜄, 更愛 kang꜄-oi꜄.
Prefigure, 預影 ue꜄-꜂ying.
Prefix, 落起頭 lok-꜂hi-t'au, 落頭頂處 lok-t'au-꜂ting-shue꜄.

Pregnant, 懷孕 waai-yan', 有身紀 ʻyau-shan-ʻki, 馱胎 tʻoh-tʻoi.
Prejudice, 偏見 pʻin-kin'.
Preliminary, 引起 ʻyan-ʻhi, ʻyan-ʻhi-ke'.
Premature, 太早 tʻaai'-ʻtso, 未熟 mi'-shuuk.
Premeditated, 豫先想出 ue'-sin-ʻseung-chʻuut.
Premises, 行 *hong.
Premium, 賞 ʻsheung, (money) 賞銀 ʻsheung-*ngan.
Preoccupy, 先得倒 sin-tak-ʻto, 先取 sin-ʻtsʻue, 住先 chue'-sin.
Prepare, 准備 ʻchuun-piʻ, 整備 ʻching-piʻ, 預備 ue'-piʻ, 整定 ʻching-ting'.
Prepay, 先交銀 sin-kaau-*ngan.
Preponderate, 越重 uet-ʻchʻuung.
Preposterous, 慌唐 fong-tʻong, 不入理 'm-yup-ʻli, 怪誕 kwaai'-taan'.
Prerogative, 獨權 tuuk-kʻuen.

Presage, (a) 兆頭 chiu'-tʻau.
Prescription, 藥方 yeuk-fong.
Presence, 面前 min'-tsʻin, (of mind) 淡定 taam'-ting', 定見 ting'-kin'.
Present, (time) 今 kum, (to be) 在 tsoi', (a) 禮物 ʻlai-mat, (to) 送 suung', 獻上 hin'-ʻsheung.
Presently, 就家 tsau'-ka, 就來 tsau'-loi.
Preserve, 守住 ʻshau-chueʻ, 保全 ʻpo-tsʻuen, 存吓 tsʻuen-ʻha.
Preserves, 糖菓 tʻong-ʻkwoh.
President, 會頭 *ooi'-tʻau, of a Republic, 總統 ʻtsung-ʻtʻung.
Press, (a) 櫃 kwai', (oil, &c.) 榨 cha', (printing-) 印書盤 yan'-shue-pʻoon.
Press, (to) 壓住 aat'-chueʻ, 逼 pik, 搾 cha', 瘟 ʻang.
Pressing, 急切 kup-tsʻit'.
Prestige, 聲勢 shing-shai'.

Presume, 膽敢 ʻtaam-ʻkom, 逞 ʻchʻing, 敢當 ʻkom-tong, 檀 shinʼ, (on) 恃 ʻchʻi, 倚恃 ʻi-shi.
Pretend, 詐 chaʼ, 貌爲 maauʼ-wai, 自稱 tszeʼ-chʻing, 自己話 tszeʼ-ʻki-waʼ.
Pretty, 好睇 ʻho-ʻtʻai, 靚 lengʼ, 美 ʻmi, (-well) 幾好 ʻki-ʻho.
Prevail, 贏 yeng, (abound) 豐盛 fuung-shingʼ.
Prevaricate, 不講心 ʼm-ʻkong-ʻsum, 閃縮 ʻshim-shuuk, 吸三吸四 ngup-saam-ngup-szeʼ.
Prevent, 阻 ʻchoh, 免致 ʻmin-chiʼ, 不俾 ʼm-ʻpi.
Previously, 預先 ueʼ-sin.
Price, 價錢 kaʼ-tsʻin, 價 kaʼ.
Prick, 攙刺 ʻchʻaam-tsʼzeʼ, (a) 條刺 tʻiu-tsʼzeʼ, 管刺 ʻkoon-tsʼzeʼ.
Pricking, 癪 tsʻek.
Prickles, 簕 lak, 刺 tsʼzeʼ.
Prickly-heat, 熱痱 it-*fai.

Pride, 傲氣 ngoʼ-hiʼ.
Pride of India, 森木 ʻshum-muuk, 苦楝 foo-linʼ.
Priest, 祭司 tsai-szeʼ, (Bud.) 和尚 woh-*sheungʼ, (Tau.) 道士 toʼ-*szeʼ, (Rom.) 神父 shan-fooʼ.
Prim, 迂腐 hue-fooʼ.
Prime, 第一 taiʼ-yat, 首 ʻshau, 上等 sheungʼ-ʻtang.
Prime cost, 本錢 ʻpoon-tsʻin.
Prime Minister, 拜相 paaiʼ-seungʼ, 宰相 ʻtsoi-seungʼ.
Primitive, 原本 uen-ʻpoon.
Primrose, 蓮馨花 lin-hing-fa.
Prince, 君 kwun, 親王 tsʻan-wong.
Principal, 頭一個 tʻau-yat-kohʼ, (-thing) 根本 kan-ʻpoon.
Principally, 大概 taaiʼ-*kʻoiʼ, 大約 taaiʼ-*yeukʼ.
Principles, 道理 toʼ-ʻli, 理 ʻli.
Print, 印 yanʼ.
Printing office, 印書館 yanʼ-shue-ʻkoon.

Prior, 先 sin.
Prison, 監房 ₍kaam-fong.
Prisoner, 監犯 kaam-*faan⁾.
Private, 私家 sze-ka, (secret) 密 mat, 秘密 pi⁾-mat, 隱 ₍yan.
Privet, (ligustrum lucidum) 山瑞香 shaan-sui⁾-heung.
Privilege, 湊巧 ts'au⁾-₍haau.
Privy-council, 內閣 noi⁾-kok⁾.
Privy, (a) 厠坑 ts'ze⁾-₍haang.
Prize, (a) 賞 ₍sheung, 賞賜 ₍sheung-ts'ze⁾, 賞犒 ₍sheung-ho⁾, (to win a) 贏 yeng.
Prize up, 撟起 kiu⁾-₍hi.
Probably, 或者 waak-₍che, (most) 大槪 taai⁾-*k'oi⁾, 怕係啩 p'a⁾-hai⁾-kwa⁾.
Probation, 試驗 shi⁾-im⁾.
Probe, (a) 鍼 ₍chum, 探針 t'aam⁾-₍chum, (to) 俾針探吓 ₍pi-chum-t'aam⁾-₍ha.
Proboscis, 象拔 tseung⁾-pat, 象鼻 tseung⁾-pi⁾.

Proceed, 前進 ts'in-tsuun⁾, 上前去 ₍sheung-ts'in-hue⁾, (from) 出乎 ch'uut, 出乎 ch'uut-oo.
Procession, (idolatrous) 菩薩出遊 p'o-saat⁾-ch'uut-yau.
Proclaim, 宣傳 suen-ch'uen.
Proclamation, (a) 告示 ko⁾-shi⁾.
Proclivity, 偏歸一便 p'in-kwai-yat-*pin⁾.
Procrastinate, 推遲 t'ui-ch'i, (COL.) 哆吊 ₍te-tiu⁾, (put off from day to day) 日推一日 yat-t'ui-yat-yat.
Procurator, 承辦人 shing-paan⁾-yan.
Procure, 搵得 ₍wun-tak, 得到 tak-₍to, 攞到 ₍loh-₍to.
Prodigal, (a) 浪子 long⁾-₍tsze.
Prodigy, 精怪 tsing-kwaai⁾.
Produce, 出 ch'uut, 生出 shang-ch'uut, 產 ₍ch'aan.
Profane, 穢褻 wai⁾-sit⁾.
Profess, 明認 ming-ying, 自稱 tsze⁾-ch'ing.

Profession, (calling) 業 ip, 事業 sze'-ip, 腳色 keuk'-shik.
Profile, 半邊面 poon'-pin-'min', 半面相 poon'-min'-'seung'.
Profit, 利益 li'-yik, (to) 賺 chaan', 利 li'.
Profitable, 有益 yau'-yik, 有賺 'yau-chaan'.
Profligate, 散蕩花消 'saan-tong'-fa-siu, (a) 敗家仔 paai'-ka-'tsai.
Profound, 深 shum, 深沉 shum-ch'um.
Profusion, 太多 t'aai'-toh.
Prognosticate, 占卜 chim-puuk, 占卦 chim-kwa'.
Programme, 預定單目 ue'-ting'-taan-muuk.
Progress, 前進 ts'in-tsuun', 上進 'sheung-tsuun'.
Prohibit, 禁戒 kum'-kaai', 禁止 kum'-chi.
Project, 凸出來 tut-ch'uut-lai, 發 faat'.
Prolapse, 墜落 chui'-lok.

Prolong, 拖長 t'oh-ch'eung, 整長 'ching-ch'eung, 阻耐 'choh-noi'.
Prominence, 凸 tut.
Prominent, 特出 tak-ch'uut.
Promissory note, 揭單 k'it-,taan.
Promiscuous mixing, 混雜 wan'-tsaap.
Promise, 應承 ying-shing, (break a) 食言 shik-in, 失信 shat-suun'.
Promontory, 海表 'hoi-'piu.
Promote, 助 choh', (a man) 提拔 t'ai-pat.
Prompt, 快捷 faai'-tsit, (to) 提醒 t'ai-'sing.
Promulgate, 播揚 poh'-yeung, 傳講 ch'uen-'kong.
Prone to, 偏向 p'in-heung', 會 'ooi.
Pronounce, 講出來 'kong-ch'uut-lai, 話出 wa'-ch'uut.
Pronunciation, 口音 'hau-,yum, 口鉗 'hau-k'im.
Proof, 憑據 p'ang-kue', (print a) 打稿 'ta-'ko.

Prop, (to) 頂起 'ting-'hi, (a) 條撐 t'iu-ch'aang'.
Propel, 推前 t'ui-ts'in, 使——行 'shai——hang.
Propensity, 偏向 p'in-heung', 癖性 p'ik-sing'.
Proper, 着 cheuk.
Property, 產業 'ch'aan-ip, 家業 ka-ip, 財 ts'oi, (nature) 性 sing', 性格 sing'-kaak'.
Prophesy, 講未來事 'kong-mi'-loi-sze'.
Prophet, 先知 sin-chi.
Propitiate, 和翻 woh-faan, 挽回 'waan-ooi.
Propitious, 慈祥 ts'ze-ts'eung, (time, &c.) 吉 kat, 好 'ho.
Proportion, (rule of) 比例 'pi-lai', 配法 p'ooi-faat'.
Propose, 陳説 ch'an-shuet', 出主意 ch'uut-'chue-i'.
Proprietor, 原主 uen-'chue, 原人 uen-yan.
Propriety, 禮數 'lai-sho'.
Prosecute, 告 ko', (pursue) 趕起 'kohn-'hi.

Proselyte, 進教 tsuun'-kaau'.
Prospect, 光景 kwong-'king.
Prospect for gold, 探金 t'aam'-,kum.
Prosper, 興旺 hing'-wong', 發達 fuat'-taat.
Prosperous, 暢盛 ch'eung'-shing'.
Prostitute, 娼婦 ch'eung-'foo, 文牛 mun-*ngau, (to) 浪用 long'-yuung'.
Prostrate, 傾倒 k'ing-'to, (one's self) 蹼倒處 puuk-'to-shue', 俯伏 'foo-fuuk.
Protect, 保佑 'po-yau', 擋梢 maan-shaau.
Protegé, 所照顧 'shoh-chiu'-koo'.
Protest, 告訴 ko'-so', 話心不服 wa'-sum-'m-fuuk.
Protestant, (Christianity) 耶穌教 Ye-soo-kaau'.
Protract, 拖長 t'oh-ch'eung.
Protuberant, 凸 tut, 凸出 tut-ch'uut.
Proud, 驕傲 kiu-ngo'.
Prove, 証實 ching'-shat, (verify) 徵驗 ching-im'.

Proverb, 俗語 tsuuk-ʼue, 成語 shing-ʼue, 箴言 chum-in.
Provide, 給 kʻup, 預備 ueʼ-piʼ, (against) 提防 tʻai-fong.
Providence, 化生保養 faʼ-shang-ʻpo-ʻyeung.
Providential, 天注定 tʻin-chueʼ-tingʼ.
Province, 省 ʻshaang.
Provisions, 糧草 leung-ʻtsʻo, 口糧 ʻhau-leung.
Provoke, 惹 ʻye, 激 kik.
Prowl, 出夜 chʻuut-*yeʼ.
Proxy, 代理 toiʼ-ʻli.
Prudence, 智慧 chiʼ-wai.
Prudent, 會思量 ʻooi-sze-leung, 好打算 ʻho-ʻta-suenʼ.
Prune, (to) 省枝葉 ʻshaang-chi-ip.
Prunes, 梅子 mooi-ʻtsze, (dried) 乾梅 kohn-*mooi.
Prussia, 布國 Poʼ-kwokʼ.
Prussian-blue, 洋靛 yeung-tinʼ.
Pry, 窺探 kʻwai-tʻaamʼ.

Psalms, 聖詩 shingʼ-ʻshi.
Psoriasis, 乾漏 kohn-lauʼ.
Puberty, (female) 天癸 tʻin-kwaiʼ, (male) 成童 shing-tʻunng, (VULG.) 發身 faatʼ-ʻshan.
Public, 公 kuung, (the) 百姓 paakʼ-singʼ.
Public spirit, 公心 kuung-sum, 義氣 iʼ-hiʼ.
Publish, (books, &c.) 出賣 chʻuut-maaiʼ.
Pucker, 縐埋 tsauʼ-maai, (the mouth) 呡埋口 mai-maai-ʻhau.
Pudding, 麵食 minʼ-shik.
Puddle, iron, 炒鐵 ʻchʻaau-tʻitʼ, (make muddy) 攪濁 ʻkaau-chuuk, (water tight) 整坭涾底 ʻching-nai-paanʼ-ʻtai.
Puff, (a) 一朕 yat-chumʼ.
Puffed up, 自滿 tszeʼ-ʻmoon.
Puisne Judge, 副臬司 fooʼ-nip-ʻsze.
Pule, 哇哇 wa-wa.
Pull, (to) 搖 mangʼ, 拉 laai, 扯 ʻchʻe, (down) 拆 chʻaakʼ.

Pulley, 縴羅 luut-₍loh.
Pulp, 釀 nong.
Pulpit, 講書檯 ₍kong-shue-t'oi.
Pulse, (lentils) 荳 *tau', (the) 脈 mak.
Pulverize, 粉碎 ⸨fun-sui'.
Pumice, 浮石 fau-shek.
Pummelo, 波碌 poh-luuk, 柚子 yau-⸨tsze', 囉柚 loh-*yau.
Pump, 欶筒 shok'-t'uung, 拖水泵 t'oh-⸨shui-₍tum, (to) 欶 shok'.
Pumpkin, 冬瓜 tuung-kwa.
Pun, 雙關取笑 ₍sheung-₍kwaun-⸨ts'ue-siu'.
Punch, (a) 鐵撞 t'it'-chong', 鷄眼鑿 ₍kai-⸨ngaan-*tsok.
Punctilious, 執細 chup-sai'.
Punctual 依期 i-k'i.
Punctuate, 點斷 ⸨tim-⸨t'uen.
Puncture, 針 chum.
Pungent, 辣 laat.
Punish, 罰 fat, 責罰 chaak'-fat.
Punishment, 刑罰 ying-fat.
Punkah, 風扇 fuung-shin'.

Puny, 矮細 ⸨ai-sai'.
Pup, 狗仔 ⸨kau-⸨tsai'.
Pupil, (of the eye) 瞳人 t'uung-*yan, (scholar) 門生 moon-₍shaang, 學生 hok-₍shaang.
Puppet show, 鬼仔戲 ⸨kwai-⸨tsai-hi'.
Purblind, 眼矇 ⸨ngaan-muung.
Purchase, 買 ⸨maai.
Pure, 清潔 ts'ing-kit'.
Purgative, 瀉藥 se'-yeuk.
Purgatory, 煉獄 lin'-yuuk.
Purify, 洗滌 ⸨sai-tik, 潔淨 kit'-tsing', 整乾淨 ⸨ching-kohn-tseng'.
Purple, 葡萄青 p'oo-t'o-₍ts'eng.
Purpose, 主意 ⸨chue-i'.
Purposely, 特登 tak-₍tang, 故意 koo'-i'.
Purse, 荷包 hoh-₍paau, 匙挿 shi-*ch'aap'.
Purser, 寫字人 ⸨se-tsze'-yan.
Purslane, 猪仔茶 chue-⸨tsai-ts'oi'.

Pursue, 追趕 *chui-ʻkohn*.
Purvey, 辦伙食 *paan-ʻfoh-shik*.
Pus, 膿 *nuung*.
Push, 推 *tʻui*, 擁 ʻ*uung*, (along, as a row of types &c.) 褪 *tʻan*ʼ.
Pusillanimous, 心怯 *sum-hipʼ*.
Pustule, 小瘡 ʻ*siu-*ʻ*chʻong*.
Put, 放 *fongʼ*, 置 *chiʼ*, (down) 擠落 *chai-lok*, (on) 着 *cheukʻ*, 按 *ohnʼ*, 安 *ohn*, (in) 插 *chʻaap*ʼ, 入 *yup*, (out) 出 *chʻuut*, (past) 收埋 *shau-maai*, (away) 除 *chʻue*, (off) 推 *tʻui*, 脫 *tʻuetʼ*.
Putchuk, 木香 *muuk-heung*.
Putrid, 腐爛 *fooʼ-laanʼ*.
Putty, 桐油灰 *tʻuung-yau-fooi*.
Puzzle, (a) 難估之物 *naan-*ʻ*koo-chi-mat*, *naan-*ʻ*kooʼ-*ʻ*ye*, (a toy) 耍圖 ʻ*sha-tʻo*.
Pygmy, 矮佬仔 ʻ*ai-*ʻ*lo-*ʻ*tsai*.
Pylorus, 幽門 *yau-moon*.

Pyramid, 尖方形 *tsim-fong-ying*, 金字塔 *kum-tszeʼ-tʻaap*ʼ.

Q

Quack, (a) 撞包先生 *chongʼ-paau-sin-shang*, *chʻongʼ-paau-seng*.
Quadrangular, 四方 *szeʼ-fongʼ*, *szeʼ-fong-ke*ʼ.
Quadrant, (or sextant) 量天尺 *leungʼ-tʻin-chʻek*ʼ.
Quadruped, 走獸 ʻ*tsau-shau*ʼ.
Quaff, 飲 ʻ*yum*.
Quail, (a) 鵪鶉 *om-shuun*.
Quail, (to) 失志 *shat-chi*ʼ.
Quaint, 古怪 ʻ*koo-kwaai*ʼ.
Quake, 振動 *chanʼ-tuung*ʼ.
Qualified, (able) 能 *nang*.
Quality, 等 ʻ*tang*, 品 ʻ*pun*, 脚色 *keukʼ-shik*, (of things) 色 *shik*, 性格 *singʼ-kaak*ʼ.
Qualm of conscience, 良心自責 *leung-sum-tszeʼ-chaak*ʼ.

Quantity, 數量 sho'-leung', (what?) 多少 toh-'shiu.
Quarrel, 爭 chaang, 鬧交 naau'-ˏkaau, 隘交 aai-ˏkaau.
Quarry, 取石山 'ts'ue-shek-shaan.
Quart, (a) 一斤 yat-kan.
Quarter, (a) 四分之一 sze'-fun'-chi-yat, 一角 yat-kok', (of an hour) 一刻 yat-hak, (of the year) 季 kwai', (of the body) 肢 chi.
Quarter, (to lodge) 歇宿 hit'-suuk.
Quartz, 白火石 paak-'foh-shek, 石瑛 shek-ying.
Quash, 拉倒 laai-'to, 撲滅 p'ok'-mit.
Quassia, 白木 paak-muuk.
Queen, 皇后 wong-hau'.
Queer, 奇怪 k'i-kwaai', 另特 lak-tak.
Quell, 滅 mit.
Quench, 滅 mit, 救熄 kau'-sik, (thirst) 解 'kaai.
Quest, 尋 ts'um.

Question, 問 mun', (a) 問話 mun'-wa', (doubt) 思疑 sze-i.
Quibble, 盤根問柢 p'oon-kan-mun'-'tai, 詰難 k'it'-naan, 爭言語 chaang-in-'ue.
Quick, 快 faai', 快快 faai'-faai', (sharp) 麻俐 ma-li', (clever) 伶俐 ling-li', (lively) 活潑 oot-p'oot'.
Quicken, (in the womb) 胎動 t'oi-tuung'.
Quicksand, 浮沙 fau-sha.
Quicksilver, 水銀 'shui-ngan.
Quiet, 安靖 ohn-tsing', (be) 靜靜 tsing'-*tsing'.
Quietness, 平安 p'ing-ohn.
Quill, 鵝毛筆 ngoh-mo-pat.
Quilt, 綿被 min-'p'i, 綿胎 min-ˏt'oi.
Quilted-coat, 綿衲 min-naap.
Quince, 木瓜 muuk-ˏkwa.
Quinine, 金鷄納霜 ˏkum-ˏkai-naap-seung.
Quinsy, 生鵝喉 shaang-ngoh-hau.

Quip, 譏刺 ki-ts'ze⁾.
Quire, 刀 to, (a) 一刀紙 yat-to-⌐chi.
Quirk, 扭計 ⌐nau-*kai⁾.
Quisqualis, 使君子 sze⁾-kwun-⌐tsze.
Quit, 離去 li-hue⁾, (-hold) 放手 fong⁾-⌐shau, 用手 lut-⌐shau.
Quite, 十分 shap-fun──, 嘥──saai⁾, ──完── uen, (not quite) 爭的 chaang-⌐ti.
Quiz, 試探 shi⁾-t'aam⁾, 嘲笑 chaau-siu⁾.
Quote, 引 ⌐yan, 引述 ⌐yan-shuut.

R

Rabbet, (to) 入柳 yup-⌐lau.
Rabbit, 白兔 paak-t'o⁾.
Rabble, 下流 ha⁾-lau.
Rabid, 狂 k'wong, 刁 tiu.
Race, (family) 類 lui⁾, 種 ⌐chuung, (to) 跑 ⌐p'aau.
Rack, (engine) 刑具 ying-kue⁾, (frame) 架 ka⁾.

Racking, 苦楚 ⌐foo-⌐ch'oh.
Radiate, 射 she⁾, 光射 kwong-she⁾, 熱射 it-she⁾.
Radicals, (characters) 部 po⁾ (roots) 根 kan.
Radish, 紅蘿蔔 huung-loh-paak.
Radius, 輻線 fuuk-sin⁾.
Raffle, 擎色 ngo-shik.
Raft, 棑 *p'aai.
Rafter, 桷 kok⁾, (purlin &) 桁桷 hang-kok⁾.
Rag, 爛布 laan⁾-po⁾.
Ragamuffin, 囉囉仔 ⌐loh-⌐loh-⌐tsai.
Rage, 忿怒 ⌐fun-no⁾.
Ragged, 襤褸 laam-lue⁾.
Rag-man, 換爛布 oon⁾-laan⁾-po⁾.
Rail, (to) 詈罵 li⁾-ma⁾, (a bird) 竹鷄 chuuk-kai.
Railing, 欄杆 laan-⌐kohn.
Railway, 鐵路 t'it⁾-lo⁾, 火烟車路 ⌐foh-in-ch'e-lo⁾.
Rain, 雨 ⌐ue, (to) 落雨 lok-⌐ue, (-water) 雨水 ⌐ue-⌐shui.

Rainbow, 天蜂 t'in-kong', 虹栱 huung-'kuung.
Raise, 起 'hi.
Raisins, 菩提子 p'oo-t'ai-'tsze.
Rally, (troops) 合翻埋 hop-faan-maai, (ridicule) 嘲笑 chaau-siu'.
Rake, (a man) 花花公子 fa-fa-kuung-'tsze, ,oh-,li-kat-tai', (a tool) 筢 p'a, 耙 楷 p'a-,ngaau.
Ram, (a) 羊牯 yeung-'koo, 羊公 yeung-,kuung, (to) 舂 chuung.
Ramble, 遊行 yau-hang, 去 逛 hue'-k'waang', 蹓 'liu.
Rampant, 嘈雜 ts'o-tsaap, 高興 ko-hing'.
Rampart, 城牆 sheng-ts'eung.
Ram-rod, 鳥鎗捅 'niu-ts'eung-ch'aap', 通條 t'uung-t'iu.
Rancid, 腥 seng, (oil) 噫 yik.
Rancour, 怨毒 uen'-tuuk.

Range in rows, 一行行列開 yat-*hong-hong-lit-hoi.
Rank, (order) 等級 'tang-k'up, 品 'pun, (merit) 功名 kuung-ming, (with) 同列 t'uung-lit.
Rank, (growth) 茂 mau', (taste) 臊 so.
Rankle in the breast, 心滾 sum-'kwan, 到心滾 to'-sum-'kwan.
Ransom, 贖 shuuk.
Rant, 狂辯 k'wong-pin'.
Rap, 拍 p'aak', (COL.) pop-pop.
Rape, 強姦 k'eung-kaan.
Rapid, 急速 kup-ts'uuk, (rapids) 灘 t'aan.
Rapture, 極喜 kik-'hi.
Rare, 希罕 hi-'hohn, 希奇 hi-k'i.
Rarities, 奇物 k'i-mat.
Rascal, 爛仔 *laan'-'tsai.
Rase, 拆平 ch'aak'-p'ing, 洗平 'sai-p'ing.
Rash, 冒險 mo'-'him, 躁暴 ts'o'-po'.

Raspberry, 蛇抱竻 she-ʻpʻo-lak.
Rat, 老鼠 ʻlo-ʻshue.
Rat-trap, 老鼠籠 ʻlo-ʻshue-*luung.
Rate, (price) 價 kaʼ, (of motion) 行法 hang-faatʼ, (first-) 頂好 ʻting-ʻho.
Rather, 畧畧 leuk-*leuk, 頗 ʻpʻoh, (in preference) 寧可 ning-ʻhoh, 更好 kangʼ-ʻho.
Ratify, 枇准 pʻai-ʻchuun, 証實 chingʼ-shat.
Rational, 合情理 hop-tsʻing-ʻli.
Rations, 粮食 leung-shik, (daily) 日粮 yat-leung.
Rattan, 沙籐 sha-tʻang, (shavings) 籐絲 tʻang-ʻsze.
Rattle, 擎 ngo, (a drum) 鈴冞鼓 ʻling-ʻlum-ʻkoo, (death-) 抴氣 ʻchʻe-hiʼ.
Rattle-snake, 响尾蛇 ʻheung-ʻmi-she.
Ravage, 刦毀 kipʼ-ʻwai.

Rave, 喪心 songʼ-sum, 發譖話 faatʼ-ngaamʼ-waʼ, (in anger) 暴怒 poʼ-noʼ.
Ravelled, 亂 luenʼ.
Raven, 烏鴉 oo-a.
Ravenous, (hungry) 餓得急 ngoh-tak-kup, (greedy) 爲食 waiʼ-shik.
Ravine, 山壑 shaan-kʻokʼ.
Ravish, 强奪 kʻeung-tuet, (force) 强 ʻkʻeung.
Raw, 生 shaang, shaang-keʼ.
Ray, (of light) 射光 sheʼ-kwong, (a fish) 鯆魚 po-*ue, 琵琶沙 pʻi-pʻa-sha.
Razor, 剃刀 tʻaiʼ-ʻto.
Reach, 到 toʼ, 到得 toʼ-tak, (with the hand) 攎到 o-ʻto, (out) 伸 shan.
Read, 讀 tuuk, (in silence) 看 hohnʼ, 睇 ʻtʻai.
Readily, 即時 tsik-shi, 易易 iʼ-iʼ.
Ready, 備 piʼ, 齊備 tsʻai-piʼ, 便 pinʼ, (money) 現銀 inʼ-*ngan, (made) 現成 inʼ-*shing.

Real, 眞 chan.
Really, 果然 ʻkwoh-in, 確實 kʻokʼ-shat.
Reap, 收割 shau-kohtʼ.
Rear, (like a horse) 骙高前蹄 ngok-ko-tsʻin-tʻai, 椿 ʻchong, (raise) 養 ʻyeung, tsʻo.
Rear, (the) 尾 ʻmi, 後便 hauʼ-pinʼ.
Reason, 道理 toʼ-ʻli, 情理 tsʻing-ʻli, (a) 緣故 uen-kooʼ.
Reasoning, 理論 ʻli-luunʼ, 辯論 pinʼ-luunʼ.
Reasonable, 有道理 ʻyau-toʼ-ʻli, 有理 ʻyau-ʻli, 合理 hop-ʻli.
Reassure, 壯 —— 胆 chongʼ —— ʻtaam.
Rebate, (a groove) 入柳 yup-ʻlau.
Rebel, (to) 作反 tsokʼ-ʼfaan.
Rebels, 逆賊 yik-tsʻaak.
Rebound, 濺開 tsaanʼ-hoi.
Rebuke, 責成 chaakʼ-shing.
Rebut, 答倒 taapʼ-ʻto.

Recall, 叫 —— 翻 kiuʼ —— faan, (to mind) 想得翻 ʻseung-tak-faan.
Recant, 反口 ʻfaan-ʻhau.
Recede, 退 tʻuiʼ, 褪後 tʻanʼ-hauʼ.
Receipt, 收單 shau-ʻtaan.
Receive, 接收 tsipʼ-shau, 接到 tsipʼ-toʼ, 受 shauʼ, (from a superior) 領 ʻling.
Recent, 近時 kanʼ-shi, kanʼ-shi-keʼ.
Recently, 近來 kanʼ-loi.
Receptacle, 藏 tsongʼ, 房 fong, 藏處 tsʻong-chʻueʼ.
Recipe, 方法 fong-faatʼ, 方子 fong-ʻtsze.
Reciprocate, 互相交接 ooʼ-seung-kaau-tsipʼ.
Recite, 玩誦 oonʼ-tsnungʼ, 念出 nimʼ-chʻuutʼ.
Reckless, 刁蠻 tiu-maan, 唔打理乜野 ʼm-ʻta-ʻli-matʼ-ʻye.
Reckon, 點數 ʻtim-ʻsho, 筭 suenʼ.
Reclaim, 攞翻 ʻloh-faan, 救翻 kauʼ-faan.

Recline, 瞓低 fun'-'tai, 'fun, 挨到 aai-'to, 挨下 aai-'ha.
Recluse, 離世獨居 li-shai'-tuuk-kue.
Recognise, 認 ying'.
Recoil, 褪 t'an', tan', 濺起 tsaan'-'hi.
Recollect, 記起 ki'-'hi, 憶起 yik-'hi.
Recommend, (a person) 舉薦 'kue-tsin', (advise) 勸 huen'.
Recompense, 報答 po'-taap'.
Reconcilable, 和得翻 woh-tak-faan.
Reconcile, 令——再好 ling' ——tsoi'-'ho.
Reconciled, 復和 fuuk-woh.
Reconnoitre, 打探 'ta-t'aam'.
Record, 錄 luuk, (to) 記 ki'.
Recount, 述出來 shuut-ch'uut-lai.
Recover, 得翻 tak-faan, (get well) 病好 peng'-'ho.
Recreate, 遊耍吓 yau-'sha-'ha.

Recrimination, 互相攻訐 oo'-seung-kuung-k'it'.
Recruit, 添補 t'im-'po, (health) 養翻吓 'yeung-faan-'ha.
Rectify, 整正 'ching-cheng', 改正 'koi-cheng, 整好 'ching-'ho.
Rectitude, 義氣 i'-hi', 正直 ching'-chik.
Rectum, 直腸 chik-ch'eung.
Recur, 又來 yau'-loi, 來復 loi-fuuk, (in speaking) 再講 tsoi'-'kong.
Red, 紅 huung, 朱 chue.
Redeem, 贖 shuuk, 贖翻 shuuk-faan, (from sin) 贖罪 shuuk-tsui'.
Redound to, 歸翻 kwai-faan.
Redress, a grievance, 申冤 shan-uen, (no) 無法 'mo-faat'.
Reduce, (bring) 令 ling', 致使 chi'-'shai, (diminish) 減 'kaam, (change) 化 fa', 變 pin', (subdue) 打服 'ta-fuuk.

Redundant, 太多無用 tʻaaiʼ-toh-ʻmo-yuungʼ, 蛇足 she-tsuuk.
Reed, 蘆葦 lo-ʻwai, 蘆荻 lo-tek.
Reel and stagger, 行動搖擺 hang-tuungʼ-iu-ʻpaai, (COL.) hang-tak-ʻpʻe-ʻpʻe-ʻha.
Reel of thread, 線轆 sinʼ-luuk, 車轆 chʻe-luuk.
Refer to, 指 ʻchi, (speak of) 講及 ʻkong-kʻaap, (apply to) 轉詳 ʻchuen-tsʻeung, 轉問 ʻchuen-munʼ.
Refine, 傾煉 kʻing-linʼ, 煉 linʼ.
Refit, 修整 sau-ʻching.
Reflect, 反照 ʻfaan-chiuʼ, 射轉 sheʼ-ʻchuen, (think) 思想 sze-ʻseung.
Reform, 變正 pinʼ-chingʼ, 改惡遷善 ʻkoi-okʼ-tsʻin-shinʼ.
Refract, 轉斜 ʻchuen-tsʻe, 撮曲 tsʻuetʼ-kʻuuk.
Refrain, 戒 kaaiʼ, 忍手 ʻyan-ʻshau, 忍口 ʻyan-ʻhau.

Refresh, 益補 yik-ʻpo, 滋補 tsze-ʻpo.
Refreshment, 滋補野 tsze-ʻpo-ʻye, 點心 ʻtim-ʻsum.
Refuge, 躲避處 ʻtoh-piʼ-chʻueʼ, 避身所 piʼ-shan-ʻshoh.
Refund, 償還 chʻeung-waan.
Refuse, 推辭 tʻui-tsʻze, 不允 ʼm-ʻwan, (not receive) 不接 ʼm-tsipʼ.
Refute, 駁贏 pokʼ-yeng.
Regain, 得翻 tak-faan, 贏翻 yeng-faan.
Regard, 顧住 kooʼ-chueʼ, (pity) 恤 suut.
Regardless, 不打理 ʼm-ʻta-ʻli.
Regards, (to express) 問候 munʼ-hauʼ.
Regatta, 鬥船 tauʼ-shuen.
Regenerate, 更生 kangʼ-shang, 重生 chʻuung-shang, 翻生 faan-shaang.
Regent, 攝政 shipʼ-chingʼ.
Regimen, 戒口 kaaiʼ-ʻhau.
Regiment, 營 ying, 旗 kʻi.
Region, 地方 tiʼ-fong.

Register, 紀錄 ʻki-luuk, (to) 上冊 ʻsheung-chʻaak᾽.
Registrar, 掌案司 ʻcheung-ohn᾽-ʻsze.
Registrar General, (in Hongkong) 華民政務司 wa-man-ching᾽-moo-ʻsze.
Regret, 惜 sik, 念惜 nim᾽-sik, (repent) 悔 fooi, 反悔 ʻfaan-fooi᾽.
Regular, 有次序 ʻyau-tsʻze᾽-tsuc᾽, 依法 i-faat᾽, 正 ching᾽.
Regulate, 定制 ting᾽-chai᾽, 整好 ʻching-ʻho.
Regulation, 章程 cheung-chʻing.
Reign, 爲王 wai-wong, 做王 tso᾽-wong, (one) 一王之世 yat-wong-chi-shai᾽.
Rein, (bridle) 轡頭 pi᾽-tʻau.
Rein-deer, 北大鹿 pak-taai᾽-luuk.
Reinforce, 添補 tʻim-ʻpo.
Reinstate, 叫翻 kiu᾽-faan, 請翻 ʻtsʻeng-faan.
Reject, 丟棄 tiu-hi᾽, 丟抛 tiu-pʻaau.

Rejoice, 喜悅 ʻhi-uct, 歡喜 foon-ʻhi.
Rejoin, (answer again) 復答 fuuk᾽-taap᾽.
Relapse, 復陷 fuuk-haam᾽, (of sickness) 復病 fuuk-peng᾽.
Relate, 說知 shuet᾽-chi, 講述 ʻkong-shuut, (belong to) 屬 shuuk.
Relations, (five) 五倫 ʻng-luun, 人倫 yan-luun.
Relation } Relative } 親戚 tsʻan-tsʻik, 相屬 seung-shuuk.
Relax, 放鬆 fong᾽-suung.
Relaxation, 舒伸 shue-shan.
Release, 釋放 shik-fong᾽.
Relent, 悔 fooi, 可憐 ʻhoh-lin.
Relevant, 關涉 kwaan-ship᾽.
Relief, relieve, 浮凸 fau-tut.
Relieve, (the poor) 救濟 kau᾽-tsai᾽, (lighten) 減輕 ʻkaam-heng.
Religion, (doctrine) 教 kaau᾽.
Religious, 敬虔 king᾽-kʻin.
Relinquish, 捨 ʻshe.

Relish, (to) 知味 chi-mi', (a) 味道 mi'-to', 滋味 tsze-mi', *mi'.
Reluctantly, 勉強 'min-'k'eung.
Rely on, 倚賴 'i-laai', 恃 'shi.
Remain, 留住 lau-chue', (over) 剩 shing'.
Remainder, 餘剩 ue-shing'.
Remand, 命—反 ming'—'faan, 着—囘去 cheuk'—ooi-hue'.
Remark, (see) 睇見 't'ai-kin', (say) 話 wa'.
Remarkable, 非常 fi-sheung.
Remedy, 治法 chi'-faat', 醫治 i-faat'.
Remember, 記得 ki'-tak, 記住 ki'-chue'.
Remind, 提醒 t'ai-'seng.
Remiss, 放縱 fong'-tsuung'.
Remit, (forgive) 赦免 she'-'min, (send) 寄 ki', (relax) 鬆 suung.
Remnants, 餘碎 ue-sui'.
Remonstrate, 責論 chaak'-luun'.

Remorse, 痛悔 t'uung'-fooi'.
Remorseless, 殘忍 ts'aan-'yan.
Remote, 遠 'uen, 疏 shoh'.
Remove, (flit) 搬遷 poon-ts'in, (put away) 除去 ch'ue'-hue', (from office) 革 kaak'.
Remunerate, 賠答 p'ooi-taap'.
Rend, 裂 lit, 扯裂 'ch'e-lit.
Render, (return) 還 waan, (make) 令 ling', 使 'shai.
Rendezvous, 聚處 tsue'-ch'ue'.
Renew } 更新 kang'-san,
Renovate } 改新 'koi-san, 整翻新 'ching-faan-san.
Renounce, 棄絕 hi'-tsuet.
Rent, 租銀 tso-*ngan, 租價 tso-ka', (to) 租 tso; (torn) 爛了 laan'-hiu.
Repair, 修整 sau-'ching, 補 'po, (go to) 去到 hue'-to'.
Repay, 還翻 waan-faan, 賠還 p'ooi-waan.
Repeal, 廢除 fai'-ch'ue.

Repeat, 再復 tsoi²-fuuk, 重復 ch'uung-fuuk, (a lesson) 背 pooi², 念 nim², 念出 nim²-ch'uut.
Repeatedly, 再三 tsoi²-saam.
Repel, 拒住 ʿk'ue-chue².
Repent, 悔恨 fooi²-han², (and mend) 悔改 fooi²-ʿkoi.
Repetition, 贅累 chui²-lui².
Repine, 怨 uen², 憂怨 yau-uen².
Replace, 補翻 ʿpo-faan.
Replenish, 滿翻 ʿmoon-faan.
Reply, 對答 tui²-taap², 回音 ooi-yum.
Report, 風聲 fuung-sheng, (give a) 回復 ooi-fuuk, (sound) (COL.) pom.
Repose, 安靜 ohn-tsing².
Represent, (stand for) 作係 tsok²-hai², 當做 tong-tso², (symbolize) 見意 kin²-i².
Repress, 禁制 kum²-chai², 遏制 aat²-chai².
Reprisals, (to make) 搶翻 ʿts'eung-faan.
Reproach, 辱罵 yuuk-ma².

Reprimand, Reprove } 責成 chaak²-ʿshing, 執責 chup-chaak², (to the face) 斥白 ch'ik-paak, 面斥 min²-ch'ik.
Reptile, 蹮蟲 laan-ch'uung.
Republic, 民主之國 mun-ʿchue-chi-kwok².
Repudiate, 棄 hi².
Repugnant, 相反 seung-ʿfaan, 相攻 seung-kuung, 逆 yik, ngaak.
Repulse, 打退 ʿta-t'ui².
Repulsive, 塊䐗 tau-mau.
Reputation, 名聲 ming-shing, 體面 ʿt'ai-min².
Request, 求請 k'au-ʿts'eng.
Require, 須要 sue-iu².
Requite, 報 po².
Rescue, 救 kau², 打救 ʿta-kau², 救出 kau²-ch'uut.
Research, 考究 ʿhaau-kau².
Resemblance, 象樣 tseung²-*yeung², 貌 maau².
Resemble, 似得 ʿts'ze-tak, 象似 tseung²-ʿts'ze.
Resembling, 猶之乎 yau-chi-oo.

Resentment, 怨恨 *uen*ˀ-*han*ˀ.
Reserve, 留有餘 lau-ˁyau-ue, (to) 存下 ts'uen-ˁha.
Reserved, 深沉 shum-ch'um.
Reservoir, 蓄陂 ch'uuk-pi, 陂池 pi-ch'i, 水井 ˁshui-ˁtseng.
Reside, 居住 kue-chucˀ.
Residence, 住家 chucˀ-ka, 宅 chaak.
Resign, 告退 koˀ-t'ui, 辭職 ts'ze-chik, (one's self) 服 fuuk.
Resigned, (submissive) 舒服 shue-fuuk.
Resin, 松明 ts'uung-ming (meng), 松香 ts'uung-heung.
Resist, 抗拒 k'ongˀ-ˁk'ue, 頂住 ˁting-chueˀ, 敵住 tik-chueˀ, 擋住 ˁtong-chueˀ.
Resolute, 堅心 kin-sum.
Resolve, 定意 tingˀ-iˀ, 立心 laap-sum, 決意 k'uetˀ-iˀ, 主意 ˁchue-iˀ, (solve) 解開 ˁkaai-hoi.

Resort, (to a place) 去到 hueˀ-toˀ, (to a person) 轉向 ˁchuen-heungˀ, (to a thing, &c.) 轉使 ˁchuen-ˁshai, (a place of) 聚處 tsueˀ-ch'ueˀ, (an escape) 去路 hueˀ-loˀ.
Resound, 響聲 ˁheung-sheng (echo) 回响 ooi-ˁheungˀ, 撞聲 chongˀ-sheng.
Resource, 所倚賴 ˁshoh-ˁi-laaiˀ, (escape) 去路 hueˀ-loˀ.
Respect, (to) 敬 kingˀ, 敬重 kingˀ-chuungˀ, (regard) 顧 kooˀ.
Respectable, 有體面 ˁyau-ˁt'ai-minˀ.
Respectful, 恭敬 kuung-kingˀ.
Respecting, 論及 luunˀ-k'ap, 至於 chiˀ-ue.
Respects, to pay, 拜候 paaiˀ-hauˀ.
Respiration, 呼吸 foo-k'up.
Respite, 歇時 hitˀ-shi.
Resplendent, 光朗 kwong-ˁlong.
Respond, 應答 yingˀ-taapˀ.

Responsibility, (負荷 foo꜄-hoh꜄) 担帶 taam-taai꜄.
Responsible, 是問 shi꜄-mun꜄.
Rest, 息 sik, 安息 ohn-sik, (to) 歇下 hit꜄-꜀ha, 抖下 ꜀t'au-꜀ha, (the) 餘剩 ue-shing꜄, ue-shing꜄-ke꜄, 其餘 k'i-ue, 重有的 chuung꜄-꜀yau-ti.
Restive, 拗頸 aau꜄-꜀keng.
Restless, 無寧耐 mo-ning-noi꜄, 俺尖 im-tsim.
Restore, 挽回 ꜀waan-ooi, 復 fuuk, (save) 救翻 kau꜄-faan.
Restrain, 禁制 kum꜄-chai꜄, 拘束 k'ue-ch'uuk.
Restriction, 限度 haan꜄-to꜄.
Result, (in) 終歸 chuung-kwai, (from) 出乎 ch'uut-oo, (the) 關系 kwaan-hai꜄, 效驗 haau꜄-im꜄.
Resume, 開翻手 hoi-faan-꜀shau, (return to) 做翻 tso꜄-faan.
Resurrection, 復生 fuuk-shang, fau-shang.

Retail, 賣碎貨 maai꜄-sui꜄-foh꜄, 零賣 ling-maai꜄, (trade) 小販 ꜀siu-faan꜄.
Retain, 留翻 lau-faan, 收留 shau-lau.
Retake, (a place) 克復 hak-fuuk, (a prisoner) 捉翻 chuuk-faan.
Retaliate, 還手 waan-꜀shau, 報翻 po꜄-faan.
Retard, 滯 chai꜄, 阻慢 ꜀choh-maan꜄, 整慢 ꜀ching-maan꜄.
Retch, 作嘔 tsok꜄-꜀ou.
Retentive memory, 好記性 ꜀ho-ki꜄-sing꜄.
Retinue, 跟班 ꜀kan-꜀paan.
Retire, 退避 t'ui꜄-pi꜄, 去 hue꜄, 歸隱 kwai-꜀yan.
Retired, 幽靜 yau-tsing꜄, 背 pooi꜄.
Retirement, 靜中 tsing꜄-chuung, 隱處 ꜀yan-ch'ue꜄.
Retort, to, 還口 waan-꜀hau.
Retrace, 回步 ooi-po꜄.
Retract, 反口 ꜀fuan-꜀hau, 食言 shik-in.

Retreat, 退 t'ui', 走 'tsau, (a) 隱處 'yan-ch'ue'.
Retrench, 減省 'kaam-'shaang.
Retribution, 報應 po'-ying'.
Retrieve, 得翻 tak-faan, 贏翻 yeng-faan, 救 kau'.
Retrograde, 倒行 'to-hang.
Retrospect, 回顧 ooi-koo'.
Return, 返 'faan, 回 ooi, 翻去 faan-hue', 翻來 faan-lai, 歸 kwai, (restore) 還 waan.
Reunite, 合翻埋 hop-faan-maai.
Reveal, 啟示 'k'ai-shi'.
Revel, 鬧酒 naau'-'tsau.
Revenge, 報仇 po'-ch'au, 雪恨 suet'-han'.
Revenue, 庫銀 foo'-ngan.
Reverberation, 回嘥 ooi-shai', (sound) 應响 ying'-'heung.
Reverence, 恭敬 kuung-king'.
Reverend, (honourable) 尊 tsuen, (elderly) 老 'lo.
Reverie, 想入神 'seung-yup-shan.

Reverse, (the) 相反 seung-'faan, 對面 tui'-min', (to) 倒轉 'to-'chuen.
Revert, 歸反 kwai-'faan.
Review, 閱 uet, 簡閱 'kaan-uet, 評 p'ing.
Revile, 譭罵 'wai-ma', 講壞 'kong-waai'.
Revise, 修改 sau-'koi.
Revive, 復興 fuuk-hing, 復生 fuuk-shang, 再旺 tsoi'-wong', (the spirits) 打醒精神 'ta-'seng-tsing-shan.
Revoke, 反變 'faan-pin', 追回 chui-ooi, 廢 fai'.
Revolt, 背叛 pooi'-poon'.
Revolting, 凄慘 ts'ai-'ts'aam.
Revolution, 周 chau, 回 ooi, (in a state) 變 pin'.
Revolve, 氹氹轉 tum'-tum'-chuen', t'um-t'um-'chuen, (旋轉 suen-'chuen), (in an orbit) 週轉 chau-chuen'.
Revolver, 連還鎗 lin-waan-ts'eung, 對面笑 tui'-min'-sui'.

Reward, 賞 ʽsheung, 賞給 ʽsheung-kʼup, 賞賜 ʽsheung-tsʽzeʼ, 花紅 fa-huung.
Rheumatism, 風濕 fuung-shup.
Rhinoceros, 犀牛 sai-ngau.
Rhubarb, 大黃 taaiʼ-wong.
Rhyme, 叶韻 hipʼ-wunʼ.
Rib, 肋 lak, 肋索骨 lak-shaakʼ-kwut, (ribs) 排骨 pʽaai-kwut.
Ribaldry, 惡聞臭氣 okʼ-mun-chʽauʼ-hiʼ.
Ribbon, 絲帶 sze-taaiʼ.
Rice, 米 ʽmai, (boiled) 飯 faanʼ, (growing) 禾 woh, (paddy) 穀 kuuk, (old man's) 糯米 nohʼ-ʽmai.
Rice-bird, 禾花雀 woh-fa-tseukʼ.
Rice-paper, 通紙 tʽuung-ʽchi.
Rich, 富厚 fooʼ-hauʼ, 富貴 fooʼ-kwaiʼ, (man) 財主 tsʽoi-ʽchue.
Riches, 財帛 tsʽoi-paak.
Rickety, 移移郁 i-i-yuuk.
Rid, 絕了 tsuet-hiu, 甪曉 lut-hiu.

Riddle, (sieve) 篩 ʽshai, (puzzle) 謎 ʽmai, (ask a) 打物一 ʽta-mat-yat, 打古仔 ʽta-ʽkoo-ʽtsai.
Ride, 騎 kʽe.
Ridge, 條脊 tʽiu-tsekʼ, (in a field) 瀝 lek.
Ridicule, 嘲笑 chaau-siuʼ, 戲笑 hiʼ-siuʼ, (an object of) 笑柄 siuʼ-pengʼ.
Ridiculous, 可笑 ʽhoh-siuʼ.
Rifled, (grooved) 入柳 yup-ʽlau.
Right, 着 cheuk, 正 chingʼ, 本等 ʽpoon-ʽtang, (side) 右 yauʼ.
Righteous, 義 iʼ.
Rigid, 硬 ngaangʼ, 梗 ʽkang.
Rigorous, 嚴緊 im-ʽkan, (森嚴 shum-im).
Rim, 圓邊 uen-pin.
Ring, 環 waan, (finger) 戒指 kaaiʼ-ʽchi, (to) 响 ʽheung, (a bell) 打鐘 ʽta-chuung.
Ring-worm, 癬 ʽsin.
Ringlets, 一學學 yat-ʽtsze-ʽtsze.

Rinse, 蜩 ʻlong.
Riot, 亂鬧 luen'-naau', 鬧事 naau'-sze'.
Rip open, 割開 tʻong-hoi.
Ripe, 熟 shuuk.
Ripple, 波紋 poh-*mun.
Rise, 上 ʻsheung, 起 ʻhi, 興起 hing-ʻhi, (get up) 起身 ʻhi-shan.
Risk, 險 ʻhim, (to) 拚 pʻoon'.
Rite, 禮儀 ʻlai-i, 禮文 ʻlai-mun.
Rival, 對頭 tui'-*tʻau.
Rive, 破裂 pʻoh'-lit, (a) 條裂 tʻiu-lit, 條裂口 tʻiu-lit-ʻhau.
River, 河 hoh, (a) 條河 tʻiu-hoh, 條江 tʻiu-kong, (Canton river is called sea) 海 ʻhoi, 條海 tʻiu-ʻhoi.
Rivet, (to) 轉釘尾 chuen'-teng-ʻmi, (mend) 碼翻 ʻma-faan, (a) 兩頭釘 ʻleung-tʻau-ʻteng.
Rivulet, 溪 kʻai, 小河 ʻsiu-hoh, 山坑 shaan-haang.
Roach, 鱒魚 ʻtsʻuun-ue.

Road, 路 loʼ, (high-) 官路 koon-loʼ.
Roam, 遊 yau.
Roar, (哮 haau), 喊 haamʼ, (of thunder) 轟轟聲 kwang-kwang-sheng, (of water) (溯洑 pʻaang-paaiʼ), (COL.) pʻop-pʻop-sheng.
Roast, 燒 shiu, (in ashes) 煨 ooi.
Rob, 搶奪 ʻtsʻeung-tuet.
Robber, 賊 *tsʻaak.
Robe, 袍 pʻo.
Robust, 壯肥 fi-chongʼ, 壯健 chongʼ-kinʼ.
Roc, 鵬 pʻaang.
Rock, 磐石 pʻoon-shek, 大石頭 taaiʼ-shek-tʻau, (to) 兩邊擺 ʻleung-pin-ʻpaai.
Rock-fish, 石狗公 shek-ʻkau-ʻkuung.
Rocket, (a) 一枝起火 yat-chi-ʻhi-ʻfoh, (falling) 九龍到地 ʻkau-luung-toʼ-ti', (a, to be caught) 炮頭 pʻaauʼ-tʻau, 花炮 fa-pʻaauʼ.

Rocking-chair, 搖椅 luuk-ʿi.
Rock-work, 假石山 ʿka-shek-shaan.
Rod, 竿 kohn.
Roe, (female deer) 麀 yau, (fish-) 魚鶿 ue-chʻuun.
Rogue, 賊仔 tsʻaak-ʿtsai, 爛仔 *laanʾ-ʿtsai.
Roll, (to) 轆 luuk, (up) 捲埋 ʿkuen-maai, (as water) 滾 ʿkwun, (a) 卷 ʿkuen.
Roller, 碾 ʿchin, 轆 luuk, (for fields) 石滾 shek-ʿkwun.
Rollicking, 反斗 ʿfaan-ʿtau.
Rolling-pin, 研麵棍 ngaan-minʾ-kwunʾ.
Roman Catholic, 天主教 Tʻin-ʿchue-kaauʾ.
Romantic, 虛幻 hue-waanʾ.
Rome, 羅馬 Loh-ʿma.
Roof, 瓦背 ʿnga-*pooiʾ, 屋背 uuk-pooiʾ, (of the mouth) 上齶 sheungʾ-ngok.
Room, 房 *fong, 廳 ʿtʻeng, (space) 地方 tiʾ-fong, 定*tengʾ.

Roost, 鷄栖 kai-tsʻai, (to) 鷥 mau.
Root, 根 kan, (and branch) 本末 ʿpoon-moot, (and rise) 來歷 loi-lik.
Rootlet, 薑 ʿkʻeung.
Rope, 繩 *shing, 纜 laamʾ, (a) 條繩 tʻiu-*shing.
Rose, 玫瑰花 mooi-kwaiʾ-fa, (monthly) 月桂 uet-kwaiʾ, (quarterly) 四季春 szeʾ-kwaiʾ-ʿchʻuun.
Rose-apple, 葡萄菓 pʻoo-tʻo-ʿkwoh.
Rose-wood, 花梨木 fa-*li-muuk.
Rosin, 松香 tsʻuung-ʿheung.
Rot, (dry) 枯槁 foo-ʿko, (damp) 霉 mooi.
Rotten, 霉爛 mooi-laanʾ, (putrid) 腐爛 fooʾ-laanʾ, (worm-eaten) 蛀爛 chueʾ-laanʾ.
Rotate, 輪轉 luun-chuenʾ.
Rouge, 脂粉 chi-ʿfun, 胭脂 in-chi.
Rough, 粗 tsʻo, 齨 haai, 肋喀 lak-kʻak.

Round, 圓 uen, 窗窗圈 t'um-t'um-‚huen, (turn) 轉 chuen', t'um-t'um-chuen'.
Rouse, 揚起 tik-‚hi, 打醒 ‚ta-‚seng, (urge) 鼓舞 ‚koo-‚moo.
Rout, 衆人亂聚 chuung'-yan-luen'-tsue', 亂走 luen'-‚tsau.
Route, 道路 to'-lo'.
Routine, 慣經 kwaan'-king.
Rover, 遊手 yau-‚shau.
Row, (rank) 行 hong, 剌 laat.
Row, (disturbance) 鬧事 naau'-sze'.
Row, (to) 櫂 chaau'.
Rowdy, 匪徒 ‚fi-t'o.
Row-lock, 槳脚 ‚tseung-keuk'.
Rub, 搓 ch'a, 擦 ts'aat', 磨擦 moh-ts'aat', (the hands) 挪挲 noh-soh.
Rubbish, 廢物 fai'-mat, 爛坭 laan'-nai, 擸擂 laap-saap'.
Rubble, 蠻石 maan-shek.

Ruby, 紅寶石 huung-‚po-shek.
Rudd, 鱒魚 ‚ts'uun-ue.
Rudder, 舵 t'oh, 舵 ‚t'aai.
Rude, 粗 ts'o, 無禮 ‚mo-‚lai, 鄙劣 ‚p'i-luet', 魯莽 ‚lo-‚mong.
Rudiment, 胚 p'ooi, 初做 ch'oh-tso'-ke', (of learning) 小學 ‚siu-hok.
Rue, (to) 悔 fooi', (a plant) 臭草 ch'au'-ts'o.
Rueful, 悲哀 pai'-ai'.
Ruffian, 兇徒 huung-t'o.
Ruffle, 縐埋 tsau'-maai.
Rug, (hearth-) 爐口氈 lo-‚hau-‚chin.
Rugged, 崎嶇 k'i-‚k'ue, 肋喀 lak-k'ak, 巖嵾 ngaam-ts'aam.
Ruin, 破敗 p'oh'-paai', 崩敗 pang-paai' 敗壞 paai'-waai'.
Rule, 規矩 k'wai-‚kue, 法度 faat'-to', (to) 管理 ‚koon-‚li, (paper) 間線 kaan'-sin'.

Ruler, 主宰 ʻchue-ʻtsoi, (an instrument) 間尺 kaanʼ-chʻekʼ.

Rumble, 轟 kwang, (COL.) tʻum-tʻum-sheng.

Ruminate, 翻草 faan-ʻtsʻo, 反齧 ʻfaan-ngit, (reflect) 心思思 sum-sze-sze.

Rummage, 找搵 ʻchaau-ʻwan, 掏亂 lo-luenʼ, chʻaauʼ.

Rumour, 消息 siu-sik, 風聲 fuung-shing, 流風 lau-fuung.

Rump, 尾根 ʻmi-kan, 尾龍骨 ʻmi-luung-kwut.

Rumple, 縐 chʻaau, chʻaau-mang-mang.

Run, 走 ʻtsau, 跑走 ʻpʻaau-ʻtsau, 踢 tekʼ, (as water) 流 lau, (off) 走路 ʻtsau-loʼ.

Runner, (official) 廰差 tʻing-chʻaai.

Running-hand, 草書 ʻtsʻo-shue.

Running-knot, 老鼠耳 ʻlo-ʻshue-ʻi.

Rupture, (See Hernia), (to) 裂 lit.

Rural, 鄉里 heung-ʻli, 鄉下 heung-ʻha.

Rush, (to) 冲突 chʻuung-tat.

Rushes, 燈心草 tang-sum-ʻtsʻo, (mat-) 鹹水草 haam-ʻshui-ʻtsʻo.

Russia, 鵝羅斯國 Ngoh-loh-sze-kwokʼ.

Rust, 銹 sauʼ, (to) 生銹 shang-sauʼ.

Rustic, 鄉下 heung-ʻha.

Rusticate, 居鄉 kue-heung.

Rustling, 沙沙聲 sha-sha-sheng, sa-sa-sheng, sö-sö-sheng.

Rut, (軌道 ʻkwai-toʼ), 車轍 chʻe-chʻitʼ.

Rye, 麥 mak, 小麥 ʻsiu-mak.

S

Sabbath, 安息日 Ohn-sik-yat.

Sable, (fur) 黑貂皮 hak-tiu-pʻi.

Sack, 囊 nong, 袋 *toiʼ, (to) 刼空 kipʼ-huung.

Sack-cloth, 粗麻布 ts'o-ma-po'.
Sacred, 聖 shing'.
Sacrifice, 祭祀 tsai'-tsze', (to part with) 捨 ꞌshe, 拚 p'oon', 拚窮 p'oon'-k'uung.
Sad, 憂悶 yau-moon', 鼻厬 pai'-ai', (how!) 可憐 ꞌhoh-lin, 可惜 ꞌhoh-sik.
Saddle, 鞍 ꞌohn, 馬鞍 ꞌma-ꞌohn.
Safe, 穩當 ꞌwan-tong', 妥當 ꞌt'oh-tong', 穩陳 ꞌwan-chan'.
Safe, (for meat) 風燈 fuung-tang, (an iron) 鐵箱 t'it'-ꞌseung.
Safflower, (colour) 花紅 fa-huung.
Saffron, 紅藍花 huung-laam-fa.
Sagacious, 伶俐 ling-li'.
Sage, (a) 聖人 shingꞌ-yan, (herb) 來路茶 loi-*lo'-ch'a, 英國茶 Ying-kwok-ch'a.
Sago, 沙穀米 sha-kuuk-ꞌmai.

Said, (the) 該 koi.
Sail, 悝 ꞌli, 帆 faan, (to) 行船 hang-shuen, 駛 ꞌshai, 駛風 ꞌshai-fuung, (set-) 開身 hoi-shan, 扯悝 ꞌc'he-ꞌli.
Sailor, 水手 ꞌshui-ꞌshau.
Sake of, 爲 wai'.
Salacious, 姣 au.
Salad, 生菜 shang-ts'oi'.
Salary, 俸祿 fuung-luuk, (a teacher's) 修金 ꞌsau-ꞌkum.
Sale, 消流 siu-lau, 消路 siu-lo', (for) 出賣 ch'uut-maai', (auction) 出投 ch'uut-t'au, (deed of) 契 k'ai', 張契 cheung-k'ai'.
Salisbury seeds, 白菜 paak-ꞌkwoh.
Saliva, 口水 ꞌhau-ꞌshui.
Sallow, 黃黃白白 wong-wong-paak-paak.
Sally, 走出 ꞌtsau-ch'uut.
Salmon, 馬友 ꞌma-ꞌyau.
Saloon, 客堂 hank'-t'ong.
Salt, 鹽 im, (salted) 鹹 haam, (Epsom) 朴硝 p'ok'-siu, (to) 醃 ip'.

Saltpetre, 鹹硝 haam-siu, 硝 siu.
Salubrious, 温和 wan-woh.
Salubrity, 好水土 ʻho-ʻshui ʻtʻo.
Salute, (to) 請安 ʻtsʻing-ₒohn, (a) 禮炮 ʻlai-pʻaau⁾.
Salvation, 救 kau⁾, 得救 tak-kau⁾, 救法 kau⁾-faat⁾.
Salve, 膏藥料 ko-yeuk-liu⁾.
Same, 同 tʻuung.
Sample, 樣子 yeung⁾-ʻtsze, 辦 *paan⁾.
Sanctify, 作聖 tsok⁾-shing⁾, 成聖 shing-shing⁾.
Sanction, 准 ʻchuun.
Sand, 沙 sha.
Sandals, (grass-) 草鞋 ʻtsʻo-haai.
Sandal-wood, 檀香 tʻaan-heung.
Sand-stone, 礪石 lai⁾-shek.
Sandwich Islands, 檀香山 Tʻaan-ₒheung-ₒshaan.
Sanguine, 心雄 sum-huung, sum-huung-kₒ⁾.
Sanity, 自在 tsze⁾-tsoi⁾.

Sap, 汁 chup, 蘂 ʻyui, ʻshui, (to undermine) 水割地脚 koht⁾-ti⁾-keuk⁾.
Sapan-wood, 蘇木 soo-muuk.
Sapindus, 無槵樹 mo-*waan⁾-shue⁾, muuk-*waan⁾.
Sapphire, 青玉 tsʻing-yunk.
Sarcastic, 譏諷 ki-fuung⁾.
Sarcenet, 綢綾 chʻau-ling, (for fans) 紙絹 ʻchi-kuen⁾, (for lanterns) 紗 sha.
Sarsaparilla, 茯苓 fuuk-ling.
Sash, 帶 taai⁾, 褲頭帶 foo⁾-tʻau-taai⁾, 腰帶 iu-taai⁾.
Satin, 緞 *tuen⁾, (native) 八絲緞 paat⁾-sze-*tuen⁾.
Satire, 譏刺 ki-tsʻze⁾.
Satisfied, 厭足 im⁾-tsuuk, 心足 sum-tsuuk, 見夠 kin⁾-kau⁾.
Saturate, 浸透 tsum⁾-tʻau⁾.
Saturday, 禮拜六 ʻlai-paai⁾-luuk.
Saturn, (planet) 土星 ʻTʻo-ₒsing.
Sauce, 醬 tseung⁾.
Sauce-pan, 煲 po.

Saucer, 茶碟 ch'a-*tip, 茶船 ch'a-*shuen.
Saucy, 輕慢 hing-maan', 傲慢 ngo'-maan', 沙塵 sha-ch'an.
Saunter, 閒遊 haan-yau.
Sausage, 猪腸 chue-*ch'eung, (dried) 臘腸 laap-*ch'eung.
Savage, 蠻 maan, (a) 野人 'ye-yan, 生番 shaang-faan.
Save, 救 kau', 拯救 'ch'ing-kau', 存 ts'uen, (gain) 賺 chaan'.
Saviour, 救世主 Kau'-shai'-'chue.
Savour, 味道 mi'-to'.
Saw, (a) 把鋸 'pa-kue', (to) 拉鋸 laai-kue', 鋸 kue'.
Saw-dust, 木糠 muuk-'hong.
Saw-mill, 解木廠 'kaai-muuk-'ch'ong.
Saxifrage, 老虎耳 'lo-'foo-'i.
Say, 話 wa', (a saying) 語 'ue.
Scab, 塊𤷪 faai'-'im.

Scabbard, 刀殼 to-hok'.
Scaffold, 搭架 taap'-*ka', 棚 p'aang.
Scald, 爛 luuk.
Scale, (series) 等級 'tung-k'up, (comparative) 配法 p'ooi'-faat'.
Scales, (for weighing) 天平 t'in-p'ing; (of fishes) 魚鱗 ue-luun.
Scaly, (in flakes) 一片片 yat-p'in'-p'in'.
Scandal, (a) 醜事 'ch'au-sze', (to talk) 講是非 'kong-shi'-ji.
Scandalized, 見醜 kin'-'ch'au.
Scandalous, 醜 'ch'au, 害情 hoi'-ts'ing, (abusive) 壞名 waai'-meng.
Scanty, 窄窄地 chaak'-*chaak'-*ti'.
Scar, 痕 han, 痕迹 han-tsik'.
Scarce, 罕有 'hohn-'yau, 希罕 hi-'hohn, 少 'shiu.
Scarcely, 僅 'kan.
Scare, 嚇勢 haak'-shai'.

Scarf, 長膊巾 ch'eung-pok'-kan, (join on) 駁 pok'.
Scarlet, 大紅 taai'-huung.
Scatter, 散開 saan'-hoi.
Scattered, 星散 sing-saan'.
Scavenger, (street) 掃街 so'-ʻkaai, 倒擸撻 ʻto-laap-saap', (house-) 倒屎 ʻto-ʻshi.
Scenery, 景象 ʻking-tseung'.
Scent, 香氣 hueng-hi', 香 heung, (to) 鼻聞 pi'-mun.
Scented capers, 珠蘭茶 chue-laan-ch'a.
Sceptical, 多疑 toh-i.
Sceptre, 圭 kwai, (a ladle-shaped) 如意 ue-i'.
Schedule, 冊 ch'aak'.
Scheme, 計謀 kai'-man.
Schism, 分門 fun-moon.
Scholar, 學生 hok-ʻshaang, 讀書人 tuuk-shue-yan.
School, 書館 shue-ʻkoon, 學館 hok-ʻkoon, 學堂 hok-t'ong.
School-fellow, 書友 shue-ʻyau.

School-master, 先生 sin-shang, (mistress) 女師 ʻnue-sze.
Science, 學 hok.
Scissors, 鉸剪 kaau'-ʻtsin.
Scoff, 譏笑 ki-siu'.
Scold, 閙 naau'.
Scolding, 啉嗶 hum-lut, (a) 閙一場 naau'-yat-ch'eung.
Scoop, (to) 挖 waat'.
Scope, 大意 taai'-i'.
Scorch, 焦 tsiu, 燶 ʻnuung, 燒親 shiu-ts'an.
Scorn, 輕慢 hing-maan', 厭棄 im'-hi', 藐視 ʻmiu-shi'.
Scorpion, 蜂蠍 fuung-hit'.
Scoundrel, 光棍 kwong-kwun'.
Scour, 潤乾淨 t'o-kohn-tseng', 嗻 ʻshaang.
Scourge, 鞭 pin.
Scout, (disdain) 厭棄 im'-hi', (to spy) 覘吓 chong-ʻha.
Scowl, 嬲色 nau-shik, 縐眉 tsau'-mi.

Scraggy, 瘦出骨 shau²-ch'ut-kwut.
Scramble, 擒爬 k'um-p'a, 手爬爬 ʿshau-p'a-p'a.
Scrap, 碎 sui².
Scrape, (to) 刮 kwaat². 刮削 kwaat²-seuk².
Scratch, 搲 ʿwa, ʿwe, 楷 ngaau, 抓搲 ʿchaau-ʿwa, 搔 so.
Scrawl, 畫花 waak-fa.
Scream } 叫聲 kiu²-sheng,
Screech } 高聲叫 ko-sheng-kiu².
Screen, 屏風 p'ing-fuung, 簾 *lim, (to) 遮蓋 che-k'oi².
Screw, 螺絲 loh-ʿsze, (cork-) 酒鑽 ʿtsau-tsuen², (miser) 蝦𧎸鑽 ha-ch'uun-tsuen².
Screw-driver, 螺絲撐 loh-sze-ning².
Screw-steamer, 暗輪船 om²-luun-shuen.
Scribble, 亂搽 luen²-ʿch'a.
Scribe, 讀書人 tuuk-shue-yan.

Scrimp, 短少 ʿtuen-ʿshiu.
Scrofula, 瘰癧 ʿloh-lek.
Scroll, 卷 ʿkuen, 手卷 ʿshau-ʿkuen, (a pair of scrolls) 對 ʿtui.
Scrotum, 腎囊 shan²-nong.
Scrub, 刷 shaat², 擦 ts'aat².
Scruple, (doubt) 思疑 sze-i.
Scrutinize, 查察 ch'a-ch'aat².
Scuffle, 爭鬥 chaang-tau².
Sculk, 竄匿 ʿch'uen-nik.
Scull, 頭殼 t'au-hok², (bare) 枯顱頭 foo-lo-t'au; (of a boat) 櫓 ʿlo, (to) 搖櫓 iu-ʿlo.
Scum, 浮沫 fau-moot, 糜 mi.
Scurf, 老坭 ʿlo-nai, (on the head) 頭坭 t'au-nai.
Scurrilous, 汚穢 oo-wai².
Scythe, 長鐮 ch'eung-lim.
Sea, 海 ʿhoi, 洋海 yeung-ʿhoi.
Sea-sickness, 嘔浪 ʿau-long², 暈浪 wan²-long².
Sea-weed, 海菜 ʿhoi-ts'oi².

Seal, (animal) 海獺 ʻhoi-chʻaat’, (to) 印 yan’, 給印 kʻup-yan’, (up) 封 fuung, (-character) 圖書 tʻo-ˏshue, 篆字 suen’-*tsze’, (the imperial) 御璽 ue’-ˏsaai.

Sealing-wax, 火漆 ʻfoh-tsʻat.

Seam, (a) 聯骨 luen-kwut, 聯口 luen-ʻhau, (in boarding) 罅 la’, (to) 聯 luen, 縫 fuung, 合埋 hop-maai

Seamstress, 揸針嘅 cha-chum-ke’.

Search, 搜檢 ʻsau-ʻkim, 搵 ʻwun.

Seared conscience, 喪良心 song’-ˏleung-sum, 無本心 ˏmo-ʻpoon-sum.

Season, 時 shi, (4 seasons) 四季 sze’-kwai’, 四時 sze’-shi.

Seasonable, 着時候 cheuk-shi-hau’.

Seasoning, 落味道 lok-mi’-to’.

Seat, 座 tsoh’, 座位 tsoh’-wai’.

Secluded, 噆 pooi’.

Second, 第二 tai’-i’.

Second-hand, 二檯 i’-*tʻoi.

Secret, 機密 ki-mat, 暗 om’, (a) 隱事 ʻyan-sze’.

Secretary, 西席 Sai-tsik, (private) 幕友 mok-ʻyau, (Colonial-) 輔政司 foo’-ˏching’-sze.

Secretion, 津液 tsuun-yik.

Secretly, 私吓 sze-ʻha.

Sect, 教門 kaau’-moon.

Section, 段 tuen’, (a cutting) 截 tsit.

Secure, 穩陳 ʻwan-chan’, 主固 ʻchue-koo’.

Security, 擔保 taam-ʻpo, 擔干紀 taam-kohn-ʻki.

Sedan-chair, 頂轎 ʻting-*kiu’.

Sedan-poles, 轎升 *kiu’-ˏshing.

Sedge, 蒲草 pʻo-ʻtsʻo.

Sediment, 渣滓 cha-tsze, 脚 keuk’.

Seditious, 擾亂 ʻiu-luenʼ.
Seduce, 挑引 tʻiu-ʻyan, 誘惑 ʻyau-waak, 引誘 ʻyan-ʻyau.
Sedulous, 勤力 kʻan-lik.
See, 見 kinʼ, 睇見 ʻtʻai-kinʼ, (look) 睇吓 ʻtʻai-ʻha, (after) 看守 hohn-ʻshau.
Seed, 種 ʻchuung, 仁 yan, ngan, 米 ʻmai.
Seek, 搵 ʻwan, 尋 tsʻum, (ask) 求 kʻau.
Seem, 似 ʻtsʻze, 顯出 ʻhin-chʻuut, (seems to me) 似覺 ʻtsʻze-kokʼ.
Seen, 見過 kinʼ-kwohʼ.
Segar, (Manila) 呂宋烟 ʻLue-suungʼ-ʻin, (a) 一口烟 yatʼ-ʻhau-ʻin.
Seize, 捉住 chuuk-chueʼ, 霸住 paʼ-chueʼ, 搶 ʻtsʻeung.
Seldom, 少可 ʻshiu-ʻhoh, 無幾何 ʻmo-ʻki-*hoh.
Select, 擇 chaak, 揀 ʻkaan, 選 ʻsuen.
Self, 自己 tszeʼ-ʻki.

Self-contradictory, 自相矛盾 tszeʼ-seung-mau-tʻuun.
Self-examination, 自省 tszeʼ-ʻsing.
Self-sufficient, 自足 tszeʼ-tsuuk.
Self-will, 執拗 chup-aauʼ.
Selfishness, 私心 sze-sam.
Sell, 賣 maaiʼ, 賣去 maaiʼ-hueʼ, (offer to) 發賣 faatʼ-maaiʼ.
Semen, 種 ʻchuung, 精 tsing.
Semi-, 半 poonʼ.
Send, 寄 kiʼ, (a person) 遣 ʻhin, 打發 ʻta-faatʼ.
Senior, 長 ʻcheung.
Senna, 槐葉 waai-ip.
Sense, 智識 chiʼ-shik, 見識 kinʼ-shik, (common) 情理 tsʻing-ʻli.
Senses, (five) 五官 ʻng-koon.
Sensitive, 情急 tsʻing-kup, 性急 singʼ-kup.
Sensual, 嗜慾 shiʼ-yuuk, 私慾 sze-yuuk.

Sentence, 句話 kue'-wa', (judicial) 批判 p'ai-p'oon', 擬定刑 i-ting'-ying, 定罰 ting'-faat, 辦 paan'.
Sentinel, 哨人 shaau'-yan.
Separate, 別開 pit-hoi, 分別 fun-pit, (ADJ.) 另外 ling'-ngoi'.
September, 英九月 Ying-'kau-uet.
Sepulchre, 墳墓 fun-moo'.
Sequester, 抄 ch'aau, 封 fuung.
Serene, 淸平 ts'ing-p'ing.
Serge, 嗶嘰 put-'ki.
Series, 次第 ts'ze'-tai', 列陳 lit-chan', 一件件 yat-kin'-kin'.
Serious, (person) 莊敬 chong-king', (affair) 關系 kwaan-hai', 重 chuung'.
Serpent, (a) 條蛇 t'iu-she.
Servant, 奴僕 no-puuk, 使喚人 'shai-foon'-yan, (boy) 事仔 sze'-'tsai.
Serve, 服事 fuuk-sze'.
Servile, 柔順 yau-shuun', 下作 ha'-tsok'.

Sesamum, 芝蔴 chi-ma, 油蔴 yau-ma.
Set, (to) 立 laap, 置 chi', 儕 chai, (as the sun) 落 lok, 入 yup, (a) 副 foo', (of people) 班 paan.
Settle, 定 ting', (accounts) 淸數 ts'ing-sho', (as dregs) 凝 k'ing.
Seven, 七 ts'at.
Seventh, 第七 tai'-ts'at.
Sever, 割短 koht'-'tuen.
Several, 幾個 'ki-koh', 數 sho'.
Severe, 嚴緊 im-'kan, 利害 li'-hoi', (grievous) 重 'ch'uung.
Sew, 聯 luen, 縫 fuung.
Sewer, 坑渠 haang-k'ue, 暗渠 om'-k'ue.
Sex, 陰陽之分 yum-yeung-chi-fun.
Shabby, 卑賤 pi-tsin'.
Shackles, 桎梏 chat-kuuk, 繚 liu.
Shad, 三黎魚 saam-laai-*ue.

Shaddock, 碌柚 luuk-*yau, 柚子 yau-ʻtsze.
Shade, 遮陰 che-yum, (lamp-) 燈罩 tang-chaauʼ, (a slight) 帶有的 taaiʼ-ʻyau-ʻti.
Shades, 陰間 yum-kaan.
Shadow, 影 ʻying.
Shaft, 竿 kohn, (handle) 柄 pengʼ.
Shaggy, 鬆毛 suung-mo, suung-mo-keʼ.
Shake, 搖吓 iu-ʻha, 搖動 iu-tuungʼ, 抰 ʻyeung, (as dice) 擎 ngo, (the head) 擰頭 ningʼ-*t'au, (hands) 揸手 cha-ʻshau.
Shall, 將來 tseung-loi, 必 pit.
Shallow, 淺 ʻts'in.
Shallows, 瀝 lek, (rapids) 灘 t'aan.
Sham, 詐僞 chaʼ-ngaiʼ, (to) 詐 chaʼ.
Shame, 羞 sau, 羞恥 sau-ʻch'i, (to feel) 見羞 kinʼ-sau, (for another) 見醜 kinʼ-ʻch'au, (disgrace) 醜 ʻch'au.

Shampoo, 泵身 ʻtum-shan.
Shape, 式 shik, 像 tseungʼ, 模樣 moo-*yeung,ʼ 形 ying.
Share, (to) 分數 fun-shoʼ, (a) 分子 funʼ-ʻtsze, 股分 ʻkoo-*funʼ.
Shark, 沙魚 sha-*ue.
Sharp, 利 liʼ, 快利 faaiʼ-liʼ.
Sharpen, 磨利 moh-liʼ.
Shatter, 打碎 ʻta-suiʼ.
Shave, 剃 t'aiʼ, (to plane) 刨 p'aau.
Shaving, 刨柴 p'aau-*ch'aai, (gum-shavings) 刨花 p'aau-ʻfa.
Shawl, 答膊蔞 taapʼ-pokʼ-ʻlau.
She, he, or it, 佢 ʻk'ue.
Sheaf, 禾束 woh-ch'uuk, (a) 一把 yat-ʻpa.
Shear, 剪 ʻtsin.
Shears, 鉸剪 kaauʼ-ʻtsin.
Sheath, 鞘 ts'iuʼ, 刀殻 ʻto-hokʼ.
Shed, a, 廠 ʻch'ong, 蓬廠 p'uung-ʻch'ong.

Sheep, 羊 *yeung, 綿羊 min-*yeung.

Sheep-fold, 羊欄 yeung-laan.

Sheepish, 錯錯諤諤 ts'ok²-ts'ok²-ngok-ngok.

Sheer, 淨係 tseng²-hai².

Sheet, (of a bed) 被單 ʻp'i-ₜtaan, (of paper) 張 ₜcheung, (-ropes) 繚繩 liu²-shing.

Shelf, 格板 kaak²-ʻpaan, 架 ka².

Shell, 螺殼 loh-hok², lö-hok², (of eggs, &c.) 殼 hok².

Shelter, 遮蔽 ₜche-pai², 庇護 pi²-oo². 庇蔭 pi²-yum².

Shepherd, 牧羊人 muuk-yeung-yan, 牧童 muuk-t'uung.

Shepherd's purse, 薺 ʻts'ai.

Sheriff, 傳票官 ch'uen-p'iu²-koon.

Shield, 牌盾 p'aai-ʻt'uun, (rattan-) 籐牌 t'ang-p'aai.

Shift, (to) 换 oon², 搬 poon, 移 i, (move) 郁 yuuk, (expedient) 計 kai².

Shin, 前臁 ts'in-lim.

Shine, 發光 faat²-kwong, 照 chiu², (upon) 照光 chiu²-kwong.

Ship, 船 shuen, (full rigged) 三枝桅船 saam-chi-wai-shuen.

Ship-building, 裝船 chong-shuen.

Ship-wreck, 破船 p'oh²-shuen.

Shirk, 躲避 ʻtoh-pi².

Shirt, 內衫 noi²-ₜshaam, (under) 近身衣 kan²-shan-i, 汗衫 hohn²-ₜshaam.

Shiver, (with cold) 打冷振 ʻta-ʻlaang-chan², (shatter) 打碎 ʻta-sui².

Shoals, 沙灘 sha-t'aan.

Shock, (shake) 震動 chan²-tuung², (violence) 勢兇 shai²-huung.

Shocking 慘 ʻts'aam, 傷心 sheung-sum.

Shoe, 鞋 haai, (pair of shoes) 對鞋 tui²-haai.

Shoe-horn, 鞋拔 haai-pat, 鞋抽 haai-ch'au.
Shoot, (to) 射 she', 打 'ta, (sprout) 出笋 ch'uut-'suun.
Shoots, bamboo-, 竹笋 chuuk-'suun.
Shop, 舖頭 p'oo'-*t'au.
Shop-man, 賣貨手 maai'-foh'-'shau, (head) 掌櫃 'cheung-*kwai'.
Shore, 岸 ngohn'.
Shore up, 撐住 ch'aang-chue'.
Short, 短 'tuen, (time) 暫時 tsaam'-shi.
Short-hand, 減筆字 'kaam-put-tsze'.
Short-sight, 近視眼 kan'-shi'-'ngaan.
Shot, 彈子 taan'-'tsze.
Should, (ought) 應當 ying-tong.
Shoulder, 肩膊 kin-pok', 膊頭 pok'-t'au.
Shoulder of mutton, 羊手 yeung-'shau.
Shout, 喝聲 hoht'-sheng.

Shove, 推擁 t'ui-'uung, 擁開 'uung-hoi, (along) 褪 t'an', (pole) 撐 ch'aang.
Shovel, 鏟 'ch'aan.
Show, 俾 — 睇 'pi — 't'ai, (point out) 指示 'chi-shi'.
Shower, 陣雨 chan'-ue.
Showy, 排場 p'aai-ch'eung.
Shred, 爛條 laan'-t'iu.
Shrew, 惡婆 ok-*p'oh.
Shrewd, 麻俐 ma-li'.
Shriek, 叫聲 kiu'-sheng.
Shrike, 伯鷯 paak-liu.
Shrill, 狠響 'han-'heung.
Shrimp, 蝦 ha.
Shrine, 神龕 shan-hom.
Shrink, 縮埋 shuuk-maai.
Shrivel, 縐 ch'aau.
Shroud, 壽衣 shau'-i.
Shrouding, 收殮 shau-'lim.
Shrouds, 上桅繩梯 'sheung-wai-*shing-t'ai.
Shrub, 矮樹 'ai-shue'.
Shrug the shoulders, 縮膊 shuuk-pok'.
Shudder, 打振 'ta-chan', 戰慄 chin'-luut.

Shuffle cards, 洗牌 ʻsai-*pʻaai.
Shuffling, 閃閃縮縮 ʻshim-ʻshim-shuuk-shuuk.
Shun, 避 piʼ.
Shut, 關 kwaan, 閂埋 shaan-maai, 掩埋 ʻim-maai, 合埋 hop-maai, (lock) 鎖住 ʻsoh-chueʼ, (stuff), 塞 sak, (seal) 封 fuung.
Shutters, 窗板 ₍chʻeung-ʻpaan.
Shuttle-cock, 踢燕 tʻek-*inʼ.
Shy, 畏縮 waiʼ-shuuk.
Siam, 暹羅國 Tsʻimʼ-loh-kwokʼ.
Sick, 有病 ʻyau-pengʼ, (stomach-) 會嘔 ooiʼ-ʻau, 想嘔 ʻseung-ʻau.
Sickle, 鐮 lim.
Side, 邊 pin, 旁邊 pʻong-₍pin, 側邊 chak-₍pin, (of the body) 小腌 ʻsiu-ʻim.
Siege, (to lay) 圍住 wai-chueʼ.
Siesta, 刞晏覺 funʼ-aanʼ-kaauʼ.

Sieve, 篩斗 shai-ʻtau.
Sift, 篩 shai.
Sigh, 引氣 ʻyan-hiʼ, 嘆息 tʻaanʼ-sik.
Sight, 眼見 ʻngaan-kinʼ, (power of) 眼力 ʻngaan-lik.
Sightly, 好睇 ʻho-ʻtʻai.
Sign, (one's name) 簽名 tsʻim-*meng, (a trace) 影跡 ʻying-tsik, (an omen) 兆頭 chiuʼ-tʻau, (a mark) 號 hoʼ.
Signboard, 招牌 chiu-pʻaai.
Signify, (mean) 有──意思 ʻyau──iʼ-szeʼ, 意係 iʼ-haiʼ, (refer to) 指 ʻchi, (make signs) 示意 shiʼ-iʼ, 會意 ooiʼ-iʼ, 諧意 haaiʼ-iʼ.
Silence, 寂靜 tsik-tsingʼ, 無聲 ʻmo-sheng.
Silent, 靜靜 *tsingʼ-tsingʼ.
Silently, 靜靜 tsingʼ-*tsingʼ.
Silk, (material) 絲 sze, (cloth) 綢 chʻau, (thread) 絲線 sze-sinʼ.

Silk-worm, 蠶蟲 ts'aam-*ch'uung.
Sill, 根 ʽch'aan, ʽch'aam.
Silly, 呆呆 ngoi-ngoi, 疳食 nup-shik.
Silver, 銀 ngan, *ngan.
Similar, 似 ʽts'ze, 相似 seung-ʽts'ze, 好似 ʽho-ʽts'ze.
Simper, 冷笑 ʽlaang-siu'.
Simple, 朴素 p'ok'-so', (minded) 蠢直 ʽch'uun-chik, (easy) 容易 yuung-i'.
Simpleton, 呆佬 ngoi-ʽlo.
Sin, 罪 tsui', 罪惡 tsui-ok', (to) 犯罪 faan'-tsui'.
Since, 從──以來 ts'uung ──ʽi-loi, (seeing that) 既然間 ki'-in-kaan, (how long?) 起有幾耐 ʽhi-ʽyau-ʽki-*noi'?
Sincere, 誠實 shing-shat, 真心 chan-sum.
Sinew, 筋 kan.
Sing, 唱 ch'eung', 唱歌 ch'eung'-ʽkoh.
Singe, 燒燶 shiu-nuung.

Single, 單 ʽtaan, 隻 chek'.
Singly, (one by one) 一一 yat-yat, 逐一逐二 chuuk-yat-chuuk-i'.
Single-hearted, 丹心 taan-sum, 赤心 ch'ik-sum.
Singular, 奇異 k'i-i'.
Sinister, 左 ʽtsoh, (bad) 使左挑 shai-ʽtsoh-ʽt'iu.
Sink, 沈落 ch'um-lok, (as a wall) 坐 tsoh'.
Sinner, 罪人 tsui'-yan.
Sinus, 穴 uet, (bay) 彎 waan.
Sip, 哶 mi, 啜 tsuet'.
Siphon, 角筒 kok'-t'uung.
Sir, 駕上 ka'-sheung', 尊駕 tsuen-ka', (Sirs) 列公 lit-kuung.
Sister, (elder) 亞姐 a'-ʽtse, (younger) 亞妹 a'-*mooi'.
Sister-in-law, 嬸姆 ʽshum-ʽmoo, (elder brother's wife) 亞嫂 a'-ʽso, (younger brother's wife) 亞嬸 a'-ʽshum, (wife's sisters) 亞姨 a'-i, a'-i, (husband's sisters) 亞姑 a'-koo.
Sit, 坐 tsoh', ʽts'oh.

Situation, 地位 ti'-wai', 所在 'shoh-tsoi', (office) 職任 chik-yum'.
Six, 六 luuk.
Sixth, 第六 tai'-luuk.
Size, 體度 't'ai-to', (capacity) 度量 to'-leung', (what?) 幾大 'ki-*taai'.
Size, (glue) 膠 kaau.
Skate, (fish) 鯆魚 poo-ue.
Skate, (to) 碾 shin'.
Skein, 札 chaat', 子 'tsze.
Skeleton, 骨體 kwut-'t'ai.
Sketch, 意筆 i'-put, (a rough) 草稿 'ts'o-'ko, (to) 繪 'fooi.
Skewer, 燒肉串 shiu-yuuk-'ch'aan ('chum).
Skill, 伎巧 ki'-'haau, 才藝 ts'oi-ngai'.
Skilled, 善精 shin'-tsing.
Skim, 撇 p'it'.
Skin, 皮 p'i, (to) 剝皮 mok-p'i.
Skin (cast off,) 蛻 t'ui'.
Skin-flint, 蝦嗸鈒 ,ha-,ch'uun-chaap.

Skip, 跳 t'iu', 跳躍 t'iu'-yeuk.
Skirt, 衫尾 shaam-'mi, (woman's) 裙 k'wun.
Skulk, &c. See Sculk, &c.
Sky, 蒼天 ts'ong-t'in, 穹蒼 k'uung-ts'ong, 天 t'in, 太空 t'aai'-huung, (in the) 空中 huung-chuung.
Sky-light, 天窗 t'in-ch'eung.
Slab, 塊石 faai'-shek, 石版 shek-'paan, 石碑 shek-pi.
Slabber, 伐伐聲 faat-faat-sheng.
Slack, 鬆 suung, (remiss) 嬾 laai-lau', (water) 水漫 'shui-maan'.
Slake, 解 'kaai, (lime) 發 faat'.
Slam, 冲撞 ch'uung-chong', 摐 p'uung'.
Slander, 譭謗 'wai-p'ong', (a) 讒言 ts'aam-in.
Slang, 市井話 'shi-'tseng-wa'.
Slanting, 斜 ts'e, ts'e'.

Slap, 打巴 ʿta-pa, (with the hand) 打巴掌 ʿta-pa-ʿcheung, 摑 kwaakʾ, 拍 pʿaakʾ.
Slash, 斬 ʿchaam, 亂斬 luenʾ-ʿchaam.
Slate, 石版 shek-ʿpaan.
Slattern, 拉歚 laai-taai, 濕霉 shap-mooi.
Slaughter, 殺戮 shaat-luuk, 屠戮 tʿo-luuk, (butcher) 劏 tʿong.
Slave, (female) 奴婢 no-ʿpʿi, (male) 僕 puuk, 奴僕 no-puuk.
Slay, 打死 ʿta-ʿsze.
Sledge, 拖轎 tʿoh-*kiuʾ.
Sleek, 滑澤 waat-chaak.
Sleep, 瞓 funʾ, 睡 shuiʾ, 打睡 ʿta-shuiʾ, 瞓覺 funʾ-kaauʾ.
Sleepy, 眼瞓 ʿngaan-funʾ, 想瞓 ʿseung-funʾ, hapʾ-ʿngaan.
Sleet, 霰雪 sinʾ-suetʾ.
Sleeve, 袖 tsauʾ.

Sleight of hand, 手法 ʿshau-faatʾ.
Slender, 幼細 yauʾ-saiʾ, 弱 yeuk, 纖 tsʿim, 朴 niu.
Slice, 片 pʿinʾ, 塊 faaiʾ, (to) 切 tsʿit, 剾 ʾlek.
Slide, 蹁 shinʾ.
Slight, (to) 輕忽 ʿhing-fut, (small) 小小 ʿsiu-ʿsiu.
Slim, 纖 tsʿim.
Slime, 泥濘 niʾ-ningʾ, 潺 shaan.
Sling, (for stones) 飛砣 fi-tʿoh, (for carrying) 絡 lok, (of rattan) 籐絡 tʿang-lok.
Slip, (to) 蹁 shinʾ, 失 shat, (fall) 跌 titʾ, (off) 滑甪 waat-lut, (grow from a) 插生 chaapʾ-shang, 嗀 pok.
Slippers, 拖鞋 tʿoh-haai.
Slippery, 滑 waat, (character) 白鼻哥 paak-piʾ-ʿkoh, 猾賊 waat-tsʿaak.
Slipstitch, 桶綫 ʿtʿuung-sinʾ.

Slit, 裂開 lit-hói, (a) 裂lit, 條裂 tʻiu-lit, 條罅 tʻiu-laʾ.
Slop, 水肙 ʿshui-ngan ʾ.
Slop-basin, 哴水碗 ʿlong-ʿshui-ʿoon.
Slope, 斜 tsʻeʾ, tsʻe.
Sloth, (the) 木狗 muuk-ʿkau, 樹懶 shueʾ-ʿlaan.
Slothful, 懶惰 ʿlaan-tohʾ.
Slouching, 氹堆 tumʾ-tui, 低頭屈屈 tai-tʻau-wat-wat.
Slovenly, 嚹穄 laai-lueʾ, (in dress) 拉獃 laai-taai.
Slow, 遲慢 chʻi-maanʾ.
Slowly, 慢慢 maanʾ-*maanʾ, 摩摩 moh-moh.
Slug, 鼻涕蟲 piʾ-tʻai-chʻuung.
Sluggard, 一身懶骨 yat-shan-ʿlaan-kwut.
Sluice, 竇板 tauʾ-ʿpaan.
Slur, 玷辱 timʾ-yuuk, 瑕疵 ha-tsʻze.
Slush, 泥漰 nai-paanʾ.
Sluttish, 苟且 ʿkau-ʿchʻe.

Sly, 搞滑 lo-waat.
Smack the lips, 答口聲 taapʾ-ʿhau-sheng, chaapʾ-ʿhau.
Small, 細小 saiʾ-ʿsiu, ——仔——ʿtsai, (very) 微 mi.
Small-pox, 出痘 chʻuut-*tauʾ, 天行 tʻin-hang.
Smalts, 洋青 yeung-ʿtsʻing.
Smart, 伶俐 ling-li, 快利 faaiʾ-li, 精巧 tsing-ʿhaau, 精 tseng, (to) 痛 tʻuungʾ, 見痛 kinʾ-tʻuungʾ.
Smash, 打碎 ʿta-suiʾ.
Smattering, to have a, 識幾程 shik-ʿki-chʻing.
Smear, 塗 tʻo, 搽 chʻa, 盪 tongʾ.
Smell, (generally bad) 臭 chʻauʾ, 隨息 tsʻui-sik, (to) 聞 mun.
Smelt, (to) (銷冶 siu-ʿye), 煉 linʾ.
Smile, 含笑 hom-siuʾ, 微笑 mi-siuʾ.
Smite, 打 ʿta.
Smith, 打(金)匠 ʿta-(kum-)*tseungʾ.

Smoke, 烟 in, 火烟 ʿfoh-in, (to, tobacco, &c.) 食烟 shik-ʿin, (emit) 出烟 chʻuut-in, (hams) 燻 fun-ʿfoh, (blacken) 燉黑 tsʻau-hak.

Smooth, 滑 waat, 繆 nauʾ, (level) 平 pʻing.

Smother, 局死 kuuk-ʿsze.

Smoulder, 尚有的燒 sheungʾ-ʿyau-ti-shiu.

Smuggle, 走私 ʿtsau-sze.

Smuggled goods, 私貨 sze-fohʾ.

Smut, 烏煤 oo-mooi.

Snail, 蝸牛 woh-ngau, 田螺 tʻin-loh.

Snake, (a) 條蛇 tʻiu-she.

Snap, (break) 斷 ʿtʻuen, (the fingers) 整手卟 ʿching-ʿshau-puuk.

Snapper, fish, 立魚 laap-ue.

Snare, 圈套 huen-tʻoʾ.

Snarl, 噬牙 shaiʾ-nga.

Snatch, 搶 ʿtsʻeung, 奪 tuet.

Sneaking, 屈氣 wat-hiʾ.

Sneer, 冷笑 ʿlaang-siuʾ.

Sneeze, 打噴嚏 ʿta-pʻanʾ-tʻaiʾ, (COL.) ʿta-hat-chʻi.

Snipe, 沙佳 shá-chui.

Snobbish, 草莽 ʿtsʻo-ʿmong.

Snore, 扯鼻鼾 ʿchʻe-pi-hohn.

Snort, 噴鼻 pʻanʾ-piʾ.

Snout, 嘴 ʿtsui, (pigs) 猪鼻 chue-piʾ.

Snow, 雪 suet.

Snub, (short) 短設設 ʿtuen-chʻit-chʻit (to) 充淡水 chʻuung-tʻaam-ʿshui.

Snuff, 鼻烟 piʾ-in, (a candle) 剪燈花 ʿtsin-tang-fa.

Snug, 安穩 ohn-ʿwan.

So, (in degree) 咁 komʾ, (in kind) 噉 ʿkom, (so and so) 某某 ʿmau-ʿmau, (so forth) 噉之類 ʿkom-chi-luiʾ.

Soak, 浸 tsumʾ, 濕透 shap-tʻauʾ.

Soap, 番梘 faan-ʿkaan.

Soap-stone, 滑石 waat-shek.

Soar, 高飛 ko-fi.

Sob, 縮氣 shuuk-hiʾ.

Sober, 醒定 ʿsing-tingʾ.

Sociable, 好相與 ʻho-seung-ʻue.
Society, (a) 會 ooiʼ, (in general) 相與聚集 seung-ʻue-tsueʼ-tsaap.
Sock, See Hose.
Socket, 寶 tauʼ.
Soda-water, 荷蘭水 Hoh-laan-ʻshui.
Sodomy, 雞姦 kai-kaan, 男色 naam-shik.
Sodomite, 契弟 kʻaiʼ-taiʼ.
Sofa, 匠 kʻongʼ, 睡椅 shuiʼ-ʻi.
Soft, 柔軟 yau-ʻnen, 脸軟 num-ʻuen.
Soil, 坭土 nai-ʻtʻo, (to) 整污 ʻching-oo.
Solanum, 茄 *kʻe.
Solder, 釬 hohnʼ.
Soldering-iron, 鈉鎚 naat-pai (kai).
Soldier, 兵 ping, 兵丁 ping-ting, 兵卒 ping-tsuut.
Sole, (of foot) 脚板 keukʼ-ʻpaan, (of shoe) 鞋底 haai-ʻtai.

Sole, (a fish) 撻沙魚 tʻaatʼ-ʻsha-*ue.
Sole, (only) 單 taan, 獨 tuuk.
Solely, 獨係 tuuk-haiʼ, 不過 pat-kwohʼ.
Solemn, 威嚴 wai-im, 嚴肅 im-suuk.
Solicit, 求 kʻan.
Solicitor, 小狀師 ʻsiu-chongʼ-ʻsze.
Solicitor, (Crown-) 國家狀師 Kwokʼ-ka-chongʼ-ʻsze.
Solicitude, 掛慮 kwaʼ-lueʼ.
Solid, 實 shat, 硬 ngaangʼ.
Solitary, 孤寂 koo-tsik, 獨居 tuuk-kue.
Solstice, (summer) 夏至 haʼ-chiʼ, (winter) 冬至 tuung-chiʼ.
Solve, 解 ʻkaai.
Sombre, 憂色 yau-shik, 陰陰沉沉 yum-yum-chʻum-chʻum.
Some, (有) 的 (ʻyau) ʻti.
Somersault, 打勉斗 ʻta-kan-ʻtau.

Something, 野 ʻye, 閒野 haan-ʻye, 有野 ʻyau-ʻye, 的野 ₍ti-ʻye.
Sometimes, 有時 ʻyau-shi.
Somnambulism, 睡中行 shuiʼ-chuung-hang.
Son, 仔 ʻtsai, 子 ʻtsze, 兒 i, (your) 令郎 lingʼ*long, (my) 小兒 ʻsiu-i.
Son-in-law, 女婿 ʻnue-saiʼ.
Song, 支曲 chi-kʻuuk, 隻歌仔 chekʼ-koh-ʻtsai.
Sonorous, 曾响 ʻooi-ʻheung, 响嘅 ʻheung-keʼ.
Soon, 就來 tsauʼ-loi, 無幾耐 mo-ʻki-*noiʼ, 挨邊 ₍aai-₍pin.
Soot, 烟煤 in-mooi, 火燖煤 ʻfoh-tʻaam-mooi.
Soothe, 安慰 ohn-waiʼ, 開鬱寧神 hoi-wat-ning-shan, (a child) 噤願 tʻumʼ-uenʼ.
Sophistry, 巧辯 ʻhaau-pinʼ.
Soporific, 致睡 chiʼ-shuiʼ, chiʼ-shuiʼ-keʼ.
Sorcery, 巫術 moo-shuut.

Sordid, 籬呫囉 lak-komʼ-haai.
Sore, 損痛 ʻsuen-tʻuungʼ.
Sorrel, 酸迷草 suen-₍mi-ʻtsʻo, (in Shi-king) 莫 moʼ.
Sorrow, 憂悶 yau-moonʼ.
Sorrowful, 鼎鳳 paiʼ-aiʼ.
Sort, 樣 yeungʼ, 般 poon.
Sot, 爛酒佬 laanʼ-ʻtsau-ʻlo.
Sottish, 死爛飲 ʻsze-laanʼ-ʻyum.
Soul, 靈魂 ling-wan.
Sound, (a) 聲音 sheng-yum, (to) 响 ʻheung, (sleep) 睏稔 funʼ-numʼ, (entire) 全 tsʻuen, 堅固 kin-kooʼ, (to try) 探 tʻaamʼ.
Soundly, 重 ʻchʻuung.
Soup, 湯 tʻong.
Sour, 酸 suen, (sullen) 鼓氣 ʻkoo-hiʼ.
Source, 源頭 uen-tʻau.
Souse, 撞 chongʼ, (in water) 洰下 yum-ʻha.
South, 南 naam, (S.E. &c.) 東南 tuung-naam, &c.

Southernwood, 青蒿 tsʻing-ho, 同蒿 tʻuung-ho, (in Shi-king) 蔞 lau.
Sovereign, 主 ʻchue.
Sow, (to) 撒 saatʼ.
Sow, (a) 猪乸 chue-ʻna.
Soy, 豉油 shiʼ-yau.
Space, 間 kaan, (room) 地方 tiʼ-fong, 笪地方 taatʼ-tiʼ-fong, (all) 週圍 chau-wai.
Spacious, 闊落 footʼ-lok.
Spade, 鏟 ʻchʻaan, (a small) 鍫 tsʻiu.
Spain, 呂宋 ʻLue-suungʼ.
Span, 揇 naamʼ.
Spanish-flies, 斑蝥 paan-maau.
Spare, (save) 愛惜 oiʼ-sik, 省 ʻshaang, (give away) 捨 ʻshe.
Spark, 火星 ʻfoh-ʻsing (ʻseng), (sparks) 火屎 ʻfoh-ʻshi.
Sparkle, 閃亮 ʻshim-leungʼ, 火飛 ʻfoh-fi.
Sparrow, 麻雀 ma-tseukʼ.

Spasm, 抽筋 chʻau-kan, 拶掣 tsaatʼ-ʻha.
Spatter, (with the hand) 澆 kiu.
Spattered, (by walking) 濃污糟 tsaanʼ-oo-tso.
Spawn, 魚鶿 ue-chʻuun.
Speak, 講 ʻkong, 講說話 ʻkong-shuetʼ-wa.
Spear, 竹篙鎗 chuuk-ko-tsʻeung, (a) 一枝鎗 yat-chi-ʻtsʻeung.
Special, 特登 tak-ʻtang, 專登 chuen-ʻtang, (extra) 額外 ngaak-ngoiʼ.
Species, 種 ʻchuung.
Specify, 話實 waʼ-shat, 逐一講 chuuk-yat-ʻkong.
Specimen, 樣子 yeungʼ-ʻtsze, 表率 ʻpiu-suut, 辦 *paanʼ.
Specious talk, 巧言 ʻhaau-in.
Speckled, 一點點 yat-ʻtim-ʻtim.
Spectacle, (a) 景 ʻking.
Spectacles, 眼鏡 ʻngaau-ʻkeng.

Spectator, 睇見之人 ʿtʻai-kinʾ-chi-yan, ʿtʻai-kinʾ-keʾ.
Speculate, 追想 chui-ʿseung, 圖 tʻo.
Speech, 話 waʾ, 說話 shuetʾ-waʾ.
Speedy, 速 tsʻuuk, 快 faaiʾ.
Spell, (to) 切音 tsʻitʾ-ɲum.
Spend, 使費 ʿshai-faiʾ, (a day) 過日 kwohʾ-yat.
Spend-thrift, 浪子 ʿlong-ʿtsze.
Sphere, 球 kʻau.
Sphex, 螺蠃 ʿkwoh-ʿloh.
Spice, 香料 heung-*liuʾ.
Spider, 蝻蠊 kʻum-*lo, 蜘蛛 ˳chi-˳chue, 壁虎 pikʾ-ʿfoo.
Spider's web, 蜘蛛網 ˳chi-˳chue-ʿmong.
Spike, 刺 tsʻzeʾ, 錐 chui, (wooden) 木丁 muuk-teng.
Spikenard, 甘松香 kom-tsʻuung-˳heung.
Spill, 流出 lau-chʻuut, 漏瀉 lauʾ-seʾ.

Spin, 紡績 ˳fong-tsik, 紡線 ˳fong-sinʾ, (round) 轉棹轉 ningʾ-chuenʾ, 窑窑轉 tʻum-tʻum-chuenʾ.
Spinage, 波菜 poh-tsʻoiʾ, 菠菱菜 poh-ling-tsʻoiʾ, 莧菜 inʾ-tsʻoiʾ.
Spindle, (鐵)綑 (tʻitʾ) tsʻuun.
Spine, 背脊 pooiʾ-tsekʾ.
Spinning-machine, 紡機 ˳fong-ki.
Spinster, 老女 ʿlo-ʿnue.
Spiral, 螺線 loh-sinʾ, 螺紋 loh-*mun.
Spire, 塔 taapʾ, 鐘樓 ˳chuung-*lau.
Spirit, 神 shan, (drink) 燒酒 shiu-ʿtsau, (animal spirits) 精神 tsing-shan.
Spiritual, 靈 ling, 神 shan.
Spit, 吐 tʻoʾ, 唾 tʻoh, löʾ, (a) 炙肉叉 chekʾ-ɲuuk-˳chʻa.
Spite, 怨恨 uenʾ-hanʾ, 怨毒 uenʾ-tuuk.

Spittle, 口水 ʿhau-ʿshui, (ejected) 口水花 ʿhau-ʿshui-ₑfa.
Spittoon, 痰鑵 tʻaam-koonʾ, 痰盂 tʻaam-*ue.
Splash, (to throw) 澆 kiu, (to rebound or splash up) 濺 tsaanʾ, tsaanʾ.
Spleen, (the) 脾 pʻi, 臁貼 lim-tʻipʾ, (feeling) 鬱氣 wat-hiʾ.
Splendid, 光亮 kwong-ₑleungʾ, 華美 wa-ʿmi.
Splice, 駁纜 pokʾ-laamʾ.
Splinter, 片 pʻinʾ, 孹 ʿnin.
Split, 打裂 ʿta-lit, 破 pʻohʾ, 劈 pʻekʾ.
Spoil, 整壞 ʿching-waaiʾ, 爛 laanʾ.
Spokes, 輻 fuuk.
Spoliation, 搶刼 ʿtsʻeung-kipʾ.
Sponge, 水泡 ʿshui-ʿpʻo.
Sponge-cake, 鷄蛋糕 kai-taanʾ-ₑko.
Spongy, 冧 pauʾ.
Spontaneous, 自自然然 ʿtszeʾ-ʿtszeʾ-ₑin-ₑin.

Spoon, 匙羹 shi-ₑkang, 羹 ₑkang.
Sport, 頑耍 waan-ʿsha.
Spot, 點 ʿtim, 玷 timʾ, 疵 ₑtsʻze, (place) 笪 taatʾ.
Spotted, 一笪笪 yat-taatʾ-taatʾ.
Spout, (of a kettle) 嘴 ʿtsui, (on a roof) 水槽 ʿshui-tsʻo, (to) 浙 chit, 噴 pʻun.
Sprain, 扭傷 ʿnau-ₑsheung, 趨親 ʿchʻau-tsʻan.
Spray, of water, 水花 ʿshui-ₑfa.
Spray ⎱
Sprig ⎰ , 枝 ₑchi.
Spread, out, 攤開 tʻaan-ₑhoi, 散開 saanʾ-ₑhoi, 鋪開 pʻo-ₑhoi, (as ink) 淰開 ʿnumʾ-ₑhoi.
Sprightly, 英敏 ying-ʿmun.
Spring, (season) 春天 chʻuun-ₑtʻin, (water-) 源泉 uen-tsʻuen, (of a machine) 機關 ki-kwaan, 連機 lin-ki, (main-) 發條 faatʾ-*tʻiu, (to) 跳 tʻiuʾ, 發 faatʾ.

Spring-water, 山水 shaan-ʻshui.
Sprinkle, 灑ʻsha, 澆 kiu.
Sprout, 萌芽 mang-nga, 淋ʻlum, 咪 muuk, (bamboo-) 竹笋 chuuk-ʻsuun, (to) 出咪 chʻuut-muuk.
Spur, 距ʻkʻue, (to) 踢 tʻekʼ.
Spurious, 僞 ngaiʼ, 假 ʻka.
Spurn, 擯棄 punʼ-hiʼ.
Spurt, 噴水 pʻunʼ-ʻshui.
Sputter, 噴口水花 pʻunʼ-ʻhau-ʻshui-fa.
Spy, (a) 線人 sinʼ-yan, 探子 tʻaamʼ-ʻtsze, (to) 打探 ʻta-tʻaamʼ, 訪事 fong-*sze, 覘 chong, hau.
Squabble, 嗌交 aaiʼ-ʻkaau.
Squad, (a) 一隊 yat-tui.
Squalid, 襤褸 laam-lucʼ.
Squall, (a) 一陣風雨 yat-chanʼ-fuung-ucʼ.
Squall, (to) 啞啞聲 ʻnga-ʻnga-sheng.
Squander, 花散 fa-saanʼ.
Square, 方 fong, 四方形 szeʼ-fong-ying, (a tool) 曲尺 huuk-chʻekʼ.

Squash, (a) 瓜 ʻkwa, hairy, 節瓜 tsitʼ-ʻkwa, bitter, 苦瓜 ʻfoo-ʻkwa, bottle, 江葡 kong-pʻoo, (to) 壓扁 aatʼ-ʻpin.
Squat, 踎 mau.
Squeak, 翳翳聲 ngit-ngit-sheng.
Squeamish, 憾飫 imʼ-ueʼ, 作悶 tsokʼ-moonʼ.
Squeeze, 榨住 chaʼ-chueʼ, 壓 aatʼ, 夾住 kaapʼ-chueʼ, (extort) 勒索 lak-sokʼ.
Squib, 起火仔 ʻhi-ʻfoh-ʻtsai.
Squint, 斜眼 tsʻe-ʻngaan, 到眼 toʼ-ʻngaan.
Squirrel, 果鼠 ʻkwoh-ʻshue.
Squirt, (a) 水浙筒 ʻshui-chit-*tʻuung, (to) 浙 chit.
Stab, 剖 kat, 攙 chʻaam, ʻchʻaam.
Stable, (a) 馬房 ʻma-fong, (firm) 安穩 ohn-ʻwan, 定實 tingʼ-shat.
Stack, (a) 禾堆 woh-ʻtui.
Staff, 枴杖 ʻkwaai-*cheungʼ.

Stag, 鹿 *luuk, 鹿公 *luuk-ₒkuung.

Stage, (a platform) 臺 t'oi, (scaffold) 棚 p'aang, (of a journey) 驛站 yik-chaam'.

Stagger, reel and, 行得啤啤吓 hang-tak-ᶜp'e-ᶜp'e-ᶜha.

Stagnant, 遲滯 ch'i-chai', 不流 'm-lau.

Stain, (a) 印迹 yan'-tsik, (to) 染污 ᶜim-oo.

Stairs, 樓梯 lau-t'ai, (stone-) 石級 shek-k'up.

Stake, 杙 tak, 椿 chong, 棟 tuung', (to risk) 捹 ᶜp'oon.

Stalactite, 鐘乳石 chuung-ᶜue-shek.

Stale, 陳 ch'an, 舊 kau', 宿 suuk.

Stalk, 竿 kohn, 枝 chi, 秆 ᶜkohn.

Stall, (for goods) 賣貨攤 maai'-foh-'-ₒt'aan, (for cattle) 欄位 laan-wai', (horse's) 馬槽 ᶜma-ts'o.

Stamen, 花蕊 fa-ᶜyui, 花粉蕊 fa-ᶜfun-ᶜyui.

Stammer, 遛口 lau'-ᶜhau, 講得肋喀 ᶜkong-tak-lak-k'ak.

Stamp, 印 yan', (the foot) 踎腳 tum'-keuk'.

Stamp Office, 印捐局 yan'-kuen-kuuk.

Stanch, (to) 止 ᶜchi, (hearty) 堅心 kin-sum.

Stand, 企立 ᶜk'i-laap, 企到 ᶜk'i-ᶜto, (up) 起身 ᶜhi-shan, 企起 ᶜk'i-ᶜhi, (aside) 企開 ᶜk'i-hoi, (endure) 抵住 ᶜtai-chue', 啉 k'um; (a) 架 ka'.

Standard, (flag) 旗 k'i, (rule) 度 to'.

Staple, (a) 鐵耳 t'it'-ᶜi.

Star, 粒星 nup-ₒsing, ₒseng.

Star-board, 船右 shuen-yau'.

Starch, 漿 tseung.

Stare, 撐眼睇 chang-ᶜngaan-ᶜt'ai.

Start, (set out) 開行 ʽhoi-hang, (by water) 開身 ʽhoi-shan, (up) 跳起 tʽiuʼ-ʽhi.
Startle, 振驚 chanʼ-king.
Starve, 制食 chaiʼ-shik, (to death) 制死 chaiʼ-ʽsze, 餓死 ngohʼ-ʽsze.
State, (condition) 情勢 tsʽing-shaiʼ, (nation) 國 kwok; (to) 講實 ʽkong-shat, 話 waʼ, 陳說 chʽan-shuetʼ, (to a superior) 禀告 ʽpun-koʼ.
Statics, 重學 chuungʼ-hok.
Station, 身分 shan-funʼ, 位 waiʼ, (on a road) 站頭 chaamʼ-tʽau, (guard's) 汛地 suunʼ-tiʼ, (position) 所在 ʽshoh-tsoi, (police) 差館 chʽaai-ʽkoon.
Stationary, 不郁 ʼm-yuuk.
Stationer's shop, 紙筆舖 ʽchi-put-*pʽo, 紙料舖 ʽchi-liuʼ-*pʽo.
Statistics, 志 chiʼ.
Statue, 偶像 ʽngau-tseungʼ.

Statute, 律例 luutʼ-laiʼ.
Stay, (to) 等吓 ʽtang-ʽha, 歇 hitʼ, 住 chueʼ.
Steady, 穩當 ʽwun-tongʼ, (stand) 企穩 ʽkʽi-ʽwun.
Steak, (beef-) 牛肉耙 ngau-yuuk-*pʽa.
Steal, 偷 tʽau, 竊 sitʼ.
Steam, 滾水氣 ʽkwun-ʽshui-hiʼ, (to) 烝 ching.
Steamer, 火輪船 ʽfoh-luun-shuen.
Steel, 鋼 kongʼ.
Steelyard, 把秤 ʽpa-chʽingʼ, (money-) 螯戥 li-*tangʼ.
Steep, 企斜 ʽkʽi-tsʽeʼ, 斜 tsʽeʼ.
Steep, (to) 浸 tsumʼ, (dip) 泧吓 ʽyum-ʽha.
Steeple, 鐘樓 chuung-*lau.
Steer, (to) 把舵 ʽpa-tʽoh, (COL.) 揸舦 cha-ʽtʽaai.
Steersman, 梢公 shaau-kuung.
Stem, 竿 kohn, 枝 chi, 莖 ʽkʽwaang, (to) 阻止 ʽchoh-ʽchi, 抵住 ʽtai-chueʼ.

Stench, 臭 ch'au’, 一棒隨 yat-puung’-ts'ui, (a vile) 臭亨亨 ch'au’-hang-hang.
Step, 步 poo’, (to) 進腳 tsuun’-keuk’, 行 hang, (in a stair) 級 k'up, 階級 kaai-k'up.
Step-father, 繼父 kai’-foo’, (-mother) 繼母 kai’-‘mo.
Stepping-stone, 踏腳石 taap-keuk’-shek.
Sterculia, 擷婆 p'an-*p'oh, 梧桐 'ng-t'uung.
Sterile soil, 瘠土 tsek’-‘t'o.
Stern, 嚴肅 im-suuk, (the) 後邊 hau’-pin, 尾 ‘mi.
Stew, (to) 會 ooi’.
Steward, 管事人 ‘koon-sze’-yan, (comprador) 買辦 ‘maai-*paan’.
Stick, (a) 條棍 t'iu-kwun’, (pierce) 刮 kat, (adhere) 黐緊 ch'i-‘kan, (fail) 不能行 pat-nang-hang, (to paste) 貼 t'ip’, (stick in) 插落 ch'aap’-lok.
Stickle, 拘執 k'ue-chup, 泥 ni’.

Stiff, 硬 ngaang’, 骾 ‘kang.
Stiffnecked 拗頸 aau’-‘keng.
Stifle, 局死 kuuk-‘sze.
Stigma, 忝辱 ‘tim-yuuk.
Still, (ADV.) 仍然 ying-in, 重 chuung’, 還 waan, (quiet) 寂靜 tsik-tsing’, 靜靜 *tsing’-tsing’, tsing’-*tsing’.
Still, (a) 酒甑 ‘tsau-tsang’.
Stilts, 駁腳棍 pok’-keuk’-kwun’.
Stimulate, 聳起 ‘suung-‘hi.
Sting, 釘 ‚teng, 針 chum, (to) 刺 ts'ze’.
Stingy, 慳 haan, 刻薄 haak-pok.
Stink, 臭氣 ch'au’-hi’, 齧臭 ngat’-ch'au’.
Stink-pot, 灰煲 fooi-‚po.
Stint, (to) 限制 haan’-chai’, (a) 工課 kuung-foh’.
Stipulate, 約定 yeuk’-ting’.

Stipulations, 條欵 t'iu-‘foon, 約條 yeuk’-t'iu.
Stir, (to) 攪 ‘kaau, (begin to move) 興起 hing-‘hi, 動身 tuung’-shan, (a) 鬧熱 naau’-it.
Stitch, (of a needle) 針步 chum-poo’, (to) 釘 teng, (fine) 鉤密 k'au-mat, (pain) 刺痛 ts'ek’-t'uung’.
Stock, (of a tree) 木頭 muuk-t'au, 樹身 shue’-‚shan, (of a musket) 牀 ch'ong, (in trade) 貨本 foh’-‘poon, (shares) 股分 ‘koo-fun’.
Stockings, 襪 mat.
Stocks, 脚架 keuk’-ka’.
Stoical, 無情 ‘mo-ts'ing.
Stolid, 鈍 tuun’.
Stomach, 脾胃 p'i-wai’.
Stomach-pump, 入喉水浙 yup-hau-‘shui-chit.
Stone, 石 shek, 石頭 shek-t'au, (of fruit) 核 wat, (to) 俾石打 ‘pi-shek-‘ta.
Stone-cutter, 打石人 ‘ta-shek-yan.

Stool, 凳 tang’, (go to) 如厠 uc-ts‘ze’, 出恭 ch'uut-‚kuung.
Stoop, 攣腰 luen-iu, 噁低 oo’-tai.
Stop, 停吓 t'ing-‘ha, 歇息 hit’-sik, 止住 ‘chi-chue’, (with the hands) 拃住 cha’-chue’, (up) 塞住 sak-chue’.
Stopper, 枳 chat.
Store, (to) 積貯 tsik-‘ch'ue, 積埋 tsik-maai, (-house) 貨倉 foh’-ts‘ong, 棧 *chaan’, 棧房 chaan’-*fong, (basement) 土庫 ‘t'o-foo’.
Stores, 積貨 tsik-foh’, (food) 伙食 ‘foh-shik.
Stork, 白鶴 paak-*hok.
Storm, 風雨大作 fuung-‘ue-taai’-tsok’, 風暴 fuung-po’.
Story, (a) 一段古 yat-tuen’-‘koo, (of a house) 層 ts'ang.
Stout, 精壯 tsing-chong’, (fat) 肥壯 fi-chong’.

Stove, 火爐 ꞌfoh-lo, 局爐 kuuk-lo.
Stow away, 裝埋 chong-maai.
Straddle, 了開脚 ngaꞌ-ʰoi-keukꞌ.
Straggle, 行散 hang-ꞌsaan.
Straight, 直 chik, 掂 timꞌ.
Straighten, 做直 tsoꞌ-chik, 整掂 ꞌching-tim.
Straightway, 即時 tsik-shi, 就正 tsauꞌ-chingꞌ.
Strain, 隔渣 kaakꞌ-cha, (tighten) 扭緊 ꞌnau-ꞌkan.
Strainer, 羅斗 loh-ꞌtau, (wine-) 酒漏 ꞌtsau-*lauꞌ.
Strait, 迫窄 pik-chaakꞌ, 淺窄 ꞌtsꞌin-chaakꞌ, 阨 ak, (a) 陜 haap.
Stramonium, 鬧羊花 naauꞌ-yeung-fa.
Strange, 奇怪 kꞌi-kwaaiꞌ, (not at home) 生外 shaang-*ngoiꞌ.
Stranger, 新客 san-haakꞌ, 生步 shaang-*poꞌ, (ꞌpo) 生面 shaang-*minꞌ.

Strangle, 縊死 aiꞌ-ꞌsze, 勒死 lak-ꞌsze, (with the hand) 揸死 cha-ꞌsze.
Strap, (a) 皮帶 pꞌi-*taaiꞌ.
Strata, 層隔 tsꞌang-kaakꞌ.
Stratagem, 謀畧 mau-leuk, 韜畧 tꞌo-leuk.
Straw, 禾稿 woh-ꞌko, 禾稈 woh-ꞌkohn.
Straw-hat, 草帽 ꞌtsꞌo-*moꞌ.
Strawberry, 蛇苺 she-mooi.
Stray, 行散 hang-ꞌsaan, 行錯 hang-tsꞌohꞌ, (from the flock) 離開隊 li-hoi-*tuiꞌ.
Streaks, 虎班紋 ꞌfoo-paan-*mun.
Stream, 流水 lau-ꞌshui, (small) 溪澗 kꞌai-kaanꞌ, 條水 tꞌiu-ꞌshui.
Streamer, 旗帶 kꞌi-taaiꞌ.
Street, 街 ꞌkaai, (a) 條街 tꞌiu-ꞌkaai.
Strength, 力 lik.
Strengthening, 補力 ꞌpo-lik.
Strenuous, 慇懃 yan-kꞌan.

Stress, 重 chuung', 重處 chuung'-ch'ue', (on) 重在 chuung'-tsoi'.
Stretch, 揳長 mang'-ch'eung, (out) 伸 shan, (as clothes) 撐開 chaang-hoi.
Strew, 撒 saat', 'sum.
Strict, 嚴緊 im-'kan.
Stride, 了脚 nga'-keuk', (long) 大步 taai'-po'.
Strike, 打 'ta, 揼 'tum, (stop) 罷 pa', (a match) 畫 waak.
String, (a) 條繩 t'iu-*shing, 帶 *taai', (a string of) 一串 yat-ch'uen', (1,000 cash) 一吊 yat-tiu', (to) 貫串 koon'-ch'uen', 穿埋 ch'uen-maai.
Strip, (a) 一條 yat-t'in, (to) 脫 t'uet', 捋 luet', 戩 'chin.
Stripe, 班紋 paan-*mun, 柳條紋 'lau-t'iu-*mun.
Strive, 爭 chaang, 相爭 seung-chaang, (endeavour) 出力 ch'uut-lik.

Stroke, (line) 畫 waak, (a blow) 打一吓 'ta-yat-'ha, (rub) 攋 lip.
Stroll, 逛 k'waang', liu'.
Strong, 有力 'yau-lik, 'yau-lik-ke', 壯健 chong'-kin', 主固 'chue-koo', (as tobacco) 揹 k'ang', (as tea, &c.) 濃 nuung, yuung.
Strop, (to) 喝利 hoht'-li'.
Struggle, 打武咁打 'ta-'moo-kom'-'ta, 勉强 'min-'k'eung, 苦爭 'foo-chang.
Strut, 岳頭行 ngok-t'au-hang.
Strychnine, 馬前 'ma-ts'in.
Stubborn, 硬頸 ngaang'-'keng, 板頸 'paan-'keng.
Stucco, 石膏 shek-'ko.
Stud, (a button) 粒鈕 nup-'nau, 雙粒鈕 sheung-nup-'nau.
Study, (to) 習學 tsaap-hok, 讀書 tuuk-shue, (a) 讀書房 tuuk-shue-*fong.

Stuff, (material) 材料 ts'oi-liu', (useless) 廢物 fai'-mat, (nonsense) 譜話 ngaam'-wa', (to) 塞實 sak-shat.

Stuffing, 入材料 yup-ts'oi-liu'.

Stumble, 踢着脚 t'ek'-cheuk-keuk', 失脚 shat-keuk', (fall) 跌倒 tit'-'to.

Stumbling block, 窒碍 chat-ngoi', 碍石 ngoi'-shek.

Stump, (a) 榾頭 kwut-t'au.

Stun, 震瘟 chan'-wan, 驚迷 keng-mai.

Stunted, 屈短 wut-'tuen.

Stupid, 憨蠢 ue-'ch'uun, 笨呆 pun'-ngoi, (boy) 笨仔 pun'-'tsai.

Stupified, 失魂 shat-wan, 昏迷 fun-mai.

Sturdy, 大力 taai'-lik.

Sturgeon, 鱘龍魚 ts'um-luung-*ue.

Stuttering, 吃口 kat-'hau, 遛口 lau'-'hau.

Sty, 猪欄 'chue-'laan.

Style, 文 mun, 文法 mun-faat', 樣 *yeung', (address) 稱呼 ch'ing-foo.

Suavity, 温柔 wan-yau.

Sub, 下 ha', 下屬 ha'-shuuk.

Subdue, 勝服 shing'-fuuk.

Subject, 臣下 shan-ha', (people) 民 mun, (of discourse) 所論 'shoh-luun', (of an essay) 章旨 cheung-'chi, 提目 t'ai-muuk.

Subject } 打服 'ta-fuuk.
Subjugate

Sublimate, 霜 seung.

Sublime, 崇大 shuung-taai'.

Submissive, 服屬 fuuk-shuuk.

Submit, 服 fuuk, 歸服 kwai-fuuk.

Subordinate, 屬下 shuuk-ha'.

Suborn, 買囑 'maai-chuuk.

Subscribe, 簽題 ts'im-t'ai.

Subserve, 供應 kuung-ying'.

Subside, 擎 k'ing, 平翻 p'ing-fuan, 息 sik.

Subsidiary, 助 choh'.

Substance, 質體 chat-ʻtʻai, 材料 tsʻoi-liuʼ, 物 mat.
Substitute, (a) 代做 toiʼ-tsoʼ.
Subtile, 靈活 ling-oot, (subtle) 巧 ʻhaau.
Subtract, 減 ʻkaam.
Subtraction, 減法 ʻkaam-faatʼ.
Suburbs, 城外 sheng-ngoiʼ.
Subvert, 傾倒 kʻing-ʻto.
Succeed, (get on) 得成 tak-shing, (follow) 繼 kaiʼ, 接做 tsipʼ-tsoʼ.
Successive, 陸續 luuk-tsuuk.
Succinct, 簡畧 ʻkaan-lenk.
Succumb, 服 fuuk.
Such, 噉 ʻkom, 如此 ue-ʻtsʻze.
Suck, 啐 tsuetʼ, 欶 shokʼ.
Suckle, 餵奶 waiʼ-ʻnaai.
Sudden, 忽然 fut-in, fut-in-keʼ.
Suddenly, 忽然間 fut-in-kaan.
Sudorific, 發汗藥 faatʼ-hohnʼ-yeuk.
Sue, 告 koʼ, (for) 求 kʻau.

Suet, 版油 ʻpaan-yau, 腰油 iu-yau.
Suffer, 抵受 ʻtai-shauʼ, 受 shauʼ, 抵捱 ʻtai-ngaai, (permit) 准 ʻchuun.
Suffering, 受苦 shauʼ-ʻfoo.
Sufficient, 殻 kauʼ, 足 tsuuk.
Suffocate, 局死 kuuk-ʻsze.
Sugar, 糖 tʻong.
Sugar-candy, 冰糖 ping-tʻong.
Sugar-cane, 蔗 cheʼ.
Suggest, 提起 tʻai-ʻhi.
Suicide, 自殺 tszeʼ-shaatʼ, 自盡 tszeʼ-tsuunʼ.
Suit, (to) 合 hop, 着 cheuk, (a, of clothes) 一腿 yat-tʻuetʼ, (petition) 禀 ʻpun.
Suitable, 着使 cheuk-ʻshai, 啱 ʻngaam.
Suite, 跟班 ʻkan-ʻpaan.
Sulky } 嬲人嘅 nau-yan-keʼ, 古毒 ʻkoo-tuuk, 鼓氣 ʻkoo-hiʼ, 黑面 hak-minʼ.
Sullen }
Sully, 玷污 timʼ-oo.

Sulphur, 硫磺 lau-wong, (flowers of) 硫磺末 lau-wong-*moot.
Sultry, 暑曀 ʻshue-aiʼ.
Sum, 共計 kuungʼ-kaiʼ, 攏總 ʻluung-ʻtsuung.
Summer, 夏天 haʼ-ʻtʻin.
Summer-house, 涼亭 leung-*tʻing.
Summit, 頂 ʻting, ʻteng.
Summon, 傳叫 chʻuen-kiuʼ.
Summons, 傳票 chʻuen-pʻiuʼ.
Sumptuous, 破費 pʻohʼ-faiʼ.
Sun, 日 yat, 熟頭 it-*tʻau, 太陽 tʻaaiʼ-yeung, (to) 曬 shaaiʼ.
Sunday, 禮拜日 ʻlai-paaiʼ-yat, ʻlai-paaiʼ.
Sundries, 什碎 sup-suiʼ.
Sun-flower, 向日葵 heungʼ-yat-kʻwai.
Sunken-rocks, 海心石 ʻhoi-sum-shek.
Sun-rise, 日出 yat-chʻuut.
Sun-set, 日入 yat-yup, 日落 yat-lok.
Sunstroke, 中暑 chuungʼ-ʻshue.

Sup, 喫 yaakʼ, 嗑啖 haapʼ-taamʼ.
Super-, 過 kwohʼ, 上 sheungʼ.
Supercargo, 班上 paan-sheungʼ, 大班 taaiʼ-paan.
Superficial, 淺 ʻtsʻin, (scholar) 充斯文 chʻuung-sze-mun.
Superfluous, 太多無用 tʻaaiʼ-toh-mo-yuungʼ, 無用 ʻmo-yuungʼ, 無爲 ʻmo-waiʼ, 蛇足 she-tsuuk.
Superintend, 督理 tuuk-ʻli, (work) 督工 tuuk-kuung.
Superintendent, 監督 kaam-tuuk.
Superior, 長 ʻcheung, 上好 sheungʼ-ʻho, (better) 更好 kangʼ-ʻho, 好過 ʻho-kwohʼ.
Supernatural, 神異 shan-iʼ.
Supersede, 廢去 faiʼ-hueʼ.
Superstitious, 溺信古怪 nik-suunʼ-ʻkoo-kwaaiʼ.
Supervene, 自至 tszeʼ-chiʼ.
Supine, 袖手 tsauʼ-ʻshau.
Supper, 晚餐 ʻmaan-tsʻaan.
Supplant, 迫用 pik-lut.
Supple, 跳疾 tʻiuʼ-tsaatʼ.
Supplement, 添補 tʻim-ʻpo.

Supply, 供給 kuung-k'up.
Support, 承住 shing-chue', (with the hand, or morally) 扶住 foo-chue', 扶持 foo-ch'i.
Suppose, 估量 ʿkoo-leung', 估 ʿkoo.
Supposing, 假使間 ʿka-ʿsze-kaan.
Suppress, 鎭壓 chan'-aat', 彈壓 t'aan-aat'.
Supreme, 至上 chi'-sheung', 最上 tsui'-sheung'.
Supreme Being, 上帝 Sheung'-T'ai'.
Supreme Court, 臬署 nip-ʿshue, nip-ʿch'ue.
Sure, 確實 k'ok'-shat, 穩當 ʿwun-tong'.
Surety, (a) 担保 taam-ʿpo.
Surface, 面 min', 上面 sheung'-min'.
Surfeit, 食到飫 shik-to'-ue'.
Surfeited, 饜飽 im'-ʿpaau, 飽饇 ʿpaau-nau'.
Surge, 浪如壁立 long'-ue-pik-laap.

Surgery, 外科 ngoi'-foh.
Surloin, 尾龍扒 ʿmi-luung-p'a.
Surly, 蠻 maan.
Surmise, 估 ʿkoo.
Surmount, 勝 shing', 勝得過 shing'-tak-kwoh'.
Surname, 姓 sing'.
Surpass, 超卓過 ch'iu-ch'euk'-kwoh', 越過 uet-kwoh'.
Surplus, 餘剩 ue-shing'.
Surprise, 驚愕 king-ngok.
Surprised, 見怪 kin'-kwaai', (frightened) 失愕 shat-ngok.
Surprising, 出奇 ch'uut-k'i.
Surrender, 投降 t'au-hong, (to prison) 投監 t'au-kaam, (give up) 付交 foo'-kaau.
Surround, 圍埋 wai-maai, 圍住 wai-chue'.
Survey, 查察 ch'a-ch'aat'.
Surveyor, 量地官 leung-ti'-koon, General, 工務司 Kuung-moo'-ʿsze.

Survive, 尚活 sheung⁾-oot, 還在世 waan-tsoi⁾-shai⁾.
Susceptible, 易感 i⁾-ᶜkom, i⁾-ᶜkom-ke⁾.
Suspect, 猜疑 ch'aai-i, 恐怕 ᶜhuung-p'a⁾.
Suspend, 掛 kwa⁾, (stop) 罷 pa⁾, 停 t'ing.
Suspense, 掛望 kwa⁾-mong⁾.
Suspicion, 思疑 sze-i.
Sustain, (suffer) 抵受 ᶜtai-shau⁾, (be fit for) 克當 hak-tong, (keep up) 扶住 foo-chue⁾, 承住 shing-chue⁾, (alive) 存 ts'uen, 養 ᶜyeung.
Sustenance, 飲食 ᶜyum-shik.
Swab, (a) 布拂 po⁾-fut.
Swagger, 誇大 k'wa-taai⁾.
Swallow, (a) 燕子 *in⁾-ᶜtsze; (to) 吞下 t'un-ᶜha, 吞 t'un.
Swamp, 爛涎 laan⁾-paan⁾.
Swan, 鵠 kuuk, 天鵝 t'in-ngoh.
Swarm, (a) 一堆 yat-tui.
Sway, (power) 權柄 k'uen-ping⁾.

Swear, 發誓 faat⁾-shai⁾.
Sweat, 汗 hohn⁾, (to) 出汗 ch'uut-hohn⁾.
Sweep, 掃 so⁾, 打掃 ᶜta-so⁾, (at a) 一掃 yat-so⁾, 一掃光 yat-so⁾-ᶜkwong.
Sweeping assertion, 話埋湊 wa⁾-maai-ts'au.
Sweet, 甜 t'im, 甘 kom.
Sweet-bread, 牛核 ngau-wat.
Sweet-potato, 番薯 faan-*shue.
Swell, (to) 腫起 ᶜchuung-ᶜhi, (a) 裝腔 ᶜchong-hong, 大駕子 taai⁾-ka⁾-ᶜtsze.
Swelling, 腫脹 ᶜchuung-cheung⁾.
Swift, 快 faai⁾, 速 ts'uuk, 疾速 tsaat-ts'uuk.
Swim, 泅水 yau-ᶜshui, 游 yau.
Swimming, (dizziness) 頭暈 t'au-wan.
Swindle, 誆騙 hong-p'in⁾, (and run) 起尾注 ᶜhi-ᶜmi-chue⁾.
Swine, 猪 ᶜchue.

Swing, (a) 鞦韆 ₍ts'au-₎ ₍ts'in₎, (to) 搖 iu, 搖擺 iu-ᶜpaai.
Switch, 鞭 pin.
Swivel, 轉楯 ᶜchuen-suut.
Swoon, 失魂 shat-wan.
Swoop, (to) 一扑抓住 yat-p'ok⁾-ᶜchaau-chue⁾.
Sword, 把劍 ᶜpa-kim⁾.
Sycee, 紋銀 mun-*ngan.
Sycophant, 白鴿眼 paak-kop⁾-ᶜngaan.
Symbol, 表意之物 ᶜpiu-i⁾-chi-mat, ᶜpiu-i⁾-ke⁾-ᶜye.
Symmetrical, 相稱 seung-ch'ing⁾, 對得好 tui⁾-tak-ᶜho.
Sympathy, 同情 t'uung-ts'ing, (with sorrow) 心酸 sum-suen, 相憐 seung-lin.
Symptom, 形迹 ying-tsik, (of disease) 病形 peng⁾-ying.
Synagogue, 會堂 ooi⁾-t'ong.
Synonymous, 同解 t'uung-ᶜkaai, 同意 t'uung-i⁾.
Syphilis, 生疔病 shang-teng-peng⁾.

Syphon, 角筒 kok⁾-t'uung.
Syringe, 水浙 ᶜshui-chit.
System, 法式 faat⁾-shik, (a set of things) 一副應當 yat-foo⁾-ying⁾-tong⁾.

T

Table, 張檯 cheung-*t'oi, 棹子 cheuk⁾-ᶜtsze, (a spread) 席 tsik.
Tablet, 牌 p'aai, 碑 pi, (ancestral) 神主牌 shan-ᶜchue-*p'aai.
Taciturn, 不多出聲 'm-ₜtoh-ch'uut-sheng.
Tack, (nail) 釘仔 ₍teng-ᶜtsai, (on) 奶住 naai⁾-chue⁾, 帶住 taai⁾-chue⁾, (in sailing) 轉篷 ᶜchuen-p'uung, 摳篷 k'au-p'uung.
Tackle, 器用 hi⁾-yuung⁾.
Tact, 智謀 chi⁾-mau.
Tactics, 韜畧 t'o-leuk.
Tadpole, 雷公魚 looi-ₖuung-*ue.
Tael, 兩 ᶜleung.
Taffeta, 絹 kuen⁾.

Tail, 尾 ʿmi, 係尾 tʻiu-ʿmi, (cue) 辮 pin.
Tailor, 裁縫 tsʻoi-*fuung.
Tailor-bird, 巧婦鳥 ʿhaau-ʿfoo-ʿniu.
Taint, 染 ʿim, 沾染 chim-ʿim.
Take, 攞 ʿloh, 拈 ning, nim, 將 tseung, 取 ʿtsʻue, 把 ʿpa, 搣 ʿkʻaai, kʻaaiʾ, (up) 執 chup, (an opportunity) 乘機 shing-ki.
Tale, 雲母石 wan-ʿmo-shek.
Tale, (a) 一段古 yat-tuenʾ-ʿkoo.
Tale-bearer, 口疏 ʿhau-shoh.
Talent, 才 tsʻoi.
Talk, 談 tʻaam, 講 ʿkong, 話 waʾ.
Talkative, 好講 hoʾ-ʿkong.
Tall, 高 ko, 身體高 shan-ʿtʻai-ko.
Tallow, 脂油 chi-yau, (ox's) 牛油 ngau-yau, (sheep's) 羊油 yeung-yau.
Tallow-tree, 烏桕木 oo-ʿkʻau-muuk.

Tally, (a) 籌 chʻau, (to) 符合 foo-hop.
Talon, 爪 ʿchaau.
Tamarind, 酸子 suen-ʿtsze.
Tamarisk, 垂絲柳 shui-sze-ʿlau.
Tambourine, 單面鼓 taan-minʾ-ʿkoo.
Tame, 熟 shuuk, 養得熟 ʿyeung-tak-shuuk, 純熟 shuun-shuuk.
Tampering, 手多 ʿshau-toh.
Tan, 硝皮 siu-pʻi, 醃皮 im-pʻi.
Tangible proof, 執據 chup-kueʾ, 把柄 ʿpa-pingʾ.
Tank, 石池 shek-chʻi.
Tanner, 皮匠 pʻi-tseungʾ.
Tantalizing, 臨陣弦斷 lum-chanʾ-in-tʻuen.
Tap, 拍 pʻaakʾ, (let out) 放 fongʾ.
Tap, (a water) 水口 ʿshui-ʿhau.
Tape, 棉紗帶 min-sha-taaiʾ.
Tape-worm, 蛔蟲 ooi-chʻuung.

Tapering, 尖 tsim.
Tapioca, 西米 sai-ʿmai.
Tar, 吧碼油 ʿpa-ʿma-yau.
Tardy, 遲 chʻi, 慢 maanʾ.
Tares, 稗 paiʾ.
Target, 靶子 ʿpa-ʿtsze.
Tarnish, 失光 shat-kwong.
Taro, 芋頭 oo-*tʻau.
Tart-fruit, 路菓 loʾ-ʿkwoh, 酸菓 suen-ʿkwoh.
Tartan, 棋盤布 kʻi-pʻoon-poʾ.
Tartar, 滿洲 ʿMoon-ʿchau, 蒙古 Muung-ʿkoo.
Task, 工課 kuung-fohʾ.
Tassel, 把繸 ʿpa-*sui.
Taste, 味道 miʾ-toʾ, (to) 舐 ʿtʻim, 嘗 sheung.
Tasteless, 淡 ʿtʻaam.
Tattered, 襤褸 laam-lueʾ.
Tattle, (to) 吸 ngup.
Tattooed, 文身 mun-shan.
Taunt, 譏誚 ki-tsʻiuʾ.
Tautology, 重覆話 chʻuung-fuuk-*waʾ.
Tavern, 酒店 ʿtsau-timʾ.
Tawdry, 光面 kwong-*minʾ.
Tawny, 老黃 ʿlo-wong.

Tax, 稅餉 shuiʾ-ʿheung, (to) 收餉 shau-ʿheung, 收稅 shau-shuiʾ.
Tea, 茶 chʻa, (leaves) 茶葉 chʻa-ip.
Teapoy, 茶几 chʻa-ki.
Tea-taster, 茶師 chʻa-ʿsze.
Teach, 教 kaauʾ.
Teacher, 先生 sin-shang, 掌教 ʿcheung-kaauʾ.
Teak, 油木 *yau-muuk.
Teal, 水鴨 ʿshui-*aapʾ, (mandarin duck) 鴛鴦 ʿuen-ʿyeung.
Tear, (to) 撕破 sze-pʻohʾ, 擘裂 maakʾ-lit, (off) 皺 chin.
Tears, 淚 luiʾ, 眼淚 ʿngaan-luiʾ.
Tease, 難爲 naan-wai, 嬈嬲 nat-nau, (comb) 刷 shaatʾ, (with a bow string) 彈 tʻaan, (oakum) 撕蔴根 sze-ma-kan.
Teasing, 囉唆 loh-soh.
Teat, 奶頭 ʿnaai-tʻau, 乳頭 ʿue-tʻau.
Tedious, 長氣 chʻeung-hiʾ.

Teeth, 牙 nga, 齒牙 ʻchʻi-nga.

Teetotum, 車歪 chʻe-ʻme.

Telegraph, (electric) 電報 tinʼ-poʼ.

Telephone, 德律風 tak-luut-fuung, 地里喚 tiʼ-ʻli-foonʼ.

Telescope, 千里信 tsʻin-ʻli-kengʼ.

Tell, 話──知 waʼ──chi, (stories) 講古 ʻkong-ʻkco, (-tale) 口疏 ʻhau-shoh, (lies) 講大話 ʻkong-taaiʼ-waʼ.

Temerity, 冒險 moʼ-ʻhim.

Temper, 脾氣 pʻi-hiʼ, 品格 ʻpun-kaakʼ, (to temper steel) 見水 kinʼ-ʻshui.

Temperate, 節制 tsitʼ-chaiʼ, 節儉 tsitʼ-kimʼ, (weather) 溫和 wan-woh.

Temperature, 冷熱分 ʻlaang-it-funʼ.

Tempest, 暴風 poʼ-fuung, 風雨大作 fuung-ʻue-taaiʼ-tsokʼ.

Temple, 殿堂 tinʼ-tʻong, 廟堂 miuʼ-tʻong, (an idol-) 神廟 shan-miuʼ, *miuʼ.

Temporary, 暫時 tsaamʼ-shi, tsaanʼ-shi-keʼ.

Temporize, 隨時轉 tsʻui-shi-ʻchuen.

Tempt, 試惑 shiʼ-waak, 誘感 ʻyau-waak, 引誘 ʻyun ʻyau.

Ten, 十 shap.

Tenacious, 把實 ʻpa-shat, 韌皮 nganʼ-pʻi, 韌 nganʼ.

Tenant, 客 haakʼ, 舖客 pʻoʼ-haakʼ.

Tench, 鯇魚 ʻwaan-*ue, 大頭魚 taaiʼ-tʻau-*ue.

Tend, (attend) 看住 hohn-chuʼ, (the sick) 服事 fuuk-szeʼ, (towards) 向 heungʼ, 致 chiʼ, 噲 ʻooi.

Tender, (soft) 腍軟 num-ʻuen, (brittle) 脆 tsʻuiʼ, up-up-tsʻuiʼ, (hearted) 軟心 ʻuen-sum, (young) 嫩 nuenʼ.

Tender, (a) 票投 piu-tʻau.

Tendon, 筋 kan.
Tenon, 榫頭 ʿsuun-taʻu.
Tendrils, 躅絲 laan-sze.
Tenor, 大意 taaiʾ-iʾ, 意向 iʾ-heungʾ, 去向 hueʾ-heungʾ.
Tense, 緊 ʿkan.
Tent, (a) 帳房 cheungʾ-*fong.
Tenth, 第十 taiʾ-shap, (part) 十分一 shap-funʾ-yat.
Tepid, 煖 uen.
Term, (time) 限期 haanʾ-kʻi, (word) 話頭 waʾ-tʻau.
Termination, 收尾 shau-ʿmi.
Terrace, 天臺 tʻin-*tʻoi, 臺 tʻoi.
Terrible, 好變關 ʿho-kaau-kwaan.
Terror, 悚怯 ʿsuung-hipʾ, 畏懼 waiʾ-kueʾ, 毂觫 huuk-tsʻuuk.
Test, 試驗 shiʾ-imʾ.
Testament, 遺書 wai-shue, (Old and New) 新舊約書 San-kauʾ-yeukʾ-shue.
Testicles, 外腎 ngoiʾ-ʿshan, 卵子 ʿluun-ʿtsze.

Testimony, 指證 ʿchi-chingʾ.
Testy, 扭頸 ʿnau-ʿkeng.
Text, (subject) 題目 tʻai-muuk, (classic) 正文 chingʾ-mun.
Texture, 織紋 chik-mun.
Than, 過於 kwohʾ-ue, 於 ue.
Thank, 謝 tseʾ, (many thanks) 多謝 toh-tseʾ.
Thankful, 感恩 ʿkom-yan, 感謝 ʿkom-tseʾ.
Thankless, 忘恩 mong-yan.
That, 個個 ʿkoh-kohʾ (Put the proper classifier, when known, instead of kohʾ), 個 kohʾ, ʿkoh, (things not numbered, as water) 個的 kohʾ-ʿti.
Thatch, 蓋茅 kʻoiʾ-maau.
The, 個 kohʾ, 其 kʻi.
Theatre, 戲場 hiʾ-*chʻeung, 戲園 hiʾ-*uen.
Theatricals, 做戲 tsoʾ-hiʾ.
Thee, 你 ʿni, (Sir, Madam, &c. are used for the 2nd person in polite discourse).
Theft, 偷野 tʻau-ʿye.
Them, 佢地 ʿkʻue-tiʾ.

Theme, 題目 t'ai-muuk.
Then, 個陣時 ʻkoh-chanʼ-shi, (afterwards) 然後 in-hauʼ, 就 tsauʼ.
Thenceforth, 自後 tszeʼ-hauʼ, 自個時起 tszeʼ-ʻkoh-shi-ʻhi.
There, 個處 ʻkoh-shueʼ, (is or are) 有 ʻyau, (is no more) 無咯 ʻmo-lok.
Thereabout, 個處左右 ʻkoh-shueʼ-ʻtsoh-*yauʼ, 左右 ʻtsoh-*yauʼ, 約模 yeukʼ-*mokʼ.
Therefore, 所以 ʻshoh-ʻi, 故此 kooʼ-ʻtsʻze.
Thermometer, 寒暑針 hohn-ʻshue-ʻchum.
These, 呢的 ni-ʻti.
They, 佢地 kʻue-tiʼ.
Thick, 笨 ʻpʻan, 厚 ʻhau, (as soup) 濃 nuung, 結 kit, (close) 密 mat, 稠密 chʻau-mat.
Thicket, 矮林 ʻai-lum, 荊棘林 king-kik-lum.
Thief, 賊 *tsʻaak, 賊佬 tsʻaak-ʻlo.

Thigh, 大髀 taaiʼ-ʻpi.
Thills, 杠 kongʼ.
Thimble, 針頂 ʻchum-ʻting, (archer's) 扳指 pʻaan-ʻchi.
Thin, 薄 pok, (rare, watery) 稀 hi, (lean) 瘦 shauʼ, 凹 nip, (-skinned) 薄皮 pok-*pʻi.
Thing, 物件 mat-kinʼ, 野 ʻye, 東西 tuung-sai, (affair) 件事 kinʼ-szeʼ.
Think, 思想 sze-ʻseung, (guess) 估 ʻkoo.
Thinly, 疏落 shoh-lok.
Third, 第三 taiʼ-saam, (a) 三分一 saam-funʼ-yat.
Thirst, 頸渴 ʻkeng-hohtʼ, 口渴 ʻhau-hohtʼ, (after) 渴想 hohtʼ-ʻseung.
This, 呢個 ni-kohʼ, (that or) 彼此 ʻpi-ʻtsʻze, (See That).
Thistle, 大薊 taaiʼ-kaiʼ, 蒺藜 tsaat-lai.
Thither, 到個處 toʼ-ʻkoh-shueʼ.
Thorn, 竻 lak, 莿 tsʻzeʼ, (bush) 竻林 lak-lum.

Thorough, 通 t'uung.
Thoroughfare, 通行 t'uung-hang, 通路 t'uung-lo'.
Thoroughly, 盡地 tsuun'-*ti', 嗮 saau'.
Those, 個的 koh'-‿ti.
Thou, 你 ‿ni, (See Thee).
Though, 雖則 sui-tsak', 雖然 sui-in, 雖 sui.
Thought, 思念 sze-nim', 念頭 nim'-t'au, 意思 i'-sze', 想頭 ‿seung-t'au.
Thousand, 千 ts'in.
Thread, 線 sin', (a) 條線 t'iu-sin', (to) 穿 ch'uen.
Threaten, 嚇 haak', 話 wa', (frighten) 恐嚇 ‿huung-haak'.
Three, 三 saam.
Thresh, 使棒打 ‿shai-‿p'aang-‿ta, 打 ‿ta, (grain) 打禾 ‿ta-woh.
Threshing-floor, 禾塲 woh-ch'eung.
Threshold, 門栱 moon-‿ch'aan (‿ch'aam).
Thrifty, 慳儉 haan-kim'.

Thrill with pleasure, 歡喜到震 foon-‿hi-to-chan'.
Thrilling, (sound) 吵耳 ‿ch'aau-‿i, 剐耳 kat-‿i.
Thrive, 發達 faat'-taat.
Throat, 喉嚨 hau-luung.
Throne, 王位 wong-*wai', 御坐 ue'-tsoh'.
Throng, 擠擁 tsai-‿yuung, 人迫 yan-pik'.
Through, 由 yau, 經過 king-kwoh', 透 t'au'.
Throw, 丟 tiu, 抹 wing, 擗 p'ek, (dice) 擲 chaak, (one's self) 投 t'au.
Thrush, (white eyed) 畫眉雀 wa'-*mi-tseuk', (black) 豬屎鴝 chue-‿shi-*cha, (a disease) 口爛 ‿hau-laan'.
Thrust, 剽 piu, (in) 插 ch'aap'.
Thuja, 圓栢 uen-paak'.
Thumb, 手指公 ‿shau-‿chi-kuung.
Thump, 搥 p'uung', 搥着 p'uung'-cheuk, 泵 ‿tum.

Thunder, 雷轟 lui-ᶜkwang, (clap) 霹 pʻek, 霹靂 pʻik-lik.
Thunderer, the, 雷公 lui-ᶜkuung.
Thunder-struck, 失驚 shat-king.
Thursday, 禮拜四 ᶜlai-paaiʼ-szeʼ.
Thus, 噉 ᶜkom, 噉樣 ᶜkom-*yeungʼ, (-much) 咁多 komʼ-ᶜtoh.
Thwart, (to) 揩阻 kʻangʼ-ᶜchoh, 啞 ngaak.
Tick, (to) 滴滴聲 tik-tik-sheng.
Ticket, 票 pʻiuʼ, piu, ᶜpʻiu, 帖 tʻipʼ, 紙 ᶜchi.
Tickle, 整癢 ᶜching-ᶜyeung, 折 chitʼ.
Ticklish, 痠軟 suenʼ-ᶜuen, (troublesome) 難料理 naan-liuʼ-ᶜli.
Tide, 潮水 chʻiu-ᶜshui.
Tide-waiter, 老太 ᶜlo-ᶜtʻaai, 簽字手 tsʻim-tszeʼ-ᶜshau.
Tidings, 消息 siu-sik.

Tidy, 齊整 tsʻai-ᶜching, 雅潔 ᶜnga-kitʼ.
Tie, (a) 帶 *taaiʼ, 條帶 tʻiu-*taaiʼ, (to) 綁 ᶜpong, (up, or on) 奶住 naaiʼ-chueʼ, (a knot) 打結 ᶜta-kitʼ (litʼ).
Tiffin, 晏餐 aanʼ-tsʻaan, (take) 食晏 shik-aanʼ.
Tier, 層 tsʻang.
Tiger, 老虎 ᶜlo-ᶜfoo.
Tiger-lily, 捲丹 ᶜkuen-taan.
Tight, 緊 ᶜkan, 行 hang.
Tile, 瓦 ᶜnga, (round) 瓦筒 ᶜnga-*tʻuung, (flat) 瓦片 ᶜnga-*pʻinʼ, (for floors) 堦磚 ᶜkaai-ᶜchuen.
Till, 到 toʼ, 及 kʻap.
Till, (to) 耕田 kang-tʻin.
Tiller, (of a boat) 舵柄 ᶜtʻaai-pengʼ.
Tilt, 塊起 tau-ᶜhi, 桶側吓 chaap-chak-ᶜha.
Timber, 木料 muuk-liuʼ.
Time, 時 shi, 時候 shi-hauʼ, (set) 期 kʻi, (at, or keep) 準 ᶜchuun.

Times, (occasions) 回 ooi, 賬 cheung', 次 ts'ze', 變 pin', 勻 wan, (three times three are nine) 三三該九 saam-saam-koi-ʿkau, 三三如九 saam-saam-ue ʿkau.

Time-server, 隨風佞 ts'ui-fuung-ning'.

Timely, 着時候 cheuk-shi-hau', (early) 早 ʿtso.

Timid } 膽細 ʿtaam-sai',
Timorous } 無膽 ʿmo-ʿtaam, 膽怯 ʿtaam-hip'.

Tin, 錫 sek'.

Tincture, 藥酒 yeuk-ʿtsau, 酒開 ʿtsau-hoi, (See Tint).

Tinder, 火煤絨 ʿfoh-mooi-yuung.

Tinder-case, 火鐮包 ʿfoh-lim-ʿpaau, (-box) 火煤箱 ʿfoh-mooi-ʿseung.

Tinfoil, 錫薄 sek'-*pok.

Tinge, 染的 ʿim-ʿti.

Tingle, 响 ʿheung.

Tinkle, 打璫响 ʿting-ʿtong-ʿheung.

Tin-plate, 馬口鐵 ʿma-ʿhau-t'it'.

Tinsel, 金花彩紅 kum-fa-ʿtsʻoi-huung.

Tint of, (tinge of) 帶有的 taai'-ʿyau-ʿti.

Tiny, 奀 ngan, 奀細 ngan-sai', 細細 sai'-sai'.

Tip, 尖處 tsim-ch'ue'.

Tipple, 飲慣 ʿyum-kwaan'.

Tiptoe, 奀高脚 ngan'-ko-keuk', (of expectation) 奀脚望 ngan'-keuk'-mong'.

Tired, 見倦 kin'-kuen', 見瘣 kin'-kooi'.

Tiresome, (tedious) 長氣 ch'eung-hi'.

Tissue, 羅紋 loh-mun, 砌成 ts'ai'-shing, ts'ai'-shing-ke'.

Title, 尊號 tsuen-ho', 官銜 koon-haam, (title to) 應得 ying-tak.

Title page, 書面 shue-min', 書名紙 shue-meng-ʿchi, 書軌 shue-ʿkwai.

Tittle-tattle, 贅話 chui'-*wa', 支支咋咋 chi-chi-cha'-cha'.

To, 與 ˊue, 過 kwoh˒, (up to) 至到 chi˒-to˒, (in order to) 欲 yuuk.
To and fro, 來往 loi-ˊwong.
Toad, 蟾蜍 k'um-*k'ue, kop˒-ˊkwaai.
Toast, (to) 炕 hong˒, 炕焦 hong˒-tsiu, (bread) 炕麵包 hong˒-min˒-ˊpaau.
Tobacco, 烟葉 ˊin-ip, 烟 ˊin.
To-day, 今日 kum-yat.
Toddle, 咄吓咄吓 tut-ˊha-tut-ˊha.
Toe, 脚趾 keuk˒-ˊchi, (of a shoe) 鞋頭 haai-t'au, (great-) 脚趾公 keuk˒-ˊchi-kuung.
Together, 共埋 kuung˒-maai, 同埋 t'uung-maai, na-maai, (united) 孖埋 ma-maai, 共 kuung˒, 同一齊 t'uung-yat-*ts'ai.
Toil, 鹹苦 haam-ˊfoo, 勞苦 lo-ˊfoo, (to) 勤勞 k'an-lo, 勞碌 lo-luuk.
Toilet, 裝身檯 chong-shan-t'oi, (lady's) 妝奩 chong-lim.

Token, 記號 ki˒-ho˒, 號 ho˒.
Tolerable, 做得過 tso˒-tak-kwoh˒.
Tolerate, 任從 yum˒-ts'uung, 容縱 yuung-tsuung˒.
Tomato, 金錢桔 kum-ts'in-kat, 番茄 faan-*k'e.
Tomb, 墳墓 fun-moo˒, (vaulted) 明塚 ming-ˊch'uung.
Tomfoolery, 蠢蠢呆呆事幹 ˊch'uun-ˊch'uun-ngoi-ngoi-sze˒-ˊkohn.
Tomorrow, 聽日 t'ing-yat, 明日 ming-yat.
Ton, 墩 ˊtan, 十六担 shap-luuk-taam˒.
Tone, 聲音 sheng-yum.
Tongs, 火鉗 ˊfoh-k'im.
Tongue, 條脷 t'iu-li˒, 舌頭 shit-t'au.
Tongue-tied, 黐脷 ch'i-li˒, 齾牙 nak-*nga.
Tonic, (med.) 補血 ˊpo-huet˒.
To-night, 今晚 kum-ˊmaan.
Tonsure, 落髮 lok-faat˒.

Too, 太 t'aai', 過頭 kwoh'-t'au, 得嘬 tak-tsai', (also) 都 ,toc.

Tool, 傢伙 ,ka-'foh, 器具 hi'-kue'.

Tooth, 牙 ,nga, 牙齒 nga-'ch'i, (a) 隻牙 chek'-nga.

Tooth-ache, 牙痛 nga-t'uung'.

Tooth-brush, 牙刷 nga-chaat', 牙擦 nga-*ts'aat'.

Tooth-pick, 牙簽 nga-,ts'im.

Tooth-powder, 牙灰 nga-,fooi.

Top, 頂頭 'teng-*t'au.

Topiary work, 屈古樹 wat-'koo-shue'.

Topic, 題目 t'ai-muuk.

Topple over, 蹼轉 p'uuk-'chuen.

Topsy-turvy, 顛倒 tin-'to, 顛頭倒脚 tin-t'au-'to-keuk'.

Torch, 火把 'foh-'pa.

Torment, 磨難 moh-naan, 磨苦 moh-'foo, (to) 難爲 naan-wai.

Torn, 裂曉 lit-hiu, 爛曉 laan'-hiu.

Torpedo, (fish) 鯆哥魚 'p'o-koh-*ue, (in warfare) 水雷 'shui-lui.

Torpid, 不仁 pat-yan, 麻木 ,ma-muuk, (insects) 蟄蟲 chat-ch'uung.

Torrent, 急流水 kup-lau-'shui, (mountain) 山灘 ,shaan-t'aan.

Torrid, 熱 it, (zone) 熱帶 it-taai'.

Tortoise, 龜 ,kwai.

Tortoise-shell, 玳瑁 toi'-*mooi', to'-*mooi'.

Tortuous, 攣捐 luen-kuen.

Torture, 拷打 haau-'ta, 行刑 ,hang-,ying.

Toss, 抛 ,p'aau, 揈 ,wing, (roll) 攎身 luuk-,shan.

Total, 一總 yat-'tsuung.

Totter, 嚀嚀吓 ,ning'-,ning'-,ha.

Tottery, 險險地 'him-'him-*ti'.

Touch, 掂着 tim'-cheuk, 摩着 moh-cheuk, (meddle) 鬥 tau'.
Touchy, 火頸 'foh-'keng.
Tough, 韌 ngan'.
Tour, 出外 ch'uut-ngoi'.
Tow, 粗蔴 ts'o-ma, (to) 使纜拖 'shai-laam'-t'oh, 拉纜 laai-laam', (at the stern) 乃住 naai'-chuc'.
Towards, 向 heung'.
Towel, 面巾 min'-,kan.
Tower, 塔 t'aap', 高樓 ko-*lau, 土府 't'o-'foo.
Towering, 頂天高 'ting t'in-ko.
Town, 邑 yup, (walled) 城 sheng.
Toys, 公仔 ,kuung-'tsai.
Trace, 踪跡 tsuung-tsik, 形跡 ying-tsik, (on paper) 印 yan', 描 miu.
Track, (a boat) 拉纜 laai-laam', (foot steps) 揾腳跡 'wan-keuk'-tsik.
Tract (small book), 小書 'siu-shue.

Tractable, 受教 shau'-kaau', 聽話 t'eng-wa'.
Trade, 生意 shaang-i', 貿易 mau'-yik.
Tradesman, 舖家 p'o'-,ka.
Tradition, 口傳 'hau-ch'uen.
Traduce, 講壞 'kong-waai'.
Tragedy, 報應戲文 po'-ying'-hi-mun, 苦情戲 'foo-ts'ing-hi'.
Trail, 拖 t'oh, (a) 拖痕 t'oh-han.
Train, (in a) 次第隨從 ts'ze'-tai'-ts'ui-ts'uung, (of followers) 從人 ts'uung-yan, (of powder) 火藥線 'foh-yeuk-sin', (of carriages, &c.) 一連 yat-lin, 一剌 yat-laat.
Train, (to) 敎養 kaau'-'yeung.
Trait, 處 ch'ue'.
Traitor, 奸臣 kaan-shan, 賣主 maai'-'chue, maai'-'chue-ke'.
Tramp, (trample) 踐踏 'ts'in-taap, 踹踏 'ch'aai-taap, 踐 'ts'in.

Trance, (in a) 入定 yup-ting`, 出神 ch'uut-shan.
Tranquility, 安寧 ohn-ning, (general) 太平 t'aai`-p'ing.
Transact, 辦 paan`.
Transcend, 超卓過 ch'iu-ch'euk`-kwoh`.
Transcribe, 抄 ch'aau.
Transfer, 挪移 noh-i, 移過 i-kwoh`, 交過 kaau-kwoh`.
Transformation, 變化 pin`-fa`.
Transgress, 犯 faan`.
Transgression, 過犯 kwoh`-faan`.
Transient } 暫時 tsaam`-shi, 無耐 ‘mo-noi`.
Transitory
Translate, 繙譯 faan-yik, 譯出來 yik-ch'uut-lai.
Transmigration, 輪回 luun-ooi.
Transmit, 傳 ch'uen, 交寄 kaau-ki`, 傳遞 ch'uen-tai`.
Transparent, 透光 t'au`-kwong, t'au`-kwong-ke`, 睇得過 ‘t'ai-tak-kwoh`.

Transpire, 露出來 lo`-ch'uut-lai.
Transplant, (rice) 插田 ch'aap`-t'in, 蒔秧 shi`-yeung, (a tree, &c.) 種過 chuung`-kwoh`.
Transport, 搬運 poon-wun`, (convicts) 充軍 ch'uung-kwun.
Transpose, 調轉 tiu`-‘chuen, 相換 seung-oon`.
Transverse, 橫 waang.
Trap, 筴 kaap`, 籠 *luung.
Trap-door, 樓口板 lau-‘hau-‘paan.
Trash, 擸撞 laap-saap`, 壞傢伙 waai`-ka-foh.
Travail, 產痛 ‘ch'aan-t'uung`, 劬勞 k'ue-lo, (to) 分娩 fun-‘min.
Travel, 出行 ch'uut-hang, 行遊 hang-yau.
Traverse, 橫過 waang-kwoh`, (go about) 週遊 chau-yau.
Travesty, 改作笑話 ‘koi-tsok`-siu`-*wa`.
Tray, 托盤 t'ok-*p'oon.

Treacherous, 詭譎 ʻkwai-kwut, 猾 waat, 欺人 hi-yan.
Treacle, 糖水 tʻong-ʻshui, (thick) 糖膠 tʻong-kaau.
Tread, 行 hang, (on) 踏 taap, 踹親 ʻchʻaai-tsʻan, ʻnaai-tsʻan.
Treason, 謀反 mau-ʻfaan.
Treasure, 銀兩 ngan-ʻleung, 錢銀 *tsʻin-*ngan, (wealth) 財帛 tsʻoi-paak, (a) 寶貝 ʻpo-pooiʼ.
Treasurer, 管庫人 ʻkoon-fooʼ-yan, (provincial) 布政司 poʼ-chingʼ-ʻsze.
Treasury, 銀庫 ngan-fooʼ, 庫務署 fooʼ-mooʼ-shue.
Treat, 看待 hohn-toiʼ, 管待 ʻkoon-toiʼ, 待 toiʼ, (discuss) 講 ʻkong.
Treaty, 和約 woh-yeukʼ, 憑約 pʻang-yeukʼ.
Treble, 三倍 saam-ʻpʻooi.
Tree, 樹木 shueʼ-muuk, (a) 喬樹 pʻoh-shueʼ.

Trellised, 欖核 ʻlaam-wat.
Tremble, 打震 ʻta-chanʼ, 打戰 ʻta-chinʼ, 戰慄 chinʼ-luut.
Tremendous, 眞正交關 chan-chingʼ-kaau-kwaan.
Trench, 壕 ho, 坑 haang, 池 chʻi.
Trespass, 犯 faanʼ, (idle people are forbidden to) 閒人免進 haan-yan-ʻmin-tsuunʼ.
Triad-society, 三合會 saam-hop-*ooiʼ.
Trial, 試 shiʼ, 試驗 shiʼ-imʼ, (to make) 探試 tʻaamʼ-shiʼ, 試吓 shiʼ-ʻha.
Triangle, 三角形 saam-kokʼ-ying.
Tribe, 族 tsuuk, 支派 chi-pʻaaiʼ.
Tribulation, 患難 waanʼ-naanʼ.
Tribulus, 蒺藜 tsaat-lai.
Tribunal, 公案 kuung-ohnʼ.
Tribute, 貢 kuungʼ, (to pay) 納貢 naap-kuungʼ, 納稅 naap-shuiʼ.

Trice, 頃刻之間 ʻkʻing-hak-chi-kaan.
Trick, 詭計 ʻkwai-kaiʼ, (to) 混 wunʼ, 整頓 ʻching-tanʼ.
Trickle, 滴滴落來 tik-tik-lok-lai.
Trident, (a) 一枝扒 yat-chi-pʻa, 三叉 ʻsaam-chʻa.
Trifle, (a) 微物 mi-mat, (to) 弄 luungʼ, (with things) 懇 ʻnun, (play) 頑耍 waan-ʻsha.
Trigger, 條制 tʻiu-chaiʼ.
Trim, 整齊 ʻching-tsʻai.
Trimmer, (a) 隨風佞 tsʻui-fuung-ningʼ.
Trimming, (fancy braid) 欄杆 laan-ʻkohn.
Trinity, 三一 saam-yat, 三合一 saam-hop-yat.
Trinket, 小件頭 ʻsiu-kinʼ-*tʻau.
Trip, (the foot) 失脚 shat-keukʼ, (up) 撬馬 kiuʼ-ʻma, 鉤脚 kau-keukʼ, (a) 遊一回 yau-yat-ooi.
Tripang, 海參 ʻhoi-shum.

Tripe, 牛肚 ngau-ʻtʻo, 牛百葉 ngau-paakʼ-ip.
Triphasia, 山枯 shaan-ʻnim.
Triple, 三倍 saam-ʻpʻooi.
Tripod, 鼎 ʻting.
Trippingly, 輕步 heng-poʼ.
Trite, 講到俗 ʻkong-toʼ-tsuuk.
Triumph, 凱歌 ʻhoi-koh.
Trivial, 小小 ʻsiu-ʻsiu.
Trocar, 放水針 fongʼ-ʻshui-chum.
Troop, 軍 kwun.
Tropic, (N.) 熱帶北限 it-taaiʼ-pak-haanʼ, (S.) 熱帶南限 it-taaiʼ-naam-haanʼ.
Trot, 跑花蹄 pʻaau-fa-tʻai, 遛花 lauʼ-fa.
Trouble, 艱難 kaan-naan, (to) 煩擾 faan-ʼiu, 勞動 lo-tuungʼ, (I will) 多煩 toh-faan.
Troublesome, 費事 faiʼ-szeʼ, (person) 惗尖 im-tsim.
Trough, 槽 tsʻo.
Trousers, 條褲 tʻiu-fooʼ, (short) 牛頭褲 ngau tʻau-fooʼ.

Trowel, 灰匙 *fooi*-shi (*ch'i).
Truant, (to play) 逃學 t'o-hok.
Truce, 暫息干戈 tsaam'-sik-kohn-kwoh.
Trudge, 驟吓 'ch'au-'ha, chuung-'ha.
True, 眞 chan, 眞實 chan-shat.
Truly, 果然 'kwoh-in, 眞正 chan-ching'.
Trump up, 揑成 nip-shing.
Trumpet, 號筒 ho'-t'uung, (COL.) hö-tö.
Trundle, 轆 luuk, 轆仔 luuk-'tsai.
Trunk, (box) 箱 seung, (body) 身 shan, 大身 taai'-shan, (elephant's) 象拔 tseung'-pat.
Trunnions, 炮耳 p'aau'-'i.
Truss, (for hernia) 小腸氣夾 'siu-ch'eung-hi'-kaap', (frame) 金字架 kum-tsze'-ka'.
Trust, 信賴 suun'-laai', (on-) 瞓 she, 過信 kwoh'-suun'.

Trustworthy, 老實 'lo-shat.
Truth, 眞理 chan-'li, 眞話 chan-*wa'.
Try, 試吓 shi'-'ha, 試一試 shi'-yat-shi', (before a court) 審問 'shum-mun'.
Tub, 木盤 muuk-p'oon.
Tube, 管 'koon, 筒 t'uung, *t'uung.
Tuber, (a) 一個種 yat-koh'-'chuung.
Tuberose, 玉簪花 yuuk-tsaam-fa.
Tuck up, 歛起 'lim-'hi, 押起 yaap'-'hi'.
Tuesday, 禮拜二 'lai-paai-'i'.
Tuft, 隻髻 chek'-*kai', (a) 一執 yat-tsap.
Tug, (to) 拖 t'oh, 拉 laai.
Tumble, 跌落 tit'-lok, 慣倒 kwaan'-to, (roll) 轆倒 luuk-'to.
Tumbler, (on the stage) 六分 luuk-fun, (glass-) 玻璃杯 poh-li-pooi.
Tumour, 肉瘤 yuuk-*lau (lo), 粉瘤 fun-*lau (lo).

Tumult, (bustle) 鬧熱 naau⁾-it, (uproar) 嘈鬧 ts'o-naau⁾.
Tune, (a) 一調 yat-tiu⁾, (to) 較線 kaau⁾-sin⁾, 較準 kaau⁾-ᶜchuun.
Tunnel, 山峒 shaan-tuung⁾.
Turban, 纏頭巾 chin⁾-t'au-kan.
Turbid, 濁 chuuk.
Turbot, 左口魚 ᶜtsoh-ᶜhau-*ue.
Turbulent, 滋事 tsze-sze⁾.
Tureen, 湯兜 t'ong-tau.
Turf, 草皮 ᶜts'o-p'i.
Turgid, 浮腫 fau-ᶜchuung, (bombastic) 張大 cheung-taai⁾.
Turkey, (a) 火鷄 ᶜfoh-ᶜkai.
Turmeric, 黃薑 wong-keung.
Turmoil, 勞碌 lo-luuk.
Turn, 轉 ᶜchuen, 反轉 ᶜfaan-chuen⁾, (as a wheel) 笛笛轉 t'um-t'um-chuen⁾, (in a lathe) 車 ch'e.
Turner, 車匠 ch'e-tseung⁾.

Turns, by, 輪流 luun-lau.
Turning-lathe, 車牀 ch'e-ch'ong.
Turnip, 蘿蔔 loh-paak.
Turpentine, 松節油 ts'uung-tsit-yau.
Turtle, 玳瑁 toi⁾-*mooi⁾, 鼈 pit⁾, 脚魚 keuk⁾-*ue.
Turtle-dove, 斑鳩 ₌paan-ₗkau.
Tush, 咪聲 ᶜmai-sheng.
Tusk, 長牙 ch'eung-nga.
Tutenag, (zinc) 白鉛 paak-uen, (white copper) 白銅 paak-t'uung.
Tutor, 掌敎 ᶜcheung-kaau⁾.
Twang, 迸聲 k'wang-sheng.
Tweezers, 鉗仔 kaap⁾-ᶜtsai, 小鑷 ᶜsiu-nip.
Twelfth, 第十二 tai⁾-shap-i⁾.
Twelve, 十二 shap-i⁾.
Twenty, 二十 i⁾-shap.
Twice, 兩回 ᶜleung-ooi, (See Times).
Twigs, 蔑 mit, 枝莖 chi-hang (ᶜk'waang).

Twilight, (eve) 黃昏 wong-fun, (morn) 昧爽 mooi-꜀shong.
Twilled, 斜紋 ts'e-*mun.
Twine, 繩仔 shing-꜀tsai, (to) 絞 ꜀kaau.
Twinge, 瘌 ts'ek꜠, (to) 扭 ꜀nau.
Twinkle, 閃 ꜀shim.
Twinkling, (a) 轉眼 ꜀chuen ꜀ngaan.
Twins, 孖生仔 ma-shang-꜀tsai, 雙生 sheung-shang.
Twist, 扭 ꜀nau, 絞 ꜀kaau.
Twitching, 扭 ꜀nau, (of the muscles) 筋轉 kan-꜀chuen, tsaat꜠-꜀ha.
Twitter, 嘶嘶聲 si-si-sheng, 吱吱喌喌 chi-chi-꜀chaau-꜀chaau.
Two, 二 i꜠, 兩 ꜀leung.
Type, 活板字 oot-꜀paan-tsze꜠, a (sign) 預表 ue꜠-꜀piu.
Typhoon, 風颶 fuung-kau꜠.
Typhus, 身虛熱症 shan-hue-it-ching꜠.
Tyrannical, 暴虐 po꜠-yeuk.

Tyranny, 霸道 pa꜠-to꜠.
Tyrant, 霸王 pa꜠-wong.
Tyro, 初學 ch'oh-hok, 亞初 a꜠-꜀ch'oh.

U

Ubiquity, 無處不有 mo-ch'ue꜠-pat-꜀yau.
Ugly, 醜 ꜀ch'au, 不好睇 'm-꜀ho-꜀t'ai.
Ulcer, 瘡瘍 ꜀ch'ong-*lau꜠.
Ultimately, 到底 to꜠-꜀tai, 到頭 to꜠-t'au.
Ultramarine, 佛青 fut-꜀ts'eng.
Umbra, 陰 yum, 影 ꜀ying.
Umbrage, 狐疑 oo-i.
Umbrella, 把遮 ꜀pa-꜀che, 雨遮 ue-꜀che.
Umpire, 斷事中人 tuen꜠-sze꜠-chuung-*yan.
Unable, 不能 'm-nang, 不會 'm-꜀ooi.
Unaccommodating, 不相讓 'm-seung-yeung꜠.
Unaccountable, 解不得 ꜀kaai-'m-tak, 欠解 him꜠-꜀kaai.

Unaccustomed, 不慣 'm-kwaan'.
Unacquainted, 不識 'm-shik.
Unadorned, 樸素 p'ok'-so'.
Unadvisable, 不合勢色 'm-hop-shai'-shik, 不好 'm-'ho.
Unadulterated, 精純 tsing-shuun,
Unaffected, 無感動 'mo-'kom-tuung', (real) 眞 chan.
Unalienable, 不俾得人 'm-'pi-tak-yan-ke'.
Unalloyed, 足色 tsuuk-shik, 正色 ching'-shik.
Unalterable, 無可更改 mo-'hoh-kang-'koi.
Unanimous, 一心 yat-sum, 無不中意 mo-pat-chuung-i'.
Unanswerable, 辭無可駁 ts'ze-mo-'hoh-pok'.
Unanticipated, 不曾想到 'm-ts'ang-'seung-to'.
Unapt, dull, 蠢拙 'ch'uun-chuet'.
Unassisted, 無人幫 'mo-yan-pong.

Unassuming, 謙遜 him-suun'.
Unavoidable, 無奈何 'mo-noi'-hoh, 無可避 mo-'hoh-pi', 不免 pat-'min.
Unaware, 不估 'm-'koo.
Unbend, 放鬆 fong'-suung.
Unbiassed, 無偏 'mo-p'in.
Unbind, 解甩 'kaai-lut.
Unblamable, 無責處 'mo-chaak'-ch'ue'.
Unblemished, 無瑕疵 'mo-ha-ts'ze.
Unblushing, 無臉 'mo-'lim, 無廉恥 'mo-lim-ch'i.
Unboiled, 未煲 mi'-po.
Unbounded, 無限 mo-haan'.
Unbridled, 放肆 fong'-sze'.
Unbusiness-like, 不合事例 'm-hop-sze'-lai'.
Unceasing, 不止 pat-'chi, 不息 pat-sik, 不歇 pat-hit'.
Uncertain, 不得定 'm-tak-ting', 不定 pat-ting'.
Unchangeable, 無改變 'mo-'koi-pin'.

Uncharitable, 無人情 'mo-yan-ts'ing.
Unchaste, 不正經 'm-ching'-king.
Uncivil, 無禮 mo-'lai, 傲慢 ngo'-maan'.
Uncle, 伯叔 paak'-shuuk, (maternal) 舅父 'k'au *foo'.
Unclean, 不潔淨 'm-kit'-tsing'.
Uncomfortable, 不爽快 'm-'shong-faai'.
Uncommon, 非常 fi-sheung.
Unconcerned, 不上心 'm-'sheung-sum.
Unconscious, 不知不覺 pat-chi-pat-kok'.
Unconstrained, 自然 tsze'-in.
Uncouth, 粗俗 ts'o-tsuuk.
Uncover, 揭開 'k'in-hoi.
Undaunted, 不喪胆 'm-song'-'taam, 無畏懼 'mo-wai'-kue'.
Undecided, 無定 mo-ting', 無定準 mo-ting'-'chuun.
Undefiled, 潔淨 kit'-tsing'.
Under, 下 ha', 下底 ha'-'tai, (to be) 在下 tsoi'-ha'.
Undergo, 受 shau'.
Underhand, 私吓 sze-*ha', 暗中 om'-chuung, 陰手 yum-'shau.
Undermine, 打地窿 'ta-ti'-'luung.
Understand, 曉 'hiu, 明白 ming-paak, 會 'ooi.
Undertake, 包承 paau-shing.
Undertaker's shop, 壽板舖 shau'-'paan-*p'o'.
Undervalue, 看低 hohn'-tai, 睇輕 't'ai-heng.
Undeserved, 不應受 'm-ying-shau'.
Undesigned, 不故意 'm-koo'-i'.
Undignified, 下賤 ha'-tsin'.
Undisguised, 顯然 'hin-in.
Undivided attention, 專一 chuen-yat, 專心 chuen-sum.

Undo, (loose) 解開 ʿkaai-hoi, (ruin) 破敗 pʻohʾ-paaiʾ.
Undoubted, 定然 tingʾ-in.
Undoubting, 無疑 ʿmo-i.
Undress, 除衫 chʻue-ʿshaam.
Undulating, 波紋樣 poh-*mun, 波浪樣 poh-longʾ-*yeung.
Uneasy, 欠安 himʾ-ohn, 唔安樂 ʾm-ohn-lok.
Unemployed, 無事業 ʿmo-szeʾ-ip.
Unequal, 不等 patʾ-ʿtang, 不相等 ʾm-seungʾ-ʿtang, 不同 ʾm-tʻuung.
Unequalled, 無雙 ʿmo-sheung.
Uneven, 不平 ʾm-pʻing, 不齊 patʾ-tsʻai.
Unexpected, 再不估 tsoiʾ-patʾ-ʿkoo, 意外 iʾ-ngoiʾ.
Unfair, 不公道 ʾm-kuungʾ-toʾ.
Unfavourable, 不遂 patʾ-suiʾ, 逆 ngaak, 不順 ʾm-shuunʾ.

Unfeeling, 薄情 pok-tsʻing.
Unfilial, 不孝 patʾ-haauʾ.
Unfinished, 未成 miʾ-shing.
Unfit, 不合 ʾm-hop, 不着 ʾm-cheuk.
Unfold, 解開 ʿkaai-hoi, 展開 ʿchin-hoi, 舒 shue.
Unforeseen, 不料 patʾ-liuʾ, 料不到 liuʾ-ʾm-toʾ, 偶然 ʿngau-in.
Unforgiving, 爭啖氣 chaang-taamʾ-hiʾ.
Unfortunate, 無彩 ʿmo-ʿtsʻoi.
Unfounded, 無根無本 mo-kan-mo-ʿpoon.
Ungenerous, 小器 ʿsiu-hiʾ.
Ungovernable, 制不得 chaiʾ-pat-tak, chaiʾ-ʾm-tak.
Ungrateful, 忘恩 mong-yan.
Unhappy, 無福 mo-fuuk.
Unhealthy, 不爽 ʾm-ʿshong.
Uniform, 通都一樣 tʻuung-too-yat-yeungʾ, 同式 tʻuung-shik, (dress) 號衣 hoʾ-i.

Unimportant, 無緊要 ʻmo-ʻkan-iuʼ, 無相干 ʻmo-seung-kohn.

Unintentionally, 無意中 ʻmo-iʼ-ʽchuung.

Uninterrupted, 流連不斷 lau-lin-pat-ʻtʻuen.

Union, 合會 hop-ooiʼ, (heart and soul) 同心協力 tʻuung-sum-hipʼ-lik, (sexual) 交媾 kaau-kauʼ.

Unison, 同音 tʻuung-yum.

Unite, 合埋 hop-maai, 連埋 lin-maai.

United States, 合衆國 Hop-chuungʼ-kwokʼ, 花旗國 Fa-kʻi-kwokʼ, 美國 ʻMi-kwokʼ.

Unity, 一 yat, 純一 shuun-yat.

Universal, 普遍 ʻpʻoo-pʻinʼ, (peace) 太平 tʻaaiʼ-pʻing.

Universe, 宇宙 ʻue-chauʼ, 宇內 ʻue-noiʼ, 天地萬物 tʻin-tiʼ-maanʼ-mat.

Unjust, 不公道 ʼm-kuung-toʼ.

Unkind, 無人情 ʻmo-yan-tsʻing.

Unlawful, 不合法 ʼm-hop-faatʼ.

Unless, 若唔係 yeuk-ʼm-haiʼ.

Unlike, 不似 ʼm-ʻtsʻze.

Unlimited, 無限 ʻmo-haanʼ.

Unload, 出貨 chʻuut-fohʼ, 卸貨 seʼ-fohʼ.

Unloose, 解甩 ʻkaai-lut.

Unlucky, 凶 huung, 不好彩 ʼm-ʻho-ʻtsʻoi.

Unmanly, 非大丈夫 fi-taaiʼ-cheungʼ-foo, ʼm-haiʼ-taaiʼ-cheungʼ-foo, 小人哉 ʻsiu-yan-tsoi.

Unmerciful, 殘忍 tsʻaan-ʻyan.

Unmitigated ⎫
Unmixed   ⎬, 盡地 tsuunʼ-*tiʼ.
Unmodified   ⎭

Unnatural, 逆性 yik-singʼ, 反常 ʻfaan-sheung.

Unnecessary, 不使 'm-ʿshai, 不使亦得 'm-ʿshai-yʾ-tak, 不必 pat-pit.
Unnoticed } 睇不出 ʿtai-'m-chʿuut.
Unobserved
Unofficial, 民間 mun-kaan.
Unpardonable, 不赦得用 'm-sheʾ-tak-lut.
Unpleasant, 不合情 'm-hop-tsʿing.
Unpolluted, 不沾污 pat-chim-oo.
Unpopular, 不得人心 'm-tak-yan-sum.
Unprecedented, 從來無 tsʿuung-loi-ʿmo.
Unprejudiced, 無偏 ʿmo-pʿin.
Unprepared, 無準備 ʿmo-ʿchuun-pi.
Unprincipled, 無道理 ʿmo-toʾ-ʿli.
Unprofitable, 無益 ʿmo-yik.
Unreasonable. 無情理 ʿmo-tsʿing-ʿli.
Unrelenting, 無可憐 ʿmo-ʿhoh-lin.

Unremitting, 不歇 pat-hitʾ.
Unrepining, 不懷怨 pat-waai-uenʾ.
Unreserved, 直白 chik-paak, 坦易 ʿtʿaan-i.
Unrestrained } 無限 ʿmo-haanʾ.
Unrestricted
Unrighteous, 不義 pat-iʾ.
Unripe, 未熟 miʾ-shuuk.
Unroll, 展開 ʿchin-hoi.
Unruly, 不守法 pat-ʿshau-faatʾ, 放肆 fongʾ-szeʾ.
Unsafe, 不穩 'm-ʿwan, 險 ʿhim.
Unsatisfactory, 不如意 'm-ue-iʾ.
Unsay, 反口 ʿfaan-ʿhau, 反轉話 ʿfaan-chuenʾ-waʾ.
Unseasonable, 不着時 'm-cheuk-shi.
Unseemly, 不合式 'm-hop-shik, 不好意思 'm-ʿhoʾ-i-szeʾ, 醜 ʿchʿau.
Unselfish, 無私心 ʿmo-sze-sum.
Unsettle, 搖動 iu-tuungʾ.

Unsightly, 貌醜 maau²-ʻchʻau, 不好睇 ʼm-ʻho-ʻtʻai.
Unskilful, 不好手勢 ʼm-ʻho-ʻshau-shai².
Unsociable, 無和氣 ʻmo-woh-hi², 冷 ʻlaang.
Unsophisticated, 不乖巧 ʼm-kwai-ʻhaau.
Unsound, 不堅實 ʼm-kin-shat.
Unspeakable, 言不能盡 in-pat-nang-tsuun².
Unspotted } 無瑕疵 ʻmo-ha-tsʻze.
Unstained }
Unsteady, 無定向 ʻmo-ting²-heung², 不穩 ʼm-ʻwun.
Unsuitable, 不着 ʼm-cheuk.
Unsurpassed, 未有勝過 mi²-ʻyau-shing²-kwoh².
Unteachable, 不受敎 ʼm-shau²-kaau².
Unthankful, 忘恩 mong-yan.
Untidy, 不齊整 ʼm-tsʻai-ʻching.

Until, 至到 chi²-tw², 等到 ʻtang-to².
Untoward } 拗頸 aau²-ʻkeng.
Untractable }
Untrue, 不眞 ʼm-chan.
Unusual, 非常 fi-sheung, 非俗 fi-tsuuk, 深 shum.
Unwarrantable, 僭分 tsʻim²-fuu².
Unwearied, 無倦 ʻmo-kuen², 無瘡 ʻmo-kooi².
Unwelcome, 不喜接 ʼm-ʻhi-tsip².
Unwell, 不受用 ʼm-shau²-yuung².
Unwilling, 不肯 ʼm-ʻhang, 不願 ʼm-uen², 不中意 ʼm-chuung-i².
Unworthy, 不堪 pat-hom.
Up, upon, 在 — 上 tsoi² — sheung², (to go) 土 ʻsheung, (get) 起 ʻhi, (raise) 舉 ʻkue.
Upbraid, 罵 ma², 鬧 naau², 譏誚 ki-tsʻiu².
Uphold, 扶持 foo-chʻi.

Upper, 上 sheung⁾, (of a shoe) 面 *min⁾.
Upright, 企 ʿkʻi, 直立 chik-laap, (just) 正直 chingʾ-chik.
Uproar, 吧嘲 pa-paiʾ, 嘈亂 tsʻo-luenʾ, 拉亂 la-luenʾ.
Upset, (to) 打倒 ʿta-ʿto, (price) 至平 chiʾ-pʻeng, 開價 hoi-kaʾ.
Upshot, 結果 kitʾ-ʿkwoh.
Upside down, 顛倒 tin-ʿto.
Upstairs, 樓上 lau-sheungʾ, (go) 上樓 sheung-*lau.
Upwards, 向上高 heungʾ-sheungʾ-ko, (of) ——零 ——ling, ——幾 —— ʿki, ——把 ——ʿpa, ——以上 ——ʿi-sheungʾ.
Urbanity, 禮貌 ʿlai-maauʾ.
Urge, 催逼 tsʻui-pik, 嘅 ngai.
Urgent, 急 kup, 着緊 cheuk-ʿkan.
Urinate, 屙溺 oh-niuʾ, 小便 ʿsiu-pinʾ.

Urine, 尿 niuʾ.
Urn, 礚 tʻaapʾ, 缸 kong.
Ursa major, 北斗 pak-ʿtau.
Urticaria, 寒粒 hohn-nup.
Us, 我地 ʿngoh-tiʾ.
Use, (to) 使 ʿshai, 用 yuungʾ, (treat) 待 toiʾ.
Useful, 便用 pinʾ-yuungʾ.
Useless, 無中用 ʿmo-chuung-yuungʾ.
Usual, 平常 pʻing-sheung. 尋常 tsʻum-sheung.
Usurp, 霸佔 paʾ-chimʾ, 搶奪 ʿtseung-tuet.
Usury, 利息重 liʾ-sik-ʿchʻuung.
Utensil, 器皿 hiʾ-ʿming.
Uterine, 同胞 tʻuung-paau.
Utmost, 至極 chiʾ-kik, 十分 shap-fun.
Utter, (to) 講出 ʿkong-chʻuut.
Utterance, 口角 ʿhau-kokʾ, 口鉗 ʿhau-kʻim.
Utterly, 清楚 tsʻing-ʿchʻoh. 盡地 tsuunʾ-*tiʾ.
Uvula, 吊鐘 tiuʾ-ʿchuung.

V

Vacancy, (office) 缺 k'uet⸢.
Vacant, 空虛 ⸢huung-hue⸢.
Vacate, 搬空 poon-huung, (an office) 卸 se⸢.
Vacation, 空閒 huung-haan, 假 ka⸢, 散班 ⸢saan⸢-paan.
Vaccinate, 閹痘 im-*tau⸢, 種洋痘 ⸢chuung⸢-yeung-*tau⸢.
Vacillate, 反覆 ⸢faan-fuuk, 朝三暮四 ⸢chiu-saam-moo⸢-sze⸢.
Vagabond, 浪蕩 long⸢ (⸢long) tong⸢.
Vagina, 陰戶 yum-oo⸢, 產門 ⸢ch'aan-moon.
Vagrant, 遊手 yau-⸢shau, 流離 lau-li.
Vague, 舒闊 ⸢shue-foot⸢, 恍惚 ⸢fong-fut, 泛 faan⸢.
Vain, 裝腔 chong-hong, 虛浮 hue-fau, (proud) 嬌奢溫 kiu-ch'e-wun, (in) 虛徒 hue-t'o.

Valance, 幅袡 fuuk-*yum.
Valerian, 孩兒菊 hoi-i-kuuk.
Valetudinary, 養病 ⸢yeung-peng⸢.
Valiant, 勇敢 ⸢yuung-⸢kom.
Valid, 妥當 ⸢t'oh-tong⸢.
Valise, 皮箱 p'i-⸢seung.
Valley, 山谷 ⸢shaan-kuuk, 谷 kuuk.
Valour, 勇氣 ⸢yuung-hi⸢.
Valuable, 貴重 kwai⸢-chuung⸢.
Value, 價 ka⸢, (of) 值錢 chik-*ts'in, (to prize) 貴重 kwai⸢-chuung⸢, (to) 估價 ⸢koo-ka⸢.
Valve, 弇 ⸢im, 蓋 koi⸢.
Vampire, (蝙蝠 p'in-fuuk), 蝠鼠 fuuk-⸢shue.
Van, 先鋒 ⸢sin-fuung, 前隊 ts'in-tui⸢.
Vane, 風信旗 fuung-suun⸢-k'i, 定風旗 ting⸢-fuung-k'i.
Vanish, 銷滅 siu-mit, (disappear) 絕迹 tsuet-tsik, 無曉 ⸢mo-hiu.

Vanity, 虛幻 hue-waan⁾.
Vapour, 氣 hi⁾, (rising) 烟蓬蓬 in-puung⁾-puung⁾, (of water) 水氣 ʻshui-hi⁾.
Vapouring, 虛誇 hue-kʻwa.
Variance, 爭 chaang.
Variegated, 斑色 paan-shik.
Various, 各樣 kok⁾-yeung⁾, 不定 pat-ting⁾.
Varnish, 明油 ming-*yau, (lacquer) 漆 tsʻat.
Vary, 變轉 pin⁾-ʻchuen, 參差 tsʻaam-tsʻze.
Vase, 花罇 fa-ʻtsuun, 花瓶 fa-*pʻing.
Vast, 甚大 shum⁾-taai⁾.
Vault, (cellar) 地牢 ti⁾-lo.
Vaunt, 誇大 kʻwa-taai⁾.
Veer, 轉 chuen⁾, 轉彎 chuen⁾-waan.
Vegetable, 菜 tsʻoi⁾, (kingdom) 草木 ʻtsʻo-muuk.
Vehement, 猛 ʻmang.
Vehicle, 載車 tsoi⁾-chʻe.
Veil, (to) 遮護 che-oo⁾, (a) 蓋面紗 koi⁾-min⁾-ʻsha.

Vein, 囘血管 ooi-huet⁾-ʻkoon, (streak) 紋 *mun.
Velocity, (relative) 快慢 faai⁾-maan⁾.
Velvet, 剪絨 ʻtsin-*yuung, 多羅絨 toh-loh-*yuung.
Venal, 買得 ʻmaai-tak, ʻmaai-tak-ke⁾, 買嘱得 ʻmaai-chuuk-tak.
Venerable, 老成 ʻlo-shing, 老 ʻlo.
Venerate, 尊重 tsuen-chuung⁾.
Venerial, 春情 chʻuun-tsʻing, chʻuun-tsʻing-ke⁾, 交合 kaau-hop, 花柳 fa-ʻlau.
Venetians, 百葉窻 paak⁾-ip-ʻchʻeung.
Vengeance, (to take) 報仇 po⁾-chʻau.
Venial, 恕得過 shue⁾-tak-kwoh⁾.
Venison, 鹿肉 *luuk-yuuk.
Venom, 毒 tuuk.
Vent, (escape) 去路 hue⁾-lo⁾, 通籠 tʻuung-ʻluung.

Ventilate, 通風 t'uung-fuung.
Ventricle, 竅 k'iu’, 寵 ₍luung, 房 fong.
Venture, 敢 ʿkom, (hazard) 拚 p'oon’.
Venus, (planet) 金星 ₍Kum-₍sing.
Veracity, 老實 ʿlo-shat.
Verandah, 騎樓 k'e-*lau, 天臺 t'in-*t'oi.
Verb, 活字 oot-tsze’, 生字 shang-tsze’.
Verbal, (spoken) 口話 ʿhau-wa’.
Verbatim, 句句相同 kue’-kue’-seung-t'uung, 逐字 chuuk-tsze’.
Verbose, 贅累 chui’-lui’.
Verdant, 青活 ts'ing-oot, 秀茂 sau’-mau’.
Verdict, 批判 p'ai-p'oon’.
Verdigris, 銅綠 t'uung-luuk.
Verge, (on the) 呢門 mun’-moon.
Verify, 證驗 ching’-im’.

Vermicelli, 粉絲 ʿfun-₍sze, 粉仔 ʿfun-ʿtsai.
Vermilion, 銀硃粉 ngan-chue-ʿfun.
Vermin, 蟲 ch'uung.
Vernal, 春 ch'uun.
Verse, (poetry) 詩 ₍shi, (a) 節 tsit’.
Versed in, 熟 shuuk.
Version, (a) 翻譯書 fuan-yik-shue, (more than one) 重譯 ch'uung-yik.
Vertex, 頂 ʿteng.
Vertical, (to be) 喺天頂處 ʿhai-t'in-ʿteng-shue’, 頂天 ʿting-t'in.
Vertigo, 頭暈 t'au-wan, (wun).
Very, 實首 shat-ʿshau, 實在 shat-tsoi’, 十分 shap-fun, 好 ʿho, 甚 shum’, 太 t'aai’, 極 kik.
Vesicle, 胞仔 p'aau-ʿtsai, 泡仔 p'aau’-ʿtsai, ʿp'o ʿtsai.
Vessel, 器皿 hi’-ʿming, (ship) 船 shuen.

Vest, (a) 背心 pooi²-‿sum.
Vested estate, 實業 shat-ip.
Vestige, 蘇痕 ‿sin-han, 痕迹 han-tsik.
Veteran, 老手 ‿lo-‿shau, 老主固 ‿lo-‿chue-*koo².
Vex, 撓 ‿naan, 煩擾 faan-‿iu, 難爲 naan-wai, (irritate) 激 kik.
Vexed, 煩悶 faan-moon², 煩惱 faan-‿no, 淹悶 im-moon².
Vial, 小玻璃罇 ‿siu-‿poh-‿li-‿tsuun.
Viands, 肴饌 ngaau-chaan².
Vibrate, 搖郁 iu-yuuk, 擺動 ‿paai-tuung², (quiver) 震 chan².
Vice, 惡端 ok²-tuen, 弊病 pai²-peng².
Vice, (a tool) 老鼠鋏 ‿lo-‿shue-*kaap².
Viceroy, 總督 ‿tsuung-tuuk, 制臺 chi²-t'oi.
Vicinity, 近處 kan²-ch'ue².
Vicissitude, 更變 kang-pin².

Victimize, 當牛使 tong²-ngau-‿shai.
Victory, 獲勝 wok-shing², 得勝 tak-shing², (a) 贏一陣 yeng-yat-chan².
Victuals, 飯食 faan²-shik, 飯 faan², 食 shik.
Vie, 鬥 tau², 爭先 chaang-sin.
View, (to) 睇見 ‿t'ai-kin², 看見 hohn²-kin², (a) 光景 kwong-‿king.
Vigorous, 壯健 chong²-kin².
Vigour, 力量 lik-leung², 精神 tsing-shan.
Vile, 醜 ‿ch'au, 惡 ok², (mean) 下賤 ha²-tsin².
Vilify, 譭謗 ‿wai-p'ong².
Village, 鄉村 heung-ts'uen, 鄉下 heung-*ha², (a) 條村 t'iu-ts'uen.
Villain, 光棍 kwong-kwun².
Villainous, 黑心 hak-sum, 奸狡 kaan-‿kaau, (ugly) 醜 ‿ch'au.

Vindicate, 保護 ʽpo-oo⸲, 表白 ʽpiu-paak, (avenge) 報仇 poʼ-chʽau.
Vine, 菩提樹 pʽo-tʽai-shue⸲, (葡萄 pʽo-tʽo).
Vinegar, 醋 tsʽo⸲.
Violate, 犯 faan⸲, (defile) 汚辱 oo-yuuk.
Violence, 強 kʽeung, (to use) 強 ʽkʽeung.
Violent, 猛烈 ʽmang-lit.
Violet, 紫羅蘭 ʽtsze-loh-laan, 菫菜 ʽkan-tsʽoi⸲.
Violin, 四弦樂器 szeʼ-in-ngok-hiʼ.
Viper, 毒蛇 tuuk-she, 飯匙頭 faanʼ-shi-tʽau.
Virago, 惡婆 okʼ-*pʽoh.
Virgin, 童女 tʽuung-ʽnue, 處女 ʽchʽue-ʽnue.
Virility, 元神 uen-shan.
Virtue, 德 tak.
Virulent, 鴆毒 shum-tuuk.
Viscera, the five, 五臟 ʽng-tsongʼ.
Visible, 有形色 ʽyau-ying-shik.

Vision, - (faculty) 眼官 ʽngaan-koon, (a) 異像 iʼ-tseungʼ.
Visionary, 甕想 uungʼ-ʽseung.
Visit, 探見 tʽaamʼ-kinʼ, 見 kinʼ.
Visiting-card, 名帖 ming-*tʽipʼ.
Visitor, 人客 yan-haakʼ, (a lady) 堂客 tʽong-*haakʼ.
Vital, 關性命 kwaan-singʼ-mingʼ, 要關 iuʼ-kwaan.
Vitals, 命門 mingʼ-moon.
Vitiate, 整壞 ʽching-waaiʼ.
Vitriol, (blue) 膽礬 ʽtaam-faan.
Vivacious } 活潑 oot-pʽootʼ.
Vivid }
Viviparous, 胎生 ʽtʽoi-ʽshang.
Vocal, 口音 ʽhau-ʽyam.
Vocation, 事業 szeʼ-ip.
Vociferate, 喧嘩 huen-wa, 嘈吵 tsʽo-ʽchʽaau.

Vogue, 時欵 shi-ʿfoon.
Voice, 聲 sheng, 聲氣 sheng-hiʾ.
Void, 空 hung.
Volatile, 會飛散 ʿooi-fi-ʿsaan.
Volcano, 火山 ʿfoh-shaan.
Voluble, 油嘴 yau-ʿtsui.
Volume, 本 ʿpoon, 部 poʾ.
Voluntarily, 甘心 kom-sum.
Voluntary, 情願 tsʿing-uenʾ, tsʿing-uenʾ-keʾ.
Volunteers, 民壯 mun-chongʾ, 義兵 iʾ-ping, (to raise rebel-) 起義 ʿhi-iʾ.
Voluptuary, 膏粱子弟 ko-leung-ʿtsze-taiʾ.
Vomit, 嘔 ʿau.
Voracious, 大食 taaiʾ-shik, taaiʾ-shik-keʾ, 貪食 tʿaam-shik, 爲食 waiʾ-shik.
Vortex, 漩水心 suen-ʿshui-sum.
Vote for, 舉 ʿkue, 願舉 uenʾ-ʿkue.
Voucher, 憑據 pʿang-kueʾ.
Vow, 許願 ʿhue-uenʾ, 誓願 shaiʾ-uenʾ.

Voyage, 水路 ʿshui-loʾ, 水程 ʿshui-chʿing.
Vulgar, 俗 tsuuk, (low) 市井 ʿshi-ʿtseng.
Vulture, 鷹 chin.

W

Wabble, 轉得鬆 ʿchuen-tak-suung.
Wadded, 綿納 min-naap.
Waddle, 咄吓咄吓 tut-ʿha-tut-ʿha, ʿleung-pin-chaap.
Wade, 涇水 kaangʾ-ʿshui.
Wafer, 火漆片 ʿfoh-tsʿat-pʿinʾ.
Waffles, 夾餅 kaapʾ-ʿpeng.
Waft, 飄流 pʿiu-lau.
Wag, (a) 好趣人 ʿho-tsʿueʾ-yan, (to) 擺 ʿpaai, 搖 iu.
Wager, 賭賽 ʿto-tsʿoiʾ.
Wages, 工錢 kuung-*tsʿin, 工銀 kuung-*ngan, 人工 yan-kuung.
Waggle, 調調佞 tiuʾ-tiuʾ-fingʾ.

Waggon, 載貨車 tsoi⁼-foh⁼-cʻhe.
Wagtail, 鶺鴒 tsek⁼-ling.
Wail, 哀哭 oi-huuk.
Waist, 腰 iu.
Waistcoat, 背心 pooi⁼-͵sum.
Wait, 等候 ͵tang-hau⁼, 等下 ͵tang-*ha⁼.
Wait on, (serve) 服事 fuuk-sze⁼.
Waiter, 事仔 sze⁼-͵tsai.
Waive, 由得 yau-tak.
Wake, 醒 ͵seng, (from sleep) 瞓醒 fun⁼-͵seng.
Waken, 打醒 ͵ta-͵seng, 叫醒 kiu⁼-͵seng.
Walk, (to) 行 hang, 行路 hang-lo⁼, (take a) 去逛 hue⁼-kʻwaang⁼, (path) 小路 ͵siu-lo⁼.
Wall, 牆 tsʻeung, 壁 pik, (a) 幅牆 fuuk-tsʻeung.
Wallow, 攣 luen, 展轉 ͵chin-͵chuen, (like a beast in the mud) 陷湴 aam⁼-paan⁼ (paam⁼), (in the water) 陷水 aam⁼-͵shui.

Walnut, 核桃 hop-tʻo.
Wampee, 黃皮 wong-*pʻi.
Wan, 白白地 paak-paak-*ti⁼.
Wand, 枝鞭杆 chi-͵pin-͵kohn.
Wander, 流離 lau-li, 週遊 chau-yau, (miss the way) 蕩失路 tong⁼-shat-lo⁼.
Wane, 衰 shui, 虧 fai, (of the moon) 月缺 uet-kʻuet⁼.
Want, 要 iu⁼, (defect) 缺乏 kʻuet⁼-fat, (destitution) 窮飢 kʻuung-ki, 坳翳 aau-ai⁼.
Wanton, 好色 ho⁼-shik, 好嫖 ho⁼-pʻiu, 放蕩 fong⁼-tong⁼.
War, 打仗 ͵ta-cheung⁼, 戰事 chin⁼-sze⁼, 交兵 kaau-ping, 干戈 kohn-kwoh.
War-vessel, 兵船 ping-shuen.
Ward, (division) 街坊 ͵kaai-͵fong, (apartment) 房 *fong, (to) 防守 fong-͵shau.

Wardrobe, 衣服櫃 ‘i-fuuk-kwai’.
Warehouse, 棧房 chaan’-*fong, 貨倉 foh’-ts‘ong.
Wares, 貨 foh’.
Warlike, 武 ‘moo, (man) 武夫 ‘moo-foo, (arms) 干戈 kohn-kwoh.
Warm, 煖 ‘nuen, 熱 it.
Warming-pan, 煖鍋 ‘nuen-woh.
Warn, 儆 ‘king, 警戒 ‘king-kaai’, 提醒 t‘ai-‘sing, 預先話知 ue-sin-wa’-chi.
Warp, 經線 king-sin’, kaang.
Warp, (to) 攣 luen, 屈攣 wat-luen.
Warped, 攣 luen, 拗 ‘aau.
Warrant, (a) 票 p‘iu’, (police) 差票 ch‘aai-p‘iu’, (to) 包保 paau-‘po.
Warren, (苑囿 ‘uen-yau’), 圍 *wai.
Warrior, 勇士 ‘yuung-sze’.
Wart, 瘊子 hau-‘tsze, 飯蕊瘡 faan’-‘yui-ch‘ong.
Wary, (be) 睇眞 ‘t‘ai-chan.
Wash, 洗 ‘sai.

Washer-man, 洗衣人 ‘sai-i-yan, (’s itch) 油蟖 yau-tsze.
Wash-stand, 面盤架 min’-*p‘oon-*ka’.
Wasp, 黃蜂 wong-fuung.
Waste, (to) 費 fai’, 浪費 long’-fai’, 嘥 saai, saai-t‘aat’.
Watch, (to) 看 hohn, (at night) 看更 hohn-kaang, 睇更 ‘t‘ai-kaang, (a time-piece) 時辰錶 shi-shan-piu.
Watches, (the five) 五更 ‘ng-kaang.
Watchful, 謹愼 ‘kan-shan’, 醒定 ‘sing-ting’.
Watchman, 更夫 kaang-foo.
Watch-tower, 更樓 kaang-*lau.
Watch-word, 暗號 om’-*ho’.
Water, 水 ‘shui, (to) 淋 lum, 瀨 laai’.
Water-caltrops, 菱角 ling-kok’, 芰 ki’.
Water-chestnut, 水栗 ‘shui-luut, 馬蹄 ‘ma-*t‘ai.

Water-closet, 厠所 ts‘ze̒-ʿshoh.
Water-course, 水溝 ʿshui-kau.
Water-cresses, 水芹菜 ʿshui-k‘an-ts‘oi̒, 西洋菜 sai-yeung-ts‘oi̒.
Water-fall, 瀑布水 puuk-po̒-ʿshui.
Watering-pot, 花洒 fa-ʿsha.
Water-lily, 蓮花 lin-ʿfa.
Water-melon, 西瓜 sai-kwa.
Water-mill, 水磨 ʿshui-*moh.
Water-spout, 龍上水 luung-sheung-ʿshui.
Watery, 淡 ʿt‘aam, 生水 shang-ʿshui, (thin) 稀 hi.
Wave, (of the sea) 浪 long̒, 波浪 poh-long̒, (to) 搖擺 iu-ʿpaai.
Waver, 反覆 ʿfaan-fuuk, 思疑 sze-i.
Waving, 浪紋 long̒-*mun, 水波紋 ʿshui-poh-*mun.
Wax, 蠟 laap, (white) 蟲白蠟 ch‘uung-paak-laap.

Wax, (to) 長 ʿcheung, 生 shaang, 成 shing.
Wax-candle, 蠟燭 laap-chuuk.
Way, 條路 t‘iu-lo̒, 道路 to̒-lo̒, (method) 方法 fong-faat̒.
Way-farer, 路客 lo̒-haak̒.
Wayward, 拗頸 aau̒-ʿkeng.
We, 我地 ʿngoh-ti̒, (our, or my) 我的 ʿngoh-ti̒, ʿngoh-ti̒-ke̒.
Weak, 軟弱 ʿuen-yeuk, (watery) 淡 ʿt‘aam.
Wealth, 財帛 ts‘oi-paak, (man of) 財主 ts‘oi-chue.
Wean, 斷奶 ʿtuen-ʿnaai.
Weapons, 利器 li̒-hi̒, 器械 hi̒-haai̒.
Wear, (clothes) 穿着 ch‘uen-cheuk̒, (a hat) 戴帽 taai̒-*mo̒, (a shawl) 蔞 lau, (out) 着壞 cheuk̒-waai̒, (well) 唅 k‘um.
Wearisome, 勞神 lo-shan.
Weary, 疲倦 p‘i-kuen̒, 疚倦 kau̒-kuen̒, kooi̒.

Weasel, 鼬鼠 yau-ʻshue.
Weather, 天氣 tʻin-hí, 天時 tʻin-shi, (good) 好天 ʻho-tʻin, (hot) 天時熱 tʻin-shi-it.
Weather-cock, 順風魚 shuun³-funng-*ue.
Weave, 織 chik.
Web, 一機布 yat-ki-po³.
Web-footed, 脚指間有膜 keuk³-ʻchi-kaan-ʻyau-*mok. 鵝掌 ngoh-ʻcheung.
Wed, 娶親 tsʻue³-tsʻan.
Wedding, 婚姻 fun-yan.
Wedding sedan, 花轎 fa-*kiu³.
Wedge, 尖橕 tsim-chaang³, (to) 搧 sip³.
Wednesday, 禮拜三 ʻlai-paai³-saam.
Weed, 野草 ʻye-ʻtsʻo, (to) 搣草 mang³-ʻtsʻo.
Week, 禮拜 ʻlai-paai³.
Weep, 流淚 lau-lui³, 哭泣 huuk-yup, (aloud) 喊 haam³.
Weeping-willow, 垂楊柳 shui-yeung-ʻlau.

Weevils, 米牛 ʻmai-*ngau.
Weigh, 稱 chʻing³, 兌 tui³.
Weighing-machine, 千斤秤車 tsʻin-kan-chʻing³-chʻe, 磅 pong³.
Weights, 法碼 faat³-ʻma.
Weighty, 重 ʻchʻuung.
Welcome, (to) 喜接 ʻhi-tsip³, 歡迎 foon-ying.
Weld, 鎔埋 yuung-maai.
Welfare, 平安 pʻing-ohn, 福 fuuk.
Well, (a) 井 ʻtseng, 眼井 ʻngaan-ʻtseng.
Well, 好 ʻho, (in health) 自在 tsze³-tsoi³, 好 ʻho, (get) 好翻 ʻho-faan.
Well done, 做得好 tso³-tak-ʻho, (meat) 好熟 ʻho-shuuk, (bravo!) 好 ʻho!
West, 西 sai, (the) 西邊 sai-pin, 西方 sai-fong.
Wet, 濕 shup.
Wether, 閹羊 im-yeung.
Wet-nurse, 奶媽 ʻnaai-ʻma, 濕媽 shup-ʻma.
Whale, 海鰍魚 ʻhoi-tsʻau-*ue, 鯨魚 kʻing-ue.

WHE   289   WHI

Wharf, 馬頭 ʿma-tʻau, 步頭 poʾ-tʻau.
What? 乜野 mat-ʿye? (that which) 所 ʿshoh.
Whatever } 乜野 mat-ʿye, 不論乜野 ʾm-luun-mat-ʿye.
Whatsoever
Wheat, 麥 mak.
Wheedle, 挪撚 noh-ʿnun.
Wheel, 輪 luun, 車輪 chʻe-*luun, (turn the) 轉車 ʿchuen-chʻe, (round) 輪轉 luun-ʿchuen.
Wheel-barrow, 手車 ʿshau-chʻe.
Wheezing, 瘕聲 ha-sheng.
When? 幾時 ʿki-shi?
When, ——个時 —— kohʾ-shi.
Whence? 由邊處 yau-pin-chʻueʾ? 喺邊處來 ʿhai-pin-chʻueʾ-lai?
Whenever, 隨時 tsʻui-shi, 每逢 ʿmooi-fuung.
Where? 邊處 pin-chʻueʾ? 邊吓 pin-ʿha? 邊位 pin-*waiʾ?

Where, ——个處 —— kohʾ-chʻueʾ (shueʾ).
Whereabout, 近邊處 kanʾ-pin-chʻueʾ.
Wherefore, 所以 ʿshoh-ʿi.
Whereupon, 就 tsauʾ.
Whet, 磨利 moh-liʾ.
Whether or not, ——係唔係—— haiʾ-ʾm-haiʾ, ——是不是—— shiʾ-pat-shiʾ.
Which? 邊個 pin-kohʾ? 邊的 pin-ʿti? (that which) 所 ʿshoh, (that by which) 所以 ʿshoh-ʿi.
While, (a) 一時間 yat-shi-kaan.
Whilst, 當——個時 tong ——kohʾ-shi.
Whimper, 㖭氣 shokʾ-hiʾ.
Whimsical, 反拗 ʿfaan-aauʾ.
Whine, 䑛聲 nge-sheng.
Whip, (horse-) 馬鞭 ʿma-pin, (to) 鞭打 pin-ʿta.
Whirl, 窗窗轉 ʿtʻum-ʿtʻum-chuenʾ.

Whirlpool, 漩水心 suen-ˋshui-sum, 倒槽水 ˋto-tsʻo-ˋshui.
Whirlwind, 旋風 suen-fuung.
Whisk, 拂 faakˊ.
Whiskers, 髯 im, 鬍鬚 oo-lim-so.
Whisper, 陰聲講 yum-sheng-ˋkong.
Whistle, (to) 吹音 chʻui-yum, 嘯 siuˊ, (a) 啤啤 pi-pi.
Whit, 絲毫 sze-ho, 一的 yat-tik.
White, 白色 paak-shik, 白 paak.
Whitebait, 銀魚仔 ngan-ue-ˋtsai, 白飯魚 paak-faanˊ-*ue.
Whites, 白帶 paak-taaiˊ.
White-wash, 灑灰水 ˋsha-fooi-ˋshui, 掃白 soˋ-paak.
Whiting, 長魚 chʻeung-ue.
Whitlow, 指甲疽 ˋchi-kaapˊ-tsue.
Who? 乜誰 mat-shui (*shui)? 邊個 pin-kohˊ?

Who, ——個個—— ˋkoh-kohˊ.
Whole, 完全 uen-tsʻuen, 一槪 yat-kʻoiˊ, 成 shing, (the) 籠總 ˋluung-ˋtsuung, hamˊ-pangˊ-langˊ.
Wholesale, 發行 faatˊ-hong.
Wholesome, 爽 ˋshong.
Wholly, 嘥 saaiˊ, 盡地 tsuunˊ-*tiˊ.
Whore, 娼妓 chʻeung-kiˊ, 老舉 ˋlo-ˋkue.
Whose? 乜誰嘅 mat-*shui-keˊ?
Why? 爲乜事幹 waiˊ-mat-szeˊ-kohnˊ? 因何 yan-hohˊ? 做乜 tsoˊ-mat?
Wick, (lamp-) 燈心 tang-sum.
Wicked, 惡 okˊ, 惡僻 okˊ-pʻik.
Wickerwork, 用籐編做 yuungˊ-tʻang-pin-tsoˊ.
Wicket gate, 筚門 pat-moon.
Wide, 廣闊 ˋkwong-footˊ.
Widgeon, 鷖 i.
Widow, 寡婦 ˋkwa-ˋfoo, 寡母婆 ˋkwa-ˋmoo-*pʻoh.

Widower, 寡佬 ʻkwa-ʻlo, 鰥夫 kwaan-foo.
Wield, 揸 cha.
Wife, 老婆 ʻlo-pʻoh, (respectfully) 妻室 tsʻai-shat, 妻 tsʻai, (your) 夫人 foo-yan, 令正 lingʼ-chingʼ.
Wig, (for women) 網巾頭 ʻmong-ʻkan, (false hair) 髮 tʻau-piʼ, (for the cue) 辮排 pin-*pʻaai.
Wild, 野 ʻye, (mad) 狂 kʻwong, (roving) 放蕩 fongʼ-tongʻ.
Wilderness, 曠野 fongʼ-ʻye, 野外 ʻye-ngoiʼ.
Wile, 詭計 ʻkwai-kaiʼ.
Will, (a) 囑書 chuuk-shue, 遺書 wai-shue, (wish) 主意 ʻchue-iʼ, 志意 chiʼ-iʼ, (future tense) 將 tseung, 要 iuʼ.
Wilful, 固意 kooʼ-iʼ, 固執 kooʼ-chup.
Willing, 肯 ʻhang, 中意 chuung-iʼ.
Willingly, 甘心 kom-sum.

Willow, 柳樹 ʻlau-shueʼ.
Wily, 乖巧 kwaai-ʻhaau.
Win, 贏 yeng.
Wince, (to) 畏縮 waiʼ-shuuk.
Wind, (to) 纏埋 chinʼ-maai, 繑埋 ʻkʻiu-maai, (up) 摺埋 chipʼ-maai, (a watch) 土鏈 ʻsheung-*lin, (an account) 清數 tsʻing-shoʼ, (an affair) 了事 ʻliu-szeʼ.
Wind, (the) 風 fuung.
Winding, 彎曲 waan-huuk.
Windpipe, 硬喉 ngaangʼ-hau, 氣管 hiʼ-ʻkoon.
Windlass, 轆轤 luuk-lo, luut-ʻloh.
Window, 窗 ʻchʻeung, 窗門 ʻchʻeung-*moon.
Window-bars, 窗遏 chʻeung-aatʼ.
Windward, 風邊 fuung-pin (pinʼ).
Wine, 酒 ʻtsau, (port) 黑酒 hak-ʻtsau, (sherry) 白酒 paak-ʻtsau, (claret) 紅酒 huung-ʻtsau.

World, 世 shai², 世界 shai²-kaai², (the whole) 普天下 ‘p'o-t'in-ha², (the present) 今世 kum-shai, (the future) 來世 loi-shai².

Worldly custom, 世俗 shai²-tsuuk.

Worm, (earth-) 黄犬 wong-‘huen.

Worms, 蟲 ch'uung, 蛇蚓 yau-‘yan, (internal) 蛔蟲 ooi-ch'uung.

Wormwood, 茵蔯蒿 yun-ch'an-ho.

Worried, 淹悶 im-moon².

Worry, (bite) 咬壞 ‘ngaau-waai² (tease) 難爲 naan-wai, 搞亂 lo-luen², 混賬 wan²-cheung².

Worse, 更不好 kang²-pat-‘ho, kang²-'m-‘ho, 重弊 chuung²-pai², 惡過 ok²-kwoh².

Worship, 崇拜 shuung-paai², 拜 paai².

Worst, 至惡 chi²-ok².

Worsted, 絨線 yuung-sin².

Worth, 值 chik, 抵 ‘tai, 抵得 ‘tai-tak, (virtue) 抵德 tak.

Worthy, 堪 hom, (man) 賢人 in-yan.

Would, 欲 yuuk, 願 ‘uen², 想 ‘seung, (-that) 恨不得 han²-pat-tak, 巴不得 pa-'m-tak.

Wound, 傷 sheung, (to) 傷親 sheung-ts'an.

Wrangle, 嗌交 aai²-‘kaau.

Wrap, 打包 ‘ta-paau, 包裹 paau-‘kwoh, 包好 paau-‘ho.

Wrapper, 包袱 paau-fuuk.

Wrath, 震怒 chan²-no², 忿怒 ‘fun-no².

Wreck, (a ship) 破船 p'oh²-shuen, 破爛隻船 p'oh²-laan²-chek²-shuen.

Wren, 鷦鷯 tsiu-liu.

Wrestle, 角力 kok²-lik, 較勝 kaau²-shing², 鬥力 tau²-lik.

Wretched, 凄涼 ts'ai-leung, 凄慘 ts'ai-‘ts'aam.

Wriggle, 攣捐 luen-kuen, 嫋娜 ˈniu-ˈnoh, (as a worm) 吵吵吓 ˈmiu-ˈmiu-ˈha.

Wring, (dry) 扭乾 ˈnau-kohn, (out) 扭出 ˈnau-chʻuut, 撚 ˈnin.

Wrinkle, 縐紋 tsauʼ-*mun, (to) 縐埋 tsauʼ-maai, chʻaau-maai.

Wrist, 手腕 ˈshau-ˈoon, 手眼骨 ˈshau-ˈngaan-kwut.

Write, 寫 ˈse, 寫字 ˈse-tsze (*tszeʼ), (down) 寫落 ˈse-lok, (an essay, &c.) 作 tsokʼ.

Writhe, 抽搐 chʻau-chʻuuk.

Wrong, 錯 tsʻohʼ, 不着 ˈm-cheuk, (all) 錯嗮 tsʻohʼ-saaiʼ, (to) 損害 ˈsuen-hoiʼ.

Wry, 歪 waai, ˈme, 斜 tsʻe, (to make a, face) 扯歪面 ˈchʻe-ˈme-minʼ.

Y

Yak, 犛牛 li-ngau.
Yam, 大薯 taaiʼ-shue.

Yama, 閻羅 Im-loh.
Yard, (of a ship) 杠 kongʼ, (measure) 碼尺 ˈma-chʻekʼ.
Yarn, 紗 sha, 線 sinʼ.
Yawn, 打喊露 ˈta-haamʼ-loʼ.
Year, 年 nin, 歲 suiʼ.
Yearn, 痛想 tʻuungʼ-ˈseung.
Yeast, 酵母 kaauʼ-ˈmo, 酒餅 ˈtsau-ˈpeng.
Yell, 大喊 taaiʼ-haamʼ.
Yellow, 黃 wong, 黃色 wong-shik.
Yes, 係咯 haiʼ-lok, 是 shiʼ.
Yesterday, 昨日 tsok-yat, 尋日 tsʻum-mat, kʻum-yat, (the day before) 前日 tsʻin-yat, (the day before that) 大前日 taaiʼ-tsʻin-yat.
Yesternight, 昨晚 tsok-ˈmaan.
Yet, 尙 sheungʼ, 重 chuungʼ, (not) 未曾 miʼ-tsʻang.

World, 世 shai⁾, 世界 shai⁾-kaai⁾, (the whole) 普天下 ⌐p‘o-t‘in-ha⁾, (the present) 今世 kum-shai, (the future) 來世 loi-shai⁾.

Worldly custom, 世俗 shai⁾-tsuuk.

Worm, (earth-) 黄犬 wong-⌐huen.

Worms, 蟲 ch‘nung, 蚯蚓 yau-⌐yan, (internal) 蛔蟲 ooi-ch‘uung.

Wormwood, 茵陳蒿 yan-ch‘an-ho.

Worried, 淹悶 im-moon⁾.

Worry, (bite) 咬壞 ⌐ngaau-waai⁾ (tease) 難爲 naan-wai, 撈亂 lo-luen⁾, 混賬 wan⁾-cheung⁾.

Worse, 更不好 kang⁾-pat-⌐ho, kang⁾-‘m-⌐ho, 重弊 chuung⁾-pai⁾, 惡過 ok‛-kwoh⁾.

Worship, 崇拜 shuung-paai⁾, 拜 paai⁾.

Worst, 至惡 chi⁾-ok‛.

Worsted, 絨線 yuung-sin⁾.

Worth, 值 chik, 抵 ⌐tai, 抵得 ⌐tai-tak, (virtue) 德 tak.

Worthy, 堪 hom, (man) 賢人 in-yan.

Would, 欲 yuuk, 願 uen⁾, 想 ⌐seung, (-that) 恨不得 han⁾-pat-tak, 巴不得 pa-’m-tak.

Wound, 傷 sheung, (to) 傷親 sheung-ts‘an.

Wrangle, 嗌交 aai⁾-⌐kaau.

Wrap, 打包 ⌐ta-paau, 包裹 paau-⌐kwoh, 包好 paau-⌐ho.

Wrapper, 包袱 paau-fuuk.

Wrath, 震怒 chan⁾-no⁾, 忿怒 ⌐fun-no⁾.

Wreck, (a ship) 破船 p‘oh⁾-shuen, 破爛隻船 p‘oh⁾-laan⁾-chek‛-shuen.

Wren, 鷦鷯 tsiu-liu.

Wrestle, 角力 kok‛-lik, 較勝 kaau⁾-shing⁾, 鬥力 tau⁾-lik.

Wretched, 凄涼 ts‘ai-leung, 凄慘 ts‘ai-⌐ts‘aam.

Wriggle, 攣捐 *luen-kuen,* 嫋娜 ʿniu-ʿnoh, (as a worm) 吵吵吓 ʿmiu-ʿmiu-ʿha.

Wring, (dry) 扭乾 ʿnau-kohn, (out) 扭出 ʿnau-chʻuut, 撚 ʿnin.

Wrinkle, 縐紋 tsauʼ-*mun, (to) 縐埋 tsauʼ-maai, chʻaau-maai.

Wrist, 手腕 ʿshau-ʿoon, 手眼骨 ʿshau-ʿngaan-kwut.

Write, 寫 ʿse, 寫字 ʿse-tszeʼ (*tszeʼ), (down) 寫落 ʿse-lok, (an essay, &c.) 作 tsokʼ.

Writhe, 抽搐 chʻau-chʻuuk.

Wrong, 錯 tsʻohʼ, 不着 ʼm-cheuk, (all) 錯嗮 tsʻohʼ-saaiʼ, (to) 損害 ʿsuen-hoiʼ.

Wry, 歪 waai, ʿme, 斜 tsʻe, (to make a, face) 扯歪面 ʿchʻe-ʿme-minʼ.

Y

Yak, 犛牛 li-ngau.
Yam, 大薯 taaiʼ-shue.
Yama, 閻羅 Im-loh.
Yard, (of a ship) 杠 kongʼ, (measure) 碼尺 ʿma-chʻekʼ.
Yarn, 紗 sha, 線 sinʼ.
Yawn, 打喊露 ʿta-haamʼ-loʼ.
Year, 年 nin, 歲 suiʼ.
Yearn, 痛想 tʻuungʼ-ʿseung.
Yeast, 酵母 kaauʼ-ʿmo, 酒餅 ʿtsau-ʿpeng.
Yell, 大喊 taaiʼ-haamʼ.
Yellow, 黃 wong, 黃色 wong-shik.
Yes, 係咯 haiʼ-lok, 是 shiʼ.
Yesterday, 昨日 tsok-yat, 尋日 tsʻum-mat, kʻum-yat, (the day before) 前日 tsʻin-yat, (the day before that) 大前日 taaiʼ-tsʻin-yat.
Yesternight, 昨晚 tsok-ʿmaan.
Yet, 尚 sheungʼ, 重 chuungʼ, (not) 未曾 miʼ-tsʻang.

Yew-tree, 櫃樹 ʻfi-shueʼ.

Yield, (submit) 歸服 kwai-fuuk, (bend) 屈 wut, (produce) 產 ʻchʻaan, (concede) 許准 ʻhue-ʻchuun, (up) 讓 yeungʼ.

Yoke, 軛 aak, (of oxen) 對牛 tuiʼ-ngau.

Yolk, 蛋黃 taanʼ-*wong.

Yonder, 個處地方 kohʼ-shueʼ-tiʼ-fong.

You, 你 ʻni, (PLUR.) 你地 ʻni-tiʼ, 你等 ʻni-ʻtang, (See Thee).

Young, 少年 shiuʼ-nin, 少嫩 shiuʼ-nuenʼ, 年輕仔 nin-hing, (of animals) 仔 ʻtsai.

Young gentleman, 少爺 shiuʼ-ye.

Young lady, 姑娘 koo-neung.

Your, 你嘅 ʻni-keʼ, 你地 ʻni-tiʼ.

Youth, (time of) 年輕時 nin-hing-shi, (a) 後生 hauʼ-ʻshaang.

Z

Zeal, 烈熱之意 lit-it-chi-iʼ.

Zealous, 發憤 faatʼ-ʻfun, 憤烈 ʻfun-lit.

Zebra, 虎斑馬 ʻfoo-paan-ʻma.

Zedoary, 高良薑 ko-leung-keung.

Zenith, 天頂 tʻin-ʻteng.

Zest, 滋味 tsze-miʼ.

Zigzag, 之字 chi-tszeʼ.

Zinc, 白鉛 paak-uen, 窩澤 woh-chaak.

Zizyphus, 棗 ʻtso.

Zodiac, 黃道 wong-toʼ, 日道 yat-toʼ, (signs of, Chinese) 二十八宿 iʼ-shap-paatʼ-suuk.

Zone, 帶道 taaiʼ-toʼ.

www.ingramcontent.com/pod-product-compliance
Lightning Source LLC
Chambersburg PA
CBHW030816230426
43667CB00008B/1245